How to Garden

Alan Titchmarsh

How to Garden
essential skills, advanced
techniques, practical
step-by-steps

BOOKS

Published in 2010 by BBC Books, an imprint of
Ebury Publishing, a Random House Group Company

The Random House Group Limited Reg. No. 954009

Addresses for companies within the Random House
Group can be found at **www.randomhouse.co.uk**

The Random House Group Limited supports The Forest
Stewardship Council (FSC), the leading international
forest certification organisation. All our titles that are
printed on Greenpeace approved FSC certified paper
carry the FSC logo. Our paper procurement policy can
be found at www.rbooks.co.uk/environment

A CIP catalogue record for this book is available from
the British Library.

ISBN 978 1 84 990090 4

Produced by OutHouse!
Shalbourne, Marlborough, Wiltshire SN8 3QJ

BBC BOOKS
COMMISSIONING EDITOR: Lorna Russell
PROJECT EDITOR: Caroline McArthur
PRODUCTION: Helen Everson

OUTHOUSE!
CONCEPT DEVELOPMENT:
Elizabeth Mallard-Shaw and Sue Gordon
SERIES DESIGN: Sharon Cluett
CONTRIBUTING EDITORS: Steve Bradley, Valerie Bradley,
Julia Britten, Jo Weeks
CONTRIBUTING DESIGNERS: Sharon Cluett, Heather
McCarry, Louise Turpin, Robin Whitecross
ILLUSTRATOR: Lizzie Harper

PHOTOGRAPHS by Jonathan Buckley except where
credited otherwise on page 287

Colour origination by Altaimage, London
Printed and bound in China by C & C Offset Printing
Co., Ltd

Contents

Introduction   7

DESIGNING A GARDEN   8

Why design matters   9
Design principles   10
The site – what have you got?   12
Your garden on paper   16
Garden shapes   20
Contemporary gardens   26
Cottage gardens   28
Wildlife gardens   30
Family gardens   32
Formal gardens   34
focus on Planning for low maintenance   36
Planting by design   39
focus on Mood   45
focus on Creating height   46
Trees   48
Shrubs   50
Climbers   52
Herbaceous perennials   54
Annuals and biennials   56
Blubs   58
focus on Screening   60
Hedges   62
Problem gardens   65
Shady gardens   66
Windy gardens   68
Dry gardens   70
Damp gardens   72

LAWNS AND HARD SURFACES   74

Choosing a surface   75
Siting a lawn   84

Preparing a site for a new lawn	86
Grass seed or turf?	89
Choosing and using seed	90
Choosing and using turf	93
focus on Protecting lawn edges	95
Feeding your lawn	96
Watering your lawn	99
Mowing the lawn	101
Scarifying, aerating and top-dressing	103

GROWING IN CONTAINERS   106

Choosing the right pot	107
Using containers	110
focus on Cottage gardens and potagers	115
Planning and designing with pots	116
focus on Contemporary style	117
focus on Small spaces	120
Compost and additives	122
focus on Toppings	124
Preparing for planting	125
Planting a container	126
Planting a hanging basket	128
focus on Planting bulbs	131
Repotting	132
Watering	134
Feeding	136
Overwintering	138

VEGETABLES AND HERBS   140

Why grow your own?	141
Planning your plot	143
Growing systems versus digging	148
Deciding what to grow	151
focus on Crop rotation	153

Tools and equipment	155
All about soil	157
focus on Compost	160
Preparing your plot	162
focus on Digging	164
focus on Intensive cropping	166
Storage	168
A–Z of vegetables	170
A–Z of herbs	228

PLANT CARE AND PROPAGATION   242

Pruning	243
Why prune?	244
focus on Vertical and horizontal growth	247
Types of pruning	248
Planning your pruning	253
Tools for the job	256
Protective clothing and safety	260
Essential techniques	262
Keeping pruned plants healthy	265
focus on Training trees	268
focus on Climbers and wall shrubs	270
Propagation	272
Plant problems and remedies	278

Index	282

Introduction

Gardening is one of the best and most fulfilling activities on earth, but it can sometimes seem complicated and confusing. *How to Garden* is clearly set out and written, I hope, in a straightforward, easy-to-understand style. I don't see any point in making gardening complicated, when much of it is based on common sense and observation. (All the key techniques are explained and illustrated, and I've included plenty of tips and tricks of the trade.)

There are suggestions on the best plants and the best varieties to grow in particular situations and for a particular effect. I've tried to keep the information crisp and to the point so that you can find what you need quickly and easily and then put your new-found knowledge into practice. Don't worry if you're not familiar with the Latin names of plants. They are there to make sure you can find the plant as it will be labelled in the nursery or garden centre, but where appropriate I have included common names, too. Forgetting a plant's name need not stand in your way when it comes to being able to grow it.

Above all, *How to Garden* is designed to fill you with passion and enthusiasm for your garden and all that its creation and care entails, from designing and planting it to maintaining it and enjoying it. For more than fifty years gardening has been my passion, and that initial enthusiasm for watching plants grow, for trying something new and for just being outside pottering has never faded. If anything I am keener on gardening now than I ever was and get more satisfaction from my plants every day. It's not that I am simply a romantic, but rather that I have learned to look for the good in gardens and in plants, and there is lots to be found. Oh, there are times when I fail – when my plants don't grow as well as they should and I need to try harder. But where would I rather be on a sunny day? Nowhere!

How to Garden will, I hope, allow some of that enthusiasm – childish though it may be – to rub off on you, and the information it contains will, I hope, make you a better gardener, as well as opening your eyes to the magic of plants and flowers.

KEY to symbols used

○	Prefers an open, sunny site	⇊	Needs well-drained soil
◑	Prefers/tolerates some shade	pH↓	Needs/prefers acidic soil
●	Prefers/tolerates full shade	pH↑	Needs/prefers alkaline soil
◆	Needs wet soil	🍂	Needs humus-rich soil
◓	Needs moist soil	❖	Season of main interest (e.g. flowers, foliage, stems, berries)
◊	Needs dry soil		

Designing a garden

Do you ever look at a garden and wonder what it is that makes it successful? It's easy to think it just evolved, as if by magic – the owner has 'green fingers', the site is idyllic, the birds sing there … That may be partly true, but for a garden to work as a whole, there has to be more to it. Every site has its limitations – awkward shape, poor soil, shady aspect – but a good garden will have disguised or overcome these. The plants will be well suited to the situation and someone will have thought about how they would change with time, and how to get the best from them. In short, the garden will have been *designed*. If it doesn't appear that way, then it's a real success.

Why design matters

Garden design has long been considered a luxury. The grand gardens of the past had designers: if you asked a dozen people to name one famous garden designer, the name Capability Brown would be sure to come up. He has a lot to answer for. Garden design was for the wealthy, with rolling acres to transform, not for the ordinary gardener.

We've come a long way since then, but even now there's a feeling that garden design is some kind of extravagance, an optional extra. Most people have relatively small gardens, and plots are getting smaller. So why, and how, is design relevant or necessary?

Design is about making the best use of the space you have; it's about practicalities and problem-solving. Of course, it's also about producing something that looks pleasing, but, like a building, a successful garden must suit its site and work well for the people who use it. Even the most basic garden will benefit from these design considerations – particularly smaller gardens, where every inch counts. Then there's the question of the garden feeling comfortable and right for *you*.

Creating a place

Designing a garden involves creating a place. It should be an agreeable place to be, and an interesting space to explore. This will mean different things to different people, but

When you're planning your new garden, you may find it helps to keep a sketchbook for jotting down ideas and plans. Include photos, magazine cuttings – anything that inspires you. It can be very therapeutic!

whatever your preferences and tastes, the first step in making a satisfying garden is to create good lines and proportions when you plan it. Understanding how to use shapes, lines and proportions effectively is a fundamental design skill. Another important piece of equipment in the designer's toolbox is an awareness of colour, light and shade – how they work, and how to manipulate them to get the effects you want. A knowledge of plants, their preferences, their behaviour and how to combine them to best effect, is hugely valuable when it comes to finding the right ones for your particular site and situation. So, whether your garden is dry, shady, damp, windy or just plain difficult, don't try to fight it. Keep it simple, work with nature, trust your instincts and begin to transform your space.

Never forget that many an excellent garden began with a difficult site. You'll be amazed how a plot can be transformed by re-thinking the space and choosing appropriate plants.

Design principles

The last thing anyone wants when they're full of enthusiasm for making a new garden is to be bombarded with a lot of rules. But garden design is about planning spaces, and it has long been accepted that certain basic principles apply to the spaces we find workable, satisfying and 'right'. If you can keep these ideas in your mind (and to many people with design flair they will be second nature), then you're more likely to end up with a garden you like and enjoy living with.

An open, sunnier area beyond a patch of cool, green shade provides contrast and an invitation to move on and explore. Bold foliage shapes and pools of bright colour give balance and seasonal interest.

These tried and tested principles of design relate to proportion, scale, movement and flow, unity, rhythm and balance. They aren't clear-cut, and often overlap. Perhaps the best way to use them is as a check-list when you are evaluating layout possibilities in the early stages. Obviously, they will have to work alongside many other considerations such as practical constraints and your personal tastes, preferences and budget.

Proportion

Echoing the proportions of your house in the garden's layout often works very well, giving house and garden a sense of belonging to each other. For example, you might use the width of a gable or the footprint of a hexagonal conservatory as a guide to the size and shape of an adjacent terrace or lawn.

Think, too, about the proportions of the different areas and the various features in your garden in relation to each other. A simplified version of the well-known 'golden ratio' – a mathematical and artistic theory used since classical times – can be a useful rule of thumb. Two lines in a certain proportion to each other – roughly speaking, one-third to two-thirds – will tend to give a pleasing effect. Try this 'rule of thirds' when deciding how to divide a space or position an entrance, and keep it in mind when planning the ratio of planting to open space – 1:2, or half as much planted area as open space, will often work out well.

You may be stuck with a plot whose proportions instinctively feel all wrong, but there's no need to despair – there are all sorts of design tricks you can use to help correct this (see pages 20–1).

Scale

People are probably the most important element in the scale equation: a garden feels better as a space if it is on a human scale. Big, open exterior spaces don't feel comfortable or secure to sit in, so smaller areas must be defined within them. Paths and steps need to be a good width – more roomy than their indoor equivalents. Pergolas and arches must be high and spacious enough not to feel oppressive.

Choose plants that are in scale with the spaces they are growing in. A tree at the top of a slope will tend to dwarf everything. Tall perennials won't work in a narrow border, nor tiny plants at the foot of a high wall.

Movement and flow

This is all about giving an incentive to explore. Particular paving patterns, such as brick paving laid lengthways along a path, seem to propel you along to the next part of the garden. Carefully chosen focal points invite you to walk a bit further. A pool of sunlight beyond a patch of shade is always enticing, while a path disappearing round a bend makes you want to know what lies beyond. A shady pergola can create a sense of mystery, arousing curiosity. Avoid 'dead ends', which discourage any sense of movement.

Unity

A sense of unity helps prevent your garden from being a haphazard jumble of the things you happen to want or need in it. Elements that give unity to a design include a theme or a style: if the house is contemporary, with clean lines and strong shapes, then carrying this style consistently through into the garden will make it all hang together. As a rule of thumb, formal areas tend to work best nearer the house, informal areas farther away from it. Restraint in your use of materials, shapes and colours can also help to unify a space. Using too many different materials, or a random mix of colours, will have the opposite effect.

Rhythm

Rhythm in garden design, just as in music, usually entails repetition of a pattern or motif. Repeating a particular plant grouping, or having two or more similar arches, steps, planted pots or other such features

Movement and flow have clearly been thought about in this garden. A series of eye-catching specimen plants and a sculpture provide focal points to lead the eye through the garden, and there is a choice of walking routes to give variety.

at intervals along a path, gives coherence and leads the eye on through the garden.

Balance

Try to avoid a lopsided effect – the feeling that one side of the garden is dominant as you walk through it.

Tall plants, major groups of plants, and focal points should be evenly distributed to right and left so that both sides look equally important. When planning your planting, take care not to have all the evergreens on one side, or the garden will look unbalanced in winter.

The site – what have you got?

A garden is rarely an entirely blank canvas. There are usually existing features, and attributes such as climate, aspect, topography and soil need to be considered at the planning stage. However beautiful your design may be in your mind's eye, the reality will be a disappointment if you ignore these 'givens'. Remember – creating a successful garden is as much about problem solving as it is about artistic vision.

Don't underestimate the advantages of a compact, partly shaded urban plot. Shelter can be a real bonus in this kind of garden, creating an ideal microclimate for exotic plants and a jungle effect.

A professional garden designer would carry out a thorough site analysis to investigate and record all the factors above. You may not want to consult a professional, but you should take the time to stand and stare, so you are fully aware of what your garden does. Do overhanging trees cut out light and rainfall? Does the soil become bone dry the moment the sun warms it up in spring? Are there any persistent damp spots? Where are the sunny places, at different times of day – in winter as well as in summer? The answers to questions like these are often your most useful guide in planning a workable layout. They are also invaluable in helping you achieve one of the most important goals in gardening: choosing the right plants for the right places.

Plot size
The design of your garden will be dictated by the size of the plot, so make a record of its dimensions at an early stage. An empty plot always appears bigger than it really is, and it's easy to think you can fit in more than it will easily accommodate, resulting in a garden that seems overcrowded. With a few rough measurements in front of you it's much easier to be realistic from the outset about what you can include.

Setting
The best gardens are those that sit well in their surroundings. This applies not only to big plots in the country, with a backdrop of woodland or rolling hills, but also to smaller, urban gardens, which might take their cue from the Victorian terraced house or contemporary studio to which they belong. Make notes and take photographs of the views from your garden – the aspects that will need screening, as well as those that could be adopted into your scheme. Also note the style of adjacent buildings, their materials, and details, which could perhaps be echoed in your design.

Shape
The shape of a plot can be deceptive. Unless your garden is a simple rectangle it may be worth doing a bit of basic surveying to get a reasonably accurate idea on paper of the shape you are dealing with. In the case of bigger plots, large-scale Ordnance Survey maps may help. These are available online, for a fee, or you can consult them in some public libraries (scales 1:1250 or 1:2500 are the best). Remember, though, that these larger-scale maps are not always up to date, so boundaries may have changed. Aerial photographs can be useful,

too. Again, your local library or public record office may be able to help. Some parts of the country are also covered by large-scale satellite photography, accessible online via Google Earth.

As well as recording the actual shape of the plot, note down and perhaps photograph any areas that feel awkward, cramped, inaccessible or generally difficult. They will need special treatment in your planning.

Topography

A flat, level site is a mixed blessing – it is easier to survey, but harder to make into an interesting three-dimensional garden. A sloping site entails more work if you need to make terraces or steps, but it can lend character to a garden, offering effortless changes of eye-level as well as contrasting views of the immediate landscape when going along the same path in different directions.

Aspect and orientation

These will be key factors in your design. Use a compass to find north, and record where the sun falls at different times of day, ideally in both summer and in winter. This will help you plan seating areas, and it will be a valuable guide for siting new trees and other tall features where they won't cast unwanted shade. Equally important, knowing which areas are sunny or shady is essential when it comes to choosing plants. Note the different types of shade, such as gloomy areas beneath deciduous trees where there will be more light in winter when the trees are bare, but where the soil is also likely to be

dry and poor. On the north side of a building, or beneath evergreens, there may well be year-round shade. Earmark any protected, 'sun-trap' areas as possible locations for plants (and people!) that love to bask.

Dappled shade around deciduous trees (here a tulip tree, *Liriodendron tulipifera*) can be a lovely effect to create. The space will be sunny in winter and inviting in a different way in summer, when the leafy canopy tempers the sun's heat and glare.

Wind direction will also be a factor, determining whether you will need to create shelter in certain areas (*see also* pages 96–7).

Climate and microclimate

Different gardens – or even parts of the same garden – have their own climatic conditions, a fact that is largely the result of aspect and orientation. Other factors, such as the surrounding topography, play their part too. For example, 'frost pockets' are particular areas that seem especially prone to frost, possibly due to some obstruction that prevents cold air from draining away down a slope. It may not be possible to 'cure' a frost pocket, but if you have identified it at least you'll know not to put vulnerable plants there. The same applies to damp spots, or places where buildings cause wind turbulence. The most successful planning and planting will take factors like these into account at an early stage.

Drainage

You'll probably be only too familiar with how your garden behaves in very wet weather. If drainage is poor, note where the worst places are, and consider installing land drains if the problem is really severe (*see* pages 72–3). Terracing slopes to make level, absorbent surfaces will help solve any problems there may be with excessive water run-off.

Soil

The type of soil you have is critical in choosing the right plants. The most important thing to find out is whether your soil drains freely (more likely on sand or chalk) or retains moisture (probably on clay). Whether the soil is acid or alkaline makes a big difference to certain plants. Many rhododendrons and camellias, and some heathers, magnolias and other popular shrubs and trees, dislike alkaline soil. Other plants – clematis, pinks and many shrubby herbs – just love it. Improving the soil in a general way is always worthwhile, but with extreme soil types it is usually best to choose plants that suit the soil you have, rather than trying to change the character of your soil radically to suit the plants.

Observation is a good rough guide to basic soil type. Notice how the soil behaves, whether existing plants (including weeds) grow well in it, and what it looks and feels like in different weather conditions. Can you dig after heavy rain without soil sticking to everything? Do puddles hang around for days? Do you tend to lose plants through summer drought or winter water-logging? Which plants appear to grow well in neighbouring gardens?

Greater precision than this may not be necessary, and more scientific soil testing is often less helpful than you might think because soil can vary quite a lot in different parts of a garden. For example, chalky soils sometimes have a 'clay cap' which makes the ground heavy and sticky in places, while acid soil can become more alkaline near buildings and paving, where there may be old mortar rubble. However, if you want to know the precise pH of your soil, testing kits are widely available.

Shingle and dense, drought-tolerant planting – a classic, practical solution that has made a success of many a sun-baked garden with poor, dry soil.

Existing plants

When taking over an existing garden, it is certainly worth saving any decent plants, especially mature trees and shrubs, that are already growing and can be renovated. Even if they would not be your first choice, they will prevent a feeling of bareness in the new garden and give it a sense of maturity from the outset. Make a list of the trees and shrubs you think may be worth preserving. This will also help you to reduce your plant bill.

Existing buildings and hard landscaping

Think about what you could do with existing garden buildings, fencing and other hard landscape structures: could they be restored, or just given a coat of paint, to make them useful in a new scheme? You may be able to save on costs by reusing existing paving, either in situ – perhaps with a new edging, different detailing or a change of emphasis – or elsewhere in the garden. Recycled paving slabs or shingle can be useful for making hard paths in a kitchen garden, or around a greenhouse, shed or compost area. Consider all the possibilities before you decide to scrap any of the structures or materials you have on the site.

Make a note of any eyesores that need to be disguised or concealed, such as an oil tank or a neighbour's shed. There are ways to screen them. (*See* pages 60–1 for ideas.)

Underground services

It is vital to establish the location and depth of any pipework or cabling that crosses the site so that you can work round it, if possible. Relocating services can be a costly operation, and with careful planning you can usually avoid it. Recently installed electricity cables, water mains and other services should have been laid to a statutory safe depth and be suitably protected, so they may not cause problems, but it's a good idea to find out where you may need to take special care when digging – inadvertent damage could have expensive consequences. With newer properties, you may be able to get hold of the architect's plan of the site showing the routes of services. Otherwise, the location of inspection covers and visible pipes and cables may offer clues.

Don't forget
You will probably have to work round existing access points to and from the house and the road, so doors and gates must be factored into your layout at an early stage. People tend to take the shortest route from A to B, even if it means cutting corners, so position paths on, or very close to, these routes.

Beth Chatto's wonderful garden sits on an unpromising combination of wet clay and dry gravel. Her secret? Choose plants to suit the conditions.

Your garden on paper

Making a plan can be a useful way to begin creating a garden design, but it isn't essential. Some lucky people are blessed with the ability to walk round a garden, immediately see what's wrong and visualize a cracking new layout. (This, incidentally, is usually much easier to do in other people's gardens than in your own!) Others feel daunted by the very idea of measuring, plotting and drawing, and would avoid planning their garden at all if that's what they had to do.

Nevertheless, a design plan – even a rough one – drawn to scale on paper can be a tremendously helpful tool. It gives you an idea of whether everything fits (before you start building or planting, and find that it doesn't), and you can play around with shapes and sizes in a way that's difficult to do on the ground. It's also a good basis for calculating fairly accurately the quantities of materials to order for hard landscaping, and it gives you a ready-made template for drawing up a planting plan and estimating the number of plants you will need.

In your survey, you'll need to plot the positions of all the existing features that will affect your design: paths, drives, fences, mature trees and inspection covers.

Measuring a plot

If you do decide to make a design plan of the whole garden, you will need a clear idea of the shape of the plot, its boundaries and the position of any important features: the house, outbuildings, trees, access points and so on. Surveying can be a complicated business, with different methods and increasingly sophisticated technology. The subject could easily fill a book on its own, so it is not covered in detail here. However, if your garden has a reasonably straightforward shape, you can use some simple surveying techniques to plot its outline on paper. For larger or more complicated gardens, or if you feel you would like to plan the garden on paper but aren't confident about measuring up, consider having a professional survey done. (*See also* pages 12–13 for other possible sources of information on your plot.)

The simplest, most accurate low-tech method of plotting a garden's boundaries and features is to use the classic surveying technique of triangulation, where you plot a point by measuring its distance from two different, known points on a base line. You can use the house wall as your base line, and the two corners

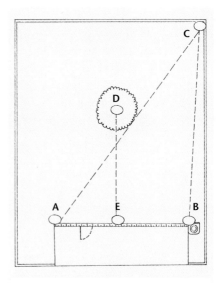

The diagram shows how to plot the corner of the site (C) by triangulation from points A and B, while the tree (D) is plotted as an offset from point (E) on the base line (AB).

Don't forget

Use metric measurements when drawing up your plan, or you will need to convert everything before you order the materials. These days, off-the-peg items, such as paving slabs, are nearly always supplied in metric sizes, with no imperial equivalents.

of the house as the points from which you measure (*see* the diagram above). First, stretch a tape measure along the wall from one end (A) to the other (B) and note down the distances from A of all doors and windows, and of the house corner (B). Then list the features you intend to plot, for example the corners of the garden (such as C), any other points where the boundaries change direction, and any significant features you plan to keep – such as a shed or greenhouse, a pond or tree. Next, fix the end of the tape at point A and measure the distance to each

Use a retractable metal tape measure for distances up to 5m (16ft) or so. For a whole garden, a surveyor's tape (up to 50m/165ft long) is best.

MAKE A WISH LIST

In creating the new garden of your dreams, it's surprisingly easy to lose sight of some of the practical things you want to achieve. So, at the outset, make a wish list of the features that you would like to have in your new garden. For a family garden, for example, your list might look like the one below – and your sketch plan could end up looking something like the one on the right.

1 A family dining area, with overhead shade, for outdoor lunches in summer
2 A water feature that can be seen from the kitchen window
3 A wildlife corner, where visiting birds can be seen from the house in winter
4 Overhead screening (a pergola) from a neighbour's upstairs window
5 Secure but attractive boundaries to keep children and dogs safe
6 A level, well-drained, grassy play area with sun for most of the year
7 A seat in the sun for morning coffee, or for a summer evening drink
8 An unobtrusive (but not too shady) place to dry the washing
9 An easy-maintenance raised bed for herbs and salad crops
10 Accessible but tucked-away storage for bicycles and tools

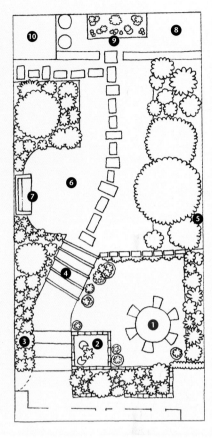

of the features on your list. Then fix the end of the tape at point B and record the distance from there to each feature. Finally, measure the footprint of any structures, and note down the diameter of the canopy of trees and major shrubs.

For plotting other features in the garden, a quicker but less accurate method is to take 'offsets' from the base line. Measure and record the distance from each feature (such as the tree, D) to the base line, being careful to make sure the tape meets the base line at right angles. Record the distance from the start of the base line (A) to the point where the offset tape meets it (E).

You can then replicate your measurements on paper, using a scale rule and a set square as described below.

Plotting the site

Armed with your measurements, and back at your work table, the next step is to turn the information you have collected into a rough site plan. You'll need a sharp pencil, a large sheet of paper, a scale rule, a set square and a pair of compasses (oh, and an eraser!). First, decide on a scale. Use the largest scale you can without making the plan unwieldy. For a small garden a scale of 1:50 will do very nicely (that is, 1cm on the plan = 50cm on the site).

Using your scale rule, draw in your base line to the correct length. Then, again using your scale rule, set the compasses to the distance from

A to your first feature. Draw an arc representing that distance from A. Do the same with the distance from B to the feature. Where the arcs cross is the position of the feature.

Build up a master plan of the garden's shape and features in this way, then make some photocopies to use as templates on to which you can roughly sketch all your design ideas.

You are now all set to experiment with as many different layouts as it takes to find the one that ticks all the boxes. *See* pages 20–5 for some design tips that may help you to get started on a layout. You will get there in the end.

Planting plans

When you've decided on a layout for the plot – whether or not you've made a design plan – it's definitely worth taking the trouble to make a planting plan for each bed and border in your garden.

On paper – away from the lures of the garden centre – it's much easier to assess how much space each plant will take up, what you can plant underneath what, how many plants of each kind you'll need, and what the effect will be throughout the year. Think about the long-term suitability of each plant, and the best combinations and groupings. The result will be more satisfying this way, and the saving you'll make on all the unsuitable impulse buys you've avoided will pay for a few more plants that will be just right.

Measuring beds and borders

A planting plan needn't be fancy, but it does need to be roughly to scale (1:50 is usually best), so measure and draw an accurate outline of each bed. Measuring a single flower bed is a piece of cake in comparison with surveying a whole garden. Rectangular beds are the easiest, of course, but do measure all four sides, as what looks like a rectangle won't always be true. For borders with one irregular side, run a tape along the straight side and then measure out from this at right angles, at 1m intervals, plotting corresponding points along the edge on the other side.

Having measured the shape of the bed, plot the dimensions on paper. Use a circle template to draw in the

plants; at 1:50 a shrub with a diameter of 1m will be represented as a circle 20mm across. Size is a knotty problem here: do you draw a tree or shrub at the size it is when you plant it, or at its eventual size? The best answer is a compromise. So a medium-sized shrub that might reach a diameter of 1.5m (5ft) within two to five years of planting would be shown by a circle 30mm across.

Label each circle as you go with the name of the plant, or number them and use a key. Link the circles representing plants of the same kind that form a group, so you only have to write the name once. You may like to sketch in a bit of detail to remind you at a glance what each plant is: jagged edges for a spiky plant like a yucca, tiny dots for a clipped box, billowy outlines for a rose. Position trees and evergreen shrubs first. It's important to get these in just the right place because

they will be with you for a long time. Shade in any evergreen shrubs that reach right down to the ground, as they won't need any underplanting. Overlap the circles where one plant is beneath another, for example a shrub beneath a tree and then a herbaceous plant at

PLANTING PLAN FOR A 6 × 2M (20 × 6FT) SUNNY BORDER
Evergreen shrubs and grasses give structure and all-year interest. Flowering shrubs and perennials, underplanted with spring bulbs, are chosen for seasonal succession.

1   *Philadelphus* 'Silberregen'
2   *Aquilegia alpina* (×6)
3   *Buxus sempervirens* 'Elegantissima'
4   *Yucca filamentosa* 'Bright Edge' (×3)
5   *Euphorbia characias* subsp. *wulfenii* (×2)
6   *Narcissus* 'Jack Snipe' (×50)
7   *Rosa* 'Winchester Cathedral' (×2)
8   *Helianthemum* 'Wisley White' (×2)
9   *Geranium* 'Rozanne' (×5)
10 *Stipa tenuissima* (×5)
11 *Mahonia* × *media* 'Winter Sun'
12 *Osmanthus heterophyllus* 'Goshiki'

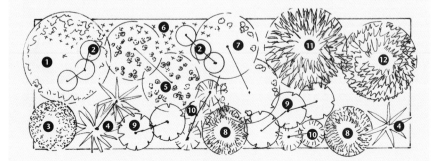

ground level. Bulbs can be shown as drifts of dots or little crosses.

Finally, list all the plants on the plan, with quantities of each. That's your shopping list.

From paper to garden

To transfer a design or a planting layout from a plan to the ground, start by converting some of the key measurements to real distances on the ground, and write them on the plan. With a planting plan, this might be the distance along the border – and the distance from the back – of the key plants, such as trees and large or evergreen shrubs. Position these key plants, in their pots, in the bed, and use them as a guide for placing the rest of the plants. You needn't measure the exact position for every single one.

Similarly, with a design plan, plot several points along the outline of a proposed path, patio or pond, for example, and join them to mark the outline with pegs and string, or with a hosepipe fixed to the ground with wire pegs or hoops. Use long canes to mark the positions of trees and other tall features, to give you a general idea of how the layout will look. As you mark out more features, it becomes easier to locate the rest. Live with this rough layout for a few days, look at it from every angle, imagine it in every kind of light and weather. When you're finally happy, mark it out more permanently with paint or a trail of dry sand.

A plastic bottle filled with free-running dry sand is a handy way of marking your layout on the ground.

If a planting plan seems a bother, remember that it is usually a much surer route to a well-designed border, with shapes and colours working well together, and the right plants in the right places.

Garden shapes

Beautiful gardens can be made on plots of any shape and size. Of course, there is no substitute for a well-proportioned space – but most gardens don't start out that way. Whether yours is standard-issue rectangular or the wackiest mix of angles or curves, you can use all sorts of tricks to alter, or enhance, its apparent size and shape. Most shapes have their pros and cons – to achieve a good layout, you just have to make sure the pros win the day.

Amazingly, this garden is only 14m (45ft) square. Strong shapes, good verticals and action-packed planting distract you from the boundaries. There's more interest here than in most gardens several times as big.

Thinking outside the box

Whatever you do, don't make the perimeter the starting point for your new design. Following the boundary lines will emphasize the shape of the plot and make it look smaller. Never, ever make narrow borders along the fences, leaving what's left as a lawn in the middle. Start, instead, from the other end of the telescope. Think not in terms of boundaries but in terms of open spaces – even small ones.

So, plan well-defined, strongly shaped spaces for the heart of your plot. The best take their cue from the shapes and proportions of the house, giving house and garden a clear sense of unity, which can be reinforced through your choice of hard landscaping materials (see pages 78–83). Other strong shapes might include a lawn in the shape of a circle, or two circles or diagonally positioned rectangles that interlock with each other.

Having determined the open areas, start to plan planting and features to give your layout structure and purpose, and to fill any 'dead space' left around the edges. This will distract attention from the garden's shape and blur the boundaries.

Using space creatively

On all but the tiniest plot, plan a walkable route so that you can stroll into the garden and return to the house a different way. It needn't all be a major path. Part of the route could cross an open space such as a lawn or paved area, and stepping-stones or narrow, bark-surfaced paths could form part of the circuit. Plan a series of interesting things along the way – specimen plants, seats, containers, a water feature – each one leading to the next.

Use changes of level to define separate areas. These can either be created by terracing an existing slope, or contrived artificially on a flat site (but don't forget that for every up there will have to be a corresponding down).

Contrasting areas of light and shade can bring changes of mood and invite you to walk on. Light and shade, and colour, can also be used to alter the apparent shape of a space by creating the illusion of distance and depth (see also page 41). Dark colours tend to recede while light colours appear nearer. You'll be amazed at the effect of painting structures black, for example; it makes a fence or shed virtually disappear. Black also makes a flattering backdrop to planting in front of it – useful for creating a sense of depth. Golden or silver foliage, or architectural plants, look really striking with a black backdrop, as do shapely bare twigs or frost-covered seedheads, enhanced by low winter sunshine.

Keeping just one long view will give an impression of distance and space in the garden. It doesn't have to be a main path: any clear sight line will do, perhaps with a focal point just visible at the far end.

Mirrors are useful tools for giving the impression of a larger space, but must be at just the right angle, and set among planting or behind trellis, to hide the edges and make the illusion work.

The awkward shape

For all sorts of reasons, some gardens are just a funny shape. Boundaries may have changed over the years, and bits of land been acquired or sold off, or sheds demolished, or a house extended. The shape of a house and its position on a plot can leave you with an awkward space, or even a whole series of them, but applying some of the techniques outlined above can help turn the situation to advantage. An awkward plot outline can prompt inventive ways of creating spaces within it that will make a more interesting and original garden than a 'standard' site such as a square or oblong. You'll soon forget you ever thought you had a difficult site.

Don't forget
'Borrowing' features such as trees from neighbouring gardens, by leaving open views to them where you can, will distract attention from your own boundaries and make your garden seem bigger.

Tips and tricks

- If you can't see the whole of a space at once, it will feel larger.
- Looking down a slope or a step makes a given area seem longer.
- An open area feels sunnier if you go through shade to reach it.
- A narrow entrance into a space will make the space feel bigger when you get there.
- A path that narrows slightly as you walk (or look) along it feels longer.
- The direction in which paving bricks or slabs are laid can make a path look longer (if they are laid lengthways) or wider (if laid crosswise).
- Still water, with its reflective surface, makes a space appear larger.

A stone lion framed by formal hedging is a focal point across the lawn, with an 'avenue' of topiary to lead the eye. The long view gives the impression of a larger space.

Square gardens

A square garden may be dead easy to measure and to plot on paper especially if it's flat, but it can be quite a challenge to turn it into something interesting. Clever planting will be one of your best allies, along with thinking in three dimensions and using strong shapes like diagonals or curves. Experiment with hexagons or octagons too – they will connect with the formal lines of the square while introducing a different directional pull.

Divide and conquer

Breaking up the garden into distinct areas is the first step in overcoming the predictability of a square space, but this needs to be done very subtly so the divisions don't look too contrived. Planting is often the best way – it's amazingly versatile and a welcome natural touch to complement and contrast with the geometry. Use plants, such as a

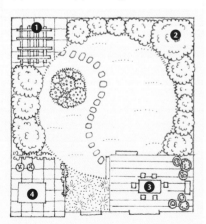

Curves and circles here counteract the 'boxiness' of a square plot. There are raised seating areas (1) and (3), with a screened utility area (4), and a pergola (1) and trees (2) for height.

Screens used to divide a garden don't need to be solid. Trellis is often ideal, allowing light and air to pass through and giving climbing plants an instant foothold.

tree or bamboo, to create height; separate spaces at a low level with a dwarf box hedge (or *Euonymus japonicus* 'Microphyllus' if box blight is a problem); or use tall grasses, the slender-stemmed *Verbena bonariensis* or a climber on a trellis to act as a semi-transparent screen.

Courtyard gardens

Though often square, these are less problematic than larger square gardens because there won't be room for major divisions of the space, and the scale is intimate enough for a real 'outdoor room'. Contemporary design (*see* pages 26–7) works very well for a courtyard garden. You'll find inspiration in the great variety of small gardens built each year for the Chelsea Flower Show. The most successful ones are those that bring together several features or incidents – perhaps a welcoming entrance, a seating area, a water feature and some cracking planting – into a coherent whole, with a unifying design theme that runs through the colours, materials and shapes used. You can create elements of surprise by having small areas hidden by planting, or by tucking a sculpture or unusual specimen plant into a corner where it can only be seen from certain angles.

Three dimensions

Height and levels are more important than ever in a square garden. If possible, set at least one part of the garden at a different level – perhaps a raised bed or semi-raised pond. Even a single low step makes a big difference if its position and shape emphasize the structure and proportions of your garden.

Long, narrow gardens

Long and narrow is without doubt the most common 'problem' shape for a garden. Look out of a train window as you go through older areas of towns and cities and you'll see them by the dozen. In the case of terraced houses, the garden will usually be the same width as the dwelling; with semi-detached houses it will be a little wider.

Either way, it's all too easy for the garden to look and feel like a passageway, particularly when there are tall wooden fences on either side and a long straight path to the end.

Making compartments

What you need to do is to turn the garden – both physically and visually – into a place to linger in, rather than one to rush through.

The tried and tested trick of dividing up the space will work a treat here. Think of the garden as a series of smaller spaces, each one related to and leading on to the next. This feeling of connectedness can be achieved by repeating hard landscape materials, or colours or particular plants. An element of the unexpected will be important as you enter the different areas, so ensure

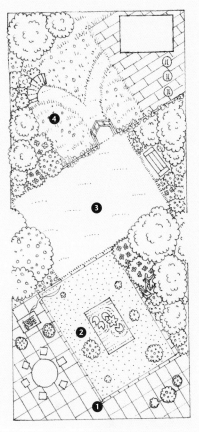

A narrow garden becomes a series of linked areas set diagonally crosswise. A patio (1) overlooks a gravel area with a pond (2), leading to a lawn (3), then through an arch to a meadow area (4).

A winding path through dense, varied planting within a framework of evergreens completely hides the boundaries of this narrow town garden.

that at least part of each space is hidden. Then consider what you want from the garden and what form you would like each area to take. Your chosen combination might be a romantic, fragrant flower garden, a play area and a compact kitchen garden; or a contemporary dining and barbecue area, a lawn with a couple of fruit trees and a small water garden. Compartments need to be linked to form a coherent whole, but preferably not by means of a straight line. Experiment with different ways of interlocking the shapes, and use diagonals, S shapes and other curves as a distraction from the parallel boundaries.

Pushing the boundaries sideways

Take every opportunity to emphasize the plot's width – perhaps by having a seat and a focal point at opposite ends of a paved or grassed area that runs across the garden, or by using a mirror to create the illusion of a space beyond the boundary. Incorporate sideways or diagonal views of things outside the garden if you can – a neighbour's tree, a distant landscape or just a patch of sky. Use trees or a structure such as an arch or pergola to lead the eye to these 'borrowed' features. And finally, use plants to disguise fences. If at all possible, make a visual link between your planting and trees or shrubs outside your garden – it will give the illusion of a much bigger planted area and help to make your boundary disappear altogether.

Triangular gardens

OK, so there may not be many gardens in the shape of a perfect triangle. But if you include all the odd-shaped plots with converging boundaries, plus the wedge-shaped pieces of garden that get left when a house is awkwardly angled on its site, they add up to a significant number of design challenges. Just as with other difficult plot shapes, the solution lies in using strong shapes to focus attention completely within the garden rather than on its corners and boundaries.

A reflective pool gives this inspired London garden another dimension. Vertical plants focus attention within the garden, while the neighbours' 'borrowed' trees blur the boundaries.

Making the most of it

With any irregularly shaped garden, figure out how to make the best use of the longest dimensions, in order to make the plot look larger. One way is to base your layout on an irregular cross shape, with the two axes running at right angles across the widest part and down the longest part of the garden. Use clever planting to create the illusion that the garden is as wide and as long as this all over, rather than

Rectangles for a triangular plot: a patio (1) opens to a lawn (2), which is linked to a gravel area with a pergola (3) – a long axial view. The 'dead end' becomes a screened utility area (4).

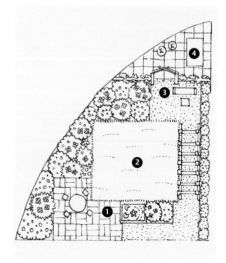

disappearing into – literally – the thin end of the wedge. Other shapes to consider are overlapping circles or squares of different sizes, or an elongated octagon or hexagon. Mirrors can also be used to make the narrow end of the plot look wider.

Wide, shallow gardens

These gardens can make you feel short of 'breathing space', with a neighbour's fence uncomfortably close to your windows. Front gardens, too, are often wide and shallow, but they tend to be less enclosed than back gardens, so the shape is less of a problem.

Creating depth

The priority with a shallow garden is to create an illusion of depth and distance. Some of the techniques for long, narrow gardens (*see* pages 22–4) work equally well turned through 90 degrees. Borrow views from beyond your garden, and use every trick in the book to make the far boundary recede or disappear. You can manipulate perspective by making a path that leads towards

the boundary slightly narrower as it runs from the house to the fence – apparently lengthening it. Changes in mood or light along a path – such as the alternating sequence of light and shade that you get beneath a pergola or along an avenue of trees – also appear to increase distance. Planting will be a key part of the illusion; you can choose and position plants to create depth (*see also* page 41) – a light-coloured shrub against a dark yew hedge or conifer will

Creating depth and distance: a clematis-clad arch leads into an open area which narrows into a path disappearing into shade.

make the distance between the two plants appear greater than it is.

The third dimension

Height too can be used as a distraction. Tall, vertical plants and structures to the sides of the garden, contrasted with shorter, horizontal ones along the end boundary, will bring the sides in and appear to lengthen the plot. Tall, interestingly shaped plants grouped around a feature at ground level, such as a pond, will subtly draw attention downwards. Tricks like this help to keep the focus of your vision firmly within the garden rather than on the too-close boundary.

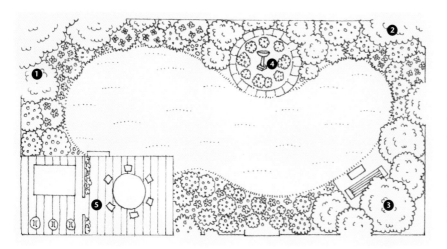

Tall planting (1), (2) and (3) brings in the sides of this wide garden, contrasting with a circle of low planting (4) around a bird bath. The deck timbers (5) are laid lengthways to suggest depth.

Contemporary gardens

The ongoing rejuvenation of many inner city areas has helped stir up a lot of interest in the design of contemporary small gardens. Outdoor spaces such as enclosed courtyards and roof gardens are a good starting point for creating clean-lined, modern outdoor rooms that don't need to worry too much about blending in with their wider setting. But when it comes to the planting in such intimate spaces, you'll realize there's nowhere to hide your mistakes – so you need to make sure everything is spot on.

Sustainable local materials and drought-resistant planting – topical themes in this 2005 Chelsea Flower Show courtyard garden, by staff and students of Chichester College.

Materials and plants

A contemporary look requires a clutter-free space with plenty of light. This applies no matter how big or small the garden, though contemporary design is particularly effective in making small spaces look and feel bigger (*see also* pages 120–1). Consider pale-coloured or reflective construction materials: metal, glass, ceramic, perhaps set off by colour-washed walls. Garden furniture should be well designed, almost sculptural, and planting will probably need to be fairly minimal and architectural (*see* box). Plants with strong shapes, such as those with spiky foliage, are well suited to contemporary gardens. Grasses really come into their own – there are so many different ones available nowadays. Plant colours used in contemporary schemes are often cool, with strong contrasts: moody blackish purple with lime green, for example. White and silver are effective, too, looking very chic against a dark background or in the shade. Feed, water, weed and dead-head regularly: plants need to be in tip-top condition for the crisp, clean look you're after.

Plant ideas for contemporary schemes

Allium hollandicum
Cordyline australis
Eryngium giganteum
Euphorbia characias subsp. *wulfenii*
Fargesia nitida
Fatsia japonica
Hakonechloa macra 'Aureola'
Helictotrichon sempervirens
Hosta sieboldiana
Iris pallida 'Variegata'
Phormium 'Maori Queen'
Santolina chamaecyparissus 'Lemon Queen'
Sedum spectabile 'Iceberg'
Sempervivum tectorum 'Atrorubens'
Sisyrinchium striatum
Stipa gigantea
Yucca filamentosa 'Bright Edge'

A detail of a Chelsea garden by Kate Gould, using materials favoured in contemporary design: brushed steel, decking and the tough perennial sedge *Carex buchananii*.

Roof gardens

Roof gardens aren't new by any means, but increasingly they are being seen as a practical option by city dwellers; in fact, a roof garden may be your only option if you live in an upstairs flat. But first, make quite sure that it will be structurally sound. It may be necessary to strengthen the existing building to take the load, so consult a structural engineer before you even think about creating a roof garden. If it works, you will have the benefit of views to die for, as well as great light and a curious sense of seclusion that ground-hugging gardens can't match. All this lends itself well to a contemporary design.

Wind is sure to be a challenge, and you will need to create shelter and shade. Construction materials need to be chosen with the location in mind. A purpose-made roof garden on a new building may have solid walls for shelter, but this may not be the case if you are adapting an existing structure. Soundly fixed trellis is light and will filter the wind, and decking is often a good choice of flooring.

Choose plants that can withstand regular buffetings. Think drought-tolerant, too. Those winds will dry plants very rapidly, especially if there isn't much depth of soil, and access for watering may not be easy. So build your scheme around undemanding plants: succulents such as sedums and sempervivums, low shrubs with felted or leathery leaves and tough, wiry grasses. Sheltered corners are ideal for sun-trap seating, and for tubs of dwarf spring bulbs and seasonal colour.

'Black' plants

Perhaps more than any other colour, black (or at least very dark) plants – sought after by nurserymen and gardeners alike – are particularly effective in a contemporary setting. Here are some favourites:

Aeonium 'Zwartkop'

Alcea rosea 'Nigra'

Anthriscus sylvestris 'Ravenswing'

Euphorbia 'Blackbird'

Geranium pratense 'Black Beauty'

Helleborus (many dark forms available)

Hermodactylus tuberosus

Ophiopogon planiscapus 'Nigrescens'

Phormium 'Platt's Black'

Phyllostachys nigra

Pittosporum tenuifolium 'Tom Thumb'

Sambucus nigra 'Gerda' ('Black Beauty')

Scabiosa atropurpurea 'Chile Black'

Tulipa 'Queen of Night'

Veratrum nigrum

Viola riviniana Purpurea Group

Clean lines, stark colours and minimal planting are typical of many contemporary schemes. In this one by Diarmuid Gavin, a similarly styled roof terrace overlooks the oval deck.

Seeking inspiration

Visiting one of the growing number of annual flower shows staged in various parts of the UK from spring to autumn is undoubtedly the best way to sample contemporary design and planting ideas, ranging from the down-to-earth and practical to the way-out and wacky. The key events are organized by the Royal Horticultural Society (RHS), which awards medals to nursery exhibits and display gardens that are constructed specially for the show. Many of the show gardens are small, and special categories such as urban gardens and courtyard gardens are chosen for their practical relevance to garden owners. Make notes, take photos and talk to the exhibitors, who are usually on hand and only too willing to share their ideas and tips. Good shows to visit (most of them are also televised) include:

■ RHS Spring Flower Show (Cardiff, April)

■ RHS Chelsea Flower Show (London, May)

■ BBC Gardeners' World Live (Birmingham, June)

■ RHS Hampton Court Palace Flower Show (Surrey, July)

■ RHS Flower Show at Tatton Park (Cheshire, July)

■ RHS Flower Show at Malvern Autumn Show (Worcestershire, September)

Cottage gardens

Garden fashions come and go, but the cottage garden seems to be a true perennial. With its luxuriance and its wide range of plants, this is a style that lends itself to the British climate and temperament. Although the exuberant planting scheme of a typical garden may look artless, its success will depend on choosing the right plants and exercising a little restraint.

Unpretentious yet dramatic, oriental poppies suit cottage gardens well. They need space, but cut them down after flowering and plant summer annuals around their crowns.

Controlled exuberance

The most successful cottage gardens do have an underlying structure, however discreet. The hand of restraint may not be obvious, and the effect is probably better if it isn't, but it needs to be there all the same, to prevent the plants from engulfing one another and to provide some contrast to the luxuriance, so it doesn't all seem indigestible. Anything harsh, modern or clumsy is out, but limited areas of open space – such as paving or soft paths – are necessary to set off the billowing planting and invite you to wander through it, while hedges and fences, or perhaps some topiary, will create a contrasting backdrop. These structural elements help to hold the garden together and extend the season of interest so there is something to enjoy in winter, when the flowers have faded.

Cottage gardens through time

Certain key elements of the traditional cottage garden style fit in well with today's enthusiasm for sustainable gardening. Keeping the ground densely covered with plants helps to save both work and water, since weeds are suppressed and evaporation is reduced. Mingling flowers with vegetables, fruit and herbs looks good and helps foil pests and diseases, while self-sufficiency – an idea born out of necessity in times past – is now finding favour again. Cottagers were great recyclers, finding decorative

Self-sowing flowers such as aquilegias and forget-me-nots are invaluable in cottage borders – especially (as here at Eastgrove Cottage) in spring, before roses take centre stage.

garden uses for household cast-offs and reusing building materials such as bricks, chimney pots and roof tiles for different purposes. Other materials would have been locally sourced: sustainable hazel or willow for wigwams and plant supports, perhaps, and hurdles for fencing and gates, or for edging beds. Willow and hazel hurdles have become popular again today, and can even be fixed to an existing close-boarded or panel fence to fit in with the cottage garden style. Choose garden furniture carefully so it doesn't spoil the effect: rustic, antique or simple bistro-style tables and chairs would be good choices.

Cottage garden planting

As to plants, the popular perception of a cottage garden is that anything goes, but the overall effect will be much more successful with a little discreet planning. As you head for yet another nursery, keep a few design principles in mind. Select some backbone plants – evergreens like holly, yew or santolina as well as strongly shaped perennials (alliums, eryngiums, irises) to add structure and texture and keep interest going through the seasons. If there's room for a tree, you may want an apple, with a clematis to climb through it, or a plum. You'll probably want plenty of 'old-fashioned' plants in the borders – perhaps aquilegias, foxgloves, hollyhocks, poppies, violas, pinks, wallflowers, sweet peas, lavender, honeysuckle ... the list goes on. Plants that self-seed (see 'Volunteers', right) encapsulate the spirit of cottage gardening and help lend

(see 'Volunteers', right)

'Volunteers'

American gardeners still use this old term to mean plants that have sown themselves. Many plants will reproduce themselves indefinitely in the right conditions – provided, of course, that you leave the flowerheads to ripen and shed their seed. This is no hardship in the case of poppies and love-in-a-mist, whose intricate, shapely seedheads are part of their charm. Plants like this can be invaluable when you are trying to create a 'cottagey' effect. True, such plants can become weeds if they are not properly managed, but they have many advantages, and unwanted seedlings are easy to pull up when small. So learn to recognize these no-fuss arrivals when they appear in your borders – every garden will have its own 'specialities'. They will be the plants that are naturally happy there; they won't need cosseting, and they'll make a harmonious backdrop that will help your planting scheme hang together – and all for free!

Some self-sowers to encourage:

Allium

Aquilegia (columbine)

Cyclamen

Erigeron karvinskianus

Eryngium giganteum

Eschscholzia californica (Californian poppy)

Euphorbia characias

Helleborus (hellebore)

Hesperis matronalis (sweet rocket)

Limnanthes douglasii (poached-egg plant)

Lunaria annua (honesty)

Myosotis (forget-me-not)

Nigella (love-in-a-mist)

Papaver somniferum (opium poppy)

Primula veris (cowslip)

Stipa tenuissima

Verbena bonariensis

Viola riviniana Purpurea Group

coherence to the planting scheme, often positioning themselves in just the right place. Whatever you choose, the overall impression should be artless – no matter how much forethought and effort have gone into achieving it.

There's nothing quite like sweet peas, one of the old-fashioned hallmarks of cottage gardening. Build a rustic structure of poles to support them and give height to the garden.

Easy cottage garden perennials

Ajuga reptans 'Catlin's Giant'

Alchemilla mollis

Anemone x *hybrida* 'Honorine Jobert'

Armeria maritima

Aster x *frikartii* 'Mönch'

Astrantia

Brunnera macrophylla 'Jack Frost'

Campanula poscharskyana

Centranthus ruber

Dianthus

Echinops ritro

Geranium psilostemon

Geum rivale 'Leonard's Variety'

Inula hookeri

Nepeta 'Six Hills Giant'

Pulmonaria

Thalictrum delavayi

Wildlife gardens

Garden design entails creating a whole environment. This involves not just the look of a garden but the life and movement that help make it a special place to be. Anyone who has a garden rich in wildlife will tell you that the creatures give them at least as much pleasure throughout the year as the plants. Watching your 'own' little ecosystem on a daily basis gives you an intimate knowledge and understanding of a host of fascinating lives and life-cycles, together with a constant sense of wonderment.

Foxgloves are ideal for a wildlife garden. They take over in early summer, when the profusion of spring flowers has come to an end, and if they are happy they will self-seed, increasing the size of colony year on year. Bees love them, too.

Designing for wildlife

First, there's no need to transform your garden into a wilderness, nor to fill it with native plants. Ordinary gardens with ordinary planting can attract a whole range of wildlife with great success, provided of course that food chains aren't interrupted by the use of pesticides such as sprays and slug pellets. Habitats, too, must be preserved and not destroyed by over-zealous trimming, strimming and obsessive tidiness – particularly in spring and summer. Good design and wildlife gardening aren't in the least incompatible, and the usual principles still apply – from creating focal points to balancing planted areas with open spaces, or choosing a mixture of plant shapes and types for interest in different seasons. There are, though, a few key features that will make a real difference to the balance of wildlife in your garden.

Planting for wildlife

Shelter and natural food for your wild guests should be your first priority. Hedges, trees and shrubs, including some evergreens for winter cover, provide not only places to hide and build nests, but also food in the shape of small insects and caterpillars, as well as winter berries. Include some native plants if you can. Many native trees, such as oak and ash, are too vigorous for the average garden, but hawthorn, birch, crab-apple and rowan are easier to accommodate, and are all attractive garden trees in their own right. Delay cutting down herbaceous plants until early spring and you may notice that in winter they attract seed-eaters, including goldfinches and chaffinches, as well as dunnocks, tits and wrens searching among them for tiny insects. Blackbirds and thrushes will keep you entertained with their enthusiastic rummaging among the dead leaves.

Boosting your garden's insect population by introducing a good mixture of different plants can be beneficial all round. With luck you will attract pest-eating predators such as hoverflies, ladybirds, spiders, lacewings and ground beetles. They are fascinating to watch at close quarters as well as being valuable gardening allies, helping to control aphids, slugs and many other pests. Open-centred flowers such as poppies, evening primroses and poached-egg flowers are good for hoverflies, while bees delight in catmint, foxgloves, eryngiums, sedums and many herbs such as thyme, mint, lavender and hyssop. Butterflies and moths use a huge range of plants as food for caterpillars or a nectar source for adults on the wing. Try *Centranthus ruber* (red valerian), *Sedum spectabile* (ice-plant), buddleia and *Verbena bonariensis*.

Wildlife and water

A pond is a magnet for all kinds of wildlife, attracting not only breeding frogs and other amphibians but also birds in search of a drink, or a plumage-restoring bath, or mud to help build their nests. Other visitors are likely to include hedgehogs and other small mammals, as well as bees and many different insects, among them several glamorous species of dragonfly and damselfly.

Another feature that will boost your garden's wildlife potential is the compost heap, a favourite hideout for centipedes, voles and the slug-eating slow-worm. Piles of logs, sticks or stones tucked under a shady hedge encourage newts, frogs and toads to lurk, and will also attract beetles, woodlice and other garden-friendly invertebrates.

A pond doesn't need to be huge or deep to make all the difference to garden wildlife, but it does need a gently sloping edge for access.

Ten shrubs for wildlife

Buddleja (butterfly bush)
Cotoneaster
Euonymus europaeus (spindle)
Hedera (ivy)
Hippophae rhamnoides (sea buckthorn)
Ilex (holly – species and varieties)
Prunus spinosa (blackthorn)
Pyracantha (firethorn)
Rosa rugosa (Ramana rose)
Viburnum opulus (guelder rose)

The outsize hips of *Rosa rugosa* – a feast for the human eye and, in hard weather, for fruit-eating birds.

Positioning a birdbox high up a tree, but with easy access so you can clean it, will give nesting birds some protection from predatory cats.

Planting generous drifts of nectar-rich plants (here, Michaelmas daisies) will help butterflies find their way to your garden.

Family gardens

A family garden is all about having something for everyone – easy to achieve if you have lots of space, but harder in a small town garden. A patio (*see* page 80), a lawn, a child-sized gardening area and a couple of well-designed pieces of outdoor play equipment form a good basis for a variety of outdoor pastimes, but the possibilities are endless.

Willow is a wonderfully easy, cheap and eco-friendly material for play structures such as a tunnel or a den like this. And building them is part of the fun, whether you're seven or 70.

Lawns

Not every garden needs a lawn (*see* pages 74–105), but if you have a young family it is likely to be a priority. As a versatile, soft-surfaced open space for play and relaxation, lawns are hard to beat. You don't want a bowling green, just a tough grass mixture that can take a lot of punishment. (If you're starting from scratch, buy a special, hard-wearing grass-seed mix.) Don't cut the grass too short or you might end up with bare patches, especially in areas of heavy wear.

Gardening with children

Lots of young children find great delight in gardening and the magic of making things grow. Children can be involved in the planning and building of a specially designed little garden of their own, where they can grow plants that produce quick results. A timber raised bed, narrow enough for short arms to reach from both sides, is simple to construct (*see* page 37). If you edge it with stout planks nailed or screwed to posts sunk into the ground it should last as long as it needs to, and will give a lot of pleasure. A semi-shaded spot could be used for a small, acrylic-glazed cold frame, where seeds can be sown and cuttings rooted. And paths surfaced with chipped bark, with a seat and small table nearby, will finish it off nicely.

Play equipment

A vast selection of play equipment made from natural materials is now available and will look far better in a garden setting than brightly coloured plastic, which never seems to mellow and can be hard to dispose of sustainably when no longer needed. You could of course

Growing organically

Many parents now choose to garden organically. As well as producing chemical-free food, this eliminates the risk of children coming into contact with potentially harmful substances such as pesticides and weedkillers.

Swimming pools

In hot weather what could be more perfect than your own swimming pool, but the design challenge is how to incorporate it without letting such a large feature dominate the garden. If you have the space, a separate, hedged enclosure is probably the best solution, ideally free from overhanging trees that will drop leaves into the water. You can plant the area exclusively for seasonal summer colour and fragrance to enjoy while you're using the pool, and forget about it for the rest of the year.

There are, however, other ways for swimming and gardening to go hand in hand. A good swimming pool installer with a little imagination should be able to offer you a tailor-made, harmonious design that is more garden-friendly than the standard bright blue rectangular box. An exciting new development is the 'swimming pond', a pool that looks and behaves like a natural pond. Aquatic plants chosen specifically to keep the water clean naturally, without the need for chemicals, are planted around the shallow margins, and there is a deeper, central area of open water for swimming. These ponds are a specialist construction job, but several companies in the UK now operate in this field.

spend thousands on a bespoke tree house or a sophisticated climbing frame, but children will have just as much fun, at a fraction of the cost, with a tunnel created from slips of living willow, a worn-out rowing boat picked up second-hand, or a sandpit made from a circle of logs set vertically into the ground or from a cleaned-up tractor or lorry tyre.

Planting for a young family

Your garden may have to cater for budding footballers and games of hide-and-seek, but that doesn't mean plants are doomed. Choice, delicate specimens may have to wait a few years, but there are hundreds of attractive shrubs and perennials for which a few knocks are all in a day's work. Don't expect miracles – any plant deserves a bit of respect, after all – but try some of these:

Ajuga reptans 'Catlin's Giant'
Alchemilla mollis
Buxus sempervirens 'Elegantissima'
Carex oshimensis 'Evergold'
Chaenomeles x *superba* 'Crimson and Gold'
Cornus alba 'Elegantissima'
Cotoneaster horizontalis
Euonymus fortunei 'Emerald 'n' Gold'
Geranium x *magnificum*
Ilex x *altaclerensis* 'Golden King'
Jasminum nudiflorum
Jasminum officinale
Lonicera nitida 'Baggesen's Gold'
Origanum vulgare 'Aureum'
Phlomis fruticosa
Rosmarinus officinalis
Sarcococca confusa
Tellima grandiflora Rubra Group
Thymus citriodorus
Verbena bonariensis
Vinca minor 'La Grave'

Football needn't make your garden an eyesore. Designer Cleve West's goal is imaginatively created from sustainable materials – an attractive feature, yet practical and robust.

Cotoneaster horizontalis – an undemanding shrub that looks presentable all year and makes a useful filler for a family garden. Birds will enjoy the berries in winter, too.

Don't forget

Water and safety are key considerations in a family garden. With very small children, even shallow open water is a potential hazard. Unless you want to go to the expense of covering it with a stout metal grille, it's best to wait until children are older before creating a pond of any depth. Some other kind of water feature, such as a fountain or bubble-jet pebble pool with an inaccessible, underground reservoir, would be much safer.

Hazardous plants

An exhaustive list of garden plants that it's wise not to eat could fill a book. It goes without saying that children should be taught about the dangers as well as the pleasures of plants. There are a few common garden plants that look tempting but are dangerously poisonous if accidentally eaten, and others that commonly cause allergic skin reactions. You may prefer not to grow these until children are older:

Aconitum	Euphorbia
Arum	Ipomoea
Brugmansia	Laburnum
Colchicum (below left)	(below right)
Daphne	Ricinus
Digitalis	Ruta
	Taxus

Formal gardens

The formal garden comes with an impeccable pedigree. Stately homes with parterres, balustraded terraces and billiard-table lawns spring to mind, but formality has a valuable role to play in many a more modest establishment. Often based on evergreen planting, the formal garden has year-round interest and can be low-maintenance. Some would say this style is more important than ever in the small, neat, town gardens that are features of many modern homes.

Symmetry and geometric shapes are critical to formal gardens but needn't look severe if combined with some informal planting – as in this 1997 Chelsea Flower Show garden designed by Xa Tollemache.

A geometric layout is what separates a traditional formal garden from the rest. Straight lines and right-angled corners are typical. Curves in the form of quarter- or semi-circles work well; other shapes may be acceptable if they are repeated symmetrically. Nothing should be free-form, abstract or (perish the thought) disorderly. The all-important architectural elements comprise good-quality, classic hard-landscaping materials (this goes for furniture and accessories too), and small-leaved evergreens – typically box or yew – clipped into wall-like hedges and topiary.

Achieving a formal garden

Formality is tricky on slopes, so if your garden isn't level, do consider the landscaping implications before you plan a formal garden. Symmetrically laid out terraces, steps and paths will probably look fantastic when it's all finished, but make sure you are prepared for the expense and disruption that will be necessary to create that kind of garden. Even if no major earth-moving is involved, achieving the precision finish that a formal garden requires will need really meticulous attention to detail at every stage of planning and setting-out, to make sure that surfaces are level and smooth, angles precise and objects symmetrically positioned – and that's before you even begin to think about the planting.

Maintenance

Think twice (at least) about your attitude to maintenance before launching into creating a formal garden. Even tiny lapses of attention are all too obvious in a garden of trim, straight lines and clean, flat surfaces. Lawns need to be in tip-top condition, gravel immaculately raked, and hedges and other topiary perfectly and precisely manicured.

Formal meets informal

Most of us probably wouldn't want an entirely formal garden, but whatever you do, don't dismiss formality altogether. Above all, it's a great foil for informality. You can create both formal and informal areas to give contrasts in mood between different parts of a garden; formality works wonderfully well closer to the house; informality at a distance. The great plantswoman and designer Gertrude Jekyll liked to plant informally within a formal structure, often working in partnership with the architect Sir Edwin Lutyens to create gardens that became classic set pieces. But you don't need to have a grand garden to use their ideas. Jekyll's use of colour harmonies in planting, for example, can be adapted to smaller gardens, or even a single border.

Show gardens – for example the small gardens at the Chelsea Flower Show – often fit loose, romantic-style planting into strongly designed, highly structural hard landscaping. You can pick up all sorts of ideas from the ways in which different designers have adapted this approach. One thing they have in common is that formal elements, such as symmetrical paths and steps, and clipped evergreens, ensure that the garden always has something to hold it together, even in winter. But, at the same time, the shapes, textures and colours change dramatically with the seasons – a pleasure that isn't easy to achieve in a wholly formal garden.

Seeking inspiration

Classic gardens to visit in the UK where you can see the formal and the informal working successfully together include the National Trust's Hidcote Manor Garden, in Gloucestershire, and the late Christopher Lloyd's garden, Great Dixter, in East Sussex. Hidcote is a collection of garden 'rooms', formal and informal, working together to create different moods and forming a harmonious and satisfying whole. Dixter has exuberant, informal planting of different kinds, all given structure by a formal framework of venerable old yew hedging. If you want to see aspects of seriously stylish formal gardening, visit Ham House in Richmond or Levens Hall in Cumbria.

Formal hedges should be dead straight. When clipping them, run a length of taut string between two canes as a guide to ensure a level top.

Topiary

Topiary has never really gone out of fashion. It appeals both to the control-freak end of the designer spectrum, for its strong architectural shapes (as in clipped pyramids, spirals and 'lollipops'), and to the quirky end, where the sky's the limit. There are many famous and much-photographed examples: topiary teapots, snails and locomotives, even a hunt in full cry.

There is something very satisfying about creating your own topiary feature, however small, and it can have a useful role in almost any kind of garden. A simple, clipped box ball or cone in a carefully chosen container makes a great focal point in even a tiny space; several of them, set along a path, give rhythm and continuity to a design.

If you're new to topiary, you'll need a pair of good secateurs and some small, sharp, one-handed shears ('sheep-shears' are ideal). Start with simple shapes, and progress to more intricate forms as you get more confident. You can buy wire frames in many different shapes, to put over the plant as a guide to clip round as it grows. Be sure to keep the plants amply fed and watered: plants that are continually clipped (especially those in containers) need to replace lost nutrients if they are to stay well furnished with healthy greenery.

Formal and informal can make excellent partners. Use topiary to contrast with meadow planting (as at Great Dixter, above) or juxtapose clean, cool hard landscaping with a tumble of foliage such as the grass *Stipa tenuissima* (left).

Planning for low maintenance

For a lot of people, garden maintenance is a necessary evil. Even keen gardeners often dislike repetitive chores such as grass-cutting and hedge-clipping. But it's actually quite simple to turn the situation to advantage. Ask yourself which tasks you least enjoy, and then spend some time re-planning the garden to eliminate the drudgery and create low-maintenance features that you know you will enjoy. After all, a garden is meant to be a pleasure and not a burden. You'll be surprised how easy it is to say goodbye to garden features that you don't consider to be worth the trouble – and how much better you'll feel when you have a garden that is right for you.

Lawns

The traditional view is that no garden is complete without a lawn (*see pages 74–105*), but looking after a lawn properly is actually quite hard work, especially in a small garden where it may get intensive wear. All that spiking, weeding, feeding and mowing can be a thing of the past if you opt for a low-maintenance alternative – perhaps paving or gravel softened by a cushion of mat-forming plants.

Hedges

Think seriously before replacing an existing hedge with fencing to save on maintenance. Hedges have so many advantages, to wildlife and the environment as well as to the look of your property. You could replace an existing, high-maintenance hedge of privet, Leyland cypress or *Lonicera nitida*, which needs regular trimming to keep it neat, with a different hedging material. Some of the best native hedging shrubs, such as yew, holly and beech, are very long-lived and can be kept looking respectable with just one cut a year.

Beth Chatto's inspired gravel garden is densely planted to suppress weeds, needs no watering, and has no grass to mow – all excellent labour-saving tactics.

Saving time and effort

There's a lot you can do to make the garden less physically strenuous to look after when your circumstances change. You might have taken on a very demanding job that leaves little time for gardening, or recently started a family. After retirement, too, the plan may be to spend more time in the garden but, ironically, that's just when the ground is beginning to seem a bit further away, or the watering can a bit heavier. Whether you are trying to cheat the advancing years or have other reasons to avoid undue exertion, here are some ideas:

■ If you are a keen gardener, turn your attention to enjoying plants on a smaller scale. A greenhouse, an upright cold frame or a potting shed can open up pastimes such as growing from seed, propagating, or growing specialist plants such as dwarf bulbs, bonsai, cacti and succulents, or alpines.

■ Re-plan borders with layered planting, which will mean minimal digging and weeding. Create a tapestry of ground-cover plants with interesting foliage, interplanted with spring bulbs. Weave in some tall, easy perennials for summer colour and some shrubs to flower in spring or autumn. Include a few evergreens – invaluable for both ground cover and winter structure.

■ Review your tool shed. Today there are many easy-to-use tools on offer that are a real boon to people who need help with lifting, bending or gripping.

Raised beds

Anyone who has gardened in raised beds will tell you how much easier they are to look after. Somehow the very idea of gardening in a confined space makes the whole business seem more manageable, and of course it's far easier if you don't have to bend double to reach your plants. Plants, too, like raised beds, as they don't have to compete against encroaching weeds or battle through compacted soil. You can plant more densely, and if the top of the bed is at a convenient height it will double as a seat, and a place to put your cup of tea.

HOW TO build a raised bed

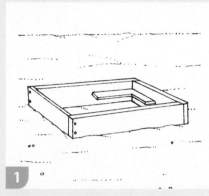

1 Cut four 150 x 50mm (6 x 2in) planks to the size and shape of bed you require. Screw them together, keeping the corners square, to create a frame. Cut four corner posts from 75 x 75mm (3 x 3in) timber. Their length should be the height of the bed plus 30cm (12in) to allow for sinking them into the ground.

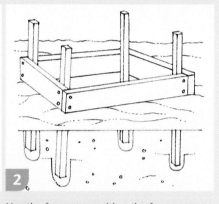

2 Use the frame to position the four corner posts, and dig post holes in the correct positions. Keep the posts upright, and sink them into the holes. For a small, temporary raised bed this should suffice, but larger, permanent structures will need the posts set in concrete.

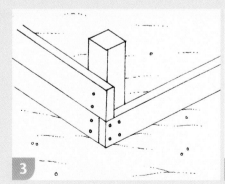

3 Build further layers of planks as in step 1 to the height of bed required. Screw the timbers to the posts as well as to each other, staggering the joints as shown.

4 Finish the top with a shelf made from the same planking, mitred at the corners and screwed to the posts. Add a 5cm (2in) layer of rubble or gravel to the bottom of the bed for drainage. Fill with a mixture of good topsoil and garden compost.

Low-maintenance planting for containers

A group of thoughtfully arranged containers always makes a garden look well cared for, but it doesn't need to involve hours of work, or cost a fortune, if you choose the right plants. Start by building up a small 'background' collection of all-season, low-maintenance shrubs and other plants, bought in 2- or 3-litre pots and potted on into your chosen containers. Use a humus-rich compost or mix in a moisture-retaining gel, and add a slow-release fertilizer. That way, they will need repotting only once a year at most. Choose frost-resistant containers in a mixture of shapes and sizes. You can ring the changes by moving them around and adding a pot or two of seasonal colour, with bulbs or bedding plants for example, when you see something you fancy in the garden centre. Avoid being a slave to watering: choose relatively drought-tolerant plants, and don't let them become pot-bound or they will dry out very quickly. Keep them out of full sun in summer. Here are some to try:

EVERGREEN SHRUBS
Buxus sempervirens 'Elegantissima'; *Fatsia japonica*; *Gaultheria procumbens*; *Juniperus communis* 'Compressa'; *Osmanthus heterophyllus* 'Goshiki'; *Skimmia japonica* 'Rubella'.

GRASSES
Carex buchananii; *Festuca glauca*; *Stipa tenuissima*.

SUCCULENTS and 'EXOTICS'
Cordyline australis; *Phormium*; *Sedum*; *Sempervivum*.

Sempervivums are a great all-year standby, needing only good drainage.

Putting together a planting scheme is a bit like painting a picture. You are using a palette of plants to create an apparently seamless (but in fact carefully contrived) blend of satisfying composition and effective colours. The composition angle is sometimes forgotten in garden planning, but it's an important component if you want your collection of plants to work together as a scheme that looks good all year. A border needs contrasts of shape, scale and texture, sequences to lead your eye, and focal points to act as punctuation marks. Without these, it can easily become a confusing, pointless jumble.

Planting by design

Everyone has their favourite plants, and we should all have the ones we like best in our gardens. But if a planting scheme is to succeed as a balanced, harmonious whole, it's also vital to recognize the role that each different plant will play as part of the team effort. But don't just make a collection of plants, with one of each kind, like specimens. Herbaceous plants, especially, make more impact when at least some of them are grouped in drifts or clumps of several individual plants.

Evergreens, bare branches and shapely seedheads emerge as summer foliage and colours fade, making a garden that is still full of visual interest in winter.

Structure

To some plants, forming the bones of a planting scheme just comes naturally. Depending on the space you have to play with, these structural plants might be formal, clipped evergreens such as domes, cubes or cones of box or yew, positioned to accentuate a path or mark corners; they could include one or more distinctive trees used as stand-alone specimens; or perhaps a large architectural plant that is so striking it simply stands out from the crowd. Climbers trained up obelisks are another option.

Structural plants should be used with two main things in mind. First, they should contrast with the many less conspicuous 'filler' plants of the growing season, serving as a framework that helps to hold the scheme together. Secondly, they should also provide structure in the dormant season. It's well worth considering how plants will contribute in winter. A few carefully chosen, distinctive plants can make all the difference between a garden that has sunk into off-season tiredness, making you look the other way, and a picture that gives pleasure whenever you glimpse it.

Grouping plants

Make structural plants your first priority when planning your border, whether on paper or on the ground. They are difficult to position correctly at a later stage, and there may well be reasons for putting them in particular places – hiding an eyesore perhaps, or aligning with something else to create a focal point. The next step is to combine them with complementary plants of different shapes, with the structural plants as the dominant feature. Take care to restrict the number of dominant plants. Adjacent planting should be a foil for these, and not steal their thunder. Group complementary plants in drifts, perhaps with an 'outlier' just beyond the end of the group for a more natural look.

Don't grade a border strictly in height, from back to front, like a team photo. Plants at the back must be visible when in flower, but a few tall grasses or alliums at the front will add depth and richness.

There are no universal rules for putting plants together, and you will develop your own techniques. A successful border will usually have been contrived – but it should always look effortless.

Shape

One of the elements that makes the plant world so fascinating is the diversity of shapes within it. The variety is almost endless, but for the purposes of planning a planting scheme, plant shapes can be simplified into a handful of groups. Generally, a recipe for a successful border will include some from each.

Vertical plants

With a small footprint in relation to their height, the best strongly vertical plants, in design terms, have distinct upright lines – tall, slender flower spikes, or sword-shaped leaves, or sometimes both. This group also includes some conifers and other shrubs and trees (*see* page 47). These emphatic plants, even those that are not very tall, can contribute valuable structure to a border.

Horizontal plants

Plants with strong horizontal shapes range from those with sideways-spreading, rounded or spoon-shaped leaves to those with flat plates of flowers or daisy-like blooms. Also in this group are shrubs with a layered or tiered effect, or with a spreading branch structure. Ideal for border edges where there is room for them to extend laterally, they also contrast vividly with the 'verticals', and the two together form an excellent basis for many a planting scheme.

Domed plants

Included in this group are compact evergreen shrubs such as dwarf hebes and santolina, and plants,

Plants with strong shapes

BOLD FOLIAGE
Cordyline australis
Cynara cardunculus
Fatsia japonica
Ficus carica
Hosta sieboldiana
Humulus lupulus 'Aureus'
Matteuccia struthiopteris
Rheum palmatum 'Atrosanguineum'
Ricinus communis

VERTICALS

Spiky leaves	Spiky flowers
Cordyline (below)	*Acanthus*
Crocosmia	*Delphinium*
Iris	*Digitalis*
Kniphofia	*Eremurus* (below)
Libertia	*Kniphofia*
Phormium (below)	*Lupinus*
Sisyrinchium	*Verbascum*
Yucca	*Veronicastrum*

HORIZONTALS
Foliage
Bergenia
Brunnera
Cotoneaster horizontalis
Cyclamen
Hosta
Rheum
Viburnum davidii
Flowers
Achillea
Euphorbia polychroma
Helenium
Rudbeckia
Sedum
Viburnum plicatum f. *tomentosum* 'Mariesii'

usually herbaceous, that grow in bun-shaped clumps. These are useful on corners where a low 'full stop' is needed.

Filler plants

Softening the lines of the more definite shapes, these plants fill gaps and help to knit a scheme together. They have a range of textures and habits from fluffy to creeping, and good examples are *Viola cornuta*, trailing campanulas and the 'wandering' perennial geraniums.

Plants for texture

LIGHT AND FLUFFY
Alchemilla mollis
Astilbe
Crambe cordifolia
Cryptomeria japonica 'Elegans Compacta'
Eupatorium maculatum Atropurpureum Group
Euphorbia cyparissias 'Fens Ruby'
Foeniculum vulgare 'Purpureum'
Gypsophila paniculata
Nigella damascena
Spiraea 'Arguta'
Stipa tenuissima
Thalictrum aquilegiifolium

BOLD AND LEATHERY
x *Fatshedera lizei*
Fatsia japonica
Rheum palmatum 'Atrosanguineum' (below)
Rodgersia podophylla
Viburnum davidii

A dramatic foliage composition, seen at its best in late spring. From top: *Polygonatum* x *hybridum* (Solomon's seal), *Rodgersia podophylla*, *Iris pseudacorus* 'Variegata' and *Hosta* 'Halcyon'.

Texture

A garden that will look good for many months of the year must draw from the whole spectrum of plant material, and that includes textures. In your beds and borders, plant groupings that exploit contrasting textures, as well as shapes and colours, will always have the edge, enabling you to get more 'plant power' out of even the smallest space. It's amazing to think of all the different textures that plants can contribute to a scheme – woolly, waxy, stiff, papery, silky, shiny, matt and many more. And it's not just the flowers and leaves: seedheads, fruits, stems and bark all add to the effect.

Colour

Any garden designer will tell you that to build a satisfying planting scheme you have to think about *all* the visual properties of a plant. But colour is the obvious one for most people, and the one they tend to feel most strongly about. Favourite colours are deeply ingrained. Colour is often a matter of 'gut reaction' or personal taste that is certain to influence your choice of plants, but in garden design try to expand your horizons and get to grips with the power of different colours to create particular effects.

Combining colours

A lot of the skill in planning a border lies in the way you combine colours. A good means of learning how to do this is to study planting schemes at flower shows and in gardens. Record, in notes and photographs, what works and why. This will also help you to manage the tricky business of getting flower colours to coincide: a colour combination is useless if the plants end up flowering at different times.

A colour wheel – a device used by artists and designers, setting out the colours of the spectrum in a circle (*see* right) – can be a helpful illustration of some of the ways in which colours work with each other. Colours that are directly opposite on the wheel make the best contrasts: lime green and purple, orange and deep blue, or red and green. Colour harmonies work best if they are chosen from colours that are adjacent to each other on the wheel: yellow, orange and red, for example.

Colour and space

As well as the emotional effects of different colour harmonies and contrasts, colour can be used to manipulate space. In daylight, warm colours – yellow, orange and red – tend to advance and look closer than they really are. White has a similar effect, which is particularly marked in dim light. Cool colours – blues and purples – tend to recede and look farther away, giving a feeling of spaciousness and distance, except in the low light around dawn and dusk, when they become prominent.

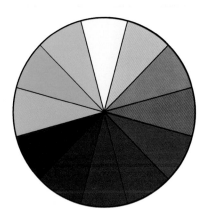

A simple colour wheel is a handy design tool showing the ways in which colours relate to each other. Colours that harmonize are adjacent to each other on the wheel, while colours that make good contrasts are opposite each other.

But remember that when planning a colour scheme you may not have a completely blank canvas. A strongly coloured existing tree or shrub such as a photinia or a forsythia, or even a high red-brick wall, may need to be factored in, and will certainly limit your palette in that area of the garden.

Using colours

The best plant combinations often come about completely by chance.

Trial and error with colours can be entertaining, and happy accidents, when plants combine themselves beautifully, do happen. But you have to wait for them, so it's a slow route to success. It definitely pays to have some clear ideas on colours and their effects at the back of your mind, well before you start to put plants together.

Blue

Of all flower colours, blue is the hardest to capture in photographs. Perhaps it is this elusiveness that helps make it such a special, and popular, colour in the garden. Everyone loves blue. Cool, calming, sophisticated and versatile, it works as a great foil for so many other colours: with yellows and whites in those long-awaited, fresh schemes of early spring; with rich reds and violet to make a jewel-like picture with all the richness of a Persian carpet; or in startling, two-colour combinations to contrast tellingly with lime green or orange. Blue also shows up well in low light, especially at dawn and dusk when it seems to come to the fore.

Purple

Sombre and rather dull on its own, purple goes brilliantly with silver and grey, and this is a good colour scheme for a dry, sunny site – perhaps a gravel garden – where you could use drought-resistant Mediterranean shrubs with tulips, irises and alliums. Purple or bronze foliage makes a rich, exciting backdrop to red flowers: the popular *Dahlia* 'Bishop of Llandaff' has just this combination. Purples and blues also make a striking but cooler contrast with lime green plants such as euphorbias or *Alchemilla mollis*.

Pink

Use paler shades of pink with white, blue and lilac in a classic pastel scheme, or darker pinks in a glowing mix of rich, sultry hues with deep blues, reds and purples. Either of these combinations works well with silver, bronze or green foliage. Pink and yellow can clash unpleasantly – beware of forsythia and flowering

The garden at Great Dixter is famous for exciting and inventive colour combinations – here alliums, honesty and campanulas contrast with golden wallflowers, in the Solar garden.

A daring Dixter partnership: *Salvia involucrata* 'Bethellii' clashing loudly with *Dahlia* 'Chimborazo'.

currant or cherry doing one another no favours in spring if planted too closely. But pale creamy yellow with a dark pink, such as a magenta cranesbill, can work very well.

Red

'Hot' borders with a red theme are eye-catching to say the least, and can be a great way to enjoy a fling of rip-roaring bold colour, especially in late summer and autumn. Purple, silver and green foliage all work well as an accompaniment, and there is a surprising number of wonderful red flowers to choose from: roses, clematis, dahlias, daylilies, penstemons and many berrying shrubs. The National Trust gardens at Hidcote, in Gloucestershire, and Tintinhull, in Somerset, both have glorious red borders. Plan a visit, or look at photographs, for inspiration.

Orange

Orange is always an exciting colour, whether used in harmonious schemes with red and yellow, or in more daring contrasts with deep blue, purple or bronze. *Ajuga reptans*, with its blue flower spikes in spring, is a good partner for orange tulips, while orange geums, poppies or pot marigolds are good with spiky blue salvias a little later in the year.

Yellow

Yellow seems to be the colour of spring in the garden – all that forsythia, all those daffodils. It can easily take over again in late summer, with sunflowers, rudbeckias and goldenrod. Some people aren't keen on yellow, and it can be difficult to use with other colours. But yellow does have a capacity to cheer things up that no other colour can rival, and it's worth thinking about how to use it cleverly. Along with white, it is great for

brightening up dull places. Use golden-variegated shrubs, for instance, to bring the illusion of sunshine to a corner that doesn't get much of the real thing. But be careful – many golden-leaved plants will only keep their bright colour if they receive a certain amount of light, reverting to green if it's too gloomy for them.

Green

This is the most soothing and restorative of all colours. Where there is no greenery, the lack of it is deeply felt. An all-green garden (daring, in a way), can be very effective, especially in shade, transforming a small town garden, perhaps, into a cool, tranquil retreat. A green scheme, however, needs

Green need never be dull. Beth Chatto's planting of shuttlecock fern (*Matteuccia struthiopteris*) with *Rodgersia podophylla* has all the textural contrast you could wish for.

careful handling because the interest will depend on plant shapes and textures, and without enough variety it could easily be dull. Ferns, hostas and shade-tolerant grasses are a good combination for a calming scheme – but admittedly it may not be to everyone's taste.

Green is a great mediator when it comes to warring colours. A meadow can contain every colour but never looks garish because of the tempering effect of the grass, and plenty of foliage in a border prevents an exciting mix turning into a messy riot of clashing colours.

White and silver

White flowers and silver, or grey, foliage (*see* page 51) really come into their own at dusk, standing out in the gloaming when other colours can no longer be distinguished. Choose plants with interesting shapes to exploit this – the steely, sharp outlines of eryngiums, the fans of variegated irises or the delicate froth of gypsophila. Distinctively shaped white plants set against a dark background, such as a yew hedge, will really stand out. A dark or shady backdrop is also ideal for the great trumpets of *Lilium regale*. Like many other white flowers, these have a swooning fragrance on summer evenings. White is a component of all the pastel colours and combines well with them. It's also a lovely fresh colour to use in spring with blues, greens and yellows.

Variegated plants

It may often seem, especially if you go to a specialist plant sale, as if every single plant has at least one variegated form – that is, one with leaves that have cream or yellow markings. From a design angle, variegated plants can be hugely useful as accent features, or to brighten dull corners. But there's no getting away from the fact that variegated plants tend to draw attention to themselves. If you overdo it you will end up with too many plants clamouring for the limelight.

Most variegated plants grow more slowly than their green-leaved counterparts, because they contain less of the green pigment chlorophyll, which enables photosynthesis – the process by which plants turn sunlight into energy for growth. Certain variegated plants are clearly suitable for small spaces but some are such weaklings that they are best avoided or you will spend your life coaxing them to cling on to theirs.

That said, there are many very good variegated plants: see a selection below.

VARIEGATED GROUND COVER FOR SHADE
Arum italicum subsp. *italicum* 'Marmoratum'

Cyclamen hederifolium

Hedera canariensis 'Gloire de Marengo'

Hedera colchica 'Sulphur Heart'

Hedera helix 'Oro di Bogliasco'

Hosta 'Wide Brim'

Lamium maculatum 'White Nancy'

Pulmonaria saccharata

VARIEGATED SPIKY PLANTS
Iris pallida 'Variegata'

Iris pseudacorus 'Variegata'

Phormium cookianum subsp. *hookeri* 'Cream Delight'

Sisyrinchium striatum 'Aunt May'

Yucca filamentosa 'Bright Edge'

VARIEGATED HERBACEOUS PLANTS
Astrantia major 'Sunningdale Variegated'

Brunnera macrophylla 'Hadspen Cream'

Euphorbia characias 'Silver Swan'

Mentha suaveolens 'Variegata'

Sedum erythrostictum 'Frosty Morn'

VARIEGATED GRASSES
Calamagrostis x *acutiflora* 'Overdam'

Carex morrowii 'Fisher's Form'

Miscanthus sinensis 'Morning Light'

Miscanthus sinensis 'Zebrinus'

VARIEGATED TREES AND SHRUBS
Acer platanoides 'Drummondii'

Cornus alba 'Elegantissima'

Cornus controversa 'Variegata'

Sambucus nigra 'Marginata'

Weigela 'Florida Variegata'

VARIEGATED EVERGREENS
Euonymus fortunei 'Silver Queen'

Ilex aquifolium 'Handsworth New Silver'

Luma apiculata 'Glanleam Gold'

Osmanthus heterophyllus 'Goshiki'

Rhamnus alaternus 'Argenteovariegata'

Viburnum tinus 'Variegatum'

White foxgloves and lupins standing out among a sea of foliage – an especially effective planting at dusk.

The design elements of a garden, like those of an interior, work in subtle ways to create a mood that you pick up on as soon as you step into the space. Colour, light, scent, sound, stillness, temperature and humidity are among the factors that make up this complex and powerful cocktail.

Light and shade

Light and shade, and the contrast between them, are key considerations in setting the mood of a particular space. Subdued light conditions promote feelings of calm, and of welcome coolness even during hot weather. Bright light can be invigorating in spring, oppressive and overwhelming in summer, relaxing and perhaps a touch wistful in autumn. You might use light and shade to create a sense of mystery, where a sunlit path disappears into dappled tree cover perhaps, or of anticipation, where a tempting patch of sunlight is seen beyond an area of shade.

Colour and mood

Use plant colour to influence the mood of a garden and experiment with some of these well-established links to see if they work for you:

Calming	white, blue
Cooling	blue, green, white
Cheerful	yellow, orange
Mysterious	purple, 'black'
Romantic	pink, white, lilac
Exciting	red, orange

Movement and sound

Gentle movement and the sound it often produces can have a soothing and relaxing effect. You can bring movement into a garden by using water – maybe just a simple bubble-jet, wall spout or solar-powered fountain. And easier still, introduce some plants that move with the slightest breath of wind, for instance a birch tree or one

of the grasses, for example the shimmering, silky *Stipa tenuissima*. (*See also* pages 110–11.)

Scent

There's no doubt that scents have a powerful effect on mood and emotions, working in complex and subtle ways to evoke memories and feelings. The whole thing is very subjective – so the best advice is just to choose those that you like best. (*See also* pages 110–11.)

Contrasting moods: ① vibrant and stimulating, with *Crocosmia* 'Lucifer' leading the cast in a late-summer border; ② cool and calming with a classic pairing of water and willow.

The third dimension, height, is sometimes neglected in garden design, but without it a garden can so easily be flat and dull. It's important to include taller features, whether plants or structures, to give the garden more variety and a sense of scale. Vertical growing also increases your available planting space and creates lots of opportunities for extra plant colour and interest.

Pergolas

A plant-covered pergola is one of the most effective design devices you can add to a garden to create height. It can also fulfil other design functions: giving a sense of enclosure to a seating area, or a strong feeling of direction if it spans a path; adding a focal point or a full stop; blotting out an unwanted view; linking a house with its garden; or blurring the distinction between man-made structure and natural planting. (*See also* pages 50, 66–7.)

Arbours

Usually an intimate structure clothed with climbing plants and sheltering a seat, an arbour is a very traditional concept, harking back to romantic trysts in medieval gardens. Arbours are usually constructed from metal or wood – normally timber, either rustic or sawn – but sometimes from living willow or woven hurdles, or even carved out of an evergreen hedge. An arbour offers great scope for creativity and originality, in the structure itself and in the plants you use to furnish it. Beautiful and functional in both traditional and contemporary settings, arbours work perfectly in even the smallest garden, both as a secluded retreat that defines a separate little space and as an inviting focal point.

Arches

An arch is used to frame an entrance, leading into the garden itself perhaps, or from one part of it to another.

Arches should be positioned where they will create an element of surprise – what lies beyond? A freestanding arch in the middle of a garden never looks quite right. Use it in tandem with an opening in a hedge or fence, a door or gateway, or a gap in the planting to either side of it, and it will make much more sense. An arch can also be used to frame a mirror to give the illusion of more space, but this trick does need to be staged very carefully to be effective, and is essential to have plenty of planting around it to distract the eye from the mechanics.

Obelisks

An obelisk is a versatile, incidental means of creating height – either as a single focal point or as one of a series. An obelisk is a reasonably quick way of giving scale and shape to a border where a tree would create unwanted shade or be too dominant. Obelisks can be solid or open, and may or may not support climbing plants. In a small garden an obelisk can be a valuable means of emphasizing height, especially if clothed with greenery, without using much lateral space. An obelisk as a plant support can be used to top a large container, planted with a flowering climber, or with clipped ivy or box for a more formal effect.

A tree can eventually be a host for climbers such as roses and clematis ① – but will require patience. An obelisk ② is a better option where height and structure are needed quickly.

Plants for adding height

SLENDER TREES
Carpinus betulus 'Fastigiata'
Fagus sylvatica 'Dawyck'
Prunus 'Spire'
Pyrus calleryana 'Chanticleer'
Sorbus aucuparia 'Fastigiata'

UPRIGHT SHRUBS
Berberis thunbergii f. *atropurpurea* 'Helmond Pillar'
Buddleja davidii 'Black Knight'
Ilex aquifolium 'Pyramidalis'
Juniperus communis 'Hibernica'
Mahonia x *media* cultivars
Phyllostachys nigra
Rosa 'Geranium'
Taxus baccata 'Fastigiata'

Tall and slender plants. ① *Taxus baccata* 'Fastigiata' and ② *Fagus sylvatica* 'Dawyck Purple'. For vertical emphasis in a border, try perennials such as *Verbena bonariensis*. and *Crocosmia* 'Lucifer' ③.

Poles

This simple means of supporting a climber is also a cheap and effective way of creating height. The pole needs to be stout, made of either hardwood or pressure-treated softwood, and well anchored into the ground. Stain it black if you want it to be unobtrusive. Then plant a climber such as a clematis, honeysuckle or climbing rose at its foot, tying it in as it grows.

Vertical planting

More than any other single feature, a tree makes a real difference to a garden, providing its own unique combination of height, shade, restful greenery and wildlife habitat. You should never need to ask yourself whether you should plant a tree in your garden, even if it is a small space. As long as you've done your homework and choose wisely, the answer will always be yes, and more than one if space allows. A number of tree cultivars tend to have an upright shape (*see* box) and are worth considering if space is at a premium.

In a border, if you are seeking height without bulk, there are several obliging shrubs (*see* box), or you could grow a climber on a pole or obelisk. There are also many herbaceous plants and grasses that have a clear emphasis on the vertical (*see also* page 82). Foxgloves, lupins, verbascums and *Eremurus* (foxtail lilies) have colourful, upright flower spikes, while good cultivars of *Calamagrostis* and *Miscanthus* are useful tall grasses with a relatively small footprint.

Trees

Planting a tree is often the easiest, most economical and most successful way to create height in a garden. Of course, it requires a little patience, but a suitable tree, thoughtfully positioned, can be invaluable, providing not only a strong focal point, but also screening, shelter, shade, perhaps flowers and fruit to enjoy, and cover for wildlife. The right tree can be important in achieving a particular design effect – for example an acer in a Japanese garden – but remember it will only be the right tree if it also suits its growing conditions.

Winter tree shapes are endlessly intriguing. This unusual but short-lived tracery, caught in perfect light conditions, belongs to *Robinia pseudoacacia* 'Lace Lady', clinging on to its leaves after an early frost.

Choosing a tree

Garden trees are a big investment, not so much in terms of cash (true, they aren't cheap – though a good tree will be worth every penny) but because they will occupy precious garden space for a long time to come. Choosing the right tree is therefore a major decision. The tree needs to be happy in the conditions you can offer it, and you must be happy to live with and look at that particular tree 365 days a year.

So, before you rush home from the garden centre with the prettiest tree you could find there this week, here are a few things to think about.

Size and spread

If space is limited, it is much better (for you and for the tree) to select a variety that is naturally compact, rather than one that is going to involve you in constant saw-and-secateur battles, or regular bills from a tree surgeon, simply to keep it within its allotted place.

Growing conditions

Some types of tree will naturally be more tolerant of dry, chalky soil; others won't mind a windy boundary; and a problematic damp spot in your garden will be meat and drink to some species. Finding out which trees are likely to enjoy life with you is not only easy, but also well worth the effort. A tree that is struggling with its growing conditions will never be an asset, no matter how well it might suit the style of your garden.

Seasons of interest

For those of us with limited space, a tree that works hard to contribute to

Right tree, wrong place

Avoid planting certain trees in particular places. For example, you may live to regret putting a thorny tree too close to where you walk or sit. And *Morus nigra* (black mulberry) will stain paving (and clothes, and children!) with its luscious but messy dark fruits. Some trees, such as some of the limes, attract aphids that exude a sticky honeydew, which you will soon know all about if you have to park your car under them.

the garden scene during two or three seasons of the year will be a better investment than a tree that has gorgeous blossom for one week and looks dull as ditchwater for the other 51. So find out if it has attractive foliage, colourful berries,

good autumn tints or interesting bark in the winter months.

Living with trees

Some trees (most notoriously willows and poplars) have questing roots that must not be allowed anywhere near buildings or drains. Many other fast-growing woodland trees, such as sycamore and beech, are almost as unsuitable for the average garden. Even some popular garden trees are less than ideal. *Robinia*, for example, has brittle branches that can snap off unannounced. Insurance companies tend to disapprove of trees planted near buildings, especially if they are of an unsuitable type. But as a general rule, most ornamental garden trees are likely to be fine, as long you plant them at least as far away from buildings as their expected mature height.

The Judas tree (*Cercis siliquastrum*) makes a fine feature for a sunny spot.

The dazzling white bark of *Betula utilis* var. *jacquemontii* – a favourite tree for contemporary gardens.

Trees for a light canopy

People are often wary of planting a tree because of the shade it will cast, and this is something worth thinking about when choosing. If you go for a tree with a spreading canopy and dense foliage, it will have a severe impact on the space around it and will affect what can be grown nearby. Beech is a notorious example, and its roots are near the surface too, so hardly anything will grow underneath. But you can avoid plunging your garden into gloom if you choose a tree with an upright (fastigiate) habit and/or one with light, fern-like foliage. There are quite a few good garden trees that fit the bill. Birches tend to have light, delicate foliage and are also quite narrow. Rowans *(Sorbus)* have slender, divided leaves and often an upright shape, so they don't cast much shade at all. Their berries come in various colours from pinkish white (*Sorbus hupehensis*) through orange and red (*Sorbus aucuparia* and *Sorbus commixta*) to golden (*Sorbus* 'Joseph Rock'). *Ginkgo* and *Gleditsia* cast light shade and are also worth considering, while for larger gardens, walnut, or ash or one of its cultivars, are very reliable. Both come into leaf late, casting little shade before midsummer – and by then you may be very glad of it. For a waterside setting in a small garden, the compact, willow-like tree *Pyrus salicifolia* 'Pendula' (*see* below) is an ideal choice. (*See also* pages 60–1.)

Shrubs

As any garden design book will tell you, shrubs are the backbone of a garden, vital for providing permanent height and structure. Getting the right shrubs in the right places is critical to a successful planting scheme so choosing and siting them are big decisions. Fortunately, if you find you've made a mistake, most young shrubs can be moved successfully while they are dormant.

Different cultivars of dogwood offer a striking spectrum of winter stem colour – here, *Cornus alba* 'Sibirica', underplanted with snowdrops.

Evergreen shrubs

Year-round structure in a garden usually relies on these, and they are also much used for screening, shelter and ground cover. Their main disadvantage is that, unlike their deciduous counterparts, most of them don't change much with the seasons, so it is best not to use too many together. But as a backdrop to other planting they are invaluable, and many of them are interesting enough to act as specimen plants, either in a border or in pots. Some, such as phormiums and yuccas (for a sunny place) or *Fatsia japonica* (for shade), are splendid architectural plants in their own right. Others, *Viburnum davidii* or *Osmanthus heterophyllus* for example, are reliable stalwarts that belong in the supporting cast. Many evergreens flower beautifully: you can grow rhododendrons and camellias in acid soil; ceanothus, cistus and hebe if you have sun and good drainage; mahonia and sarcococca for fragrant flowers to cheer you in winter.

Deciduous shrubs

Many deciduous shrubs are also grown for their flowers. This is all very well for as long as the flowers last, but you will get much more value from your shrubs if you choose from the many multi-taskers that also contribute to the garden when they aren't in flower. Luckily this isn't

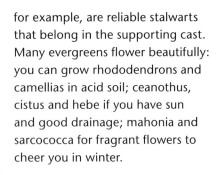

Surprisingly hardy, yuccas are among the boldest 'statement' shrubs.

difficult. Some – in particular certain popular dogwoods – have colourful winter bark. Others have been bred or selected by growers for their coloured foliage (*see* box, opposite). Then there are shrubs that produce spectacular autumn berries to keep you (or your garden birds) happy well into winter.

Growing and pruning shrubs

Provided they are in a position and soil that suit them, and are properly watered and fed, most shrubs are easy to maintain. Many gardeners struggle with pruning, but remember that you aren't actually obliged to prune at all, and if you aren't sure it may be better to leave well alone. A basic knowledge of the whys and wherefores of pruning, however, is useful because you will then know how to tailor shrubs to the design of your garden, keeping them to the size and shape you want. So get to know the principles and you will soon understand why, when and how to prune.

Controlling size and shape

It's usually best with shrubs to remove some branches completely each year. This benefits the plant, thinning the growth to let in air and light, and keeping the centre of the bush vigorous. Generally speaking, reserve light trimming for hedges and topiary. Most shrubs, if trimmed only lightly, will develop a surface covering of foliage and a dead, woody centre. They lose their individual character and look dull and artificial (not to say downright silly, in extreme cases).

Encouraging growth and flowering

A grasp of basic pruning techniques will help you to get the best from your plants. Many shrubs, for example, need to be encouraged to keep producing new growth to perform well, and this is stimulated by pruning. Some shrubs flower better on new branches, so they need an annual pruning to keep them youthful and productive (buddleias, roses, caryopteris). Likewise, many shrubs grown for their foliage produce larger, brighter leaves on young growth (cotinus, ornamental elders). This will be at the expense of flowering, but the upside is a splendid foliage plant. Shrubs grown for colourful stems (certain dogwoods, and ornamental brambles such as *Rubus thibetanus*) have brighter bark colour on young wood. Some shrubs (daphnes, sarcococca and other naturally compact evergreens) need no pruning at all; others require removal of the oldest wood to keep them reasonably young at heart.

Removing some of the tired old wood from a weigela in autumn to promote vigorous new growth.

Shrubs for colour

SHRUBS WITH RED/PURPLE/BRONZE FOLIAGE

Acer palmatum 'Bloodgood'

Berberis thunbergii f. *atropurpurea* 'Helmond Pillar'

Corylus maxima 'Purpurea'

Cotinus coggygria 'Royal Purple'

Physocarpus opulifolius 'Diabolo'

Pittosporum tenuifolium 'Tom Thumb' (evergreen)

Salvia officinalis 'Purpurascens' (evergreen)

Sambucus nigra 'Gerda' ('Black Beauty')

Viburnum sargentii 'Onondaga'

Weigela florida 'Wine and Roses'

SHRUBS WITH GOLDEN/YELLOW FOLIAGE

Berberis thunbergii 'Aurea'

Choisya ternata 'Sundance' (evergreen)

Cornus alba 'Aurea'

Escallonia laevis 'Gold Brian' (evergreen)

Euonymus fortunei 'Emerald 'n' Gold'

Lonicera nitida 'Baggesen's Gold' (evergreen)

Philadelphus coronarius 'Aureus'

Physocarpus opulifolius 'Dart's Gold'

Rubus cockburnianus 'Goldenvale'

Sambucus racemosa 'Sutherland Gold'

Spiraea japonica 'Goldflame'

Viburnum opulus 'Aureum'

SHRUBS WITH SILVER/GREY FOLIAGE

Artemisia 'Powis Castle'

Atriplex halimus (evergreen)

Brachyglottis (Dunedin Group) 'Sunshine' (evergreen)

Convolvulus cneorum (evergreen)

Elaeagnus 'Quicksilver'

Hebe pinguifolia 'Pagei' (evergreen)

Helianthemum 'Wisley White' (evergreen)

Helichrysum italicum 'Korma' (evergreen)

Hippophae rhamnoides

Lavandula angustifolia 'Imperial Gem'

Phlomis fruticosa (evergreen)

Santolina chamaecyparissus 'Lemon Queen' (evergreen)

Teucrium fruticans (evergreen)

Climbers

Climbers have a valuable role to play in all gardens, but they are especially useful for packing in interest and flower power where space is short. Grown over arches, arbours and pergolas they make wonderful garden features, adding height and seasonal colour (and often fragrance). You can train a climber up a pole or an obelisk for an attractive vertical focal point if there's no space for a tree, and in awkward spots it's possible to grow less vigorous climbers in containers.

Climbers as planting partners

Some climbers are never happier than when scrambling through shrubs and up into trees, and they can even be planted in the same hole as long as food and water are plentiful. Clematis are ideal for this, as they like to flower in the sun but have their feet in the shade. A vigorous flowering shrub such as a forsythia or a large philadelphus is the perfect host, and the clematis flowers will stop the shrub from looking dreary in its 'off' season.

Self-clinging climbers on walls

Areas of blank wall, especially in shade, cry out for planting to make them more interesting. Some plants have adhesive pads or aerial root hairs that enable them to climb up walls happily without you having to

wobble about on a ladder, rigging up support for them. Provided the wall is perfectly sound, with no patches of crumbly mortar or render, self-clinging climbers such as ornamental ivies, *Euonymus fortunei* 'Silver Queen', or the climbing

Clematis – king of climbers. There is one for every situation and season. If you have room for only one, choose reliable, free-flowering forms such as *Clematis* 'Warszawska Nike', which produces its gorgeous velvety blooms over many weeks in summer and autumn.

Train climbing roses horizontally to encourage them to flower well.

hydrangea *Hydrangea anomala* subsp. *petiolaris* will do no harm to the structure. Keep them in check and prune them from time to time to keep them well away from gutters, windows and roof tiles. To get them started, fix the stems lightly to the wall with adhesive tape or Blu-Tack®, or hold them in place with the unobtrusive plastic fixings intended for electric and telephone cables. In dry weather, spray the wall with water from time to time to help the plant adhere.

Wisterias need a lot of space and a lot of pruning – but when they are in the right place, and well looked after, they're in a class of their own. This one has a perfect setting near the loggia at Wayford Manor, Somerset.

Climbing roses

There's nothing like a climbing rose – especially if it's scented – to catch the mood of an old-fashioned country garden. Some of them have only a short flowering season, so partner them with another climber, such as a clematis or jasmine, to keep the interest going. For maximum flowering, train the rose so it makes a permanent framework of horizontal stems. The aim is to expose them to the sun, which will help them to ripen and flower well. Fix wires along a wall or fence; for a pillar, pergola or arbour train the young stems in a spiral round and round the post and then along the top of the structure. Tie them in with soft green or brown twine that won't cut into the soft stems as they grow, and trim off unwanted stems. Flowers will appear on side-shoots, and should be dead-headed as soon as they fade – some go brown and continue to cling to the shoots, spoiling the display. Reliable, fragrant climbers include: *Rosa* 'Compassion' (peach-pink) *below top*, *R.* 'Golden Showers' (yellow) and *R.* 'Madame Alfred Carrière' (pink-tinged white) *below bottom*.

Some climbers for pergolas

◼ *Clematis* 'Huldine' The pearly-white flowers of this vigorous and sun-loving summer-flowering clematis look best when viewed from below with the sun behind to show up their attractive pinkish undersides – so it's perfect for pergolas. C. 'Huldine' is also a good companion for roses, honeysuckle and other climbers. Cut the plant hard back in late winter for the best display the following summer.

◼ *Cobaea scandens* This tender annual is a good bet for a new pergola in its first year, while you wait for permanent planting to establish. If you sow seed in early spring and keep the plants frost-free until the weather is warm enough to plant them out, they will race away, and by late summer your pergola will be dripping with subtle purple bell-shaped flowers that will last until autumn frosts.

◼ *Rosa* 'Adélaïde d'Orléans' Good foliage, abundant creamy-white flowers and lax stems that are easy to tie in make this delicately fragrant old-fashioned rambler rose a good plant for a romantic pergola. It combines well with blue or purple clematis such as the free-flowering *Clematis* 'Étoile Violette' or the old favourite C. 'Jackmanii'.

◼ *Wisteria sinensis* A good wisteria can turn a large, stout pergola or a spacious house wall into a classic set-piece for a traditional garden. Its plentiful, fragrant, hanging flower trusses are a delight to sit under in early summer, and the foliage stays attractive all season. Wisteria buds break quite late, which means they don't blot out too much spring sunshine but you have the benefit of shade when you really need it, in midsummer. Make sure the pergola is tall enough for the hanging flowers to be above head height, and be prepared for a vigorous pruning job twice a year when the plant is mature. Wisterias on a house wall should be tied in to horizontal wires secured by vine eyes fixed into the wall.

See also pages 46–7.

Herbaceous perennials

This is the most versatile plant group in the garden designer's palette, offering long-lasting plants for every season, purpose, colour scheme and mood. Whether you are looking for an elegant 'statement' plant or ground cover, something to feed the birds in winter or a reliable source of cut flowers for the house, there will always be a herbaceous perennial to fit the bill.

What are herbaceous perennials?

Strictly speaking, all plants that go on from year to year, including shrubs and trees, are perennials. Among gardeners in temperate climates, however, the terms 'herbaceous plant' and 'perennial' are used to mean non-woody plants with stems and leaves that die back to ground level in autumn, leaving a rootstock that remains alive to produce new growth next year.

Using perennials

The herbaceous border, that stalwart of the English garden, has become rather a thing of the past, with its need for high maintenance to keep it looking its best through many months of the year. In its place we have the mixed border, which is a much more practical, varied and long-lasting tapestry of plants of different kinds, with interest for every season. Herbaceous perennials play an important part in this kind of

Check over your herbaceous perennials in early spring, dividing any congested clumps like this kniphofia. Re-plant small healthy pieces in improved soil.

planting, complementing shrubs, bulbs and perhaps annuals too, in a variety of ways. They provide reliable 'furnishing' for the spaces between, or in front of, shrubs, and at ground level they disguise the dying foliage of spring bulbs and keep the soil covered to discourage weeds and retain moisture. They provide seasonal accents of colour from spring to autumn, many of them have interesting foliage, and some have attractive, architectural skeletons that will enhance the garden over winter, remaining in place until cut down in spring.

A planting design always looks stronger if you use groups of plants rather than single ones, and this applies particularly to perennials. It is often recommended that they are planted in groups of three or five. In many cases it's easy to increase your stock by splitting clumps up (*see* photograph above), and in this way you will have a supply that enables you to repeat groups of your tried and tested favourites in different places. Such deliberate repetition will help to give coherence and unity to your planting scheme.

Growing perennials

Most perennials are relatively easy to grow in reasonable soil, and as there is such a wide choice, if one plant doesn't seem to like your garden it won't be difficult to find something broadly similar to try instead. The pot-grown perennials you find in garden centres can be planted at any time of year, provided they are watered well if the weather is dry.

Maintenance is fairly light if you steer clear of perennials that are too vigorous and remember to stake tall plants, such as delphiniums, early in the season. Work through each border once a year – early spring is a good time – so you can split up clumps that are getting too large, or that are dying off in the middle. Simply lift the clump and either pull it apart into individual crowns or chop it vertically into pieces with a sharp spade, making sure that each little clump has some healthy young shoots emerging from it. Refresh the soil by adding some compost, and replant the best divisions. Keep the border weed-free: mulching with compost or fine chipped bark in winter or early spring will help with this, and feed the plants too. The only other requirement is that you cut down the stems after flowering. This keeps the border looking fresh, and will also encourage some perennials to flower again.

Star performers

Easy but interesting to propagate, herbaceous perennials have long attracted the passion of enthusiasts up and down the land. As a result there are literally thousands of different cultivars to choose from. Some plant groups, such as hostas, peonies, heucheras, irises and daylilies, could single-handedly fill several gardens, such is the bewildering variety of different forms. Some of these are almost indistinguishable from one another, but others really stand out from the crowd. In designing gardens it's invaluable to get to know the forms that are 'good doers' because these will really earn their space, while others, however beautiful, may grow half-heartedly and never make a real impact. A good guide to the best performers is the RHS Award of Garden Merit (*see* box). This award scheme applies to all plants, not just perennials, but it is particularly useful for telling the sheep from the goats in this very large group.

Perennials aren't just for summer. This dark hellebore, a choice late winter flower, is a very good partner for snowdrops.

Annuals and biennials

Among the best sources of bright summer colour, annuals and biennials can be relied upon to keep the show going when perennials are taking time out. These wonderful seed-grown plants include many old garden favourites – foxgloves, forget-me-nots, poppies, wallflowers, marigolds and sweet peas – as well as plants that produce some of the most attractive seedheads, such as honesty and love-in-a-mist. Short-lived they may be, but gardens simply wouldn't be the same without them.

Love-in-a-mist (*Nigella damascena*) is one of those useful, welcome self-seeding annuals that pop up unexpectedly every year, yet it is seldom in the wrong place. Its seed-heads are as pretty as its flowers.

Growing annuals and biennials

This large category is divided into several groups for growing purposes. Hardy and half-hardy annuals usually grow from seed, flower, produce seed, and die – all in the same year. Biennials take two, or even three, growing seasons for the same process. And sometimes certain tender perennials are treated as annuals, since they are invariably killed by autumn frosts.

Hardy annuals can be sown outdoors where they are to flower, either in spring or in some cases in autumn, to get a head start. Some of them self-seed once established, leaving you to remove any surplus self-sown seedlings (*see* page 29). Half-hardy annuals are so called because they can't stand cold weather. Sow them in pots and bring them on in a frost-free place, gradually hardening them off so you can plant out after the last frost.

Biennials such as sweet williams and wallflowers are often sown in the vegetable plot in early summer, then thinned and grown on until autumn, when they should be big enough to move to the flower bed. Again, some of them – foxgloves and honesty for example – are adept self-sowers. You can always move the seedlings to where you want them to flower (although they will often have a better idea).

Using annuals

Some annuals, such as cosmos, zinnias and antirrhinums, will soon

Sarah Raven's cutting garden at Perch Hill in spring. Wallflowers – biennials grown from seed the previous year – provide colour and fragrance for garden and house.

make large, statuesque plants that are ideal for filling the gaps when early perennials have finished. Plant breeders are producing more and more dwarf versions of familiar annuals, which are good for patio pots, but in mixed borders it is best to go for larger plants, and fewer of them, as this looks more natural. Some gardeners still enjoy 'bedding out' – using nothing but annuals in the style of old-fashioned public parks – to create the traditional 'riot of colour' from early summer until the first frosts.

Using biennials

Biennials such as forget-me-nots and wallflowers (traditionally grown with

Early summer annuals and biennials at Perch Hill (see opposite): Iceland poppies (*Papaver nudicaule*), Californian poppies (*Eschscholzia californica*) and white foxgloves.

tulips) can also be used for bedding, neatly filling the period after earlier spring bulbs have finished. Sweet williams are good for cutting, too, and they look great in rows – brightening a vegetable garden or featuring in a dedicated cutting garden. Foxgloves, honesty, sweet rocket and other more informal biennials are good for wild areas, or to precede summer perennials in a border, where their lush late-spring foliage will conveniently mask the unsightly leaves of dying bulbs.

Don't forget

Plants of many kinds bloom for longer if their spent flowerheads are removed, but dead-heading is particularly important in prolonging the life of annuals such as sweet peas, marigolds and petunias. An annual plant's aim in life is to flower and set seed to reproduce itself, but if you frustrate its attempts to do this by removing dead flowers, seeds can't form, and it will just keep on trying by continuing to throw out new flowers.

Climbers from seed

Annuals that climb make quick, colourful cover for garden structures such as arches and pergolas while you wait for permanent planting to mature and take their place. They are useful for creating height in a border, trained up a decorative obelisk or an informal wigwam of tall twigs. Sweet peas and nasturtiums are probably the most familiar annual climbers, but several others are readily available such as *Cobaea scandens*, morning glory (*see* page 53) – a sun-lover that produces beautiful sky-blue trumpets every morning in late summer – and Canary creeper, with its unusual toothed yellow flowers. Climbers such as the Chilean glory flower *Eccremocarpus scaber* (below) or the flamboyant *Ipomoea lobata*, are ideal for an (almost) instant touch of the exotic, with their hot colours, quick growth and enthusiastic response to a warm summer.

Bulbs

Bulbs take some beating. They're colourful, economical on space, easy to grow and relatively cheap. They give quick results and may well go on for years, multiplying to make a dazzling seasonal impact, with plenty left over to lift and plant elsewhere in your garden or pass on to your friends and relations. The most familiar bulbs flower in spring, and colour is never more welcome than at this time. But don't neglect the more unusual ones that flower later in the year.

Tulips and wallflowers are a classic pairing – here, *Tulipa* 'Dillenburg' with *Erysimum latifolium*.

Bulbs in borders

Many spring bulbs make perfect partners for herbaceous plants in borders, providing cheerful colour amidst the young foliage of the awakening perennials. But when you're thinking about what to partner with what, do consider how the bulbs will look when they have just finished flowering and are at their tattiest. Eventually, of course, they will become dormant and you can forget about them until next season, but in the meantime how do you avoid having to look at their unlovely dying leaves? Whatever you do, don't cut them off yet. It's fine to pick off the dead flowerheads, but the fading leaves and stem will

The season's barely started, but with cyclamen, chionodoxas and hellebores there's no shortage of colour.

feed and fatten the bulb so it can flower again next year. A good tip is to partner bulbs with a deciduous shrub or a perennial that will be coming into strong growth just in time to hide the dying foliage. If you're clever you can arrange it so that the new leaves of the companion plant complement the bulbs' flowers – try orange tulips with a purple elder (*Sambucus nigra* 'Eva') or the dark-leaved *Geranium pratense* 'Black Beauty'; or partner deep blue hyacinths, *Anemone blanda* or scillas with golden-leaved plants – for example *Philadelphus coronarius* 'Aureus'.

Bulbs in grass

Big daffodils are usually the first victims of spring gales and rains. Even if they come through those unscathed, they look messy for weeks after flowering and you find yourself itching to mow them down

The delicate snakeshead fritillary (*Fritillaria meleagris*) – wonderful for naturalizing in damp grassland.

too soon. Instead, go for a low, carpeting effect, with drifts of the smaller varieties of narcissi and other early-flowering little bulbs, which will shine jewel-like in the early spring sunshine, then die off politely without causing any untidiness. Many will self-sow over the years, creating a natural-looking tapestry in the grass. Crocuses are a familiar example but the petals open only when the sun shines, and the birds and mice do love them. *Anemone blanda* – blue, white or pink – makes quite an impression and has pretty, ferny foliage. For a reliable haze of blue in any weather, even in partial shade, choose one of the various kinds of scilla and chionodoxa.

To give your little spring bulbs the best possible setting, keep mowing until late autumn so the grass is short enough not to drown them when they're in flower. If you need to mow in winter, remember to avoid the areas where the bulbs are.

Bulbs in containers

A packet of bulbs planted in an attractive pot will probably cost you less than a bunch of flowers and is certain to last longer. Feed and keep them watered for a while after flowering, and many kinds will give you a second or third year's display without repotting.

Pots of bulbs near doorways or just outside windows are lovely at any time of year. They can be put in place at just the right moment for you to enjoy the flowers as they open, then replaced with something else when past their best. For late winter try *Cyclamen coum*, early varieties of snowdrop or *Iris*

'Harmony' in a warm, sunny place. A little later come the early, bright miniature daffodils such as *Narcissus* 'Tête-à-tête' or *Narcissus* 'Jack Snipe'. For a wider range of colours, choose hyacinths or tulips, generously planted in groups of at least 10 or 15, to fill the container. Pack them in closely for greater effect, but don't let the bulbs quite touch each other.

For summer pots, tubs and borders there are lilies (such as fragrant *Lilium regale*), gladioli, and the remarkable *Galtonia candicans*, a sort of tall, white, summer-flowering hyacinth. When planting bulbs in containers, choose large ones filled with a soil-based compost so they don't get top-heavy.

Screening

For a garden to be the secluded haven of your dreams, it must at least create the illusion of being a place apart, a beautiful retreat where the outside world seems far away. Your outdoor space can be enclosed by fences and hedges up to a certain height, but you may need to adopt specific tactics when you want to blot out taller intrusive features.

Screening with trees

A thoughtfully positioned tree can be ideal for screening, but first there are careful choices to be made. You don't want to wait patiently for the tree to be tall enough to do its job, only to wish you'd chosen something else.

Think twice before you plant an evergreen tree to make your garden more private. Sometimes, when you have a difficult screening problem to solve, evergreens are the only answer, but they do have their disadvantages.

Mature evergreen trees block out not only the unwanted views but also the sky and the sunlight, all year round, and they severely limit what you can grow beneath their canopy. Some evergreens look much the same all year, so choose one that will offer seasonal variety. This might include berries (holly or yew), catkins (evergreen oak) or interesting cones (*Abies koreana*). *Prunus lusitanica*, the Portugal laurel, is mostly seen as a shrub or hedging plant, but it makes a good bushy tree, laden with fragrant, fluffy cream flower spikes in late spring. *Arbutus unedo*, the strawberry tree, is unusual in having flowers and fruits at the same time, with attractive bark as a further bonus.

Often a deciduous tree is a better bet, letting in precious sunshine in winter when privacy in the garden

Plants for screening. ① The black stems of *Phyllostachys nigra* make a good feature in contemporary gardens. ② *Prunus cerasifera* 'Nigra' blossoms early in the year. ③ Yew hedging topped with a rambler rose makes a secluded retreat.

Trees and shrubs for screening

Ceanothus 'Concha'
Crataegus x *lavalleei* 'Carrierei' (below)
Crataegus persimilis 'Prunifolia'
Phyllostachys nigra
Prunus cerasifera

may be less important, while giving welcome shade and leaf cover in summer. However, some trees, such as apple, walnut or ash, come into leaf relatively late, while others, such as horse-chestnut, lose their leaves early in the autumn. If screening is important, choose something that has a long season of leaf cover, or that blossoms before the leaves open, extending the tree's season of useful screening. Think about the shape of the tree, too. One with a low, spreading canopy may give better protection from a neighbouring window (though it will cast more shade), while a tall, slender tree (*see* page 47) may be more effective in blotting out an eyesore such as a phone mast without excluding too much light.

Structures for screening

Even for the most patient, there may come a time when you need some screening and you need it *now*. This often happens when an extension or new building springs up on a neighbouring plot, and you suddenly lose your view or are overlooked by new windows. Buying mammoth shrubs and trees to restore calm is certainly possible, but they will cost an arm and a leg (and a lot of grey hairs worrying about whether they are going to establish successfully). A pergola or trellis may be a much better option, giving a measure of screening straightaway, with cover improving all the time as plants grow to clothe it. To prevent a seating area from being overlooked by an upstairs window, an overhead pergola with the beams set fairly close together is probably the best solution.

Don't forget

If you are trying to block out something large, always position screening, such as trellis panels, close to your own viewpoint – rather than immediately in front of the offending object.

Shrubs as trees

Plant a shrub that will grow big enough to hide an unsightly feature, and it takes up half your flower border. Plant a tree, and you may well find that within a few years you have blocked out not only your neighbour's washing, as intended, but also your sunshine and your view. The choice of trees that can easily be kept compact is limited, but some shrubs can be pruned to behave like trees. Just remove the side shoots gradually, from the bottom up, as the plant grows. That way you have the best of both worlds: your privacy, and planting space underneath. Try it with these:

■ *Cornus mas* Very early, delicate golden flowers in spring, and good autumn leaf colour, make this an asset to any garden. The variegated form is worth finding if you can.

■ *Cotinus coggygria* Any variety of this familiar foliage shrub makes a good bronze- or purple-leaved specimen as a shrub or small tree.

■ *Euonymus* Spindles such as *Euonymus europaeus* and *Euonymus planipes* make nice little trees with good autumn colour, and the curious fruits can be seen near eye level.

■ *Sambucus* There is a whole range of ornamental elders – variegated, cut-leaved, golden and purple – with one for every planting scheme. They are usually pruned hard to encourage vigorous foliage, but they will make a decent tree if you remove young shoots from the base of the plant.

■ *Viburnum rhytidophyllum* Usually seen as an enormous, rather dull shrub, this evergreen comes into its own as a multi-stemmed tree, exposing the felted undersides of the bold, crinkly leaves as well as the attractive russet bark. Its striking swags of shiny red and black berries are anything but dull, but it needs a partner to bear fruit.

Climbers creating cover. ① A climber such as this white-flowered solanum will make a living 'roof', providing shade and privacy for alfresco dining. ② Just standing under a pergola clad with the vigorous and reliable *Clematis* 'Perle d'Azur' is pure joy.

Hedges

Versatile, long-lived and beneficial to wildlife, a well-planted hedge is a joy forever – well, for quite a long time. Planting hedges involves a short spell of hard work and then a degree of patience while they get established, but the end result will justify the investment many times over. Whether you want a simple screen or a thorny barrier – plant a hedge.

The base of a hedge can be a 'dead space', where weeds can easily gain a foothold. The problem has been solved here with a planting of trouble-free purple dog violets (*Viola riviniana* Purpurea Group).

Plants for hedging

■ *Buxus sempervirens* (box) Less popular than it used to be owing to the increasingly widespread disease box blight, box has always been one of the traditional plants for formal evergreen hedges, and it is very good in shade. A slow-growing form, *Buxus sempervirens* 'Suffruticosa', is the classic dwarf hedging used to edge beds, and for knot gardens. It's very easy to root from cuttings if you need a lot of it. When buying box, first inspect the plants closely and look out for leaves that have turned brown, a symptom of box blight. With established box, sometimes whole branches die off, especially in damp weather. Cut off affected parts and burn them. *Euonymus japonicus* 'Microphyllus' is a good substitute.

■ *Fagus sylvatica* (beech) Though deciduous, beech hedging provides cover for most of the year, keeping its dead leaves until early spring. It is lovely when the fresh green leaves break a few weeks later. *Carpinus* *betulus* (hornbeam) is similar to beech, but better in heavy soil.

■ *Ilex crenata* 'Convexa' You would probably never guess, but this is a kind of holly. Tiny, rounded evergreen leaves and small black berries make it look more like box, and – if you can find it – it is a good alternative hedging.

■ *Lonicera nitida* This familiar small-leaved evergreen works well for hedges up to about 1.2m (4ft) but tends to flop if you let it get much higher. It grows fast and needs clipping once a month in summer. If it gets out of hand, it will respond to hard cutting back.

■ *Phillyrea angustifolia* A bushy broadleaved evergreen, related to the olive, this is another good alternative to box if box blight is a problem (*see Buxus*, left).

■ *Taxus baccata* (yew) This is the king of hedging, and not as slow-growing as people think. It makes a sleek, dark green, slender hedge – a flattering formal backdrop for any planting scheme – and it only needs

Copper beech is excellent if you want a hedge that changes with the seasons. The young foliage, almost coral, gradually settles to a deep bronze-purple, which gives way to russet tones in winter.

clipping once a year (late summer is best). It can usually be renovated by cutting back, however old the plants. Two disadvantages: it isn't good on very damp soil, and it is poisonous to livestock.

■ *Thuja plicata* (western red cedar) This makes an attractive evergreen hedge rather similar in style to the notoriously rampant leylandii (x *Cupressocyparis leylandii*) but more manageable. Unlike leylandii it will re-sprout after cutting back if it becomes too large. It needs clipping twice a year, once in spring and again in late summer.

Sshhh!

Unless you have hedges of enormous size, try to clip them with hand shears rather than a power trimmer. Tackle the job in two or three sessions if it seems like hard work, but for the average garden hedge, light, sharp, modern shears aren't arduous to use and they are much less antisocial – and greener – than the noisy (and often unnecessary) alternative. They also give a cleaner cut, reducing the risk of introducing disease through crushed plant tissue. And you'll be able to hear the birds singing while you do it.

Restoring a hedge

You can renovate old, thin or misshapen hedges of native plants such as yew, hawthorn, holly, privet and hazel with good results. Cut back one side at a time over two winters (spring is better for evergreens) and you will have a good, thick hedge again far sooner than if you had planted from scratch. Many conifers, such as the giant x *Cupressocyparis leylandii* and the similar *Chamaecyparis lawsoniana*, will not tolerate hard pruning at all, and it's better to remove them if they have got out of hand.

HOW TO plant a hedge

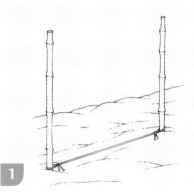

1 Order bare-rooted hedging plants of your chosen variety. Plant on a dry day from late autumn to early spring when the soil isn't frozen or waterlogged. Begin by stretching a line between two or more posts to mark the position of the hedge.

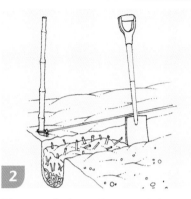

2 Dig a trench about 30cm (12in) deep and wide, breaking up the soil at the bottom with a fork. Add compost and a slow-release fertilizer to the soil you have just removed and then also to the base of the trench.

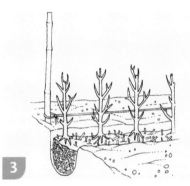

3 Space the plants along the line in a single row, 30–50cm (12–20in) apart. For a very high hedge the plants will need more room to grow, so give each one enough space by setting them out in a staggered row farther apart – up to 60cm (24in).

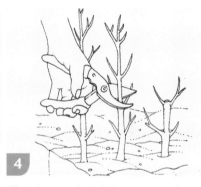

4 Fill in the trench with the mixture of topsoil and compost, firm with your foot, and water in well to settle the roots. To encourage the new hedge to thicken from the base, cut all the plants back to 15cm (6in) after planting.

Native hedging

Gardeners and farmers are now choosing to plant mixed native hedges because they are so good for wildlife. These hedges provide nesting sites and winter berries for birds, and habitats for insects, as well as interest for people. Native hedging is usually bought as small, inexpensive bare-rooted plants in winter, when they are dormant. You can buy these by mail order – look in gardening magazines or online –and plant immediately unless the ground is frozen. Typical species might include:

Acer campestre (field maple)
Cornus sanguinea (dogwood)
Crataegus monogyna (hawthorn)
Euonymus europaeus (spindle)
Ligustrum vulgare (wild privet)
Prunus spinosa (blackthorn)
Rhamnus cathartica (buckthorn)
Viburnum lantana (wayfaring tree)
Viburnum opulus (guelder rose)

'No problems, only solutions,' goes the optimistic saying. But talk to anyone who is battling to establish a garden on a waterlogged or gale-torn site and they could be forgiven for thinking the opposite. The important thing to remember if you have a difficult garden is that it's always much easier and less costly to adapt the garden and planting to the site rather than the other way round. There are very few places where literally nothing will grow – it's just a question of finding plants that will tolerate and even enjoy your conditions. Adopt a flexible approach and the solution will present itself.

Problem gardens

There are always practical challenges to be met when you're making or maintaining a garden. Poor soil, pests and diseases, and the wrong sort of weather are common grumbles, but we gardeners derive great satisfaction from outwitting the gremlins and succeeding against all the odds.

Not just for Christmas – hollies (here, *Ilex aquifolium* 'J.C. van Tol') may grow quite slowly when young but, once established, they are reliable stalwarts for year-round interest on all sorts of difficult sites.

At one time, specific types of 'problem' plot would have discouraged even the most intrepid gardener, bent on creating the one-size-fits-all, conventional garden (lawn, bedding plants, roses, shrubbery) that used to be the template for every suburban plot. But today's gardens are far more individual and, with a little imagination, creative solutions and the right planting can transform even the most unpromising site.

Improving the soil is fundamental to meeting almost every kind of garden challenge. Adding organic matter, in the form of compost, well-rotted manure or a proprietary soil conditioner, will add moisture-retaining body to dry soils, and nutrients and air to wet ones. It will nourish starved ground in the shade cast by trees, especially evergreens, and encourage plants to make the large, healthy root systems that they need for stability in windy gardens.

Aided by regular cultivation and the removal of weeds, a sterile building site will gradually transform itself into a fertile garden.

Survivors

Each kind of problem garden will have its own plant solutions, but there are some naturally tough and robust plants that seem able to cope better than most. So don't despair before you've tried growing some of the following:

Trees

Acer campestre; Betula pendula; Carpinus betulus; Crataegus x *lavalleei* 'Carrierei'; *Ilex aquifolium; Sorbus aria* 'Lutescens'; *Sorbus hupehensis*

Shrubs

Buxus sempervirens 'Elegantissima'; *Cornus alba* 'Elegantissima'; *Cotoneaster simonsii; Euonymus fortunei* 'Emerald Gaiety'; *Hebe pinguifolia* 'Pagei'; *Ilex aquifolium* 'Handsworth New Silver'; *Jasminum nudiflorum; Lonicera pileata; Lonicera* × *purpusii* 'Winter Beauty'; *Osmanthus* × *burkwoodii; Osmanthus heterophyllus* 'Variegatus'; *Phlomis fruticosa; Potentilla fruticosa* cultivars; *Prunus lusitanica; Rosa* 'Fru Dagmar Hastrup'; *Rosa glauca; Rosmarinus officinalis; Sambucus nigra* cultivars; *Sarcococca confusa; Viburnum opulus* 'Compactum'

Climbers

Clematis 'Comtesse de Bouchaud'; *Clematis* 'Etoile Violette'; *Clematis tangutica;* × *Fatshedera lizei; Hedera helix* 'Duckfoot' ; *Hedera helix* 'Parsley Crested'; *Humulus lupulus* 'Aureus'; *Lathyrus latifolius; Lonicera periclymenum* 'Graham Thomas'; *Rosa* 'Compassion'; *Solanum crispum* 'Glasnevin'; *Vitis coignetiae*

Herbaceous plants

Anthemis tinctoria 'E.C. Buxton'; *Campanula poscharskyana* 'Stella'; *Centaurea montana; Centranthus ruber; Digitalis purpurea; Doronicum orientale; Erigeron karvinskianus; Eryngium giganteum; Euphorbia amygdaloides* var. *robbiae; Geranium macrorrhizum* 'Album'; *Geranium* × *magnificum; Iris sibirica* 'Tropic Night'; *Papaver orientale; Sisyrinchium striatum; Stachys byzantina; Veronica umbrosa* 'Georgia Blue'; *Viola riviniana* Purpurea Group (*See also* box, page 55.)

Bulbs

Allium hollandicum, Chionodoxa luciliae; Crocus tommasinianus; Cyclamen hederifolium; Leucojum aestivum; Narcissus 'Jack Snipe'; *Nectaroscordum siculum; Scilla siberica; Tulipa* 'Ballerina'

Grasses

Carex buchananii; Carex oshimensis 'Evergold'; *Luzula sylvatica* 'Marginata'; *Miscanthus sinensis* 'Morning Light'; *Stipa tenuissima*

Shady gardens

People often talk about shade as if it were the worst of all gardening difficulties. It's true that what will grow in a garden overhung by large trees or shaded by tall buildings may be limited, but there are things you can do to help lighten the darkness. Choosing the right plants makes all the difference – remember that some very beautiful plants are shade-lovers.

Shade under trees

Dense shade under trees can be a problem, because as well as making the garden dark, the trees mop up moisture and goodness from the soil, leaving nothing to sustain your precious plants underneath. It may be worth consulting a qualified tree surgeon about raising or thinning the crowns of the trees to let in more light. Don't despair, though, when it comes to planting. Many spring bulbs and natural woodland plants are perfectly adapted to life under trees, and if you keep them well supplied with what they need by watering and mulching, you won't go wrong.

Shade from buildings

Many town gardens consist of a small plot shaded by large buildings, which may seem like an insoluble problem. But in gardening terms this kind of shade is easier to work with than shade under trees.

Dealing with shade in these circumstances begins when you're planning the hard landscaping. Think in terms of pale colours to reflect the maximum amount of light. This also applies to your house: white doors and window frames will act as bright focal points when seen from the garden. Cream or white rendered walls – on the boundary or the house – will also reflect light. When considering paving, avoid drab grey-green colours and opt for warm, golden hues instead.

Suggesting a pergola or arbour in a shady garden may seem to be making the problem worse, but you could paint that cream, too. You should be prepared for more frequent repainting than with bare wood or a dark colour, but that is a small price to pay. If you plant it up with deciduous climbers, they will let the sunlight in for six months of the year but give you a beautiful, leafy retreat for hot summer days.

Unwelcome in the wild, Spanish bluebells (*Hyacinthoides hispanica*) are irrepressible in gardens.

See page 7 for Key to symbols.

Plants that thrive in a shady garden

Euphorbia amygdaloides var. *robbiae*

●❖SPRING

H 50cm (20in) S indefinite

This is one of that valuable group of plants for places where you think nothing will grow. Once established, it gives dense, dark-green ground cover all year, erupting, in early spring, into a froth of flowerheads of the freshest acid lime-green. It goes particularly well with dark-blue or purple flowers such as periwinkles and violets.

Fatsia japonica

●⭷❖YEAR-ROUND

H 2m (6ft) S 2m (6ft)

There's nothing quite like this plant – except its more ivy-like hybrid offspring, x *Fatshedera lizei*. Both are wonderful architectural plants for shade. *Fatsia japonica*, with its huge, shiny leaves, makes a great focal point (and is fine in a large pot) while x *Fatshedera* is more of a climber. Both look good growing from a carpet of contrasting foliage such as ferns and variegated hostas.

Pulmonaria 'Lewis Palmer'

◐⭷❖SPRING

H 30cm (12in) S 30cm (12in)

There are many different pulmonaria cultivars, but this has to be one of the best. Its large, rich blue flowers appear in early spring, and the white-spotted leaves help brighten shady places after flowering is over. If the foliage gets mildew, just cut all the leaves off and a crop of fresh ones will soon appear.

Rubus thibetanus

●⭷❖WINTER TO SPRING

H 2m (6ft) S 1.5m (5ft)

Its former cultivar name, 'Silver Fern', aptly describes this upright deciduous shrub (a kind of bramble, but don't dismiss it because of that), with a fountain-like arrangement of upright stems. Each season's its new stems are covered with a white bloom, making them stand out against a dark background, especially in winter. It is very low-maintenance: just remember to cut down its old stems in late spring to make way for new, whiter ones. Don't plant it near a path or seat – it's prickly.

Ruscus aculeatus

Butcher's broom

●⭷❖WINTER TO SPRING

H 50cm (20in) S 90cm (3ft)

You will sometimes find this British native growing wild in shady woods, but it is seen more and more in gardens. It is a rather spiky-leaved evergreen shrub with tiny star-shaped flowers. The female form has splendid, large red berries in winter. Some nurseries also sell a hermaphrodite form, which doesn't need a male partner to bear fruit.

Vinca difformis

Periwinkle

●❖WINTER TO SPRING

H 30cm (12in) S indefinite

Never waste lovely rich soil on the larger periwinkles like *Vinca difformis* and *Vinca major* cultivars – they will repay you by growing with such vigour that they will soon begin to overwhelm their neighbours. But like the versatile euphorbia (*see* top left) they will put up with poor conditions and make a weed-smothering carpet. *Vinca difformis* has very pale bluish-white, starry flowers that will light up a dark corner. *Vinca major* flowers are violet-blue.

Windy gardens

It's easy to underestimate the destructive power of wind in a garden. Even light winds can damage young plants and slow their growth, and gardeners on exposed sites know only too well the frustration of constant battles against prevailing winds.

Many of us will occasionally suffer gale damage to trees or buildings, especially now that climate change is bringing more frequent bouts of rough weather. All in all, creating shelter is becoming more important than ever, and giving this a bit of thought at the planning stage can turn your garden into a far more pleasant space – for both you and your plants.

Wind direction

In the UK, the strongest winds tend to come from the west and south-west. If you are making a new garden on an exposed site, you will probably need to create shelter on that side of the garden first, to give your new plants protection from harsh gales.

Cold air is also worth taking into account, and planting for shelter on the north and east sides of your garden will help to reduce the effects of cold winds and frosty air. Some springtime favourites – for instance, magnolias, camellias and lilac – are particularly susceptible to frosts. Fruit trees, too, will crop less heavily – or not at all – if the blossom suffers frost damage. Giving plants like these a sheltered site may save their flowers from being browned and disfigured by frosty nights at the wrong time.

It is often assumed that town gardens will be sheltered, but tall buildings and the gaps between them can sometimes give rise to unexpected eddies and turbulence that can be quite detrimental. Whatever your situation, take time to notice the prevailing winds in your garden and the problems they cause, so that you can remedy the situation effectively.

Creating shelter

Fencing may not be the best choice for a very exposed boundary. A solid fence, especially, will be vulnerable to gale damage unless very strongly built. More important, a solid barrier can create a surprising amount of turbulence on its 'sheltered' lee side.

Broom, red and white valerian, seakale and California poppies contribute to a colourful and tough planting scheme for a seaside garden.

In windy places, semi-permeable fencing is better. This might be posts and rails, 'hit-and-miss' fencing, woven hurdles, sturdily fixed trellis, or a picket fence – though not all of these provide much privacy.

A hedge, or – depending on the space available – a mixed shelter belt of trees and shrubs, offers the best of both worlds. It forms an opaque barrier (once it is mature) and it provides very good shelter because it effectively filters the wind, slowing it down and reducing its force without creating eddies on the lee side. A windbreak such as a mixed hedge will effectively protect the plants on that side for a surprisingly long distance – up to ten times the height of the windbreak.

Seaside gardens

Coastal gardens are a special case and lend themselves to particular plants. Strong, salty winds and, usually, little tree cover for shelter or shade, mean that plants have to take everything that the sea can throw at them, and this rules out many traditional garden favourites. But the advantages of seaside gardens include brilliant light, more equable temperatures, less occurrence of fungal disease and fewer problems with difficult shade. The coasts of south-west England have some enviable gardens that are home to all sorts of exotics and other plants that would struggle inland, and the tempering effect of the sea is felt even in gardens facing into cold easterly winds. Hebes, lavateras, escallonias, fuchsias and hydrangeas are among the shrubs that usually enjoy seaside life. Trees can be difficult to establish, but hawthorns and pines are reliable or, for something more unusual, try eucalyptus or the feathery tamarisk.

See page 7 for Key to symbols.

Wind-tolerant plants

Cotoneaster horizontalis

⚐ ❖SUMMER TO WINTER
H 1.2m (4ft) S 2m (6ft)

Cotoneasters are sometimes dismissed as boring but they are stalwarts in difficult conditions. Bees love them, and there are abundant berries to cheer you and the birds in winter. The small-leaved *Cotoneaster horizontalis* can be grown as a freestanding low shrub or against a wall, perhaps with a wind-tolerant climber such as *Clematis tangutica* trained through it for summer interest.

Euphorbia polychroma

○ ⚐ ❖SPRING TO AUTUMN
H 30cm (12in) S 50cm (20in)

This widely available euphorbia puts up with all manner of adverse conditions. Its acid-yellow flowerheads stay looking presentable from spring through to autumn, by which time the leaves have taken on coral tints. It appreciates some sunshine and good drainage, and is compact enough not to get blown over by the wind.

Geranium 'Ann Folkard'

○ ⚐ ❖SUMMER TO AUTUMN
H 50cm (20in) S 1.2m (4ft)

A long flowering season and striking black-eyed magenta flowers make this vigorous perennial a reliable and attractive choice for mixed borders. It has a scrambling habit, weaving among other plants for support, and is particularly useful for covering the dying foliage of spring bulbs. It dies back to a central crown in winter, so it is not permanently invasive.

Hippophae rhamnoides
Sea buckthorn

○ ⚐ ❖SUMMER TO WINTER
H 3m (10ft) S 3m (10ft)

This resilient shrub combines an iron constitution with an elegant exterior. Its narrow silver leaves suggest a delicate treasure but its natural habitat is by the sea and it puts up with gales and poor soil uncomplainingly. Grow several in a group if you have space. You will need males and females growing together so that you (and the birds) will benefit from orange berries in autumn.

Juniperus communis

○ ⚐ ❖YEAR-ROUND
H and S vary according to cultivar

Windy hillsides are fine for most junipers, which come in an array of shapes and sizes, from ground-covering *Juniperus communis* 'Green Carpet' to the tall, slender 'Hibernica' and 'Schneverdingen Goldmachangel' (above), similar in form to 'Hibernica' but more yellow. *Juniperus communis* 'Compressa' stays as a neat flame shape 60cm (2ft) high, working well in pots.

Rosa rugosa

○ ⚐ ❖SUMMER TO AUTUMN
H 1.5m (5ft) S 1.5m (5ft)

Most pests and diseases are unknown to this vigorous, hip-bearing rose and its cultivars (above, 'Alba'). It has single or double blooms, pink, magenta or white, with crinkly foliage. *Rosa spinosissima* (formerly *Rosa pimpinellifolia*), the burnet rose, also tolerates wind.

Dry gardens

Dry gardens are not all bad news – far from it. Light, sandy and chalky soils warm up faster than heavy clay in spring and are much easier to work, especially in damp weather. However, very free-draining soils are susceptible to summer droughts. As ever, the answer lies in the soil – and in the planting.

Improve your soil

There is a lot that you can do to improve dry, free-draining soils. Start by digging in all the organic matter you can – your own garden compost, well-rotted animal manure or a proprietary soil conditioner (now available through council-run composting schemes). Adding humus helps the soil hang on to any moisture that comes its way. Mulching is also important. A surface mulch applied in late winter, before the soil dries out, makes all the difference in the critical spring growing season, ensuring that plants coming out of dormancy have moisture when they need it most. You can use a woodchip mulch (again, try your local council), chipped bark, compost or even grit or slate chippings. Replenish it when it gets thin. Anything that reduces evaporation from the soil will help. A surface covering like this will also make your garden look well tended, setting off your plants to perfection as well as keeping down weeds.

Choose the right plants

Many of the plants we grow in our gardens hail from climates much warmer and drier than ours, so when choosing plants for dry gardens it's much better to go for things that would, given the choice, actually prefer to live that way. Top of the list are probably plants from Mediterranean climates, a category that includes many herbs and other aromatic shrubs, spiky or grey-leaved perennials, and bulbs. These are well adapted to managing without water: some have succulent leaves that retain water, others have waxy or leathery leaves that resist evaporation, or silvery, hairy ones to protect them from the sun.

Plants are often overlooked as a tool for retaining soil moisture, but ground-covering shrubs and perennials make a very effective living green mulch, covering and shading the soil in just the same way as well-rotted organic matter.

Subtle colours and contrasting shapes combine in this thoughtfully composed planting scheme for a gravel garden.

See page 7 for Key to symbols.

Star performers for a dry garden

Euphorbia myrsinites
○ ◇ ‖ ❖SPRING
H 15cm (6in) S 45cm (18in)

Euphorbias are the stars of the dry garden, with dazzling, lime-green flowerheads that are a welcome feature in early spring. *Euphorbia myrsinites* has succulent leaves that make it especially drought-tolerant – good for the front of a bed on top of a retaining wall. (Wear gloves when you cut euphorbias, as their sap is a skin irritant.)

Rosa 'Roseraie de l'Haÿ'
○ ◇ ‖ ❖SUMMER
H 2m (6ft) S 1.5m (5ft)

Attempting to grow roses on poor, dry soil can be frustrating, but try this one. It can make a big bush, but if you have the space it's one of the best for adverse conditions, even resisting blackspot and greenfly. Ideal for the back of a bed, it has a long season of fragrant, double magenta flowers and slightly crinkly, fresh green foliage. Trim and dead-head it occasionally during the summer.

Rosmarinus officinalis
○ ◇ ‖ ❖YEAR-ROUND
H and S vary according to cultivar

This old-fashioned aromatic shrub comes in many different guises. *Rosmarinus officinalis* 'Miss Jessopp's Upright' does what it says on the tin, while 'Severn Sea' is compact, low and arching, with bright blue flowers. All types of rosemary love warm, dry conditions and poor soil.

Sedum 'Herbstfreude'
○ ◇ ‖ ❖AUTUMN TO WINTER
H 50cm (20in) S 90cm (3ft)

Commonly known by its English name 'Autumn Joy', this is a real workhorse of a plant. Its contribution lasts for months, from succulent grey foliage, then coral-coloured plates of flowers in late summer, to bronze seedheads in the winter. Plant several – that way, your borders won't look as if they have lost the plot in late summer.

Sisyrinchium striatum
○ ◇ ‖ ❖SUMMER
H 50cm (20in) S 30cm (12in)

This easy, 'spiky' plant has fans of sword-shaped leaves that add structure, and produces stems studded with cream flower bobbles that blend well with just about everything. For something a bit special try the variegated cultivar *Sisyrinchium striatum* 'Aunt May'.

Tulipa 'Ballerina'
○ ◇ ‖ ❖SPRING
H 50cm (20in) S 15cm (6in)

Tulips like nothing better than a good baking, and in the right conditions this tall, elegant orange variety will thrive year after year.

Damp gardens

On a hot summer's day, as you trudge round with a watering can, the idea of a damp garden might sound idyllic. But for a lot of people, a damp garden means clay – probably the most detested of all soil types: sticky and stodgy and crippling to dig, flooding easily and suffocating all but the most amphibious of plants. Yes, clay can be a pain, and it can be hard work to make something of it. But clay that has been successfully improved and well worked gives very good results, making a fertile, moisture-retentive soil that will support a wide variety of plants.

Eupatoriums, rudbeckias and persicarias – all moisture-lovers, here joining forces for an autumn display in Beth Chatto's damp garden.

Improving the soil

Most damp soils contain clay particles; these are very small and create a dense, heavy, airless mass. The answer is to mix in coarse materials to break the soil up and help it to drain better. Adding grit – sold in garden centres as horticultural grit or coarse grit – will open up the soil structure and improve drainage. Digging in organic matter helps too, so add home-made compost or any other soil-improving source of humus. This will also encourage worms – always a good thing, particularly in heavy soil where the tunnels they make will improve aeration and drainage.

Laying drainage

In extreme cases, it may be necessary to improve the situation using structural methods such as laying land drains and soakaways. This works both for persistent damp spots and for entire damp gardens – though it can involve serious toil. However, it is only worth doing on

Trees for damp gardens

Alnus incana 'Aurea'
Alnus glutinosa 'Imperialis'
Amelanchier lamarckii
Betula nigra
Crataegus laevigata
Gleditsia triacanthos 'Sunburst'
Mespilus germanica
Sorbus aucuparia

sloping sites, because if the waterlogged ground is level there won't be anywhere for the water to drain away. You might just have to get used to wearing wellingtons, and to growing plants that enjoy these conditions.

Moisture-loving plants

That takes care of the back-breaking bit. Now for the good news. There are dozens of plants that love having wet feet, and you'll make life far less frustrating for yourself if you choose these for your damp garden. Just one word of warning, though. Many damp-loving plants do grow very

Slug and snail control

Unfortunately, damp gardens tend to be popular with slugs and snails. These days conventional slug pellets are increasingly frowned on because they may also harm other creatures, but there are less damaging alternatives, from biological control to copper bands. Natural predators of slugs and snails include frogs and toads, slow-worms, ground beetles, thrushes and hedgehogs, so encouraging these allies will help control the problem. You can make choice areas less attractive to slugs and snails by spreading grit, and keep damp, dark corners tidy so they have fewer breeding places. Torchlight forays to pick slugs off your plants at night, especially after rain, are perhaps the most successful measure, and that way – or by using beer or citrus-peel traps – you have the satisfaction of knowing you've caught the culprits. Lastly, there are plants that slugs don't go for, so try bergenias or *Tellima grandiflora* as ground cover instead of hostas, and grow those plants that are slug delicacies in pots, where it's easier to keep the pests out.

fast, so keep an eye on the thuggish ones and don't let them smother more delicate neighbours.

See page 7 for Key to symbols.

Key choices for a damp mixed border

Cornus alba 'Elegantissima'
○ ◐◖◗ ❖YEAR-ROUND
H 2m (6ft) S 3m (10ft)
True to its name, this vigorous dogwood (one of many for damp soil) looks good all year. 'Sibirica Variegata' is very similar but more compact – but either shrub can be kept to size by annual spring pruning, usually removing a third of the stems at the base. This also encourages it to produce glowing red stems – its star feature. Silvery spring buds open into white-variegated leaves.

Dryopteris wallichiana
● ◐◖◗ ❖SPRING TO AUTUMN
H 90cm (3ft) S 75cm (30in)
This deciduous fern has an upright form, with dark brown ribs and scales that are particularly striking against the yellowish green of the emerging fronds. Even when these become darker green, this fern makes a wonderful focal point, planted singly or in groups.

Eupatorium maculatum Atropurpureum Group
○ ◐◖◗ pH↑ ❖SUMMER TO AUTUMN
H 2m (6ft) S 1.2m (4ft)
This tall, hardy clump-former is a good backdrop to a mixed border. It comes into its own in late summer, when it bears clouds of dusty pink flowers. After fading gradually to silvery brown, they stay intact well into winter.

Persicaria amplexicaulis 'Firetail'
○ ◐◖◗ ❖SUMMER TO AUTUMN
H 1.2m (4ft) S 1.2m (4ft)
Useful for making substantial clumps in the middle or back of a border, this robust perennial has glowing, long-lived, pinkish-red pokers.

Rodgersia aesculifolia
◐◖◗ ❖SPRING TO SUMMER
H 1.5m (5ft) S 1.2m (4ft)
The various rodgersias are great architectural foliage plants, which you will be lucky enough to grow only if your soil is moisture-retentive or if you have water to plant them beside. The leaves resemble those of horse-chestnut, and plumes of frothy white or pink flowers are a bonus. Some shade is usually better than full sun.

Viburnum opulus 'Compactum'
○ ◐◖◗ 🐦 ❖SPRING AND AUTUMN
H 1.5m (5ft) S 1.2m (4ft)
This is a small version of the native shrub guelder rose, with lobed leaves and hydrangea-like lacecap flowers in spring. These are followed by generous bunches of jammy red, translucent berries that the birds don't seem to want to touch until they're really desperate for food.

Lawns and hard surfaces

Ask any child, or adult for that matter, to make a quick sketch of a house and they'll inevitably draw a square building with a path leading to the front door and lawn on either side. It's our idealized view of home – a welcoming place where we feel secure, and a garden is an integral part of this ideal. But it's not just about plants, it's also about having an outdoor living area where children can play and adults can relax. In most gardens about two-thirds of the space consists of lawns and hard surfaces, so it's important they look good and are of practical use. Artists paint a picture and then choose a suitable frame. Garden design differs in that the 'frame', or hard landscaping, needs to be made first and then the picture 'painted' with plants.

Choosing a surface

Lawns, paths, patios, terraces and decks are the flat surfaces that make up our garden, or link its various parts. While lawns and paths are easily defined, the distinction between patios, terraces and decks is blurred, and in practice they often perform similar duties. The design and the materials that go into the construction of garden surfaces are determined by their situation as well as your personal preferences and budget. Consider the visual effect you want to achieve and always balance it with the practicalities.

If you're planning a new lawn or area of hard surfacing, begin by thinking about how you'll use the space – for example, a patio for entertaining is quite different from a utilitarian place where you hang the washing or keep the bins, and the aesthetic, practical and financial decisions you make should reflect this. Also, bear in mind the amount of work involved, both in the area's construction and its long-term upkeep. Try to be realistic in your aims: it's no good hankering after a lush green sward if you're a couch potato, because it will require too much aftercare. Likewise, there's no point in establishing a super-fine lawn if the kids play football on the grass – it simply won't withstand the wear. Consider that your needs are likely to change over time and plan for any adaptations you may want to make later on.

This informal stepped path (above) is understated and rustic, with plants left to creep naturally among the cobbles. In contrast, a groomed lawn (below) is striking and stately.

Lawns

The lawn is so much more than just an expanse of grass to be looked at and admired. It's marvellously refreshing to relax on or beside the lawn on a warm day, gazing up at the blue sky and watching birds and

Take time out to relax and enjoy your lawn after a long, hard day. It's incredibly soothing and therapeutic.

insects going about their daily lives. And a lawn is wonderful for the senses – rich green seems to have a calming effect, and at the height of summer, there's nothing quite like walking barefoot on freshly mown grass for making you feel good.

A lawn is easily adapted according to your needs, your budget and the time you're willing or able to devote to its upkeep. If you want an immaculate, carefully manicured area, complete with parallel stripes, you'll need a fine grass mixture and plenty of time at your disposal. If, on the other hand, you have children who want to play on the grass, you'll require a lawn that can pretty much take care of itself. Inevitably, if it

This circular lawn, surrounded by an edging of bricks, makes the perfect calm companion to the mixed shrubby planting around it.

gets plenty of use it will become worn in some areas and need restorative care at the end of the summer, but grass is a resilient plant and by choosing a hardwearing mixture you should be able to have a lawn that can stand a reasonable amount of wear and tear without too much long-term suffering. Mine does!

You can create a lawn on any garden soil, either by sowing seed or laying turf. Whatever you choose, a lawn needs a minimum level of attention without which it will struggle. Care

Lawns: the pros and cons

- Grass is an evergreen, resilient, natural landscaping material.

- Lawns fit in with any garden design.

- The plain green colour of a lawn links different garden elements together and acts as a cool, soothing foil to the brighter flower colours.

- A lawn creates a sense of calm openness that is a perfect complement to the planted areas, which might otherwise seem quite full and busy.

- Turf is easy to lay.

- The shape and make up of a lawn can be tailored to suit the area to be covered and its usage.

- Freshly mown grass feels good underfoot and smells lovely.

- Grass releases oxygen, so it's good for the environment. It's also wildlife friendly.

BUT...

- A fair amount of hard work is needed to keep it looking good.

- Sunshine and good drainage are both required, so you need to ensure the site is suitable (*see* pages 84–5).

- Lawns need mowing at least once and sometimes twice a week, apart from in the depths of winter, and regular edging.

- A lawn will turn brown and straw-like in prolonged dry weather and needs spring and autumn feeds to keep it healthy and green.

- To remove the build-up of thatch a lawn needs annual scarifying.

- You may have to treat a lawn for moss, weeds, and pests and diseases.

- A lawn may need restorative work where it receives heavy use.

Grass makes a great playing surface for kids. It might suffer within this willow playhouse in summer, but can recover during the winter months.

Pots of ornamental topiary flank the stone steps that lead to a perfect lawn complete with stripes – the centrepiece of this formal garden.

includes regular mowing, occasional raking and spiking, and an annual or twice-yearly feeding and weeding session. If you're not prepared to do this amount of work, it makes good sense to consider an alternative to grass. You also need to work out the logistics of cutting the grass (whether you can get a mower onto the area) and the conditions it will be growing in (especially the type of soil, *see* pages 157–8).

Flanked by vibrant flowers and foliage, this stone path provides a breathing space in a lush garden, as well as leading you to a welcome seating area.

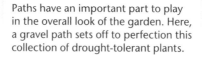

Paths have an important part to play in the overall look of the garden. Here, a gravel path sets off to perfection this collection of drought-tolerant plants.

Paths

Just like lawns, paths vary according to their position and use. If a path simply links one place to another, such as the house to the garage, it can be straight and functional. If, however, it's intended to lead the eye into the garden and encourage you to enter and explore the space, it plays a large part in the design of the garden as a whole. Depending on your overall plan for the garden, it could still be straight, leading you directly to one spot, or it could meander and become a point of interest in itself. The materials that are used to create a path should reflect its purpose.

Concrete, paving stones, bricks, gravel and bark chippings, or a combination of these, are all commonly used to make paths, and all produce a different result. For a heavily used path that leads

In a wildflower meadow, mown grass paths are the best choice. These complement the natural look and can be created as and when they're needed.

Paths: the pros and cons

■ A path serves a practical purpose, allowing you to go from A to B without wearing out the lawn and while keeping your feet clean and dry.

■ It can also be a wonderful design feature, particularly a winding path. It can create a vista and, with careful siting of a seat, give you somewhere to enjoy a moment of relaxing contemplation.

■ A well-designed path can create an illusion of width or make the garden seem longer.

■ The surfacing can be used to create interesting effects – for example, it can bring light to a dark area.

BUT...

■ Paths need careful attention in both siting and laying. If you don't plan carefully, it could mean you lay the path in the wrong place and end up walking on the lawn after all.

■ A path that is too wide, made of the wrong material or badly placed, can dominate the garden or make it seem cramped or unattractive.

■ Paved paths need laying properly with a hardcore foundation, so that there's no chance of them lifting or settling. Paths made from loose materials such as gravel are easier to lay but still need thorough preparation.

■ You need to check a path regularly to make sure frost damage isn't making the sides crumble away.

■ Regular sweeping, cleaning and sometimes weeding are necessary.

Stepping stones keep most foot traffic off the grass on this narrow strip of lawn, which would otherwise be subject to wear. They also tempt you to walk on down through the garden to find out what's there.

to the utility area of a garden, such as the dustbins or washing line, a hardwearing material is most suitable, whereas a path that winds through a shrub border is more for decoration than day-to-day use and might be more attractive surfaced with bark chippings. Depending on what they're made from, paths can be high maintenance (gravel) or low maintenance (concrete or paving).

Underlining the transition from a formal garden to a more relaxed area, this path cleverly changes from neatly laid pebbles enclosed by brick edging to chunky natural stone.

Greener driveways

Where an outdoor surface gets a lot of heavy wear, such as a driveway, you may be tempted to install a large area of concrete or paving at the expense of your front garden. However, be aware that this results in loss of habitat for wildlife and increases the risk of flooding. This is because all the rain that falls on the hard surface either runs straight into the drains, which could overflow, or sits on the top, rather than being absorbed by the soil and vegetation. A hybrid surface is much better for the environment and is less likely to cause flooding. If you do opt for a hard surface after all you could install a green roof to compensate.

Geometric shapes and crisp lines predominate in this garden and are matched by the smooth slate patio surface. The pale wooden loungers highlight the limited colour palette.

A sheltered patio makes a wonderful dining area and the wooden pergola above offers plenty of opportunities for planting ornamental climbers.

Patios

The word 'patio' was originally used to describe an inner courtyard, surrounded by the living quarters of a building. Today, it is used more generally to refer to an outdoor seating area that is usually attached to the back or side of a house and is frequently paved.

Patios are a very popular way to extend the living space into the garden. Most are built with the idea of providing an alfresco dining area and so should be large enough to fit a table and chairs with ease. They can be very simple or more complex, with walls, raised planters, steps and other decorative details. The most popular material for patios is paving, because it's versatile, flat and long lasting, but other materials, including brick, wood or gravel, are perfectly acceptable, depending on the effect you want to achieve.

The most convenient place to build a patio is beside the house. This allows for easy access from the kitchen and other rooms, and encourages you to use the patio on every suitable occasion. However, it's important to take into account shelter, privacy, sun and shade when deciding on its position. It's no good having a beautiful patio that's in the shade from four o'clock in the afternoon and receives the full blast of all the cold winds. While you can create some form of screening to reduce the effects of wind, you will feel the lack of sun on all but the very hottest of days.

Patios: the pros and cons

■ A patio provides additional space for rest, relaxation and entertaining.

■ A seating area near the house gives you a vantage point from which to enjoy the rest of the garden.

■ Patios dry off quickly after rain, meaning you can go outside without getting wet or muddy, or damaging the grass.

■ A paved area can provide the ideal place for a small child to play on a warm day, under the watchful eye of a parent near by.

■ A patio can form part of the overall design of the garden, providing structure and form, especially through the winter.

BUT...

■ The better-quality or more unusual paving materials can be expensive.

■ Paving must be properly laid with a fall to allow drainage and a good foundation. If you don't do this yourself, it can be costly.

■ Seating areas need careful siting to avoid too much sun/shade/overlooking.

■ A patio will need cleaning, sweeping, and possibly weeding and moss and algae treatment.

■ Paving may deteriorate, especially if it has been badly laid. It can also become unstable and uneven, eventually creating a trip hazard.

■ Inexpensive, poor-quality materials will discolour over time.

■ Unless it's on the level, a patio will need railings or some sort of barrier as a safety measure.

This inviting terrace, looking down over the water, contains a variety of materials but their use is subtle, which avoids a busy or distracting result.

Terraces

A terrace can be a level area created on a hillside, a raised seating area, a patio on a rooftop or even a large balcony. The word has many connotations, but in a garden situation it usually refers to a raised, flat seating area: a patio that sits at the top of a sloping garden could easily be called a terrace.

Like a patio, a terrace can be constructed from a range of materials depending on its situation and use. Privacy, shelter and comfort are also equally important on a terrace. If, however, the terrace is an integral part of the house – for example, if it's built above some ground-floor rooms – its design will be dictated by building constraints.

A generous-sized terrace forms a useful bridge between two garden levels.

Decking: the pros and cons

■ Decking can be set at almost any level without too much difficulty. The framework rests on legs that can be made shorter or longer as necessary.

■ Wood is warm to the touch and very soft and tactile.

■ When correctly treated, wood is long lasting and ages beautifully. It can also be stained to match other structures in the garden.

■ There are numerous possible patterns when it comes to laying the planks: herringbone, geometric, squares, diagonals, to name but a few.

■ It's a cheap, easy alternative to paving and can be fitted over the top of an existing paved area to save digging it up.

BUT...

■ Wood bleaches in the sun and when not properly pre-treated it can twist and buckle as it ages.

■ If damaged, it breaks up and splinters, which can cause injury.

■ Wood becomes very smooth with use, which makes it slippery, especially when wet. A deck that's in constant shade will need cleaning with a pressure washer now and then and may need to have chicken wire tacked over the surface so it can be walked on safely. That said, you'll bounce if you fall on decking, but you won't on slippery York stone!

■ Decking requires annual cleaning and regular maintenance to ensure that it stays safe.

■ It may need treating every year with a preservative to stop it from decaying and may fall prey to wood-eating insects.

Roof gardens

A roof garden is a definite plus in a crowded city or town, but it can be created anywhere and provides a uniquely private and secluded space. Even so, there are some very important practical considerations that must be taken into account before building one, as the last thing you want is for the roof to tumble into the sitting room or the water that you're giving your plants to find

Wood, metal and large architectural plants link the two levels of this contemporary two-storeyed roof terrace, which also manages to be in keeping with the old-fashioned soft yellow of the London brick walls.

its way into the neighbour's house. It makes sense to have a structural engineer assess the space to ensure it's safe and have it designed and built by a professional who has had experience of such projects.

Decking

A deck is basically a patio or terrace made from wood. In countries where wood is readily available, it has always been a popular material for using in the garden. For example, wooden verandas are traditional and commonplace in Australia and many parts of the United States, where they complement the wooden houses to which they are attached. Decking is an extension

A secluded spot in the garden is the ideal site for a deck. Making good use of a small area, this one even has a built-in pond and walkway.

This combination of decking steps and landings offers the ideal solution for a big drop between house and garden.

of this idea and is particularly suited to waterside houses or homes that have a garden that slopes away from the house.

In recent years, 'decking' has come to refer to a particular type of surface built from narrowish planks that have longitudinal ridges cut into them. This is usually surrounded by a banister arrangement of some sort and supported on strong beams and uprights. However, a deck can be made from any sort of wood and it can be arranged in a variety of ways. It's extremely versatile and is a wonderful way of creating a level seating area on any patch of land, no matter how uneven. It can be built against a building to give access over a low area without resorting to steps, and may have several levels to provide extra interest and make the space appear larger (*see* right).

Siting a lawn

When planning the shape and position of a new lawn, you'll need to take into consideration the suitability of the site. The amount of sun the area receives, the type of soil in your garden and good drainage are all key to a successful lawn. That's not to say that the site has to be perfect – there's plenty you can do to improve what nature has provided. But you do need to assess the area first, so you know what you're dealing with and can make improvements if necessary.

Lawn aspect

The direction your garden faces influences the amount of light your lawn receives and the kind of weather it has to deal with. Cold winds tend to come from the north and east, wet ones from the west and south west. Facing south means dealing with hot sun, while facing north may mean long periods without sun, especially in winter.

Being a horizontal surface, a lawn is less likely to be damaged by wind and weather than taller garden plants, but it will still be affected by deep shade and too much water, or the opposite – long sunny spells and drought. If your proposed lawn is going to be in full sun, you need to factor in strategies to stop it turning brown in summer. In practice, this means leaving it longer when you mow (so that the leaves shade the roots) and watering when necessary. If, on the other hand, it's going to receive lots of rain and you can see that the drainage isn't good, you'll need to attend to this before laying or sowing the lawn.

Shade and drought

It's best not to site your lawn in a very shady part of the garden, because grass is a hardworking plant that needs plenty of sun to survive. Buildings and structures such as fences or walls may shade

This gently sloping, well-drained site, with areas that are shaded for only part of the day, is ideal for growing a healthy lawn. Lawns on steeply sloping sites are best avoided as they will be extremely difficult to mow.

the site for part of the day and they may also produce a rain shadow (*see* below), which means a lack of water in the area affected. Watch how the sun moves around during the course of the day. If the area gets about half a day's sunlight, this type of shade may not present problems. Similarly, it is possible to cope with smaller rain shadows, especially if you provide a little extra water in the area when needed.

Trees that overhang the lawn are more likely to create permanent problems. The shade they cast can make growth difficult for the grass, and lack of light will lead to elongated, weak shoots that are easy prey for fungal diseases. Also, falling leaves in autumn can smother the grass, excluding light and

The position of a lawn plays a key part in its success. An open site that gets sun for much of the day is best. Planting trees at the back of borders rather than in the lawn tends to reduce the number of problems.

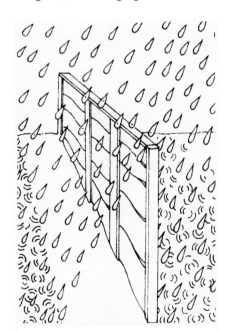

Fences and walls create rain shadows: soil that is sheltered from prevailing rain will always be very dry. It's unlikely to be suitable for grass unless you're prepared to water regularly.

heating up as they decay, leading to fungal problems and rot. Trees can cause other problems too – they're thirsty plants, so the ground beneath them can be very dry; conversely, after heavy rain they may drip water onto the lawn and create localized wet spots. If the trees belong to you, consider some judicious pruning to lighten the canopy and reduce areas of heavy shade. You could also rejig your lawn so it's away from the heaviest shade. If the trees belong to a neighbour, you may need to ask if you can do some pruning, and again redefine the edges of the lawn away from the darkest areas.

Deciduous trees that overhang the lawn can pose real problems, including fallen leaves, which block light and cause diseases.

Preparing the site for a new lawn

You've probably already realized that there's no shortcut to having a good lawn. Proper preparation leads to healthy grass growth, but lack of it can leave the grass struggling to survive. There are two ways to make a lawn: sowing seed or laying turf (*see* pages 89–94). Both will give a good result. Whichever method you choose, you'll need to prepare the site in the same way before you start.

Clearing the site

On pages 18–25 you were shown how to design, plan and mark out an area with pegs, string and sand before creating a new area of lawn or hard surfacing. Now's the time to do the heavy work. First, clear the area of any previous occupants such as trees, shrubs and flower beds.

If there's already a neglected lawn in place, you'll need to get rid of the existing grass before you can start again. There are two ways you can do this: either undercut the turf, separating it from the soil's surface with a flat spade (make sure that you don't take too much soil with it); or, you could kill off the grass using a herbicide. If you choose the first option, you can turn the old turves into a valuable source of topsoil (*see* box, right); if the latter, you'll have to wait between six and eight weeks before sowing or laying turf. Spot-treat or dig out weeds that appear during this time.

Digging is the key to improving almost every site. This stony soil will also need thorough raking to ensure that the grass has an even surface to grow on.

Making a turf stack

To make topsoil from your old turves, stack them upside down in a bricklaying pattern in a quiet corner of the garden. Within six months to a year, the grass will have rotted down and you'll have reasonably fertile soil.

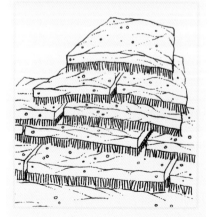

Other surfaces, such as paving, concrete or brick, will need to be completely removed, including any hardcore foundation. This is heavy work, and you may prefer to have it done by an outside contractor. Old paving slabs, blocks or bricks can be lifted and reused elsewhere, but concrete will need breaking up before it's taken away.

Digging

Once you've cleared the site, it's time to start digging. It sounds like hard work – and it is. You may be tempted to skip this stage, but for the sake of your future lawn, please don't! Digging is one of the most important steps to a healthy, happy, long-lasting lawn. There are various ways to dig – some are harder work than others. If your soil is in good shape, simple digging will be fine for preparing the site for a lawn, but if you have very heavy or light soil, it will be worth doing a really thorough job using the single digging method (*see* below). If all this sounds like too much hard work, you could hire a rotavator, although these baulk at really hard ground, too.

Simple digging This basic method involves digging the whole area over to the depth of a single spade blade, turning it over and breaking it up as you go. With heavy or stony soil, you can also use a fork for this process. This type of digging prepares the surface layer for sowing seed, but it does nothing to affect the lower level, so it's recommended only where drainage is already good or where you know that the soil has been well cultivated in the past. For example, if you're making a lawn in an area that was previously flower borders or a vegetable patch, simple digging will nearly always suffice.

Single digging A more systematic method, this is good preparation for areas that haven't been cultivated for a long time and where drainage is poor.

Work across the site, opening a trench, removing the soil into a barrow or a heap out of the way, then using a fork (or even a pickaxe) to break up the lower layer. Use the soil from the next trench to fill the previous one and so on across the area until you've dug the last trench. Fill this with the soil from the first. In the process of single digging, you can add soil improvers – well-rotted compost or farmyard manure – if needed. If the drainage is really poor, such as in a heavy clay soil, forking this in or adding gravel or hardcore to the layer below will help the upper layers to drain quickly.

Levelling the site
A level lawn is a lovely lawn, whereas high and low patches result in areas of scalping (where the grass is removed down to the roots) and long grass, which are not at all pretty. It's much more difficult to get rid of lumps and dips when the grass is growing, so spend plenty of

HOW TO single dig

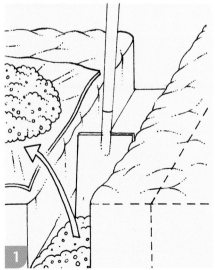

Dig a trench to about one spade's depth and width. Place the soil you've dug on some thick plastic sheeting and set aside as you will need it later. Remove any weeds as you go along.

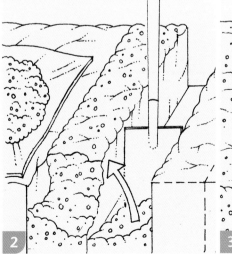

Dig another trench next to the first and put the soil from it into the first trench. Add any soil improvers if necessary (*see* above). Continue in this way until you get to the final trench.

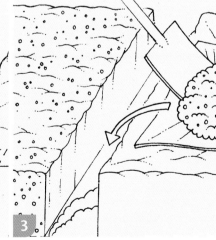

Fill the final trench, which will now be empty, with the soil on the plastic sheeting that was taken from the first trench. Go over the whole area and break up any lumps with the spade or a garden fork.

After digging, draw a garden rake across the exposed soil in order to level the site and remove obstacles such as large stones and other debris from the surface.

time getting the soil level now. Be really fussy about it, because as the ground settles uneven areas will appear in any case.

After digging, rake the area level and remove surface stones, old roots and so on. Stand back regularly to check the site from different parts of the garden. Even out any particularly high or low spots by transferring soil from one to the other.

Levelling the topsoil

The topsoil is the fertile layer of soil. It's like the cream on the milk and is what the grass will grow best in, so don't risk mixing it with the subsoil (which will look and feel different). If the soil levels have to be altered by more than 5–8cm (2–3in) for levelling purposes, the best approach is to scrape off the topsoil and stack it away from the area being landscaped. Carry out the levelling work required, working with the subsoil until the levels are almost correct, then bring back the topsoil and spread it evenly over the area to cover the subsoil. This should create the best possible root zone for the new lawn.

If your lawn area is very uneven or shallow – that is, if the topsoil is less than 15–22cm (6–9in) deep – you may need to bring in new topsoil. Always mix the imported

After rough raking, treading is vital to create a firm bed for the seed or turf. Finally, you'll rake the area over to make it really level and smooth for sowing.

soil with the existing soil on the site, because no two soils have identical properties. Mixing will also ensure that drainage will occur through all the levels.

Feeding

When the soil is level, it's a good idea to add some grass fertilizer, sprinkling it at the recommended rate, before going on to the next step. This will ensure it's thoroughly mixed in to the soil, ready for the new grass to use as it grows.

Firming the soil

In between the rough raking to level the surface and the final raking that will produce the seedbed finish, you need to firm the soil enough to stop it settling too much the first time it gets rained on. This involves walking over the whole area using tiny, close steps with all your weight on your heels. Don't tread on a wet day or when you're in a hurry. Take your time and be particular about covering every inch. Yes, your neighbours may think you've gone potty, but you'll have the last laugh when you have a beautiful lawn.

Final raking

After treading, you'll need to rake again to even out any spots that settled as you walked over the area and to remove stones. But here let me offer a word of caution. The longer you rake, the more stones will come to the surface. You are not aiming to create a fine dust, more a surface that looks like the top of a fruit crumble, while leaving the under surface firm enough to enable the grass to root strongly and deeply.

Grass seed or turf?

When it comes to laying a new lawn, you have the choice of whether to sow seed or lay turf. The decision is really a matter of convenience, time, finances and what you want from the lawn.

Timescale and suitability

Seed is much cheaper than turf, and it's very quick and easy to sow, but it takes time to grow and tends to remain dormant if the weather conditions aren't right for germination. When it does appear, it takes about six weeks to reach the stage where you can walk on it (by which time weeds will have grown up alongside the new grass plants) and you shouldn't expose it to heavy use for the first 12 months. Turf, on the other hand, creates an instant lawn – well, it might take you a day or two to lay it – and it can be walked on in two or three weeks. It also covers the ground completely, so suppressing weed growth to a greater extent than seed.

There is a range of turf types available, but this is limited compared to the variety of seed mixtures, each formulated for specific situations and uses including family, shady, and drought-tolerant (*see* pages 90–1). If you can put a tick next to any of these specific requirements, you might be advised to choose seed.

Don't forget

Although traditional lawns are composed of grass, there are also several non-grass lawn options available.

If they are to grow into a thing of beauty, both turf- and seed-based lawns need very careful looking after in their first few months and regular attention thereafter.

Maintenance

Both seed and turf need a certain amount of cosseting during their first few months. Before it has anchored itself into the soil beneath, turf is particularly susceptible to drought and needs regular watering if rainfall is low. It's important not to let the turves dry out as they'll shrink and gaps will appear all over the lawn. If they dry out too much, the grass will die.

Seed is most vulnerable before it germinates, because it's a popular food with birds; they also like to take dust baths in the exposed soil, which will disturb the emerging seedlings. Like turf, seed needs watering in dry spells (*see* page 92).

Choosing and using seed

When buying lawn seed it's important to consider the type that's best suited to your garden and your individual needs. The best lawns are created using a combination of grasses that have different habits of growth. While individually these grasses might not produce a wholly satisfactory lawn, when blended they complement each other.

Buying grass seed

Grass seed is nearly always sold in mixes that have been specially formulated for particular situations. There's a vast choice available, so you should work out exactly what your requirements are before you buy. First, consider what the conditions are like in your garden (shady, sunny, damp, dry) and what type of lawn you want (luxury, hardwearing, drought-tolerant, and so on). That way, you can get the right seed mixture and it will be more likely to grow well. Just a few of the seed mixtures available are described here.

Luxury mixtures These result in the classic green, velvety carpet desired by so many. A well-tended luxury lawn will steal the show, but it cannot withstand heavy use and needs regular, careful maintenance to remain looking beautiful. Luxury-grade mixtures include fine-leaved, compact grasses such as hard fescue (*Festuca longifolia*), chewings fescue (*F. rubra* subsp. *commutata*) and sheep's fescue (*F. ovina*).

All it needs is a good eye and a steady hand to broadcast grass seed, though measuring and marking the area will produce a more even result.

Lawn seed mixtures: the pros and cons

LUXURY GRASS SEED MIXTURE
Produces a beautiful rich, neat green carpet and is highly ornamental.

BUT...
■ A luxury lawn will not stand up to heavy wear so is unsuitable for a family garden or areas of heavy traffic.
■ It will not tolerate neglect.
■ Luxury mixtures are more expensive than hardwearing ones.
■ Luxury-grade lawns are slower-growing than hardwearing mixtures.
■ Bumps and other irregularities show up more than on hardwearing mixtures.

HARDWEARING GRASS SEED MIXTURE
Highly resilient, tolerates neglect, is quicker to establish, more forgiving and less expensive than a luxury lawn.

BUT...
■ It doesn't have the luxuriant 'bowling green' appearance.
■ Some mixtures can grow too quickly, so regular mowing is essential.
■ Some inferior mixtures can die off with close mowing.

MIXTURE CONTAINING MICROCLOVER
Eco-friendly, sustainable option: drought-tolerant and comparatively low-maintenance; microclover keeps grass green without using fertilizer. Less prone to weed growth and diseases.

BUT...
■ Microclover will dominate the lawn at certain times of the year.
■ It does not produce as neat a sward as many all-grass mixtures, especially when viewed at close quarters.

Hardwearing mixtures Also known as utility-grade or general-purpose formulations, hardwearing mixtures are ideal for family gardens. They stand up to children's games, bicycles and plenty of foot traffic, although they're still subject to wear if overused or under-tended. They're made up of thick, closely knit turf based around perennial ryegrass (*Lolium perenne*), used for its strength and ability to recover, and broad-leaved turf grasses.

Shady mixtures Many grasses require sun so if your garden is shady you'll have to choose a special blend. Shade-tolerant mixtures include hard fescue (*Festuca longifolia*), browntop bent (*Agrostis capillaris* syn. *A. tenuis*) and creeping red fescue (*Festuca rubra* subsp. *rubra*).

Microclover and grass mix Mixtures containing microclover are a relatively new and environmentally friendly alternative to an all-grass lawn. Resembling clover but with smaller leaves, microclover has

For a family garden that takes a lot of wear, select a resilient seed mixture that contains plenty of ryegrass.

many advantages: it's very drought-resistant and can smother most other lawn weeds. Also, as the roots decay, the clover releases nitrogen, which fertilizes the grass and keeps it looking green year round. The effect will be lower maintenance and lower cost, and fewer chemicals need to be used. Unlike other grass-alternative plants, microclover can be clipped with a conventional mower. Never use ordinary weedkiller with these mixes as it will also kill the microclover.

Sowing grass seed

Sow grass seed in late summer to early autumn or in late spring. The end of the year is most likely to be better because long, dry spells are rarer at this time, but spring is also a perfectly acceptable time for sowing if the weather isn't particularly cold or dry. Choose a time when the soil is moist but not waterlogged, and when the weather is reasonably warm but not too hot.

Protect the seed
Make every attempt to keep birds off the seed until it germinates (seven to ten days in warm weather, but up to three weeks if you sow in spring). The seed may have a bird repellent in it, but otherwise lay

Microclover combined with grass seed makes an excellent green, drought-resistant lawn.

Grass seed will usually start to germinate one to three weeks after sowing, depending on the weather.

twiggy pea-sticks across the area to discourage dust-bathing. You could decorate them with something shiny, such as strips of parcel ribbon, aluminium foil or old CDs. Or, with a smallish area, you could lay horticultural fleece across it – this provides warmth and also allows light through for germination. Peg it down at the edges to ensure it doesn't sail off in the breeze. Avoid netting, which can trap birds.

Watering

It's best not to water grass seed before it germinates – if you do, you'll have to continue watering regularly or the seedlings will die, whereas if you leave it the seed will simply remain dormant until the conditions are suitable for growth. However, once the seed has started to germinate, it's vital to provide some water in dry spells to keep the young seedlings going. Water well but gently, ensuring the soil is thoroughly soaked. If you sprinkle water lightly across the surface you'll do more harm than good, as the grass roots will not be encouraged to grow deeply in search of moisture.

Rolling or treading

After sowing, keep off the lawn completely for at least six weeks – or until the seedling grass is about 3cm (1½in) high – then roll it (you can hire a roller from your local hire shop if you don't have one);

Try to keep off newly sown lawns for as long as possible, ideally six months or so.

alternatively, you can tread over the ground instead. This causes branching of the plants right down at the base, which makes the lawn look much thicker almost instantly. It also resettles any soil that was lifted with the germinating grass and firms the seedlings into the soil. Pick off any stones that have risen to the surface before you roll or tread.

The first cut

Try not to walk on the lawn at all if you can help it for the first few months – for best results, it shouldn't be subjected to heavy traffic for about six months. You may notice weeds germinating in the new lawn while the grass is still starting to grow, but don't worry about them. Most will die when you begin to mow.

The lawn is ready for its first cut when the grass reaches about 5cm (2in) high. Set the blades high, so you remove only the top third of the growth (*see* page 101).

Don't forget

Put any leftover seed in an airtight glass jar and store it in a cool, dark place. You can then use it to fill in any bare patches later.

Don't forget

You can buy a combination of lawn seed and fertilizer, which will provide your young lawn with all its nutritional requirements for the first few months of its life.

Alternative sowing methods

If you're concerned about sowing the lawn unevenly, there are several alternative sowing methods you could try. Whatever method you use, you need to prepare the seed bed and rake after sowing in the same way (*see* pages 86–8).

One method involves making a frame out of four 1m (40in) bamboo canes strapped together. Place the frame at the edge of the seed bed, weigh out the amount of seed required for 1 square metre (details will be given on the seed packet), then scatter this evenly within the square. Once you've sown one area, move the frame over the lawn surface to the next square metre and repeat the process until you've covered the whole lawn, then rake it lightly in. A faster method would be to use the bamboo frame simply as a test square. Measure the required amount of seed and scatter it in the square, as before. If you feel confident that you can judge the area and density accurately by sight, you could then copy the effect over the whole lawn.

Another sowing method is to use a machine called a distributor, sowing half the seed in one direction and half at right angles to this.

Choosing and using turf

If you're buying turf, always seek out a reputable dealer. Cheap turf will be a false economy, as it may have come from anywhere (even a meadow that's about to be built on) and you'll be importing weeds as well as some very coarse grasses that will be difficult to eradicate later. If possible, inspect the turf before you buy it. It should be a healthy green, not too long and weed free.

Buying turf

Turf is sold by the square metre. It's usually delivered in strips measuring about 100 x 30cm (40 x 12in). Ideally, arrange to have it delivered just before you want to lay it. It will be rolled up into neat bundles when it arrives, and it's important to unroll it as soon as possible so it doesn't begin to turn yellow (through lack of light) or go mouldy (as the lack of air and increased heat cause fungal spores to flourish). Don't leave it rolled up for longer than a couple of days. It's a good idea to water the rolls you don't immediately need.

Good turf consists of fine-quality grass on a fertile soil base. It comes in rolls and should be laid as soon as possible. Turf must not crack when rolled up and should show healthy green grass when unrolled.

Laying turf

Turf can be laid almost any time of the year as long as the ground isn't too dry, frozen or soaking. Autumn and spring are best. Summer can be too dry (unless you're prepared to water heavily and regularly) and it's probably best to avoid doing it in winter as it's often too cold or wet.

When laying turf (*see* page 94), stagger the joints between the turves and try to place any offcuts in

Water is vital for newly laid turf. The grass roots have been severed and exposed to the elements for at least 24 hours so they need all the help they can get to recover from the shock.

Don't forget

When laying turf, don't step all over your carefully prepared surface. Use wooden planks on top of the newly laid turves; they also help to firm the turf down to make good contact with the soil.

1

2

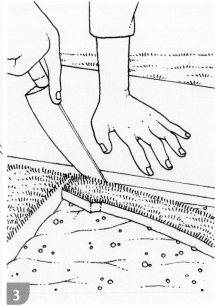

3

Prepare the ground thoroughly so that it's level before you lay the turves (*see* pages 86–8). Kneeling on a plank (never on the prepared soil or newly laid turf), lay the first roll of turf in a straight line and pat it down lightly in contact with the soil using the head of a garden rake. Add the next roll, butting the short ends together and, again, pat it into position.

When you've finished the first row, start on the second row. Stagger the joints between the turves like joints in brickwork. Repeat until the whole area is covered with turves. The final pieces laid at the lawn edges should be large pieces. Always try to have the small offcuts in the centre of the lawn, never at the edge, where they will receive more wear.

Use an old kitchen knife or half-moon cutter to trim any excess turf and to form the shape of the lawn – either straight or curved – then sweep the surface of the turves to remove debris, and water well. Keep off the grass until it has rooted down into the soil. You can test this by peeling back the corner of turves. If you can't lift them, then the grass has rooted down.

the centre of the lawn rather than around the edges, where they're much more likely to dry out or become dislodged.

Aftercare

In damp weather there will be no need to water the turf, but in dry spells, turn on a lawn sprinkler every few days so the turf does not have a chance to dry out and shrink. Alternatively, you can use a perforated hose (also known as a seep hose), which has small holes all along its length and is designed to supply water with a steady drip

straight into the soil. The water needs to soak through the turf and into the soil below; it's particularly important to keep the bottom of the turf and the surface of the soil moist to encourage the grass roots to penetrate into the soil as quickly as possible. This method of watering is better than using a sprinkler, which wets the surface of the turf but, unless left in place for a considerable time, may not penetrate to any depth.

Keep off the new turf for about two or three weeks if possible to give the grass a chance to establish and root into the ground.

The grass will be ready for its first cut when it reaches about 5cm (2in) high. Set the mower blades high so you remove only the top third of the growth. Once the turf has established in position (about six weeks), you can apply a weed-and-feed preparation all over if you notice any weeds starting to come through.

Don't forget

If there are bumps or hollows in your newly turfed lawn, don't try pushing them down with the back of a spade. Instead, lift the turf and remove or add extra soil.

Protecting lawn edges

Lawn edges are very vulnerable to scalping, which occurs when the grass along the extreme edge of the lawn is cut too low. What tends to happen is that when the edge of the lawn is being mown, one wheel goes into the border or the hover cushion of air is disrupted, the mower tilts over and cuts the grass much shorter than intended. One of the easiest ways to avoid scalping and other edge damage is to introduce a firm, solid border around the lawn. This makes mowing and trimming this area much quicker and easier, and does away with the need to re-cut the edge every spring.

There are various methods of edging lawns; some are short-lived while others are much more long term. A fairly permanent but costly option is to install an apron of bricks or paving slabs bedded into cement; make sure that when the edging is in place it's just below the level of the lawn so it doesn't foul the mower blades.

Ready-made lawn edgings

Most DIY stores and garden centres have a selection of ready-made lawn edgings; you can also buy them from mail-order companies and of course specialist firms on the internet. Commonly used materials include corrugated metal, rigid plastic, and bamboo or 'log' rolls.

These are all easy enough to fit yourself. Some come with spikes along their bottom edge. Alternatively, you may need to insert pegs at regular intervals and then slot the edging between the lawn edge and the pegs. Ideally, use a rubber mallet to drive the spikes or pegs into the ground so you don't damage the edging.

Decorative edgings

If you want to define the edge of your lawn in a more decorative way, you could choose from a range including miniature picket fences and willow hurdles, intricate cast-iron work or slightly cheaper black-coated steel. Many decorative edges provide only a little protection for the lawn itself, but they look pretty and can be used to prevent border plants flopping over the grass, which in itself is a good thing, as grass dislikes being shaded and smothered.

There is a wide variety of lawn edgings available to suit every style of garden.
① Chunky white gravel chips contrast with an aluminium edging strip.

② A traditional brick edge creates a tidy finish between slate chippings and lawn.
③ Old brick edging looks rustic and perfectly complements the lavender.

Don't forget

With any lawn edging, once it is fixed in place, go along the lawn side and backfill any gaps with soil – the grass will soon grow into it.

Feeding your lawn

Once planted, your grass plants depend on you to provide the balanced nutrition they need to survive and thrive. In most gardens, nutrient levels are less than ideal. Also, nutrients may be washed (leeched) through the soil by rainwater or during summer watering and so sink out of range of the roots, or other plants may compete for food. With grass, in particular, the quantity of leaf we remove with every cut means that the plants really do need regular boosts if they are to grow well.

The leaves of a plant manufacture their own food from sunlight by a process called photosynthesis. This provides the essential sugars and starches that the plant requires to live and to grow. So plants really rely on their leaves.

Lawns need spring and autumn feeds to keep them in tip-top condition. Some gardeners prefer to feed every six weeks between spring and autumn for a really lush sward.

To manufacture its food efficiently, a plant also needs minerals and trace elements from the soil, which are taken in by the roots in a watery solution. The main requirements are for nitrogen (N), phosphorus (P) and potassium (K), plus minute amounts of copper, iron, boron, magnesium, manganese, zinc and molybdenum. The correct quantity of each of these will enable the plant to thrive. Reduced amounts of any or all of them will limit the rate of growth to some degree. If the plant suffers from complete lack of any one of these nutrients, it will show distinct signs of the deficiency in its growth or leaf coloration. Similarly, if the plant has too much of one kind, this may also show in the type of growth that it makes.

The effects of mowing

Every time you reduce the leaf area of your grass plants through mowing, you partially remove the plant's ability to produce its own food; if you like a trim lawn you might do this twice, or even three times a week in summer. If you were to treat any other plant in the same way it would be unlikely to survive.

Mowing also takes its toll on the soil in which the grass is growing. In the normal course of events in a garden (or anywhere else that plants grow for that matter), nutrients are recycled naturally as leaves fall to the ground and gradually decay, returning any goodness they contain to the soil, which replenishes its reserves. During mowing, it is standard practice to remove the grass clippings (see page 102). This prevents a build-up of old material (thatch) that could lead to diseases taking hold; it also looks neater and avoids treading bits of grass into the house. However, it also means that the soil is being robbed of nutrients with every mowing.

Over time, the soil nutrients that a lawn needs for balanced growth will all become depleted. Nitrogen, which is responsible for growth and

You can scatter lawn fertilizer by hand on a dry, still day or use a distributor (see page 98). Wash hands well after application or wear gloves.

the greenness of the grass, becomes exhausted at a much faster rate than phosphorus and potassium, because it drains away more quickly with heavy watering. Without feeding, the grass will start to turn paler green and the growth will become thin and sparse. This gives weeds the opportunity to establish, which causes increased competition for light, water and remaining nutrients.

Redressing the balance

To have a healthy lawn, you need to feed it on a regular basis to add what you have effectively taken away with mowing. The lighter and more free-draining the soil is, the more fertilizer the lawn will need. It's vital to time the feeding so that the grass can benefit from it. Luckily, the grass fertilizer manufacturers take the guesswork out of this by giving their products names like 'Spring feed' or 'Autumn feed'. They also provide details on how to use their products – always follow their guidelines when you apply feed: too much can be as detrimental as too little, causing leaf scorching or even killing the grass.

Spring feed Spring feed tends to contain a higher level of nitrogen (N), as it promotes strong, vigorous leaf growth in the early stages by replacing what has been washed out of the soil during winter. Phosphorus (P) and potassium (K) will also be present in this feed to prevent the growth being too soft (fast growth produces more delicate leaves – think lanky), which makes it vulnerable to damage, and to encourage new root development.

Autumn feed In autumn feed, the nitrogen content is reduced so that the growth becomes harder (slower growth produces tougher leaves) and is able to withstand the winter temperatures better.

Luckily, grass responds remarkably quickly to being fed, especially if soluble fertilizers are used. The lawn becomes a rich, deep-green colour – a visible sign of its improvement in health – and the nutrients help it to build up a greater resistance to lawn pests and diseases and keep it growing more vigorously.

When to feed

It makes life easier if you can time feeding the lawn to coincide with the right weather conditions, so watch the forecast and pick your moment. Ideally, the soil should be moist when you feed the lawn, but if

the grass is dry when you apply the fertilizer you'll need rain within about 48 hours, otherwise the fertilizer may scorch the grass. If no rain is forthcoming, you'll need to water instead. Liquid and dry soluble formulations are mixed with water before application, so are less likely to produce scorching in dry weather.

How to feed

Feed is sold as a powder or in granules, which are scattered evenly on the lawn, or in a water-soluble form, which is watered in. Organic alternatives to chemical feeds are available, made from a variety of ingredients including seaweed, bonemeal, blood and fish, and these are less likely to cause scorching.

Feeding is simple but must be done with care, especially if you use a powdered or granular feed. These fertilizers are highly concentrated and if applied at the wrong rate, or spilled onto the lawn by mistake, they can kill the grass.

Before you begin, measure out the amount of fertilizer recommended for your size of lawn. Apply half of the total amount of fertilizer in one direction, then the remainder at right angles to the lines of the first. This method makes distribution much more even than if you were to apply the whole lot at once.

While you can use a bucket and scatter the granules by hand (wearing rubber gloves), to ensure

Liquid lawn feeds are great for a pick-me-up as they deliver nutrients to the grass plants very quickly. They're also the easiest and safest to use.

HOW TO feed using a distributor

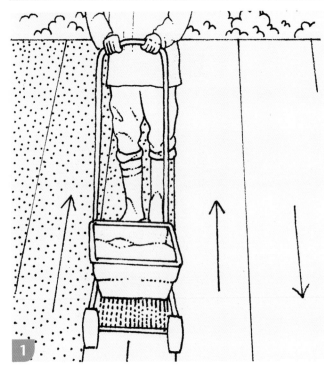

1 Pour half of the fertilizer you need over the base of the distributor and set the calibrator to deliver the feed at half the recommended rate. Walk up and down the length of the lawn at a steady pace. Take great care not to overlap the previous pass. Turn off the distributor when you turn at the end of each pass and turn it on again when you start the next pass.

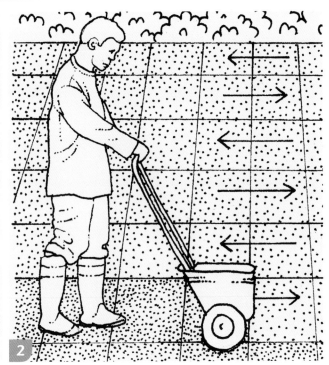

2 Pour the remaining half of the fertilizer in the distributor and repeat the process shown in step 1, but this time apply the fertilizer across the width of the lawn. Again, be very careful not to overlap the previous strip of turf. After you've finished distributing the feed, clean out the distributor thoroughly. Any fertilizer left in the machine may get damp and cause corrosion.

an even application it's better to use a specially designed distributor. Even then, you need to take care not to overlap areas of lawn, as you'll see the difference when the grass starts to grow. Before you begin, wheel the distributor on a hard surface or path to avoid dumping high concentrations of fertilizer on the lawn as the application begins.

Distributors make easy work of applying lawn feeds, grass seed, weedkillers and other granular formulations. Ensure you use the recommended quantities.

Watering your lawn

For most of us, rain is an inconvenience and we're only too happy when it stops. However, our plants (including grass) need rain to survive. We might feel it's been raining for hours, and it's easy for us to think that there has been plenty to satisfy the garden, but the only real way to find out is to dig down into the soil. In summer, you may find that only the very top few inches are wet – and evaporation from the surface soon gets rid of that, leaving the lawn dry again before long.

Why water is important

Like us, plants can't live without water: all of their functions depend upon it. Every cell within every plant is filled with a water-based solution that makes it firm and strong – a bit like a balloon filled with water – and all the systems within the plant, including those that transport nutrients around, rely on water to function. Plants even need water to provide their food, because they don't 'eat' their nutrients, they 'drink' them from the soil.

You may remember from your school biology lessons that water, which holds dissolved nutrients, moves around the plant through a continuous system called osmosis. The roots absorb water at one end and the leaves and other structures lose it at the other – like a siphon. A lack of water at the roots slows down this system and the cells

within the plant start to lose their balloon-full-of-water rigidity, which we see above the surface as wilting. At this point, watering usually leads to the recovery of the plant, although it may suffer some damage to the tips.

Extreme water shortage causes the cells to lose contact with each other and, at this stage, the plant has reached its 'permanent wilting point', beyond which it cannot recover, no matter how much water is applied. One of the problems with grass is that because it is shallow rooted it is one of the first plants to suffer in a drought. However, it is also, by nature, hugely resilient and capable of speedy recovery.

Current concerns about water conservation mean that only new lawns should be watered during prolonged dry spells.

Do you need to water?

Rainfall in Britain is generally sufficient for grass to survive, but there are occasional prolonged dry periods when it may suffer. A well-grown lawn can lose up to 20 litres (4.5 gallons) of water per square metre (10¾ square feet) of surface area each week in summer through evaporation alone. If you know you live in an area of low rainfall, it makes sense to seed your lawn with a drought-tolerant mixture that will survive the hard times.

The feeder roots of grass plants tend to be concentrated in the top 10cm (4in) of soil. The heat from the sun causes evaporation at the surface and this means feeder roots are vulnerable during a dry spell, as this is the first part of the soil to dry out. You can help the grass to root deeper into the soil, where the water will be available for longer, by spiking the lawn every autumn to relieve any compaction (*see* pages 103–4).

Applying the water

In recent years, water shortages have led to hosepipe bans. This has made us all more aware of our need to conserve water, but also of a lawn's capacity for recovery even after prolonged drought. As a result, established lawns are generally left to cope in spells of drought.

Newly established lawns are the exception to the rule and should not be allowed to dry out. Check to make sure that you have a sprinkler licence and that no hosepipe ban is in force at the time you need to water. Applying water in the evening means it has time to soak in while the temperatures are lower and

A drought-stricken lawn becomes yellow and patchy. Although the grass should recover when rain returns, this type of stress may allow weeds and diseases to take hold.

evaporation is less likely. There's a fine line between applying enough water and flooding the grass, so make sure you get it right.

Sprinklers There is a vast range of sprinklers available in garden centres, including static, rotary and oscillating bar varieties. Although a sprinkler is a convenient form of watering – you can leave it on and walk away – it isn't necessarily the most efficient: it loses a lot of water when in use (especially on a windy day) and tends to wet only the upper layer of soil. This results in the grass roots staying near the surface, which won't help them during future dry spells, and a lot of the water will be lost rapidly through evaporation.

Hosepipes A hosepipe is very versatile and if you simply lie it on the lawn and set it on a trickle it will do a more efficient job than a sprinkler. You need to move it every half hour. This way, you don't need to water the whole lawn every day, because the soil is wet enough to last longer. Having water deeper in the soil encourages the roots to grow downwards with it, making them more likely to survive in the future. Remember, 2.5cm (1in) of water on the surface can penetrate to a depth of 10cm (4in) if it's allowed to soak down.

Perforated hoses Also known as seep hoses, these are similar to hosepipes but they have holes along their length (also, they're often made of a rough black material). You attach them to the tap and they leak all along their length. The great thing about them is that if they're laid on the lawn they will deliver water to a huge area without much evaporation and no waste. It's important to keep them clean as the holes can block.

Watering cans You'll probably have one already, but you need to be extremely dedicated to water anything but the tiniest of lawns this way. They do come in useful for spot-treating very dry areas.

Don't forget

Even if there's no hosepipe ban as such, many water authorities now have restrictions on what you can use in the garden and may ask for extra payment for certain activities, such as sprinkler use. It's worth finding out what yours allows before you buy any new watering kit.

Tips for dry spells

If you're experiencing a dry spell, there are several things you can do to help your lawn survive without watering.

■ Feed the lawn (*see* pages 96–7) and remove weeds regularly to keep the grass growing vigorously and to remove competition for the available water.

■ Let the grass grow longer than usual so that it shades its own roots. This reduces evaporation from the surface.

■ Leave the clippings on the lawn as a mulch to retain moisture. This will help for a few weeks, but it's not good to do this continuously (*see* page 102).

Mowing the lawn

If your garden is looking a little scruffy you can give it an immediate facelift simply by mowing the lawn. It's incredible how this relatively simple task can transform the overall look of a garden. A lawn can be mown up to 50 times a year, so the quality of the mowing will have a huge influence on the quality of the lawn you produce. Mowing encourages the grass plants to spread and anchor down into the soil, as well as making the lawn pleasant to walk on. It can also eliminate many weeds and coarser-leaved grasses.

Frequency

How often you should mow is largely determined by the weather conditions and grass type, but generally you need to take the first cut in early spring and continue until early autumn, with the occasional light trim in early winter if it's mild. If the grass, soil or both are very wet, mowing is inadvisable. The ideal is to cut little and often, which keeps the grass healthy without allowing it to get too long, and before weeds start to grow.

A petrol-driven rotary mower is ideal for small to medium-sized lawns. When you're doing the first cut of the year, raise the mower blades to avoid shocking the grass.

Don't forget

As a rule of thumb, you'll need to mow the lawn about once a week in spring, autumn and extended dry spells in summer and twice a week when the grass is growing vigorously in summer. A lawn should never be cut shorter than 1.2cm (½in) or left longer than 3cm (1½in), or the grass will be weakened or taken over by coarse grasses respectively.

How close to cut

An average lawn should be mown to a height of 2.5cm (1in) in summer; leave it slightly longer (about 3cm/1½in) in very dry conditions. Top-quality lawns consisting of fine-leaved grasses can be half this height. If you've had to miss a couple of mowing sessions, perhaps if you've been on holiday, the temptation is to try to get the grass back to the correct height in one cut, but this is a big mistake – taking away such a large amount of its growth reduces its vigour. As a general rule, never remove more than one-third of the grass in any one cut. It's better to bring the grass back down to its regular cutting height by lowering the height of the cut in stages over the next two or three mowings.

Very close cutting on a regular basis – for example, mowing short once a week instead of longer twice a week – will weaken the grass and expose the soil between its stems, which will encourage weed seeds to germinate and invade bare areas.

Make sure you empty the grass out of the mower regularly; rather like a full hoover bag, a full grass box impairs the mower's ability to pick up lawn clippings.

an RCD (Residual Current Device) when working with electricity – it really isn't worth taking any risks.

Removing the grass

Ideally, grass clippings should be removed from the surface of the lawn, either by collecting them in a grass box attached to the mower or by raking them from the lawn for composting. Although it makes good sense to leave clippings on the lawn when the weather is very hot and dry, to reduce moisture loss, generally it isn't advisable.

There are two main reasons for not leaving clippings. First, if clippings are allowed to accumulate they form a layer of dead or rotting grass called thatch. The new grass will tend to root into this layer rather than the soil below, which makes the lawn susceptible to drying out in summer and waterlogging in winter. Fungal infection is also much more likely where the thatch has built up, because there is less airflow at soil level.

The second reason is that clippings encourage worm activity. While this is welcome in flower beds, it's not the case on a lawn. The worms will try to draw the dead and dying grass clippings down into the soil, leaving worm casts on the surface. These little mounds of soil are not only unsightly but they can be destructive – you'll need to brush them to flatten them out before mowing the lawn, otherwise the soil causes excessive wear and tear on the mower's cutting blades. Also, since the casts are made up of soil from below the lawn they often contain weed seeds.

The perfect striped lawn

Are you aiming for stripes? If so, you'll only get a striped lawn with a mower that has a roller fitted to it, as it's the angle at which the grass has been bent over that makes the stripes look a different colour.

To ensure you get an evenly striped rectangular or square lawn, start by mowing a strip along two opposite ends, then, starting at one of the other edges, mow up and down, turning the mower in your previously mown strips at each end. With a lawn that has an irregular shape, mow all around the edge to begin with. Next, mow your first row right through the centre, then mow up and down out to one side. Return to the centre and mow up and down out to the other side.

How to mow

For best results, mow around the entire edge of the lawn, then mow up and down methodically to cut all the grass evenly. If you've a petrol mower, fill it with fuel and oil on a hard surface, not on the lawn – spillages will cause brown spots. If you have an electric mower with a cable attached, start near the power point and mow away from it, as this keeps the cable away from where you're cutting and it's gradually drawn out as you work across the lawn. Always use a circuit breaker or

Scarifying, aerating and top-dressing

Once the lawn is growing well, you need to undertake routine maintenance to keep it looking its best. As well as mowing the grass regularly to keep it neat, and weeding and feeding regularly, you should maintain good hygiene by removing any dead material that accumulates and making sure the lawn drains well. For these tasks you'll need a garden fork and spade, a spring-tine and garden rake, a hollow-tined aerator and a stiff broom.

Scarifying the lawn using a spring-tine or fan rake to remove moss and thatch is a satisfying and energetic job; you'll be amazed at how much material you gather in a single session.

Scarifying

The process of scarifying improves the overall health of the lawn and is best carried out once a year. It involves deep raking of the lawn's surface, which allows air to get to the grass roots and at the same time prunes the roots. This encourages a much more finely branched root system, which in turn improves the grass's ability to absorb nutrients and water. It also removes thatch (dead and decaying grass) and moss from the lawn's surface.

On a larger lawn, it's considerably quicker to use a mechanical scarifier, available in tool-hire shops. They have rotating, knife-like blades that rip out the thatch.

How and when to scarify

Scarifying is simple: just tug a rake (preferably a spring-tine rake) through the lawn so that the tines repeatedly pull at the tangled mass of grass. If there is thatch and moss on the surface, work across the lawn in one direction and then rake a second time at 90 degrees to the first raking. After scarifying, remove and dispose of all the debris from the lawn's surface.

Scarifying is best done in early autumn, about two weeks after treatment for moss. Don't do it before killing moss, or you'll simply spread moss further around your lawn. You may be able to combine scarifying with collecting up autumn leaves. Alternatively, you could combine it with mowing in late summer, when it can be a good way of weakening weeds spreading through the lawn by means of long, trailing shoots. The raking draws up these shoots and mowing soon afterwards cuts them off.

In late spring or early summer, you can spot-scarify to remove patches of dead moss. It's important not to scarify the whole lawn at this time of the year though, or you risk setting it back for the whole summer.

Aerating

Unless they're regularly aerated, most lawns will eventually begin to suffer from compaction as the soil settles and becomes denser, and any air trapped between the soil particles is driven out. Without air, the grass roots are unable to function efficiently. Although we

Make small, deep holes in your lawn using a garden fork to improve air supply to the grass roots, increase drainage and ease compaction.

can't see what's happening underground, the growth above ground will provide some clues. The grass will be stunted, with fewer new leaves forming so that the lawn looks sparse, and the grass may start to turn a pale greenish yellow rather than being a healthy dark green.

Aerating a lawn is simply a method of getting air back down to the root zone in the soil so that the roots can breathe and the lawn can grow again. The most effective way to do this is by creating deep, narrow holes in the lawn. These enable air to get deeper down into the soil and they can greatly improve drainage. Regular attention to drainage is particularly important for lawns on heavier soils, which are much more prone to compaction than lighter, sandy soils.

How and when to aerate

Basic aeration or spiking is best done once a year in early autumn, after scarification. It's quite tiring work, and compaction is unlikely to be bad throughout your lawn, so it's probably not worth doing the whole area – just choose the places where you know the children play, or where you stand to hang up the washing, or where you've seen water lying for any length of time. To aerate a lawn, drive a garden fork into the soil in compacted areas so that the tines penetrate to a depth of 7cm (3in).

There are also several specialist pieces of equipment available that help with aeration. A hollow-tined aerator consists of a set of hollow, finger-like spikes that you push into the soil at intervals of 15–20cm (6–8in) and to a depth of about 15cm (6in). A plug or core of soil from the lawn is squeezed up into the hollow tine, leaving a small, narrow hole in the ground. The next time you insert the hollow-tined aerator into the ground, this plug is expelled onto the lawn surface. Once an area has been treated, collect up the cores, which can be stacked to make compost. Hollow-tining is the most effective form of aeration and needs doing only every three years or so in areas of heavy compaction.

Slitters and solid-tine aerators are also available. The slitter cuts narrow slits and its blades also do some pruning of the grass roots as they're pushed into the soil. Mechanical aerators make life a lot easier if you have a large area to do and they are available from tool-hire shops.

Pricking

Pricking is when only the top 2.5cm (1in) or so of soil is penetrated. It is done with a slitter or solid-tine aerator in spring or summer to ensure that food and water can get into the soil near the grass roots, where it's needed.

Applying top-dressing

The last piece of the annual lawn-care jigsaw puzzle is to apply a top-dressing in autumn, after scarifying and aerating. This task is often bypassed altogether, which is a pity as top-dressing is very beneficial for the lawn, particularly on heavier soils such as clay. The benefits are that it fills holes and hollows so scalping (*see* page 95) is avoided, and it encourages the grass to produce new roots and runners. It can also improve drainage and moisture retention. When a sandy top-dressing mixture is used on heavy soil, it improves drainage, and when a loamy mix is used on light soil, it improves the lawn's water-retaining potential.

Top-dressing a lawn involves covering it with a thin layer of good-quality topsoil, or sand and some organic material, such as peat-substitute. (Don't confuse lawn top-dressing with border top-dressing, where fertilizer is sprinkled around plants.) The layer should be thin enough for you to be able to see the blades of grass poking through it. If it's any thicker, you'll smother the grass. If you want to add more than 1.5cm (½in) – say in a deep hollow – apply it in two stages with a two- to three-week interval between the first and second application, to avoid weakening the grass.

Making and applying top-dressing

To make top-dressing, you'll need the following proportions of peat-substitute, loam and sand. You may need to get rid of lumps first by using a fine garden sieve. Make about 1.3kg (3lb) dressing per square metre (10¾ square feet) of lawn.

■ Heavy soil – 1 part peat-substitute: 2 parts loam:4 parts sand.

■ Loamy soil – 1 part peat-substitute: 4 parts loam:2 parts sand.

■ Light soil – 2 parts peat-substitute: 4 parts loam:1 part sand.

To apply, make small heaps of the dressing with a spade and use the back of a rake to ease it into the holes made by aeration and any small hollows in the lawn's surface. Peat-free multipurpose compost is a good peat-substitute.

Put the finishing touches to your autumn lawn-maintenance routine by filling shallow dips with a top-dressing. The grass will soon grow back through.

Growing in containers

Any garden will benefit from the addition of plants growing in pots. They bring colour and interest to any outdoor space, however small, and alongside the ornamental plants you can even create a kitchen garden in a plot the size of a kitchen sink! Containers are frankly indispensable: if you like to ring the changes, you can rearrange everything without having to dig it up first, and you can grow plants that won't thrive in your garden soil (so if you want to grow azaleas, but are stuck with chalky soil, containers are the answer). What's more, with containers you can create a garden from next to nothing.

Choosing the right pot

You can grow plants in practically any container, from a large cooking pot to an old boat. The only requirements are that the container can hold enough compost to meet the plants' needs and that there are drainage holes in the base. But you do need to be aware that some shapes and materials suit certain situations or types of plants better than others.

Containers come in all shapes, sizes, colours and materials. These striking pots, made from coloured concrete, look fabulous in this contemporary garden, but may look out of place in a traditional or rural setting.

The first consideration when you buy a container for a plant has to be the plant itself. Work out how long the plant will be in the pot, because there needs to be enough room for the roots to grow without becoming choked. The container must be stable so it won't fall over in the wind, particularly if the plant is tall. If the plant is likely to need a stake to keep it upright, you'll need sufficiently deep compost to allow for this.

Pot shape

When creating a display, think about the effect you want to achieve and consider the balance of plants in relation to the container. A tall, narrow pot is ideal for a spiky plant or one that can cascade over the sides, but would be inappropriate for a tall, thin plant, which would look top-heavy and precarious. Similarly, a chubby urn suits an unruly mass of foliage, while neat, carpeting plants would make the display look too bottom-heavy. A formal, square planter is ideal for a trimmed, geometric look, such as topiary. A long, rectangular window box or a relatively shallow trough suits smaller plants such as bedding and herbs or alpines, both as a seasonal or a longer-term display.

Consider also the practical aspects of certain container shapes. For example, a pot that tapers towards the top isn't a good choice for permanent plantings, because it can be almost impossible to extract the plant when it comes to repotting and you can damage the rootball. A broad, shallow container poses other problems: the lack of depth means that the plant's roots can't penetrate deep to search for water, and the large surface area provides the opportunity for maximum evaporation of water from the compost. A narrow-based pot would be unsuitable for tall plants (especially in a windy spot) as it would lack stability and may blow over.

Size of container

The size of the container in relation to the plant needs careful consideration. If the pot is too small, the roots will become cramped, which will result in the plant's growth slowing down, drying out and reduced flowering. Conversely, if the pot is too big for the plant, the amount of fertilizer and water in the compost will overwhelm the plant. As you choose your container and the plant to go in it, bear in mind that the plant will grow, so you'll need some idea of the ultimate size of pot the plant will need. The smallest pot you use should be 8–9cm (3–3½in) wide and deep.

If you have a large pot that you want to use but your plant is still small, you can cheat by putting a small pot containing your plant inside the larger one. Simply fill in the rest of the space with compost or an upturned plant pot, or both.

If they're smaller than this they'll dry out frequently. If you're growing a large plant such as a tree, you'll need a container that's about 45cm (18in) across and 30cm (12in) deep. Weight is also an issue: heavy pots are more stable than lighter ones, but they're also more difficult to move around. From a safety point of view, weight is particularly important if your containers are on a balcony or roof. You don't want pots to be so light they blow over but on the other hand there may well be weight restrictions.

Materials

When choosing a container, always bear in mind the planting and style of your surroundings. A traditional design calls for classic materials such as stone, while a modern setting requires a contemporary feel, which you can achieve with metal or bright colours for instance. A vibrant planting scheme suits a muted container that will not clash with or distract from the plants. You should also consider the different qualities of the various materials.

Terracotta and glazed earthenware

Traditional terracotta pots look lovely in almost any setting. It's a natural material, so it blends in quickly and ages well. The fact that it's porous means that algae and moss, which live on moisture that seeps through the material, colonize the outer surface, giving the pot an ancient appearance. The main disadvantage of terracotta is that you need to water plants regularly to prevent them from drying out. Glazed earthenware containers are also very attractive and there's a wide choice of colours and designs. They're particularly good where you want to create an Oriental or Mediterranean feel. Stand this type of container on pot feet to make sure it has sufficient drainage.

Wood

Troughs, tubs and barrels made of wood all have a natural look and feel that allows them to blend into most informal garden schemes. They're of moderate durability, but last better if you line them with thick plastic sheeting such as a pond liner, or apply a layer of waterproof coating to reduce drying out of the compost. If using plastic, make sure you puncture the sheeting to allow drainage. The main problem, particularly with half-barrels, is that the wood itself must be kept damp. If a barrel dries out, the wood will shrink and the band will fall off, causing the individual pieces to fall apart.

Stone and concrete

Stone is a popular choice for containers, as is reconstituted stone (stone that has been crushed and mixed with cement and then moulded) and concrete, which is sometimes textured. These containers tend to be heavy and traditional in design – ideal for the

A row of vibrant tulips in tall, striking terracotta containers flanks a path that leads up to a front door, offering a cheery welcome and softening the hard lines of the paving. Part of the attraction of this display lies in the repetition of plant and pot.

> **Don't forget**
>
> Not all terracotta or earthenware is frost-proof. Frost can cause the pot to flake or shatter completely, so look for containers with a 'frost-resistant' tag (these may cost slightly more, but will be worth it in the long run).

cottage-garden effect – and are long lasting and wear well. They're not easily moved once they've been planted, so are best used in a permanent position. They usually have good drainage, although they may need to be raised up on blocks or feet. Like terracotta, they lose moisture through the sides, which means that moss and algae will soon build up and give the container an aged effect. You'll have to water regularly in summer.

Metal

Troughs and pots made of metal look particularly good in a contemporary or minimalist setting, where the container is an integral part of the design or needs to be a focal point.

This classic stone urn, with its detailed ornamentation, is offset perfectly by the simple planting: a red-leaved phormium, which provides height and structure, and pretty, small-flowered daisies.

The weight varies depending on the style of the container, but some can be quite heavy.

The big disadvantage of metal is that it does not fare well in a sunny situation, where the container quickly heats up and damages the roots inside. It's possible to get round this by plunging the plant (still inside another container) into damp compost or shredded bark in the metal pot. The material surrounding the plant's pot then acts as insulation against the heat.

Plastic and resin

Plastic pots come in all shapes and sizes and are very flexible, because you can drill as many drainage holes as you want in the base, paint the outside to match your colour scheme, or give the pot a metallic finish so you can enjoy the appearance of metal without the disadvantages. Plastic pots are useful where you may want to change the display regularly, because they're light enough to move around without too much trouble. The disadvantage of plastic is that it will eventually discolour and go brittle, especially if positioned in direct sun. Also, the sides of plastic pots are thin and offer the roots little protection from winter cold. Black plastic absorbs heat, which can damage the plant's roots in summer.

Resin is incredibly light (about the same weight as plastic) but looks very convincingly like stone, pottery, wood or whatever else it's been designed to resemble. Pots made of resin are resistant to frost and heat, and they're easy to drill into when it comes to creating drainage holes.

The beauty of this combination lies in the contrast in form and texture between the tall, sleek metal pot and the tufted grass. Also, the cool, grey and bluish tones create a contemporary, minimalist feel.

Improvised containers

Architectural salvage yards are a wonderful source of interesting materials and unusual containers – chimney pots, for instance, are ideal for trailing plants, and clay drainage pipes are perfect for alpines and herbs, especially invasive ones like mint. You can choose a container to fit in with your personality or design. If you're a keen gardener, you might want to plant up an old watering can. If you like fishing or sailing, or live near the sea, there are all sorts of things from small boats to lobster pots that you could use, although they may need lining with plastic sheeting so that they can hold compost.

Using containers

Containers of all types are ideal for creating a movable feast of colour. Plants can be brought forward as they come into their prime and then moved back to recover once their period of interest is over. These seasonal plants may form the whole display or you could group them around a few permanent evergreen plants, which act as a foil to the changing colours.

Patio displays

This is one of the most popular places for containers, bringing the garden closer to the house and enlivening stark expanses of paving slabs. You may want to follow a certain theme and use containers of the same material. For instance, to create a cottage-garden feel

A collection of foliage plants can be just as decorative as a flowering display. Here, lush greens are set off beautifully by deep purples and light, shimmery or soft, silver-leaved plants.

(*see* page 115) you could use traditional terracotta pots in different sizes: these will blend naturally into the garden setting without making more of a statement than the plants inside them.

Alternatively, you may want to have the containers play a key role in the display – they may be bold in colour or design, or may be made from a distinctive material, such as metal. If you're opting for a varied, changing, seasonal display, make sure that the pots you're planning to

use aren't so large or heavy that they can't be moved around the garden; bear in mind that compost and water add greatly to the weight. Probably the most commonly used plants for a rotating display are spring bulbs, which look wonderful while in bloom but can get untidy as they die down. Once the flowers have passed their best, the pots can simply be moved to an out-of-the-way area for the leaves to die down naturally, nourishing the bulbs for next year's display.

Hanging gardens

A hanging basket or wall planter is an excellent way to liven up a blank wall, create a welcoming reception by the door or simply extend your gardening area (*see* pages 128–130). You can choose to tie it into the overall theme of the garden or take

the opportunity to use a burst of colour wherever it's needed.

A traditional hanging basket contains a mixture of species, including tall, bushy and trailing plants in several colours. Today, there is more of a preference for single varieties of plants, in one colour or a mixture. The advantage of this is that you know all the plants inside the basket have the same needs and preferences in terms of light, watering and feeding. It makes looking after it a lot easier.

Hanging baskets vary from open wire constructions to rigid plastic shapes. If you use one with open sides a good liner is essential. Traditionally, baskets were lined with naturally occurring sphagnum moss, but because moss needs to be conserved, a pre-formed, shaped insert or other liner is preferable (*see* pages 128–130). There are also plastic baskets available, with an external saucer attached underneath to catch excess water and provide a supply of moisture for the roots; the disadvantage of these solid constructions is that you can't plant through the sides.

Table and window displays

Window boxes are ideal for adding an extra growing area close to the house where space is limited, particularly where there isn't a garden. Use smaller plants such as summer bedding or alpines for such displays. You can also create your own herb garden in a window box or in pots on the windowsill. The attraction of growing herbs in this way is that they're close at hand: you can pick them fresh, without having to trudge down the garden in the

This pretty display features small pots of white and grey-green foliage plants, including pelargoniums, echeverias, gauras and dianthus.

rain. In addition to their culinary and medicinal uses, herbs (in particular thyme) are often very fragrant and the scent will drift in through the open window in summer; basil is reputed to deter flies from entering the room.

Wood and plastic are the most common materials for window boxes and both can look very attractive. Plastic is easier to maintain, and wood really needs lining with plastic (with drainage holes) to prevent the moisture from causing rot. Watering and feeding are vital to keep the plants growing and healthy in such a small amount of compost. The watering will be particularly important if the box is in a sunny, south-facing site. Before planting a window box, make sure you'll be able to open the window easily once the box is in position and that the box is safely attached so there is no chance that it will fall.

An arrangement of smaller containers on a table on a patio, terrace or balcony means you can

enjoy a constantly changing display of single, good specimens or groups of attractive plants closer to eye level. If you move the table close to a window, you can enjoy the display without even having to go outside. Low, alpine-type plants, pretty grasses, succulents (*see* page 135), very small shrubby plants or dwarf bulbs (*see* page 131) are all ideal for planting in shallow, wide containers or matching pots. You can liven up the display by adding pebbles, larger rocks or even seashells to the containers.

Don't forget

It's best to fill hanging baskets or wall planters when the plants are young, especially if you want to grow some of them through the sides. The main difficulty with growing plants in this way is that the compost dries out quickly, particularly when exposed to wind and sun, so they need lots of watering.

A welcoming entrance

If you have the space – and provided it's not going to become a safety hazard – a healthy container of plants or a collection of plants is a really welcoming sight beside the door, particularly if you don't have a front garden. Plants add colour and interest to the doorway, as well as softening the hard lines of the building and paving.

At the back of the house, a container by the door brings the garden right up to the house itself and provides a display that can be appreciated even on cold or wet days. Spring bulbs are a good example of this, because pots full of bright flowers always lift the spirits and you can place them where you can see them from indoors without going outside into the cold.

Screens and windbreaks

Patios are not always as private or sheltered as you'd like them to be. Your seating area may be over-looked by neighbours, or it may be in the line of a draught blowing round the side of the building. This means that for at least part of the year you may want to screen the patio so you can sunbathe or eat in comfort and privacy.

Containers are ideal for providing a screen or a windbreak – they can be placed so that the plants block the eye-line or disrupt the airflow without creating a solid barrier, like a hedge. They're also more flexible, as you can move them around according to your needs (mounting big containers on castors makes them easier to move). It could be that you need the screen in one place if you're sitting or lying down relaxing, but in another if you're at the table eating, so moving the screen will give you flexibility and double the coverage. If you're creating a screen around a balcony, roof garden or other exposed site, you'll need to use plants that will withstand wind (*see* page 69).

A bright display of summer-flowering plants grouped around a front door is a lovely way to greet guests. At the end of the season, the pots can be moved to a less conspicuous spot and replaced with others in their prime.

Balconies are often edged with railings that you can see through when you're sitting indoors. The trouble with seeing out is that other people can see in, and there are times when you might prefer a little more privacy. Much will depend on the type of railing, because the more ornamental it is, the less you'll want to obscure it completely or overwhelm it with too fussy a planting. Trailing flowering climbers across a railing will help create some privacy without forming a heavy barrier. It may be possible to install a mesh screening material inside the railings to screen the view and keep out the prevailing wind, or to fix a small

trough to the top of the railing and grow trailing plants that drape down to the ground.

Pots in borders

There are several good reasons for planting a container in a garden border, even though it might not initially seem the most obvious place to put one. First, it's a good way to control the growth of a plant that might otherwise grow too large for your garden: the container will restrict the plant's roots and therefore the top-growth, keeping the whole plant considerably smaller than if it were planted in the border, where it would have a lot of space to grow.

A tiny urban courtyard has been transformed into a private, leafy oasis. Every inch of space has been used – large pots are filled with brugmansia and palms, and a clematis cascades over the trellis.

Another advantage is that you can use a container to add height to the border without using a really tall plant. It provides interest, adds a further dimension to the planting and can make the border seem longer, drawing the eye to a point beyond. You can either bury it partway in the soil or stand it on a single slab set on the soil surface to lift it higher.

Finally, plunging a container plant into a border is a good way to help it survive a dry spell. If you're going on holiday in summer, try planting your pots to about half their depth in the garden soil. The lower temperature will keep the pot cooler and neighbouring plants will shade the container, slowing down the rate of evaporation from the compost. The compost can also establish a capillary link with the soil beneath so that it can draw moisture up from within the soil to help the plant survive.

Unsightly spots

Most of us have an awkward, shady, paved corner next to the house, shed or garage. Container plants can bring cheer to these dark, gloomy situations and really make a difference to your living space. It's vital to choose plants that can withstand the shade (*see* page 67). As a rule of thumb, the darker green the leaf the more the plant can tolerate low light levels. Conversely, pale, silvery leaves – for example those of many Mediterranean plants – are usually a sign that the plant prefers full sun. If your shady corner is really dark, or if it is windswept as well, it's a good idea to keep two containers planted up – put one on display in the problem area and move the other to a brighter spot so that it can recuperate. Remember, you can make an area appear lighter by painting surrounding walls or fences white or another light colour and by using pale gravel or paving. You could also fix an outdoor mirror nearby to reflect what little light there is.

A tiny, narrow passageway has been transformed into a lush jungle. The walls, which have been painted white to reflect light, provide shelter for these exotic container plants.

Passageways are common problem areas – they tend to be confined and draughty and may also lack light. In this situation, long, narrow troughs are ideal because they don't take up much space across the width. If you want to cover a wall, the container will have to be deep enough to accommodate the root system of a permanent plant.

There are very few properties without at least one unsightly manhole in the garden. They're large and unattractive yet we have to have access to them, so the best we can do is disguise them. It's particularly important in this situation to consider the weight of the container when it's full of compost: you don't want to break the manhole cover and you need to ensure that you'll be able to lift the container easily – it will be too late to find out that you can't shift it if you have a drainage problem! Rectangular troughs are available that have been designed to cover the average manhole cover completely, and these are ideal for planting with small, alpine-type plants. However, any round, oval or square container will do the job or else a collection of smaller pots.

Water features

It's perfectly possible to have a complete water feature within a container, from a still pool with a single water lily to a tiny bubbling fountain. The sound of water is pleasantly relaxing and therapeutic and adds interest to the area, however small it may be. You can convert a large ceramic pot or metal container into a water feature by plugging the drainage hole and painting the inner surface with a waterproof coating or lining it with a pond liner; a wooden half-barrel also makes an attractive water feature.

Cottage gardens and potagers

The term 'cottage garden' brings to mind a pretty little cottage (probably thatched) in the country, with climbing plants rambling round the door and a jumble of flowers in the garden. Many plants that create this cottage-garden effect grow happily in containers, where they can provide a spectacular display throughout the summer.

A woody shrub or climber, such as a rose, clematis or wisteria, can form the basic structural framework of this display. To this you could add annual climbers, such as Spanish flags (*Ipomoea lobata*) and sweet peas (*Lathyrus odoratus*), and other annual plants including argyranthemums, verbenas and gazanias – all of these will provide a mass of colour and flower throughout summer.

The potager takes the theme further by introducing vegetables into the mix. This is the old idea of a kitchen garden, where a small plot of land would supply fruit, vegetables and herbs for cooking as well as flowers for the house. If you want to try this idea, you'll probably need several seed catalogues to help you seek out the ornamental forms of vegetables such as Swiss chard, beetroot, peas and beans.

Sowing seed and cultivation

Many annuals dislike being moved, so it's best to sow the seed into the containers and just let the plants grow *in situ*. You can sow single varieties or a mixture, but be careful not to sow too thickly as this will lead to overcrowding problems and the likelihood of fungal diseases. As an added bonus, many seed-grown annuals produce enough seed themselves for you to save for next year's sowing.

Once the plants are growing, keep them well watered and regularly dead-head the blooms throughout the summer to keep them flowering. Once they begin to set seed, flower production will decline; if you want to keep some seed for the following year, let the seedpods develop, but be prepared for flowering to slacken off. If you don't want to save any seed, remove the seedheads to keep the plant producing flowers for longer. Flowers need moderate feeding but vegetables are greedier.

Containers and supports

Terracotta and stone pots look fitting in a cottage-style garden; terracotta-coloured plastic will do too, as the pots will soon disappear under the foliage. If you grow taller plants such as sweet peas or runner beans, they'll need supporting; to continue with the rustic theme, try to use supports made of a material that will blend in, such as a willow or hazel wigwam.

This is not low-maintenance gardening, but the rewards will be huge as you look out over your home-grown display.

Terracotta lends itself to the cottage-garden style as it looks natural, blends into the surroundings and ages well. ① Old chimney pots make perfect improvised containers when filled with flowers such as these pelargoniums. ② A potager in a large terracotta tub contains lettuce, courgettes and sweet peas for cutting.

Planning and designing with pots

Spend a little time thinking about what effect you'd like to create with your containers and what you're hoping to achieve. Just as you consider colour schemes and other design elements in the home, so you should give some thought to the garden before you get planting. Position containers where they can be most enjoyed and where they're easy to water and maintain.

Containers are frequently used as key focal points in the garden – they're designed to encourage you outdoors, highlight a particular location or distract the eye from a less attractive feature near by. In a minimalist garden, a single planted container may be the main feature. A particularly distinctive container will certainly draw the eye, or the planting itself can be the chief attraction. For the latter, plants need to be bold and bright, either in a single colour, in complementary colours, or in a brilliant mixture of hues. Some plants have a distinctive pattern of growth that makes them architectural, others put on a fantastic show of flowers.

Like a terrace of beautifully designed, identical houses, repetition and uniformity can work very well in the garden. Here, pelargoniums in tall terracotta pots are interspersed at regular intervals by low troughs of mind-your-own-business.

Practical considerations

TIME
There's nothing worse than watching a glorious container garden deteriorate because you haven't the time for the constant watering and feeding. If you're short of time, limit yourself to fewer, larger, deeper containers, which require less attention than smaller, shallower ones. Think about installing a timed irrigation system so you won't have to worry about watering, particularly if you're away a lot.

SAFETY
If you have young children or pets, the containers (and the plants themselves) will need to be robust. And avoid hips or berries that are poisonous – yet always irresistible – to little fingers! Don't buy large or lightweight containers for narrow flights of steps, especially at the front of the house, otherwise you'll find you've created an obstacle course or a stack of dominoes rather than a container garden.

ACCESS AND POSITION
Think about where you're going to position the containers – somewhere that is accessible for regular maintenance. If this happens to be a particularly sun-baked, shady or windy site, you'll need to limit your selection of plants to those that tolerate such conditions (*see* pages 65–73).

Optical illusions
If your garden is fairly short, you can deceive the eye and make the viewer think it's longer than it is by using progressively smaller containers as you go away from the house. Fill them with small-leaved plants that produce small flowers in pale colours and preferably a few that have misty flower stems that are more difficult to focus on. Plants that fade into the distance make the garden appear longer. Large pots of bold foliage and flowers in strong colours shorten the visual effect, so are best used close to the house or window. Height in the foreground also makes the garden seem longer.

Harmony and rhythm
To create a sense of harmony, try to use the same type or colour of pot throughout the area rather than a hotchpotch of styles – green plastic, terracotta and metal will just look messy together. Repetition of plants and containers through the design will give a sense of rhythm – an underlying theme that makes the whole design work. This may be a series of pelargoniums in pots up a flight of steps or the repeated use of plain green plants, which may also serve as a foil for the more colourful ones. In the garden, this task is done by a lawn, which balances the areas of colour and gives the eye a period of rest before the next burst of interest. In a large display, balance areas of bright colour by a similar-sized area of green.

Contemporary style

There are all sorts of ways to create a contemporary feel in a garden: with particular materials, colours, shapes, lighting, and of course plants – or any combination of these.

Contemporary design changes all the time, but there are some recurrent themes: modern materials, minimalist planting and bold and/or dramatic colour. There have been many 'black' plants introduced to meet this demand (although most are actually very dark green or red) and they look stunning in silver, bronze or white containers. The range of weather-resistant paints is also increasing steadily and there should be a colour to complement any scheme.

The importance of shape

Form is an essential element of contemporary style. Bold, sculptural planting in large containers instantly gives a modern feel. Palms and palm-like plants such as the Chusan palm

(*Trachycarpus fortunei*) are ideal for this, as are the Japanese maples, silver birch (*Betula pendula*), the dogwood *Cornus kousa*, contorted hazel (*Corylus avellana* 'Contorta') and magnolias. For a uniform effect you can use topiary such as box (*Buxus*). To soften the edges of severely shaped containers, grasses are effective.

Effective lighting

Good lighting will bring a container display to life at night. You can use uplighting beneath a well-shaped plant such as a Japanese maple to show off the intricate branches and leaves, or downlighting to give an effect like moonlight falling on a collection of plants beneath. If you have a containerized water feature, you can use lighting to highlight reflections or movement of the water. Light can be set within the water itself or near by, to shine onto it. Solar power makes lighting within plants much easier, because there is no restriction on where the lights can be placed as long as the panel gets enough light during the day to recharge.

Outdoor lighting from mains electricity should always be installed by a qualified electrician, and must be completely waterproof.

Dark-leaved plants

Aeonium 'Zwartkop'

Alternanthera dentata 'Purple Knight'

Anthriscus sylvestris 'Ravenswing' (black Queen Anne's lace)

Begonia × *tuberhybrida* 'Mocca' series

Capsicum annuum 'Black Pearl'

Heuchera 'Obsidian'

Heuchera villosa 'Palace Purple'

Iresine herbstii 'Purple Lady'

Lychnis × *haageana* 'Lumina Bronze Leaf' series

Ophiopogon planiscapus 'Nigrescens'

Pelargonium 'Bull's Eye' series

Pennisetum glaucum 'Purple Baron'

Pennisetum glaucum 'Purple Majesty'

Salvia lyrata 'Purple Knockout' (syn. 'Purple Volcano')

Sambucus nigra 'Eva' (elder)

Solenostemon scutellarioides 'Chocolate Mint' (coleus)

To achieve a contemporary look, use containers and plants that are simple, strong in form and architectural.
① Conical containers filled with hostas are striking and unusual.
② A red-leaved phormium, *Phormium tenax* 'Dazzler', set in a tall, concrete pot, makes a strong focal point.
③ Galvanized-steel containers with inset lights planted with *Imperata cylindrica*.

Grouping containers

Containers work well when they're grouped together. From an aesthetic point of view, the grouping is like an over-sized container, allowing you to select both flowering and foliage varieties that will complement each other. Evergreen plants can act as permanent fixtures in the grouping and you can move seasonal, flowering plants into the group as they come into their prime and out again as they start to fade and lose their attraction.

Groups of containers give maximum diversity – you can include seasonal and permanent plantings in the display and a vast range of shapes, sizes, colours and textures.

As well as looking attractive, standing groups of containers close together has a practical benefit because it reduces moisture loss and therefore the need for watering. This is because the leaves form layers that trap moisture underneath and create a more humid environment for all the plants in the group.

Year-round and transient displays

It's important to work out when you want the display to look good. If you want to admire it all year round, the display will need to contain evergreen plants to form a framework that other, more transient plants can be built around.

Flowering bulbs will give a burst of colour from midwinter through to mid-spring. In summer, you can use bedding plants, climbers, summer bulbs, shrubs and perennials. In autumn, fill pots with perennials, late bulbs and corms, and plants for autumn colour or berries. Over winter, opt for winter-flowering shrubs, hellebores and structural plants, which look particularly striking covered with frost or snow.

By hiding smaller spring bulbs underneath your winter bedding, you can have a change in the display without any extra work. The bulbs will come up and flower just as the winter display starts to look tired.

Deep-purple petunias, white daisies, trailing *Convolvulus sabatius* and soft, grey-green foliage combine to create a restful display that has a soothing effect on the senses. The pale clay pot complements the understated arrangement perfectly.

A fiery grouping of red-hot flowers, black foliage and spiky architectural foliage in vibrant pots immediately grabs attention.

Colour schemes

One of the major considerations of choosing plants for containers is colour, so always give some thought to the effect or mood you want to create when planning a display. Flower colour is obviously a key element of seasonal planting schemes, but foliage is extremely important too – it provides a useful foil to set off other plants and can in some cases be the main attraction.

For a bright, attention-grabbing display, select plants at the hot end of the colour spectrum: reds, oranges, yellows, pinks and reddish purple. These vibrant colours look good in pots that are warm and muted in colour, such as terracotta, browns or yellows. Alternatively, if you're feeling brave, go for pots in a contrasting colour, such as a deep blue or green. For a highly modern, minimalist planting, opt for a shiny metallic container, such as burnished copper. Remember, you can tire of hot, exciting colours so they're probably better for seasonal rather than longer-term displays.

If you intend to create a peaceful area in which to unwind, choose plants in relaxing colours – blues, mauve, blue-purple, pale pink, white and lemon yellow are all calming. Combine them with green foliage plants, such as hostas, or white-variegated plants if you want to lift the scheme. Blue, white, silver, dark-brown or green containers will complete the cool effect.

Plants with gold, silver, bronze or even purple leaves are ideal for creating a metallic effect in a modern setting and you can team them up with either matching or contrasting containers.

A white and green combination looks fresh and clean and is easy to live with. White flowers are superb for shady areas, as they stand out.

Gardens are getting smaller, and nowadays many homes in towns – especially new houses – have only a tiny outdoor space to call their own. This is ideal for busy people who have little time or enthusiasm for gardening, or for older people who may have downsized from a large garden. Yet even the smallest garden can work brilliantly well, provided it is thoughtfully planned and has a simple, cohesive design.

'Less is more'

This may be an overused phrase, but it really does apply when you're dealing with a very small garden. Visual tricks may make the space seem bigger, but in terms of how much you should actually fit in there's a definite limit. To look and feel right, any garden needs some open space, and if you cram in too many features you will end up with an overcrowded, cramped garden that is hard to maintain and no pleasure to be in – like a room with too much furniture. When allocating space to particular features, always remember to allow enough 'elbow room' – space to move about around a table and chairs, for example, and room to pass comfortably through doors and gates, even when you're carrying a basket full of wet laundry or a large sack of compost.

Planting opportunities

A small town garden surrounded by buildings may be shadier than you would wish (*see* pages 66–67), but it will also be sheltered. This gives you the opportunity to grow a range of foliage plants that would not stand up to the drying and damaging effects of wind in a more open site.

Try dramatic ferns such as tree ferns or *Matteuccia struthiopteris*, or the evergreen native fern *Polystichum setiferum*, with *Vinca minor* (lesser periwinkles) for spring and hostas for summer. Golden foliage is excellent for adding brightness to semi-shaded areas, though many golden plants will darken to green if the shade is very deep. Shapely white flowers such as *Zantedeschia aethiopica* (arum lilies), *Clematis* 'Marie Boisselot', *Dicentra spectabilis* 'Alba' or the white foxglove *Digitalis purpurea* f. *albiflora*, take on a starring role in shady places, while

Small but perfectly formed. This is a tiny area of a tiny garden, but it has everything a satisfying design needs – structure, focal points, variety and year-round interest.

foliage plants such as the white-variegated honesty, *Lunaria annua* var. *albiflora* 'Alba Variegata', or *Arum italicum* subsp. *italicum* 'Marmoratum' show off their intricate patterning much better in low light.

Vertical planting also comes into its own in a small garden. Climbers of all kinds, trained up obelisks or trellis screens, will emphasize the third dimension, height. Closer to the ground, it's a good idea to include spiky plants and slender, upright grasses such as *Calamagrostis* x *acutiflora* 'Overdam' or *Miscanthus sinensis* 'Morning Light' to lead the eye upwards from the limited ground space. Raised beds also make good use of the vertical space, and can be planted with treasures such as auriculas and other specialist plants that demand to be seen close-up.

Hanging baskets and window boxes

A small garden is likely to have a close relationship with its house. Window boxes and hanging baskets connect the two even more closely and are an invaluable way of increasing limited

Space-saving equipment

Manufacturers of all kinds of garden paraphernalia now cater better than ever for gardeners with limited space. If you shop around you will find ingenious space-saving versions of all those things you thought you didn't have room for, such as:

- Slimline water butt
- Lean-to mini-greenhouse
- Folding wheelbarrow
- Seat with tool storage box underneath
- Folding willow obelisk
- Folding tables and chairs

planting space. Use them for fragrant plants, which you can appreciate both indoors and out, or for a supply of culinary herbs within easy reach of the kitchen. Sunshine isn't essential, as long as you choose suitable plants. Indeed, containers in very sunny spots can dry out rapidly on hot days, but those sitting in the shade require much less attention.

In tight spaces, simple ideas generally work best. ① A highly original herb garden makes a unique feature of a shady passageway. ② The sunny wall of a cottage lends itself to conventional planting – well-maintained hanging baskets bursting with summer colour.

All-year-round greenery for small spaces

- *Fatsia japonica* This is the ultimate architectural evergreen, with great hand-shaped leaves that cast interesting shadows. Cut it back each spring if you want to keep it bushy, and don't let it get too dry.

- *Ilex aquifolium* The many variegated cultivars of holly work equally well as shrubs or small trees. They are shade-tolerant, and can be kept to size by pruning once or twice a year.

- *Laurus nobilis* Bay is a favourite for courtyards, entrances and other small spaces. It will look smart all year round if you keep it pruned to shape in summer. Prune it with secateurs, not shears, to avoid unsightly brown edges on leaves cut in half.

- *Osmanthus* x *burkwoodii* This dark broadleaved evergreen has dense foliage, and fragrant white blossom in early spring.

- *Pittosporum tenuifolium* With their attractive pale-green leaves and dark stems, pittosporums never become oppressive. There are cultivars with pretty purple or variegated foliage.

- *Taxus baccata* Yew is one of the plants that are suitable for the fashionable Japanese technique of 'cloud pruning', which results in a tree with tightly clipped blobs of foliage (the clouds) linked by short stretches of bare trunk from which all shoots are removed. The effect is much lighter than that of solid, clipped yew.

Composts and additives

When potting or repotting a plant always use fresh, sterile potting compost. Garden soil should never be used: it compacts easily, offers poor drainage, contains insufficient nutrients and might harbour pests, diseases and weeds. Home-made compost from your compost heap is not recommended either – unless the composting process was very efficient, weeds and diseases may still be present. A specially formulated compost provides a much better growing medium for containers. There are two main types: loam-based and loamless composts.

If you love rhododendrons but can't grow them in the garden as the soil's too alkaline, simply plant them in a pot of ericaceous compost and use rainwater instead of tap water.

Loam-based composts

For plants that are going to stay in the same container for a few years, a loam-based compost (also called soil-based) will be your first choice because it retains both water and nutrients well. The most commonly available loam-based composts are John Innes formulations. All of these are based on a standard recipe and contain 7 parts sterilized loam, 3 parts peat and 2 parts sharp sand mixed with general fertilizer and a little lime. The composts are numbered 1 to 3 (often abbreviated to JIP1, JIP2 and JIP3), each containing increasing amounts of fertilizer; the one you use depends on whether you're potting small, medium or large plants.

John Innes No. 1 Ideal for fine-rooted, slow-growing plants (for example alpines) and young plants.

John Innes No. 2 A multipurpose mix that is good for permanent plantings of average vigour (except acid-lovers).

John Innes No. 3 For permanent large, vigorous plantings such as trees, larger shrubs, climbers, fruit and tomatoes, all of which benefit from the added nutrients.

Ericaceous compost Made without lime for those plants that require an acidic growing medium, such as rhododendrons, azaleas, camellias and pieris.

Loamless composts

A loamless (or soilless) compost is an ideal growing medium for plants that will be in containers for only a few months, such as seedlings and spring and summer bedding. It often holds more water than a loam-based compost, so makes a good choice for small containers, hanging baskets and window boxes, which dry out quickly, particularly in summer. Also, it's lighter and cleaner than loam-based composts, making it easy to handle and a better option for large pots (which will be easier to move) and balconies (where weight may be an issue). Traditionally, a loamless compost was peat-based. However, for environmental reasons peat-substitutes based on other natural materials, such as coir (coconut husk) or composted bark, are preferable. If allowed to dry out, a loamless compost is difficult to re-wet, so it's important to keep it

My own preference is to mix equal parts of loam-based compost and loamless compost to produce a mix that combines weight and nutrient retention with a more open texture.

moist at all times. Also, loamless composts do not hold as many nutrients as loam-based composts, so you'll need to feed the plants more often.

There are three main types of loamless compost available:

Multipurpose compost
The most widely used type of compost, this is a general formulation that is good for general short-term potting, for young seedlings or cuttings, for houseplants that need repotting frequently and for summer bedding containers and hanging baskets.

Seed and cutting compost
This is light and open, enabling the tender young roots to grow easily. It contains a little nutrition to see the plant through its early days but not too much or it could burn the roots.

Bulb compost
This also has a light, open texture. However, it contains little or no nutrition because the bulb doesn't need any until it's dying down, when you have to apply it separately.

Compost additives
There are various specialist products you can add to the compost at the planting stage to improve conditions in the container. You'll be rewarded with longer-lasting, healthier plants.

Controlled-release fertilizer
This releases food into the compost gradually. It usually comes as small, resin-coated pellets that begin to work once they're in a moist environment. Ideally, they need to stay dark and damp to continue

working, although they're also affected by temperature and stop releasing food if it's cold (there is no need for them to work in winter). They can last from 3 to 24 months.

Water-retaining crystals
These are very useful in summer, when plenty of water is needed but may be in short supply. On a hot day, a hanging basket in a sunny spot may need watering twice a day to stop the plants wilting. If you're out at work, this will be difficult, so using these in the compost provides a buffer to see them through. The tiny crystals absorb water and swell to many times their original size. They then release the water slowly back into the compost as it's needed.

Water-retaining crystals, which should be added at the planting stage, greatly reduce the amount of watering required in summer. Add water to the crystals before you put them into the compost. If you put them in afterwards, the compost comes erupting out of the container like a volcano as the crystals swell.

It's well worth adding grit or sand to a container of compost if the plants you're intending to grow require excellent drainage.

Grit and sand
These are good for plants that require free drainage. Both are heavy materials, so they also provide stability to the container. However, they contain no nutrients, so you will have to feed more often to compensate.

Perlite
This can be used in place of sand or grit and consists of light, white granules that are sterile and durable. Perlite helps with drainage, aeration, moisture retention and insulation. Add about 20–25 per cent perlite in the compost mix.

Vermiculite
This naturally occurring, sterile material helps to improve aeration and drainage. It also absorbs nutrients, preventing them from being washed out, and then releases them as required. Add around 20 per cent vermiculite by volume to the compost. The disadvantage of vermiculite is that it has a pH of 7–8, making it unsuitable for ericaceous plants.

A layer of mulch placed over the top of the compost after planting serves several purposes: it reduces the amount of moisture lost to evaporation, so stops the compost from drying out too quickly; it helps to prevent weed seeds from germinating; and – as long as the depth is sufficient (approximately 5–7cm/2–3in) – it stops vine weevils from laying their eggs in the surface of the compost.

There are various toppings available and you can choose one to match the situation and design. Visually, a mulch adds something because it can complement the colour scheme and, if a pale-coloured or reflective material is used, it can help to increase light levels around the lower part of the plant.

Gravel

Long lasting and easy to use, gravel shows off plants well and is available in a range of colours to complement pot, plant or house. However, it tends to sink into the soil so you'll need to top up occasionally. Gravel should be well washed before you use it, as it can be quite alkaline.

Slate

The cool grey-blue colour of slate makes it ideal for a relaxing planting scheme. It usually comes as small, flat chips which lie neatly on the surface, but like gravel it's a loose material and so it can go everywhere if the pot falls over or if you water with a hose.

Bark

This is light, natural and easy to apply but, if it dries out, individual pieces can be blown off the container. Small creatures can also easily burrow their way through it. Bark can be acidic, so it's better used for topping acid-loving plants such as rhododendrons, azaleas, camellias and pieris.

Glass pebbles

These are good at reflecting light, so are especially useful for plants in dark spots, and they look handsome in a modern setting.

Don't forget

Toppings will prevent you from seeing if the compost is moist. You'll have to feel through it with your fingers to tell.

Cocoa shells

Clean and easy to work with, cocoa shells are also lightweight and smell delicious. However, don't use them if you have pets, particularly dogs, because they contain theobromine, which can be highly toxic if ingested.

Weed-proof fabric

This is hardly attractive, and it does need anchoring firmly, but it is very good at stopping weeds, and adult vine weevils can't lay eggs through it. To improve its appearance, cover it up with one of the other materials described here.

Natural toppings come in many forms and can be decorative as well as practical.
① Gravel and larger pebbles combine well or can be used on their own.
② Shells make a good improvised topping, particularly for coastal gardens.
③ Slate is striking in minimalist displays.

Preparing for planting

Give your plants the best possible start by spending a bit of time preparing the pot properly for planting. Before reusing any pot, dispose of all old compost as it may harbour pests, diseases or moss, which will survive to infect the new compost. Then give it a good scrub in water laced with mild disinfectant.

At the nursery, the plants you buy will have been grown on until they reach a good size for sale; in most cases, the rootball just about fills the pot it's in, which means that you'll probably have to repot it fairly quickly.

Tools

A few simple tools are all you need for planting and maintaining your container plants (*see* box, right).

To keep your tools in good working order, make sure you clean them thoroughly after use, particularly if they've been in contact with plant sap, as they can discolour and rust if left dirty. At least once a year, it's worth doing a maintenance check to see if wooden handles have been damaged; they may need sanding down to remove splintered wood. You can rub wooden tools over with linseed oil and wipe an oily cloth over the metal blades or prongs to protect them. If you use a watering can or trigger sprayer to apply fertilizer or chemicals, make sure they're washed out thoroughly before the next use so that there's no chance of contamination.

Providing drainage

Holes in the container base are essential in order to prevent the plant's roots from sitting in wet compost, which makes them soggy and causes them to rot. The number of drainage holes required increases with the size of the pot. Generally, you need 2.5cm (1in) diameter of drainage hole for every 30cm (12in) diameter of compost surface. Good drainage is especially important when growing herbs or alpines, which dislike sitting in water.

Compost can sometimes clog single holes and prevent water from getting through. To prevent this, gardeners often put crocks (broken flowerpots) into clay pots before planting. This can provide a perfect hideaway for adult vine weevils to occupy during the daytime, leaving them free to climb the plant and feast at night. They then lay their eggs in the upper layer of compost and the hatching larvae eat the roots. To prevent this, lay a piece of fine mesh across the base of the pot before putting in crocks and compost; a pair of old tights or a small piece of newspaper, cut to shape, will do just as well. As an added precaution, stand pots on pot feet to keep holes from clogging with garden debris. If weight is an issue, you could use polystyrene packing chips instead of crocks.

If the container is made of wood, you'll need to use waterproof paint or line the inside with plastic to protect the wood from rot. Puncture holes in the plastic to allow excess water to drain.

It pays to wash and disinfect pots at the end of the season. Store them somewhere dry so that they're clean and ready for spring.

Tools for planting

- **SECATEURS**
For trimming shoots for early training, pruning and taking cuttings

- **LOPPERS**
For cutting larger, thicker stems

- **GARDENING KNIFE**
For taking cuttings

- **TROWEL**
For making planting holes in compost

- **WATERING CAN (with rose) and TRIGGER SPRAYER**
Essential for regular watering of container plants

- **DIBBER**
For pricking out (planting) seedlings and young plants

- **STIFF BRUSH**
For getting rid of any residue inside a pot that has been used before

- **HAND FORK**
For breaking up compacted soil, mixing additives into the compost and dividing and separating plants

- **GLOVES**
To protect against sharp thorns and keep hands clean

- **DRILL WITH A WIDE BIT**
For making drainage holes in the bottom of a container (if necessary).

Planting a container

After cleaning the pots and ensuring good drainage, you're ready to plant. Whatever container you're using, with the exception of open-sided hanging baskets (*see* pages 128–130) the basic planting method and principles are generally the same. Always water the plants thoroughly before planting. It's also beneficial to soak porous containers in water.

Bare-root and root-balled plants

Woody plants such as trees, shrubs and climbers are sold in various forms. Bare-root plants are grown in open ground and are lifted without any soil or compost around their roots – roses are often sold like this. Root-balled plants are also grown in open ground but the roots are surrounded by soil when lifted and they're often wrapped in hessian or netting for protection.

When planting a window box, think about viewing the display from inside and outside the house and include a mixture of bushy and trailing plants.

Trees and sometimes shrubs are available in this way. Both bare-root and root-balled plants are normally available in late autumn and winter, when they're lifted from the ground during their period of dormancy. They need planting quickly, before the roots can become damaged.

Container-grown plants

Container-grown plants are the most expensive (and increasingly common) type of plants to buy, but they're also the most reliable. They've spent all their lives in pots and establish more easily than other types because their root systems are more developed. Container-grown specimens may be planted whenever you're ready or when you can see roots coming out of the base of the pot.

Bedding plants may be sold as 'plugs', which have been grown in multi-cell packs or in polystyrene strips. Remove the plants carefully to avoid damaging the roots.

Containerized plants

Containerized plants are started off in the open ground but are later potted up into a container for sale. You can usually tell containerized plants by the fact that the soil falls away when the pot is removed. Treat containerized plants as for bare-root, and plant as soon as you can.

A wheelbarrow is useful for carrying plants to the container for planting. It's best to plant large tubs *in situ* as they can be very heavy once filled.

The permanent container

If you're planning to keep a plant in a container for a long time, your choice of compost and container are particularly important. The compost must be nutrient-rich (*see* pages 122–3) and you need to select a shape that will enable you to remove the plant easily when it comes to repotting. If you intend to use a stake, ensure your chosen container is sufficiently deep to contain it. Follow the basic planting method shown opposite and add a support if the plant needs it.

For climbers, the planting and staking method depends on the type of plant and its support. If you intend to grow the plant up trellis that is fixed onto the wall, position the plant slightly off centre in the container, to bring the plant closer to the wall, and begin to train it immediately, tying in all the main stems to form a framework. If you're using a support that will stay in the container, place the plant centrally; if there are several plants, spread them evenly around the pot so that each one has equal access to the support.

If you're using a single stake, position it against the rootball at the planting stage. If you're using a frame, fill the container and firm the compost around the plant, then position the frame over, or next to, the plant. Position the stems against the support and tie them into place.

The seasonal container

If the container is going to be needed for a short period only – for example, a display of summer or winter bedding, spring or summer bulbs, or seasonal herbs – you have a greater selection when it comes to choosing a container, because the plants' roots are unlikely to fill the space in such a short time. Herbs and bedding favour John Innes No. 1, which gives the plants stability and nutrients, and bulbs thrive in bulb compost, but for short-term plantings a general multipurpose compost is perfectly adequate. As with permanent displays, drainage is important (*see* page 125).

Don't forget

The top layer of compost in an established pot plant is likely to contain weed seeds. Before repotting (*see* pages 132–3), carefully scrape the upper surface off the old compost, and discard it. You can replace it with fresh, sterile compost up to the mark of the old compost on the plant's stem.

HOW TO plant a basic container

1 Half fill a clean container with a layer of compost mixed with additives such as water-retaining granules and controlled-release fertilizer. Water the plants.

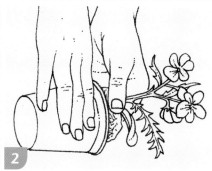

2 Remove the plants from their pots by tapping the pot on a firm edge to free the rootball. If the plant is pot bound, you'll need a little more effort to release it.

3 Gently loosen the roots at the base and at the sides of the plant with your fingers to encourage the roots to grow outwards and downwards.

4 Place the plant on the compost mix to check on the depth. Allow about 1cm (½in) between the plant's 'neck' and the top of the container. Add more compost if needed.

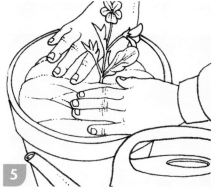

5 Fill around the sides and in between the plants, firming gently as you go. Add more compost until the surface is covered. Water well. You may find that watering makes the compost sink down and you may need to top up or fill gaps with a little more compost.

6 Add a layer of mulch over the surface of the soil to help retain moisture, suppress weeds and keep the roots a little cooler in summer (*see* page 122). Place pot feet underneath the container; keeping the base of the pot off the ground aids drainage and prevents waterlogging.

Planting a hanging basket

The major difference between planting an open-sided hanging basket and other containers is that you can plant through the sides, covering the entire basket with foliage and flowers. Planting can be more fiddly than with other containers, but provided you plant correctly, hang the basket in a sheltered site and water and feed frequently you'll be rewarded with glorious displays in areas that are otherwise frequently neglected.

A pre-formed fibre liner is useful for lining an open-sided basket before planting. Simply pop it into the basket and press it into position.

Types of basket

There are many different types of hanging basket available, from those with solid sides that need no liner to the traditional mesh variety. Open-sided baskets create a lovely all-round effect, as you can plant through the sides in layers as well as at the top. They used to be made of galvanized metal, but today they're usually made of plastic or plastic-covered wire. The disadvantage of open-sided baskets is that moisture can evaporate from the whole surface area, so the compost will dry out quickly and you'll need to water regularly. Also, they're more difficult to plant up than closed-sided ones.

Closed-sided baskets can contain plants only at the top, which means that they're easier to plant up than an open-sided type and no liner is required. Also, closed-sided baskets are easier to water, as they often have a small saucer attached, which means there is a small reservoir. The disadvantage of this type of basket is that you can't create the full, all-round effect possible with an open-sided basket. When planting, remember to use trailing plants that will spill over the sides and cover them, and bear in mind that the plastic may go brittle if the basket is positioned in full sun.

How to plant

The type of hanging basket determines how you plant it. If it's the closed-sided type, you can plant only into the top. These tend to be smaller than other baskets, so opt for smaller plants, including some that will trail down the sides (*see* opposite). If your basket has open sides, plant through the sides as well as the top (*see* opposite, far right, and page 130).

You can use multipurpose compost, John Innes No. 1 or a mixture of the two for planting, depending on whether weight is an issue. The multipurpose compost is lighter than John Innes No. 1, but it dries out more quickly and contains fewer nutrients. You can compensate for this with water-retaining crystals (*see* page 123), but you'll have to feed plants regularly. Water plants well before planting.

Basket liners

A basket liner prevents compost from falling through the mesh in an open-sided basket. It also helps to keep plant roots cool. There's a wide range of lining material available, including pre-formed shapes made of various materials.

Fibre liner This may be made from compressed wood, waste fabric fibres, old wool or coir (coconut husk fibre). It may be pre-formed into a bowl shape that will just drop into your basket, or cut out into a star shape that you press down to fit your basket by overlapping the individual pieces. You can cut your own holes in the fabric for planting through. A fibre liner is inert, so has no effect on nutrition or water retention, and may be dyed green with vegetable dye to make it less noticeable. Some of the coconut fibre liners have a latex coating to help with water retention.

An attractive, closed-sided basket contains a bright winter display consisting of skimmia and pansies with ivy trailing down the sides.

For a full, rounded effect such as this you need to use an open-sided basket, where you plant through the sides as well as the top. This glorious, red-themed display makes use of every dimension and includes petunias, verbena, diascia and lobelia.

Compressed paper pulp liner

Made from recycled paper, this type of liner is pre-formed to drop into the basket. It may also have pre-cut holes for planting through. A compressed paper pulp liner is treated to ensure the liner doesn't turn soggy as you water it. It is an inert material, so like a fibre liner has no influence on nutrition or water retention.

Sisal/jute mix liner

This type of liner is either pre-formed or cut into a star shape that you lay in the basket and arrange to fit. Some have a polypropylene backing to help with water retention and they are occasionally coloured green with vegetable dye for moss effect.

Sphagnum moss

A natural material, sphagnum moss has been used for hundreds of years to line planted containers. It has an attractive appearance and excellent water-holding qualities. However, moss is more difficult to work with than a pre-formed liner – it's a loose material and you need to line the basket with a layer of moss about 3cm (1¼in) thick before adding the compost. Avoid using sphagnum moss wherever possible, since the bogs in which it grows need to be conserved.

How many plants?

When planting a hanging basket, you want to achieve a full effect, which may involve including more plants than you think. It's tricky to say exactly how many plants to include in a hanging basket, as it depends on the size of plant, its stage of growth and the style and size of basket. However, as a rule of thumb, if you're using small plants such as strip bedding in a 35cm (14in) open-sided basket, you should include approximately 15 trailing plants (two layers of five through the sides and a row around the top), one dominant central upright plant and perhaps another three to five smaller upright plants.

HOW TO plant a hanging basket

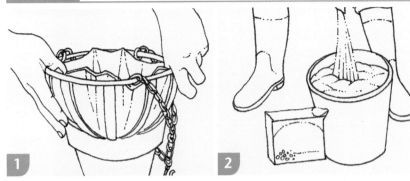

1 Place the hanging basket on an empty flowerpot to keep it steady. Lay the liner in place in the basket, tuck in the folds and press it in position.

2 Put compost in a bucket and add pre-soaked water-retaining crystals (*see* page 123). Add slow-release fertilizer and mix it all together thoroughly.

3 If the plants are in strips or trays, separate them by pulling them apart carefully. Otherwise, tap the plants out of their pots.

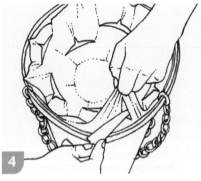

4 To plant through the sides of the basket, make a cut in the liner for each plant using a knife. Add a layer of compost mix.

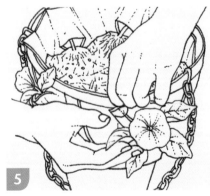

5 Plant through the holes. You can do this from the outside, compressing the rootball of each plant to push it through the gap, or from the inside, carefully feeding the shoots through the hole. Build up another layer of compost around the sides and plant as you go.

6 Place trailing plants around the sides at the top and upright, bushy plants in the centre of the basket. Add more compost, leaving a small depression in the centre of the basket for watering. In summer, water the basket at least once a day and feed approximately once a week.

Hanging the basket

The easiest means of attaching a hanging basket to the wall is a bracket, but it's important to make sure that it's sufficiently strong to take the weight of the basket once it's been filled with compost and plants and watered. Allow time for any adhesive to set before putting any weight on the bracket.

There are rotator devices available, which operate silently by solar power, rotating the basket through 360 degrees to ensure the basket receives an equal amount of light all round. This results in even growth rather than a one-sided effect. Some baskets come complete with a pulley system, which allows you to raise and lower the basket, so you can water and dead-head easily. They operate on a spring-and-ratchet system and some also include a swivel motion so you can rotate the basket.

Evergreen succulents such as these echeverias form a tight globe and make an unusual hanging display.

Bulbs often do better in containers than in the open ground, because they're grown in the perfect medium with good drainage. The main problem with bulbs is the short flowering period, but if you plant carefully you can extend the display time.

Bulbs need planting at different depths, according to their size. Most bulbs should be planted in a depth of soil that is around twice their own height, so a bulb that is 5cm (2in) high needs planting 10cm (4in) deep. Amaryllis and nerines are exceptions, and should be planted with the 'nose' of the bulb just above the soil surface. Cyclamens should be planted with the upper third of the bulb visible above the surface.

For a display that will last several weeks by flowering in succession, plant bulbs at different depths, in layers. Take a large container, add drainage and a layer of compost. First, insert the larger bulbs, such as tulips, then cover them with compost. Next, add a layer of medium bulbs, such as miniature daffodils, cover these with compost, then finally add small bulbs, such as crocuses, snowdrops, grape hyacinths or dwarf irises, and top with a final layer of compost. The crocuses will come up and flower first and then, as they die down, the daffodils should take over. As they fade, the tulips should be getting ready to flower so you will have had colour for much longer than if you just used a single type of bulb in each container. Leave room for an imaginary bulb between each bulb that you plant to prevent overcrowding as they grow.

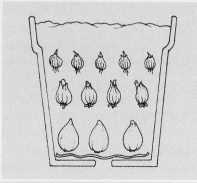

Bulbs provide a splash of colour in spring.
① Tulips and the miniature daisies *Bellis perennis* make a cheery pair.
② Miniature daffodils, crocuses and hyacinths make a pretty, fragrant display.
③ Snake's head fritillaries and plum-coloured pansies are stunning in pink pots.

To plant in layers, insert large bulbs at the base of a pot, then a layer of medium ones, then some smaller ones, with compost between each layer. The bulbs will then flower in succession.

Repotting

A plant needs repotting if it has been in its container for some time and has outgrown it. The most obvious signs that repotting is necessary are when you see roots coming out of the drainage holes in the container base or at the surface of the compost, the water runs straight out of the bottom of the pot when you water, and the plant seems constantly on the point of wilting.

The plant may also need repotting if the compost lacks nutrients (*see* pages 136–7). The leaves may drop off or change colour to pale green, yellow or brown, flowering and growth may be poor and the plant will eventually die. If you leave it pot bound for too long, the growth will slow right down, and (due to this lack of vigour) the plant will become much more susceptible to pests and diseases (*see* pages 278–281). It may have one final burst of flowers in an attempt to make seed that will ensure survival of the species and then it will die.

You can repot plants every year to keep them growing well, ideally in spring as they begin a new surge of growth. Conifers have two growth surges a year, in spring and autumn, and just before either of these is ideal. House and conservatory plants may need repotting more frequently, depending on their rate of growth and how much room you have for them, particularly while they're young. As they age, they will reach their mature size and then grow only very slowly. That doesn't mean that they will not need any more repotting, because they will still use up the nutrients, you just won't need to do it as often.

How to repot
Select a new container that is about 5cm (2in) larger all round the rootball than the old one and fill it with fresh compost. Try to use compost of the same (or similar) material to the existing growing medium (*see* pages 122–3). This will help the plant roots to establish in their new surroundings more quickly.

When a plant is ready for repotting, squeeze or tap the container to loosen the rootball, place your hand over the compost for support, turn the pot upside down and slip the plant out carefully.

Camellias are easy to maintain and can live for years in a large pot without being repotted. However, they do benefit from top-dressing with ericaceous compost in spring.

To remove the plant from its existing pot, loosen the roots from the sides of the pot without damaging them. Place your hand over the compost to support the weight, then turn the pot upside down and pull it upwards off the roots. If it won't come off easily, tap the edge of the pot (still inverted) on a surface such as a table very gently. When you repot a conifer, you may see greyish mould around the roots. Don't worry, it's meant to be there. These are 'friendly' fungi called mycorrhizae that live together with the plant in a symbiotic arrangement where both benefit.

If you have a large, heavy pot, lay the container on its side and gently tap the rim of the container with a block of wood, then ease the pot away from the plant. Or, use a hosepipe on a low-pressure setting to wash as much compost as possible out of the container to release the roots, then ease the plant free of the container. If the plant is well and truly wedged in a plastic pot, you may have to cut the pot using scissors. If it's wedged in a terracotta pot, you may have to break the pot to get the plant out, but try washing the roots with a hose first. To repot, plant as you would for a new plant (*see* pages 126–7 and right).

Top-dressing plants

Large patio plants such as trees and shrubs don't need repotting each year (every three years or so will do), but to keep them healthy and encourage flowering it's good to give them a top-dressing annually in spring. Top-dressing is very useful for climbers, which are particularly difficult to repot.

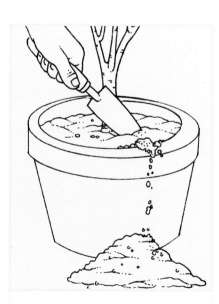

To top-dress a plant, scrape away the upper layer of compost (about 5cm/2in) and replace it with fresh compost that contains slow-release fertilizer. Water thoroughly.

HOW TO repot a container-grown shrub or tree

1 Lay the plant on its side and gently slip the pot away from the plant. If the plant is wedged in firmly, you'll need to loosen the rootball first by tapping the container rim with a block of wood or sliding a long knife between the pot and the compost. Alternatively, use a hose on a low-pressure setting to wash the roots away from the sides of the container.

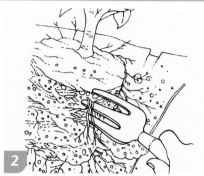

2 You may see a thick coil of roots that form a solid pot shape around the plant, depending on how pot bound it is. Using a hand fork, gently prise the congested roots from the solid mass so that they can grow into the surrounding compost once replanted in the new container. Any thick roots that will make repotting difficult can be shortened.

3 Prepare the new, slightly larger pot for planting. Place a layer of mesh then crocks at the base of the pot, covering the drainage hole (*see* page 125), then add a layer of compost to cover. Place the plant in the centre of the pot, spreading out the roots.

4 Fill the gap between the pot and the plant with more compost, firming lightly. When potting is complete, the surface of the rootball should be about 2.5–5cm (1–2in) below the rim of the pot to allow for watering. You can prune the top-growth by about one third.

Choosing a container

When choosing a new container, aim for a pot that is approximately 5cm (2in) larger all round than the previous one. It may be tempting to go for a very large pot with the idea that it will save your having to repot too often, but it's a false economy – too great a difference between the pots will check the growth of the repotted plant. A quick-growing plant will need moving up every year, usually in spring, but a slower one may need to move up only in alternate years. If you don't repot a plant that year, it will need feeding to make sure it has enough nutrients.

Watering

One of the most important aspects of care with container-grown plants is watering. Plants in containers dry out far quicker than those growing in the open ground because their roots are restricted and can't extend to seek out water in the soil.

Quantity

The amount of water a plant requires depends on a number of factors. Bright sun and wind seem to just suck the moisture from the plants and compost, so you'll need to water more frequently in sunny or exposed areas. If you have a hanging basket with moss sides or a porous container such as a terracotta pot you'll have to replenish water lost through the container's sides and top. Compost is also a key factor: if it's very free draining it means watering more often. Finally, you need to consider the plant itself. Some plants need more moisture than others. Generally, the larger the plant and the larger the surface area of the leaves the more water the plant will require.

You need to keep the compost in the container damp all the way to

Hanging baskets need masses of water throughout the summer. To reduce the amount of watering you have to do by hand, install a drip irrigation system. This can be connected to an automatic timing device.

the bottom, all the time, to ensure that there is always enough water for a plant's demands. Roots cannot survive in dry soil and will die off, reducing the amount of food and water the plant can take up, making it unstable. As an approximate guide, a very large container – such as a half-barrel 1m (40in) in diameter and filled with plants – can use up to 6 litres (1.5 gallons) of water a day in dry weather.

Frequency

Basically, you should water your plants whenever they need it. A small container that is fully planted, such as a hanging basket in a sunny position, may need watering twice a day, while a large container in a partially shaded site may be happy with watering on alternate days. You have to get to know your plants and their requirements and take into account where the pots are placed in the garden. Don't water by the clock.

The point of no return

A plant's cells are full of water and depend on it to maintain their structure. Without enough to keep them plumped up, the cells begin to shrink away from their neighbours – we see this as wilting. When the gap between these cells becomes too great to rebuild, it has passed the 'permanent wilting point', which means that even when the plant is watered again it is unlikely to recover.

When watering, make sure you soak the compost thoroughly rather than giving just a light sprinkling. The water needs to soak through the compost and reach the plants' roots.

Plants benefit more from a really thorough soaking than from a short watering that penetrates only the upper layer of compost. The latter encourages all the roots to become concentrated towards the top of the pot, making the plant unstable. As the plant can't take all its needs for a day in one go, water has to be available for as long as possible. There needs to be enough water in the pot for the plant to draw upon as and when it needs it but not so much that the roots sit in water, or they may rot. If you're short of time, or go away in summer, consider fitting an automatic irrigation system that will come on every day. You can install a timer switch and set it to come on overnight. There are also several other things you can do to help your plants survive without you while you're away.

Timing

The best times to water are in the evening and early morning. If you water in the middle of the day, you are unlikely to do any real harm (in spite of those who suggest that it can cause scorching), but most of the water put on will have evaporated long before the plant can use it. Watering in the evening or early morning, when the air is cooler and the sun is lower, allows time for the water to soak through the compost and reach the roots. Slugs feed at night and can travel around much more easily when there is a film of moisture everywhere. If you water in the evening, be prepared to have slug-control measures in place.

If your plants dry out, most will recover from a brief dry period once they're watered, although the thinner the leaf, the quicker it will reach the point of no return. Check the compost regularly and add a little more water each time until you can see the plant recovering. Little and often is the key. The very worst thing you can do to a dry plant is keep soaking it or leave the roots standing in water for too long, because you simply exchange dehydration for drowning. If the compost is too wet, there is no room for air in it and without air, the roots can't breathe.

Some loamless composts can 'shrink' and be difficult to re-wet once they have dried out. This is one of several reasons why I like to combine loam-based and loamless mixes (*see also* page 122).

If your containers are in an exposed, sunny position you may need to water twice a day in summer. Always water thoroughly.

If you're away a lot, or don't have time to water regularly, choose plants that can get by without you for a while. Succulent plants (above) retain a lot of water in their plump leaves, which means they can survive for longer between waterings.

Feeding

A container plant can survive for some time without feeding, but if left too long the rate of growth and overall health will begin to suffer. It may start to look paler, flower less and produce shorter shoots. If the lack of food continues, the plant will become susceptible to pest and disease attack. Gradually, flowering will stop, growth will slow down and the plant may look yellow and sickly.

Plants in containers need more regular feeding than those in the open ground to keep them healthy and growing vigorously. A general fertilizer is fine for most plants.

What plants need

Plants require a number of minerals and trace elements to grow well. The major nutrients are: nitrogen (N) for shoot and leaf growth; phosphorus (P) for root growth; and potassium (K) for flowers, fruit and winter hardiness. If you look at the back of a fertilizer pack, it should give the N:P:K ratio in the product, which will vary according to the purpose of the feed. Additional major nutrients include magnesium, calcium and sulphur and trace elements such as iron, copper, manganese, boron, zinc and molybdenum.

How much fertilizer you apply and when you start feeding after planting will depend on the compost you used in the container (see pages 122–3). Loamless composts normally contain fewer nutrients than loam-based ones, so the plant will need additional food much sooner. On average, you should apply a feed about three or four weeks after planting in loamless compost, because the plants should be growing quickly in their new home and may be very hungry. For plants that need a special boost, you can apply a short course of seaweed-based fertilizer: seaweed is very rich in trace elements and acts like a tonic for an ailing plant (almost as an antibiotic would for humans).

Plants have a natural cycle, with periods of fast growth, slow growth and near-dormancy (they are never entirely dormant). They need the most feeding during the period of active growth, less during the slow growth and none when they are at their slowest. Aim to get into a habit of feeding your container plants once a week during spring and summer, maybe on a particular day so you don't forget. This will help keep the growth rate constant and

If leaves start to look sickly it could well be that the plant is suffering from a nutrient deficiency of some kind. This illustration shows leaves suffering from various common deficiencies, in clockwise order starting from the bottom left: potassium, phosphate, nitrogen, manganese and iron, magnesium.

the plant healthy. Little and often is far better than overdosing them once a month, which will lead to surges of growth, followed by periods of relative inactivity. Nutrients will gradually leach out of the container as you water and especially during periods of heavy rain, so if you notice a change in the colour of the leaves, you may need to increase the feeding for a while.

Fertilizer types

A general fertilizer will contain a balance of the three major nutrients (N, P and K), along with a range of minor nutrients, and is designed to keep most plants healthy. It is ideal for shrubs, trees and other long-term container plantings. However, you may need to correct a nutrient deficiency or promote a certain type of plant growth and this is where specific fertilizers can help. For instance, if you're growing plants such as camellias or azaleas that need acid conditions, you need a fertilizer that contains more iron. These are usually sold as 'ericaceous' or 'acid-loving' formulations.

If you're growing tomatoes, peppers or other fruiting plants, a fertilizer that is high in potassium (K) will help, as it aids the production of flowers, fruit and seeds. A plant that is being grown entirely for its foliage will look better if you apply a feed that is high in nitrogen (N), as this benefits all the top-growth and will improve the colour of the leaves.

There are many different ways in which you can apply fertilizer. It comes in liquid or solid, granular or powder form. Most types are applied to the roots but some are applied to the leaves. Foliar feeds are particularly useful for plants such as bromeliads that cannot absorb fertilizer easily through their roots.

Liquid fertilizer Liquid feeds are easy to use, but some may be washed out of the base of the container along with the excess water. It is usually a ready-to-use concentrated formulation that you dilute to a recommended strength. Pour the appropriate amount of liquid fertilizer into the measure, then add it to the watering can. Fill the can with water, stir the contents with a stick to mix them together and water the plant in the usual way.

Fertilizer sticks and pellets Fertilizer sticks are simply pushed into the compost and become activated on contact with water, releasing feed gradually into the surrounding soil. Don't push them too close to the roots, or they may cause a localized concentration of

If you don't have time to give your plants a regular liquid feed, you can pop fertilizer sticks into your hanging baskets and other containers in spring. They release fertilizer very slowly as and when it is needed.

A liquid feed that is high in potassium is ideal for tomatoes and other fruiting plants, because it encourages growth of flowers, fruit and seeds. Make sure you use the correct amount stated on the bottle.

food and scorching may occur. Pellets are sprinkled on the surface of the compost.

Soluble powder or crystals These need to be dissolved in water before application. Measure the crystals or powder into the scoop provided, add to a watering can full of water and stir well until dissolved.

Controlled-release granules or pellets These work continuously and save you having to remember to feed. You need to mix them with the compost before planting. The instructions will normally give a quantity of granules per litre volume of compost, so you'll need a container of a given volume (for example 5 litres) that you can fill with compost.

Don't forget

Always read the instructions on the pack of fertilizer and try to stick to the recommended rates of application – at least until you get to know your plants and their needs.

Overwintering

Container plants are particularly vulnerable to cold weather because they're isolated from the insulating properties of garden soil: it's the difference between having a cotton blanket or a feather duvet. If the plants are not frost hardy you'll need to move the containers indoors or lift the plants and pot them up for overwintering indoors. Even hardy plants may need some protection, and if the pots aren't fully frost-proof they will need to be covered or taken indoors.

Pelargoniums, fuchsias and other half-hardy perennials need to be taken indoors over winter. Cut them back to about half their height: this removes leafy growth that might otherwise turn mouldy.

Frost, wind and snow

Frost can kill parts of the plant directly or indirectly. Directly, it causes the outer cells of the plant to freeze solid and split, or the liquid inside the cell to freeze and expand, which we see as a blackening of the shoot tips or new (tender) leaves. Indirectly, it can kill parts of the plant if they cannot thaw gradually. For example, if the early morning sun falls on frosted camellia flowers, the heat causes the cells to rupture as they thaw out too quickly. Frost causes most damage in winter or early spring, when plants have just started into growth.

Strong, cold winds can also cause damage by burning the outer leaves of a plant. The combination of low temperatures and wind speed causes desiccation (drying) because the moisture is being drawn out of the leaves faster than it can be replaced by the roots, which leads to the characteristic brown scorching on the leaf surface. Conifers and broad-leaved evergreens suffer most from drying winds. Shelter is important, so make the most of any that you have by moving the most sensitive plants out of the wind. Buildings can retain heat, as well as offering shelter from wind. The wind chill problem is made worse if the rootball is frozen, because there is water present but in a solid, rather than liquid, form that the plant can't use.

Snow is usually less of a problem than frost and drying winds, because thick snow is a good insulator against the cold. However, the weight can cause branches to fall and plants to split apart, so however pretty it looks, it's worth knocking it off your smaller plants.

It is particularly harmful when the thaw increases its weight and when it re-freezes.

Water

Even in winter, plants need a regular supply of water to stay alive. Long periods of cold can leave plants without adequate water and although their systems can slow right down, the absence of water will eventually kill them. The best approach is to insulate containers to ensure that any water present doesn't freeze.

Conversely, plants will suffer if there is too much water. Inadequate drainage will leave the roots sitting

A young hebe shoot has been damaged by early morning frost in spring. The shoot tips have turned black and the leaves have withered and turned brown.

> ### Don't forget
>
> Plants give off moisture, so never wrap your plants in plastic for longer than a few hours: the plant's moisture will condense on the inside of the plastic and, if the temperatures fall, it will freeze, sticking the leaves to the wrapping and thereby causing more damage than if you had no wrapping there at all.

in sodden compost over winter. Too much water leaves no room for air, and without air, the roots cannot breathe. If the roots cease to function, they will rot and die, and the first you will know about it is in the spring when the leaves open and then die off. Drainage is crucial and to make sure your pots are going to drain properly, you may need to stand them up on bricks or pot feet over winter. If you notice that a pot is full of water, lay it on its side for a day to let it drain out, then stand it up again.

Lifting tender and half-hardy plants

You won't be able to keep tender or half-hardy plants outdoors over winter, because they'll be killed by frost, but you can take them indoors and plant them outdoors the following year. Dig the old plants up in autumn before there's a frost, cut the tops down to about 15cm (6in)

and put them in containers in a frost-free greenhouse or conservatory. You can replant them outside again in late spring after risk of frost has passed, usually mid- to late May.

A handsome terracotta urn filled with sculptural grasses and berrying and trailing evergreens – here, *Carex comans*, skimmia and ivy – takes on a beautiful, ethereal quality when rimed with frost.

If you're expecting a big freeze, it's well worth insulating your outdoor tubs with bubble wrap, as prolonged periods of frost can kill even fully hardy plants. The compost can be covered for a few days at a time.

Frost-protection materials

In winter, the part of the plant that is most at risk of damage from both wet and cold is the roots, so protecting these should be your main priority. There are various forms of insulation you can apply if you want to leave containers out year round.

BUBBLE WRAP
■ Bubble wrap is useful for insulating around the sides of your containers. You'll need a piece that is long enough to wrap all the way round the pot (once or twice), then simply tie it in place with string. As long as it is not covering the surface of the compost,

the bubble wrap can stay in place until the weather warms up a little.

NEWSPAPER
■ Crumpled newspaper is very easy to use as an emergency means of protecting the roots. Simply open out a large plastic bag (a black bin bag is ideal) and stand the container inside. Take single sheets of newspaper and scrunch them loosely, then pack them around the pot until the bag is almost full. Draw the top of the bag together and tie it around the stem of the plant. You can open it up again during the day to

allow air to the roots, but don't let the paper get wet.

FLEECE
■ Horticultural fleece is an invaluable weapon against cold in the winter. It's light, folds down quite flat and allows light and air through (so the plant can still photosynthesize and breathe). Draped over the top of a plant it can help withstand several degrees of frost, especially if you use more than one layer. If you realize that your camellia flowers have been hit by frost, you could help prevent damage by putting fleece over the top before the sun hits the blooms.

Vegetables and herbs

Anyone can grow their own veg. In fact, it's all too easy to get bitten by the veg-gardening bug: perhaps the children want to try growing a few beans or courgettes in a tub; or a neighbour has raised one too many tomato plants and is longing to palm off a couple on you; or you spot a tray of lettuce seedlings at a car boot sale or garden centre. Beware, these little beginnings may ignite a passion that simply grows and grows.

Why grow your own?

Recently there has been a resurgence in vegetable gardening. It is difficult to pinpoint why, but it is probably a combination of factors: getting fed up with the same sterile-looking produce offered in the supermarkets; feeling a need for the tranquillity offered by pootling about in the garden; or realizing that the jet-setting lives led by many of our shop-bought fruit and veg cannot be good for us, them, or the planet. Whatever the reason, growing vegetables brings a multitude of rewards.

Even if you don't have acres of space, you can grow vegetables. For those who have plenty of room, the veg-growing bug can result in an entire garden being given over to edible produce. All power to your potager!

Taste

Nowadays we are used to being able to buy all sorts of vegetables in the shops, all the year round. We can have tomatoes in winter and courgettes in early spring. But where is the taste? All the greenhouse heating and lighting in the world hasn't been able to recreate the wonderful flavour of a home-grown tomato picked and eaten just as it reaches ripe perfection, or a cucumber sliced into a salad while still warm from the greenhouse. The thought of the amazing sweetness of a sweetcorn cob so fresh that it might have been bent over a pan of boiling water while still on the plant, should start to make your mouth water. Or what about the simple pleasure of shelling young peas and broad beans and trying not to eat them all before they reach the colander?

Convenience

Aside from their great taste, there are practical advantages to raising your own vegetables. You can ensure that you have a fresh supply of the family's favourites on your doorstep (or just down the road at the allotment), and you can also save money by growing vegetables that are more expensive to buy,

The owner of this vegetable garden is making the most of his restricted space. Growing vegetable plants in tiers on a sunny wall makes sense because most won't grow higher than 30cm (12in) or so, which means you can fit in plenty of containers. If growing crops in pots, you must pay great attention to feeding and watering.

such as asparagus and artichokes. As you tend them every single day of their lives, you will know exactly what your vegetables have been exposed to in terms of chemicals and other undesirables. While this is particularly important for those of us who have children to feed, it is also nice to know that you aren't putting anything unnecessary into your own body. And while we're on bodies, gardening is excellent exercise, getting you out into the fresh air and toning up muscles you didn't know you had.

Reality check

After all the words in praise of vegetable gardening, a few of warning: it does require commitment. It's no good bunging in a few plants and hoping for the best, you do need to plan, prepare, plant and cherish. It is also important not to be too ambitious – if you have never grown veg before, don't try to be self-sufficient in year one. In fact, unless you really have a bee in your bonnet, it is best to accept that some things are always more sensibly bought at the local greengrocer or supermarket, and to concentrate on those vegetables that are really worth growing at home. And a final spoiler – a lot of gardening is about waiting: if you are reading this in midsummer, you won't see all your dreams come to fruition until next year. The best time to start planning a vegetable patch is in the autumn or winter, so you can do the necessary preparations in time for the start of the growing season in spring.

Planning your plot

If you have the luxury of space in your garden, you will be able to choose a sheltered site, with a good sunny aspect and free-draining soil for growing vegetables. This is the ideal, but some of us who have limited space or are allocated an allotment can plan an equally productive plot by following a few simple rules.

This is a vegetable garden with designer flair. Although it is only a tiny corner, this plot has a greenhouse, compost bin and cloches, as well as a selection of healthy vegetables in raised beds.

Site

Vegetables have to grow fast and steadily to produce an abundant, healthy and tasty crop. To do this they need fertile soil that drains well after rain. They also do best with plenty of sun and water and protection from wind. Keep this in mind when you select your spot. Don't worry if you don't have all these conditions in one place, as long as you have a bit of sun the rest can be created or provided with a little bit of extra preparatory work. In addition, although vegetables are traditionally grown in one place in the garden, if you have several small sites with great vegetable-growing prospects it is always possible to divide your plants between them. You can even grow a wide range of vegetables in containers.

Vegetables don't have to be grown in long rows. If you need only a few plants, grow only a few. As well as being neat and decorative, these clearly defined vegetable beds are easy to look after.

They might not always look perfect, but nothing beats the taste of home-grown carrots – delicious. If you pull a few that seem rather small, you can always eat them raw in a salad and leave the others in the ground to grow a little bigger.

Sun Most vegetables need plenty of light and warmth. Although some leafy varieties, such as lettuce and rocket, may cope in a little shade, if you haven't got sun, the choice of what you can grow will be limited.

Soil Soil that is full of nutrients is a must because vegetable plants are fast-growers and are always hungry. Ideally, the soil shouldn't be too stony (root veg in particular protest at stones, forking and becoming tough and inedible) and should be easy to work (or dig). *See also* page 157 for information on soil types.

Water Vegetables need regular and sufficient supplies of water. If your plants suffer water gluts or shortages, your crop will be nowhere near as abundant or as tender or tasty as it could be. Hedges and trees are notorious water-thieves, and walls may cause a rain shadow, which means that plants on the lee side don't receive any water when it rains. (This is something to bear in mind when selecting your site for growing vegetables.) Of course, you can still plant in these drier places, but you will have to be prepared to provide a good proportion of the water under your own steam. Invest in water butts, and also mulch the soil to retain moisture in these areas.

Frost pockets

While the term 'frost pocket' might sound quite attractive, your vegetables will not like to be in one. On a frosty day, take a look around your garden as the sun warms it up. You can easily spot the frost pockets – they are the places where the ground stays white and frozen longer than anywhere else.

Just as hot air rises, so cold air sinks. Low areas get much colder than higher areas, and low areas hemmed in by hedges or buildings will be even worse, as the cold air cannot escape. On a slope, making a gap in a hedge or fence can help alleviate the problem. Even after the likelihood of frost is passed in late spring, don't forget that these areas are still probably the coldest in the garden. If part of your vegetable bed is in a frost pocket, remember that hardy veg like broad beans and brassicas will cope in these colder areas, while potatoes or runner beans won't fare so well.

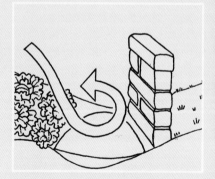

Cold air collects at the bottom of slopes or where a wall or other obstruction slows its passage. Avoid growing the more tender vegetables in such sites.

Overwintering vegetables, such as leeks and Brussels sprouts, can cope with a fair amount of frost without being killed or even spoiled.

Low box hedges and neatly trimmed box balls provide permanent structure in this vegetable garden. They also provide excellent shelter for the crops, but do bear in mind that hedges make their own demands: their roots will grow into the vegetables' space, taking nutrients and water from the soil.

Drainage Roots need air as well as water. If the soil is waterlogged (*see* box) the roots will suffocate, which means the plant they are supporting will not be able to grow. Choose a well-drained site for your vegetables or improve the drainage; this can be done by incorporating plenty of manure or compost (*see also* page 158) or by making raised beds (*see also* pages 148–50). At the other end of the scale, very free-draining soil can be equally bad – when the water runs away too quickly, the roots don't get a chance to drink. Surprisingly, the solution

for very free-draining soil is the same as for poor drainage: add some organic matter.

Exposure The perfect vegetable bed is one that is sheltered from strong, cold winds which will batter and bruise your precious crops. However, it also needs a reasonable breath of air through it to ensure pollination of certain plants, and to make it less inviting to pests and diseases. You can make an exposed site more comfortable for your vegetables by erecting a simple fence or planting a low hedge at a sensible distance.

Waterlogged soil

If you suspect your soil is poorly drained, have a closer look: mosses and rush-type plants growing in it are a giveaway, as are puddles forming and hanging about after rain. Dig a hole between 30 and 60cm (12 and 24in) deep and pour in a bucket of water; the water should drain away reasonably quickly. If the water is still there an hour or more later, you have a problem with drainage. Take heart, though, it could be that there is simply a 'pan' below the surface. This occurs when soil has been compacted by frequent walking on it, or through regular digging to the same depth.

THE SOLUTION
Make the hole a little deeper and check the consistency of the soil as you go. If you come across an area that is difficult to dig and very compacted, dig through it and try the bucket of water trick again. If it drains away more quickly this time, digging deep and adding composted material is the answer (*see also* pages 164–5). Otherwise, raised beds (*see also* page 148) are your best option – especially for those who want to grow veg in a spot where there is a high water table.

Layout

The easiest way to grow vegetables is to plant them in a traditional layout: that is in straight rows in straight-sided, not-too-wide beds with paths in between. There are many good reasons for this. Veg are plants that need lots of attention – in the form of weeding, feeding, tying up, and harvesting. If they are planted all higgledy piggledy about the place, tending them can get tiresome. Then there are the gaps that appear as you harvest the crops – these are easier to fill if they are a regular shape, plus new seedlings coming up won't get hoed along with the weeds by mistake. Narrow beds will help you to reach the plants and avoid the temptation of stepping on the soil, which will only compact it and spoil all your earlier hard digging work (*see also* page 164). However, if you really want a layout that is both pretty and practical, a potager could be the answer (*see* box, page 147).

The layout shown and described here is the ideal for vegetables. Adapt it to suit your needs and the size and shape of your plot.

You will need:

■ **Three or four main beds** – Make your main beds any length you like; the optimum width is about 1.2m (4ft), as this allows you to reach the middle without treading on the soil. Three is the perfect number as it enables straightforward rotation of crops (*see also* page 153). Run paths between the beds for easy access all around the plot.

■ **One permanent bed** – This is for perennial crops, such as asparagus and globe artichokes, which stay in place year after year.

■ **Compost bins** – Site bins within easy reach of the veg beds to make them easy to fill, turn over, and empty. Have three separate bins on the go to keep the compost-making process simple (*see also* page 160).

■ **Cold frames and/or cloches** – These are useful for raising and hardening off young plants before they are planted out into permanent beds. Cold frames are usually 1.2m x 60cm (4ft x 2ft) and made of aluminium with glass or plastic panes. Their permanent site should be reasonably bright and sheltered. Cloches are the portable version and can be moved around the vegetable patch to offer protection for rows of young plants as required.

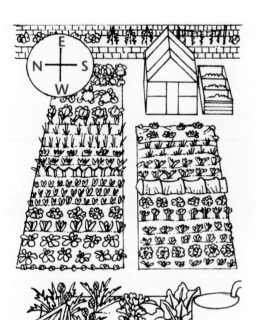

There is a good reason for every aspect of a traditional vegetable garden, from the direction the rows run – north/south to get the most sun for shorter veg plants growing behind tall ones, to the position of the greenhouse and compost heaps – easy to access but not in the way.

Careful thought has gone into the design of this plot. The wooden structures provide shelter for the vegetables and support for fruit trees; they also ensure that the vegetable garden looks interesting, even during the winter months.

■ **Greenhouse** – Although a greenhouse is not essential, the more you get bitten by the veg-growing bug, the more you will want one, and once you have one, you will fill it…easily. Get one as big as you can afford (larger ones retain heat longer and are easier to work in) and position it so its longer edges run north to south to make the most use of summer light. Position it out of the full blast of the wind, as this will cool it very quickly.

■ **Water** – Where you have a sloping greenhouse roof you can install a drainpipe and waterbutt, or two, to collect rainwater as it runs off. Put them by sheds and garages, too, or anywhere that water can be collected and put to good use. You will also almost inevitably need an outside tap, in a convenient position for filling watering cans or using the hosepipe.

Herbs

No vegetable garden is complete without a selection of herbs, and the majority of these do very well in containers. Some are short-lived and need to be sown regularly or bought as small plants (very cheaply) from a garden centre or supermarket. These include basil, parsley and coriander. Others will survive for a long time in a pot, needing only an annual pruning or tidy up. Mint, marjoram, chives, bay, sage and thyme fit into this category.

If you buy potted supermarket herbs, don't forget to harden them off slowly before putting them outside – they will be very delicate to begin with.

It is a common misconception that all herbs need a hot sunny position

Potagers

Vegetables lend themselves very well to a formal layout, but that doesn't mean your creative side has to be suppressed. Potagers are vegetable gardens that have been planted to make the most of the decorative qualities of the plants, such as blocks of purple-leaved cabbages punctuated with wigwams of red-flowered runner beans, and swirls of lettuces with different foliage textures and colours surrounding a square of onions or sweetcorn. You can add flowering plants too: it is best to stick to annuals – companion plants such as marigolds are good choices – as you will probably want to dig the whole plot over, flowers and all, at the end of the season. Although the design of your potager can be as complex as you like, don't lose sight of the fact that you will need space to weed and harvest the vegetables, and that some won't appreciate being shaded out by taller neighbours.

on poor dry soil. Though most do, there are exceptions: parsley prefers cool light shade, mint needs plenty of moisture, and chives like rich soil. Their individual requirements can be met easily by growing them in pots.

Parsley is among many herbs that do well in a container. It will also tolerate some shade.

Somewhere to put your prunings, weeds and dead plants is essential in a vegetable plot. A compost bin is also a means of recycling the goodness contained within spent plant material.

Growing systems versus digging

Years ago, no one would have considered growing vegetables without spending hours double digging the plot (*see* double digging, page 165). Most of us still automatically think that a vegetable garden means digging, and lots of it. However, there is a growing feeling among some veg enthusiasts that cultivation of the soil can break up its natural structure, destroying or damaging both the harmless and the helpful soil organisms and creating the kind of conditions that weeds love. It is true – tradition is not always right and ideas do change. So what are the advantages and disadvantages of each approach?

There is something wonderfully satisfying about digging over your plot, breaking up hard clumps of earth and removing weeds and old vegetation. This work is done in the autumn and winter – and doing it will keep you warm!

The benefits

Digging allows you to assess the texture and condition of your soil. You can use it as an opportunity to remove large stones, perennial weed roots and rubbish, to break up hard clods of earth and pans (*see* waterlogged soil, page 145) and to incorporate organic matter (*see* page 158). After the main preparation work is done in autumn/winter, a quick fork over the soil surface once or twice in early spring, before you plant your first vegetables, will bring more weed seeds up and you can hoe off any that germinate. This attention to detail will enable you to start with a reasonably weed-free patch. Make no mistake, weeds are unwanted intruders.

No-dig systems

No-dig systems rely on simply building up a layer of growing material above the soil surface; this is generally organic matter with added natural fertilizers, into which the vegetables are planted. The benefits of this method are the comparative ease of preparation and that the valuable nutrients and soil organisms are not destroyed or disturbed. In addition, weed seeds are not disturbed and therefore, if they haven't already, they are less likely to germinate.

Deep beds and raised beds

Deep beds are for the real diggers among us – they are created by a version of double digging (*see* page 165). However, it's claimed that they have the advantage of yielding more crops per square foot of ground than conventionally cultivated plots. Experiment if you wish!

Dig down to two spades' depth, loosening the soil and working in large quantities of well-rotted organic matter as you go. Make the

Digging over a vegetable plot gives you a chance to make adjustments to the soil in order to improve its health and growing abilities. Here, horticultural sand is being added to heavy soil to improve drainage and aeration.

A raised bed provides these lettuces with optimum nutrition (plenty of organic matter has been added) and discourages some pests.

beds narrow so you can work from both sides without needing to step on the soil. If you need to fork the beds over between crops, do it from the paths alongside, or put down a temporary plank to spread your weight and avoid squashing down the soil in the bed with your feet.

This might start to sound a bit complicated, but an easier way to make a deep bed is to make a raised, or semi-raised, bed. Think of it this way: you dig to one spade's depth in your soil and then put a raised bed of one spade's depth over the area – two spade's depths, half the work. Raised beds are also a form of no-digging, in that you create your growing area above the soil surface, but many advocates break up the soil surface anyway to assist drainage, before filling the beds with soil and organic matter in which to grow their plants.

Don't forget

What about those of us who don't like digging at all, or even those of us who have no soil to dig in but still want to grow some vegetables? Well, it's good news. Vegetables are like the hare in the story about the tortoise and the hare. They grow away very quickly, using up all their energy as they go. They don't put down an extensive root run for the future, and they collapse exhausted at the end of the season, having given their all. So, despite frantic activity above ground, they need little space for their roots, and canny vegetable growers profit from this exuberance: even those gardeners who have plenty of space in their veg beds have reason to plant up some in pots. It could be that the sunniest wall for ripening tomatoes and aubergines is beside the patio, or that the lettuces always become slug fodder unless they are raised above ground level, or that the soil in the vegetable garden is infected with clubroot (see page 184). Even if you have very limited room – or no garden at all – pots will enable you to grow some of your favourite greens. And, of course, pots are essential if you want to grow your culinary herbs on the kitchen windowsill.

Although these little hurdle beds won't last as long as raised beds made from planks, they are more ornamental so are a good solution for making raised beds where your vegetable garden is in full view. Fixing the hurdles to wooden-sided beds will prolong their life.

This raised bed uses planks joined at the corners and held in place with posts, either set in concrete or hammered into the soil. You can also use railway sleepers and do away with planks and posts altogether. Although railway sleepers are pricey and heavy to manoeuvre into place, they last for years, need little or no other fixing, are great to sit on, and generally do the job just fine.

YOU WILL NEED:

■ Planks – 15 x 5cm (6 x 2in) multiplied by the bed's length

■ Posts – 7.5 x 7.5cm (3 x 3in) multiplied by the bed's height plus 10cm (4in) or so to fix them into the concrete

■ Screws (nails may be quicker, but they are less secure)

■ Hardcore or gravel – a bag or two should do

■ Ready-mixed concrete

■ Tools, including a drill, a spirit level and a carpenter's square

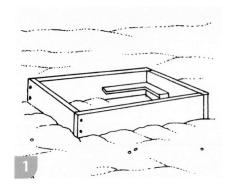

1

Decide where to put your bed; the ground needs to be reasonably level. Position and then screw the planks together for the first layer, butt-joint the timbers at the corners and use the builder's square to make sure these corner joints are straight.

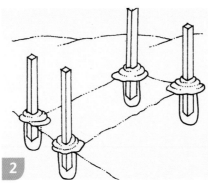

2

Dig four holes for the corner posts, using the first layer of planks as a guide for their positions. Add a handful of gravel to each post hole to allow any water to drain away. If your raised bed is very long, you may need to add some extra posts along the sides for strength.

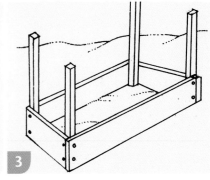

3

Set the posts into the holes on top of the gravel, check they are straight using the spirit level and add the mixed concrete. While the concrete is setting around the posts, position the first layer of planks in place. Make sure they fit snugly and are straight and level.

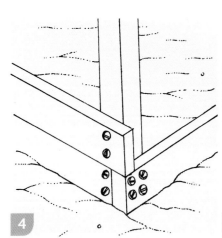

4

Once the concrete is set, build up the rest of the raised bed with planks, layer by layer, until you reach the height you require. Stagger the joints at the corners and screw the planks to each other and to the corner posts as you go.

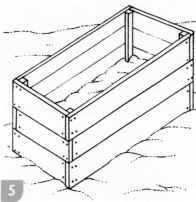

5

When construction is complete, loosen the surface of the soil inside the bed using a fork, then add a layer of gravel or hardcore a couple of centimetres (1in) deep. This is optional, but sensible if you have poorly drained or heavy soil beneath.

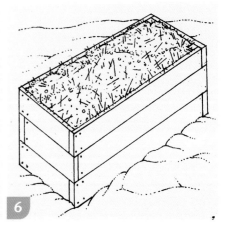

6

Fill the bed with a mixture that is half topsoil and half humus-rich material, to get your vegetable off to a good start. Overfill the bed to allow for settling.

Deciding what to grow

One of the easiest times to get carried away is when you sit down with vegetable seed catalogues or take a trip to the local garden centre and wander around all those consoles filled with tempting seed packets. Unplanned buying is a well-known phenomenon among gardeners of all ages and stages – and whatever you might think now, you will fall victim. However, you can limit the distance you fall by making as many of the decisions about what seeds to buy before you ever open a catalogue, browse the internet, or leave the house.

Well, you'll be smiling when, after a few weeks, you go out to the veg plot and return with the makings of a home-grown meal in your trug!

Top of the list
Everyone has different likes and dislikes, so tailor your choice of veg to suit your taste. These lists are intended to give you some inspiration; when you have a shortlist of candidates, read more about your choices in the A–Z of Vegetables, which starts on page 60. It gives details of the varieties of each vegetable and how to grow them – be prepared to rework your list a few times over.

Favourites
Chillies
French beans
Mangetout and sugar snap peas
New potatoes
Radishes
Runner beans
Sweetcorn
Tomatoes

Easy
Courgettes
Garlic
Onions and shallots
Rocket
Salad leaves in variety, but not necessarily lettuce
Spinach

Pricey in the shops
Asparagus (perennial)
Sprouting broccoli

Unusual and difficult to buy in the shops
Carrots of the not-orange kind
Globe artichokes (perennial)
Kohl rabi
Potatoes of the heirloom varieties, such as Pink Fir Apple
Swiss chard

To enjoy young and tender
Beetroot
Carrots
Courgettes and summer squashes
Leeks
Parsnips
Turnips

Swiss chard is hardly ever available in the shops. It is best picked and cooked straight away as it wilts soon after picking and the large leaves are easily damaged.

More difficult to grow

Calabrese
Cauliflowers in interesting colours
Celery
Cucumber
Florence fennel

Herbs for flavour

The following need virtually no care and are generally bought as small plants:

Chives
Fennel
Marjoram
Mint
Rosemary
Sage
Thyme

To add variety

Aubergines
Brussels sprouts
Celeriac
Endive or chicory
Kale
Land cress
Peppers

With just a few herb plants you can flavour your cooking for most of the year, so you don't need much space to get a worthwhile crop. They are easy to look after, and when planted in a herb wheel like this they also make an attractive feature. Just make sure that herbs you grow together have the same growing requirements.

To grow as mini veg

Here is a selection of currently available baby vegetables, but new ones are constantly coming on the market:

Beetroot 'Pablo'
Cabbages 'Redcap', 'Shelta'
Calabrese 'Kabuki'
Courgette 'Supremo'
French beans 'Ferrari', 'Stanley'
Leek 'King Richard'
Parsnips 'Dagger', 'Lancer'
Squash 'Sunburst'
Sweetcorn 'Minipop', 'Minor'
Turnips 'Primera', 'Tokyo Cross'

To inspire the kids

Children are often very keen to get involved in gardening and, of course, parents are keen to encourage them. Don't forget, though, that even one week of waiting for something to happen seems like forever to a child, so grow vegetables that are quick to mature. Help children to choose types of vegetables that they like to eat and give them the best possible spot to grow them or they'll soon become discouraged. Tomatoes, salad leaves, and baby vegetables are a good start.

Salad leaves

If your lettuces never get beyond providing local slugs and snails with tasty food on which to produce yet more offspring, try something else. Nowadays, the variety of other plant leaves that can be sown as salad crops is astonishing:

Baby spinach	Oriental leaves
Beetroot leaves	Purslane
Dandelions	Rocket
Endive	Sorrel
Lamb's lettuce	Sprouting seeds
Land cress	Watercress
Mixed salad leaves	

Because they grow quickly and are soon harvested, it is quite possible to grow salad leaves in a container or hanging basket – where they can be within easy reach of the kitchen.

Unlike 'harvest' and 'dig', which everyone understands, the term 'crop rotation' seems to cause quite a bit of confusion. It needn't. Crop rotation, while very important, is not nearly as complicated as some might think. The very simple idea behind it is that you don't plant the same crop in the same bit of ground more than one year in three (or four).

Crop rotation is good for vegetable production in two main ways.

First, it is a great natural method of preventing diseases taking hold – think of it as a kind of quarantine, if you like. For example, members of the cabbage family (brassicas) can suffer from root diseases. If you continuously plant cabbages, broccoli, sprouts, and so on in the same spot, you are continuously feeding these root diseases. If you move your brassicas each year, the root diseases will 'starve'.

Second, it makes the maximum use of soil nutrients and other resources, such as manure, which are needed in varying amounts by different crops.

For example, peas and beans love a bit of muck, but carrots and parsnips don't and are happier in a bed that has been manured one or two years before.

How to rotate

The traditional way to rotate crops was to divide the plot into four equal parts, growing potatoes in one quarter, other root veg in another, peas and beans in the next, and brassicas in the last. (With salads and other quick crops planted in the gaps between rows of bigger, slower crops.) However, this traditional system doesn't take into account 'modern' crops, such as sweetcorn and courgettes, and the fact

that many people don't think it is necessary to grow maincrop potatoes. But the general principles are still sound; simply divide the plot into three and grow these newcomers with the peas and beans, or tuck them in around the other beds. An example of how this would work in practice is shown in the diagram below, with the various categories of vegetables moving from top to bottom.

If you grow your vegetables in small beds where it's not practical to follow a strict rotation, try to avoid growing the same crop on the same patch of ground every year (or two, if possible) to keep the beds in good health.

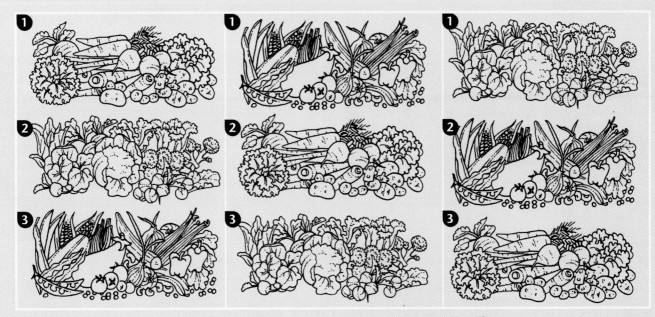

Year One
Grow roots in bed 1, brassicas in bed 2 and other vegetables in bed 3.

Year Two
Grow other veg in bed 1, roots in bed 2 and brassicas in bed 3.

Year Three
Grow brassicas in bed 1, other veg in bed 2 and roots in bed 3.

Now you know what you are aiming for, it's time to get down to the nitty gritty of vegetable gardening – the ground preparation and the planting and aftercare of your vegetables. Although it can be tempting to rush the preparation in order to get to the fun bit, time spent in the beginning will repay you – and you may even find that you enjoy it.

Tools and equipment

If you have any sort of garden, you have probably already accumulated some tools; if they do the job and are pleasing to use, look no further. If you need any new implements, perhaps for digging a vegetable garden from scratch, go to your nearest garden centre or DIY store and have a look at what's on offer. Weigh up price with quality. There is rarely any need to spend a fortune, as a spade will be doing a job of work, not looking pretty in the shed.

When it comes to buying tools, it's all too easy to get carried away. Bear in mind that any tool you have in your shed will only be useful if it is used.

Digging

For digging the soil, you need a spade and a fork. Generally, forks are more versatile. Spades are good for digging lighter soils, but on heavy or stony soil, forks are less likely to get stuck, and they are excellent at ferreting about under the soil surface, loosening clumps and destroying pans of compacted soil (*see* page 145).

Forks and spades come in a variety of sizes and weights, and have either a T-handle or a D-handle – choose what is more comfortable for you. Wooden shafts have a degree of 'give' that metal does not – a relief if you are constantly digging into stony ground.

Weeding

Hoes are the traditional tool of choice for weeding vegetable beds. The draw, or chop, hoe has its blade at a right angle to a longish shaft. As the name implies, it is used to chop down weeds, which it does very well. It isn't a precision instrument, so be careful around rows of delicate young seedlings. For these areas, use an onion hoe, which has a short handle and finer blade. Get down onto your knees to use it and ease it carefully around your plants. A push, or Dutch, hoe has a slightly angled blade at the end of a long shaft. The blade is pushed just under the soil surface, slicing through weeds as it goes. All hoe blades need to be sharp, otherwise they uproot rather than decapitate. Uprooted weeds are not dead: they are only too pleased to re-root, given the opportunity.

A Dutch or push hoe is one of the vegetable gardener's most hardworking tools. Through the growing season it could be in almost daily use, so make sure you choose one that you find comfortable, and sharpen its blade regularly.

Raking

The only rake you need for veg is the type with short parallel teeth. This is used to level the soil surface in preparation for planting. Don't pick an ultra-light one, as it will bounce over the soil surface, making you do all the work.

Hand tools

The most useful hand tool is a trowel, which you use for planting and surreptitious weeding. Choose one with a decently shaped blade (nice and long) that has good sharp edges. A hand fork comes in second place, but is good for planting, removing stubborn perennial weeds and a bit of spot hoeing. For removing more stubborn, deep-rooted weeds a daisy grubber may be useful. There are any number of cheap and nasty hand tools on the market. They make gardening a chore and soon break – if you ask for a set as a gift, make sure you specify the make.

Garden knives, secateurs, and a pair of well-fitting gloves all come in handy, too.

Other important items

For watering and administering liquid feed, you will need a watering can. If you plan to use weedkiller, have a plastic watering can labelled specifically for the purpose. Waterbutts are useful, even in a small garden, and hosepipes are invaluable in a larger one. An outdoor tap is almost indispensable.

Most likely you will need a wheelbarrow. Get one with pneumatic tyres as they run more smoothly. Make sure the space between the handles is wide enough for your hips and hands – they often seem to be made for stick-thin people. If your plot is very small, a flexible plastic tub-trug will do an adequate haulage job, but it does make life tough on your back.

Seed bed preparation is best done with a parallel-toothed rake. This is satisfying work, and when well done provides the perfect nursery for your young vegetables. Don't over-rake or the surface will become 'caked' when it rains.

After a while you will get to know the tools that you find most useful. Forks, spades and trowels are likely to be high on the list.

Rotavators

While they do have their place, particularly on larger plots, rotavators are not all good news, and they may not cultivate deeply enough. On the upside, they will slice up annual weeds, on the downside, they chop through the roots of perennial weeds, effectively propagating them and encouraging new growth (*see* page 162). If you must use one, hire rather than buy, just to be sure it helps, and that you can handle it.

All about soil

Despite outward appearances, soil is an immensely complex and dynamic material, full of living organisms, chemicals, minerals, and decaying matter. As a vegetable gardener you are interested in the topsoil and, to a lesser extent, the subsoil. Depending on where you live, these are made up of varying amounts of loam, sand, chalk (limestone), clay and/or peat. To get the best from your soil, it is good to know a bit about its make-up (*see* box).

Soil types – benefits and disadvantages

If you have loam, you are lucky. Loamy soil is well drained but moisture retentive, and it is naturally fertile. It is easy to dig, it is not easily compacted, and it warms up quickly in the spring, enabling you to get off to an early start with your planting. In short, gardeners and most plants love loam.

Sandy soil is often described as light soil. It is made up of large particles, with lots of air spaces, and it feels rough to the touch; water drains out of it very quickly, washing nutrients with it as it goes. Like loam, though, it is easy to dig and warms up quickly.

Chalk soils are made up of fine particles and are reasonably fertile and well drained. Chalk soil is also shallow, which means you might also get to know your subsoil quite well (*see* digging, page 164). There

Know your soil

If you are unsure of your soil type, the easiest way to assess it is to go out into the garden and have a feel. The texture of soil reveals a lot about its make-up. The soils shown here are the five basic types, but it is possible to have something that consists of a mixture of them, or even to have different soil types in different parts of your garden.

① Sandy soil is light: very loose, dry and gritty. If you grab a handful of it, it tends to flow out through your fingers.

② Clay soil is heavy: it is sticky and nearly always feels damp, except during drought when it becomes as hard as iron.

③ Chalk soil tends to be pale and lumpy. The lumps are pieces of chalk. Chalk soil dries out quickly and doesn't clump together.

④ Loam is dark brown and just looks good. It is soft in texture and when it is moist it can be squeezed into a handful but crumbles up again easily, without being sticky.

⑤ Peat is even darker than loam, and it holds water very well. If you grab a handful after rain, you can squeeze water out of it like a sponge.

are various terms used to describe chalk soil, including limey, calcium (calcified), or simply alkaline.

The particles that make up clay are very fine, so the soil has few air spaces. It tends to retain moisture and nutrients, but during dry weather it bakes hard. If you have clay soil, you are likely to dig up clumps of gooey stuff that could be used to create something on a potter's wheel. Peaty soil tends to go

with moorland environments and is naturally low in nutrients. It absorbs moisture, but also drains quickly and can be made more fertile with relative ease.

Alkaline or acid?

Like everything else in life, soil has a chemical balance that makes it anything from very alkaline to very acid. The scale used to measure soil acidity or alkalinity is called pH –

and it varies from pH 1 (very acid) through pH 7 (neutral) to pH 14 (very alkaline). Luckily, the extremes (1 and 14) are rare. The chemical balance of the soil can make certain nutrients unavailable to plants, so it has an impact on how well they grow. Most vegetables will produce their highest yields on neutral soil, although members of the cabbage family (brassicas) prefer growing in slightly alkaline soil for best results.

The most effective way to find out the pH of your soil is to buy a testing kit from the garden centre; these are cheap, easy to use and accurate enough for our purposes. You can also make some deductions as follows: chalky soil is alkaline, peaty soil is acid. With plants that prefer acid soil, the leaves tend to go yellow when they are grown on neutral or alkaline soils (because they can't get the iron they need).

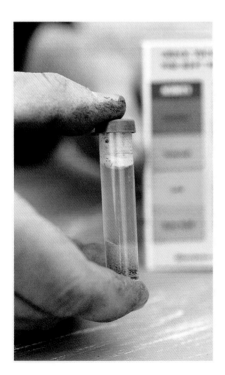

Testing kits to find out the pH of your soil are widely available at garden centres and are simple and fun to use. Follow the instructions carefully, otherwise you may get a false reading. This result indicates that the soil is neutral to slightly acid.

Altering the pH

While you can slightly influence the pH of your soil, drastic alterations are not only expensive, they are also only a temporary fix and so are not recommended. A garden that has been well tended over many years with the addition of plenty of compost and manure, will have become slightly more acid; the traditional 'remedy' for this is to add lime. This can be normal lime, Dolomitic lime, which contains more nutrients, particularly magnesium, or calcified seaweed – which has all the trace elements in it as well.

Adding lime

If your soil is slightly acidic and you want to add lime to make it more neutral, do this in the early autumn, well before the time in late autumn that you want to dig in your compost or manure. You need to allow a few weeks for the lime to slowly leach into the soil, otherwise it will scorch your plants and may not have time to alter the pH. Adding lime at the rate of about 500g per sq metre (1lb per sq yard) will alter the pH by one point, depending on the variety of lime you choose (the container it comes in will tell you how much to use for the area you wish to treat). Personally, I'd only add lime on a regular basis to acid soil where I wanted to grow brassicas; it also discourages clubroot (*see* page 184).

Improving your soil

Although tinkering with pH levels helps to increase fertility by releasing nutrients, the addition of organic matter is by far the most important way of improving your soil structure and nutrient content, followed very closely, especially for veg, by using a fertilizer to increase productivity.

Organic matter

After clearing the site, the first step in preparing your patch is to dig in organic matter. Also known as humus, organic matter is anything that was once a growing plant and is now decaying. It comes from the compost that you make from your garden and kitchen waste and the manure produced by herbivorous animals. When it is ready to put on the garden, it is soft with a flaky or crumbly texture. Even if it once came out of a cow or horse, it doesn't smell unpleasant (if it does, it isn't rotted enough). It has umpteen benefits:

■ It acts like a sponge, holding onto moisture so the ground doesn't dry out too fast, especially in dry, hot summers and periods of drought.
■ It creates lots of tiny air spaces that allow excess rainwater to drain away faster, thereby preventing the soil from becoming waterlogged.
■ It makes the soil 'softer' and 'looser' so that roots are able to spread through it more easily.
■ It contains flourishing colonies of beneficial soil bacteria that break the material down to humus and release valuable trace elements – often severely lacking in ground that's been cultivated over some time using only fertilizers.

You know you are a real gardener when you start to look forward to adding manure to the soil. When well rotted, this material is truly a gardener's gold.

Before sowing another crop where one has just been cleared, always give the ground a sprinkling of general-purpose fertilizer and rake it in to feed the soil.

Feeding the soil

Vegetables are raised intensively and, although it is wonderful, organic matter doesn't provide enough of the main nutrients to keep hardworking, heavy-cropping plants supplied, so you need to use fertilizer as well. There are two types of fertilizer, those that you add during soil preparation, which are covered here, and those that you give as regular feeds during the growing season, which are described on page 47. Soil-preparation fertilizers are in the form of pellets, powders and granules; these break down slowly in the soil hanging about so the growing plants can make use of them as needed. Using fertilizer doesn't mean you have to throw your 'organic' principles out of the window, as there are plenty of organic fertilizers on the market derived from natural sources.

General-purpose fertilizers

These offer a balanced feed, containing roughly equal quantities of NPK (*see* box). Use them to ensure that your crops get a bit of everything they need. Sprinkle it evenly over the soil and lightly work it into the surface when preparing the patch in late winter or early spring, and when you've cleared a row of crops in summer and are going to replant. Perennial veg, like artichokes and asparagus, appreciate it at the start of the growing season (mid- to late spring), too. Follow the instructions on the packet, but as a rough guide use about a handful per square metre.

Nitrogen-rich fertilizers

Designed to help the plant in its leaf production, they include chicken manure pellets, hoof and horn, and seaweed meal. Apply chicken manure pellets before sowing or planting green veg. Hoof and horn is slow-acting and organic; it is best applied very early in spring. Seaweed meal, which should appeal to vegetarians, is also rich in potassium and is a renewable resource; rake it in before planting in spring.

Phosphate-rich fertilizers
Beneficial for establishing strong root systems. Although bonemeal contains plenty of phosphates, it tends not to be available to the plants; blood, fish and bone provides a better source of food.

High-potash feed
This is given to produce flowers and fruit. It is usually sold as sulphate of potash, which is appreciated by heavy-cropping, fruiting plants, such as tomatoes. Organic high-potash feeds are also available.

Organic or not?

Nowadays, gardeners are much better educated about the pros and cons of using chemical and other means to enrich the soil. 'Natural' fertilizers do a good job and feed soil micro-organisms too, but it can be tempting to use chemicals because they are often cheaper and very quick-acting – think of it as being like an instant sugar-fix and it won't seem quite so attractive. Inorganic fertilizers also work independently without interacting with the soil, which can become lifeless in the long run. Even the faster-acting organic feeds will do more for the health of your soil than the pure chemical ones.

Perhaps we should also consider the ethics behind manufactured fertilizers. For example, the chickens that provide the chicken manure pellets might be factory farmed, and there is no putting a pleasant slant on blood, fish and bone. Manure from animals can also contain chemicals, such as antibiotics and dewormers. To my mind, if you are going to eat it, it seems best that veg is produced as wholesomely as possible.

Now you know the benefits of organic matter, you'll understand why you need a compost bin (or three). Learning how to make good compost is one of the most useful things a vegetable grower can do.

The main principle in making good compost is to use plenty of different material: mix fine waste such as grass with coarse waste such as potato peelings; use dry waste such as unprinted paper and cardboard with wet waste such as annual weeds and crop trimmings. This mixture contains a careful balance of air and moisture, providing suitable conditions for the bacteria that rot down the heap. The bacteria are responsible for creating heat as they work and this heat increases their numbers. Worms and other organisms in the mixture also help the decaying process.

There are some people who say they compost everything, right down to the kitchen sink, and it all comes out as a beautiful, rich, brown, sweet-smelling humus. Well, lucky them. In reality, almost any kitchen or garden waste can go into the bin, except

This neat compost bin, complete with hinged lid, is simple to make and will repay a few hours' work with years of service.

cooked food and meat, which may attract rats. And it goes without saying, don't put cat or dog muck into the mix as it contains harmful pathogens.

To speed up the compost-making process, make sure that everything is well mixed. I reckon life is too short to keep turning it later. If you have added woody material, you may have to return it to the heap for another session, as it is much slower to rot down.

The ideal is to have three bins: one is rotting down, one is being added to, one is ready for use; two will do, though. Top of the range are the wooden bins, which look great and do a good job. You can also use the wide-bottomed plastic bins that look a little like Daleks; drill some more holes in them for drainage, and water their contents regularly to speed things up.

Who would have thought this pretty little doll's house was a repository for all the garden's waste materials?

HOW TO make a wooden compost bin

The ideal wooden bin is 1m (3ft) square or bigger. The bin shown here is made from planks attached to posts. The planks are held in place on three sides with screws or nails, and at the front they are slid into batten guides, so you can empty the bins with ease. There is no need to secure it to the ground. This step-by-step describes one bin. If you want more, you can simply add them on at the side, using two more posts and adding three sides of planks.

YOU WILL NEED:

■ Planks – 15 x 2cm (6 x ¾in) by 1–1.4m (3–4ft)

■ Battens – 5cm (2in) square by 1–1.4m (3–4ft)

■ Posts – 10 x 10cm (4 x 4in) by 1–1.4m (3–4ft)

■ Screws or nails (nails are quicker but are less secure)

■ Tools, including a drill or hammer, a spirit level and a carpenter's square

1 Decide where to put your bins; ideally the ground should be reasonably level. Lay two posts, cut to size, on the ground and start to attach the cut planks to them, either with screws or nails. Leave a small gap about 8–10cm (3–4in) at the bottom to ensure that the bin sits level.

2 Make the second side in exactly the same way as the first.

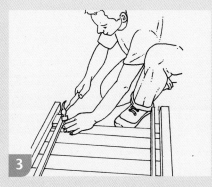

3 Measure and cut two battens to fit 2.5cm (1in) behind what will become the front two posts. Nail or screw them in place.

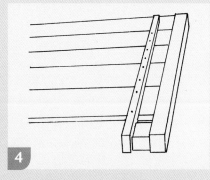

4 Put a small piece of wood at the bottom of each batten guide for the lowest sliding plank to rest on.

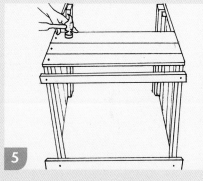

5 Use temporary battens to hold the two sides in place while you attach the planks. Check the corners stay square.

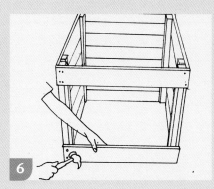

6 Cut and attach a strengthening plank to the top and bottom of the bin front.

7 Cut and fit the sliding planks.

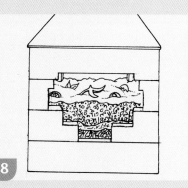

8 Add compost – mix the material well and dampen it down if necessary. Lay a tarpaulin over the top to retain the heat.

Preparing your plot

Now you are fully armed with all the information you need, it is time to get out there and prepare your plot. It may seem a bit boring, but the hard work that you do now will stand you in good stead for years and years to come. Do preparation work in good time for planting in spring – this means starting in autumn, if at all possible.

First time around

If you are creating a new patch, you must first remove any grass and/or weeds, and then – just as important – dig in loads of organic material.

When faced with an uncultivated piece of ground, a lot of people make the mistake of hiring a rotavator and pushing it around to chop up weeds or turf. They then bury the lot and start planting straight away. Don't do it! Strange as it sounds, rotavating propagates perennial weeds; it does this very efficiently by chopping their roots into hundreds of root cuttings, all of which turn into new plants, and

Spend some time digging out large stones and builder's rubble. This can be a hard job, but you'll regret it if you don't do it.

it does nothing to discourage the destructive soil pests that are usually prevalent in old grassland.

Grass and weeds

If your proposed vegetable garden is covered with grass, your first job is to strip off the turf. Use a spade and skim it off the ground in slices 4cm (1½in) thick so you get most of the roots,

too. Stack the pieces upside down in an out-of-the-way corner of your garden and over 18 months or so they will turn into good fibrous loam that you can recycle back onto the garden. If instead of grass you have rough or overgrown ground to contend with, dig out brambles, tree seedlings, perennial weeds and any annual weeds with seedheads; you can leave smaller, non-seeding annual weeds, as they can safely be dug back in.

Organic material

Once the majority of the weeds have been removed, dig the ground roughly, using a fork. Take out large stones, roots, and any other rubbish. Now dig it over again, this time using a spade, working in as much well-rotted organic matter as possible. A barrow-load per square metre/yard isn't too much when you're breaking in new ground; a bucketful per metre/yard is enough for ground that's previously been well cultivated but allowed to run wild for a time. If you've only just started gardening and haven't made any of your own compost, phone around local livery

Once you have marked out the site of your plot – in this case a circular herb bed – you need to remove what's there. If it's grass, begin by stripping the turf around the perimeter. This reveals the shape of your bed in the flesh and offers you a final opportunity for fine-tuning.

stables, mushroom farms, smallholders, and so on to see if they have any organic material to spare.

Relax (a bit)

Leave the ground alone for several months so that birds and other natural predators can remove soil pests and slugs or snails. It's a good idea to fork over the area occasionally to expose more pests so that predators can continue to reduce the population. This also helps to reduce your weed population, as it brings dormant weed seeds to the surface where sunlight 'triggers' them to germinate. Hoe off these new crops of weed seedlings or flame-gun them before they have time to set seed or become established. The more of this you can do before you start to cultivate a new plot, the easier it will be to manage the patch later. Also, this is the time to add lime, if necessary (*see* page 158).

Now for the fun bit

Before planting, fork over the ground, removing any last-minute weeds, sprinkle on a general-purpose fertilizer (*see* page 159) and rake it in, removing any stones and roots as you go so the ground ends up clean, level and ready to go.

Regular maintenance

The soil used for growing annual vegetables benefits from a little attention every time it falls vacant.

Spent mushroom compost doesn't contain many nutrients, but it is a great soil conditioner.

Autumn

Each autumn, as soon as summer crops have been cleared, spread well-rotted organic matter on those areas that won't be used for growing root vegetables, such as parsnips, carrots or potatoes, next year. A few weeks later, hoe off or otherwise remove re-emerging weeds from the soil surface.

Winter and spring

Continue digging and adding organic matter over the winter and early spring as winter crops are harvested and cleared, so that by spring the whole plot is ready to go.

Summer

Even in summer it's worth doing a little light soil improvement every time you clear rows of salads or other short-term crops. Clear away the old roots and leaves, plus any weeds, taking care not to disturb adjacent rows of plants, then sprinkle some organic general-purpose fertilizer over the bare soil and work it lightly into the ground with a rake before sowing or planting your next crop. This replaces lost nutrients and makes sure growing conditions are back up to scratch so the whole space stays as productive as possible all season.

FOCUS ON Digging

The main purpose of digging is to break up the soil and to incorporate organic matter. Single digging (digging to the depth of a spit – the spade blade) is sufficient for most purposes, but very heavy or poor soils may require more drastic action (double digging).

HOW TO single dig

Single digging is excavating soil to a spit deep and moving it along the bed. As you move the soil it is easy to take out the roots of persistent weeds, break up large clumps of earth and remove large stones and other debris. It gives you a chance to assess the health of your soil and learn a little more about its character, such as how well drained it is, or whether there are pockets of clay or chalk that might need breaking up a bit more thoroughly.

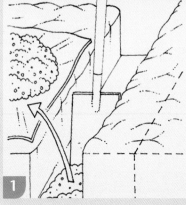

1 Dig a trench to one spit's depth and width. Place the extracted soil on thick plastic sheeting (or in a wheelbarrow). Leave it there as you will need it later. Remove any weeds as you go along.

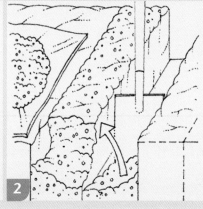

2 Dig another trench next to the first and put the soil from it into the first trench. Add any soil improvers if necessary. Continue in this way until you get to the final trench.

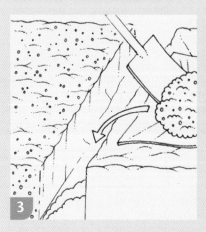

3 When you've extracted the soil from the final trench, fill it with the soil you've kept from the first trench. Go over the whole area and break up any lumps with the spade or a garden fork.

Invest in a good-quality wheelbarrow: it will make light work of transporting weighty compost around the garden.

HOW TO double dig

Double digging involves cultivating the soil to the depth of two spits. If you have a bad pan in your garden or very poor soil that is full of debris, such as builder's waste for example, you might decide to double dig – a few days later, when you are nursing your backache, you might regret your decision. But double digging has its place, and can do some good by loosening the subsoil without bringing it nearer the surface. If you do feel your plot would benefit, why not do it over a few years, focusing on one area at a time?

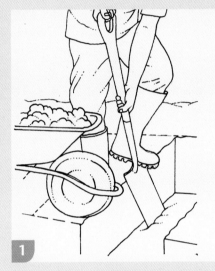

1 Using a spade, make a trench as for single digging. Remove the soil to a wheelbarrow (or large sheet of plastic). You will need this later.

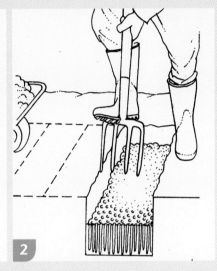

2 Fork over the base of the trench, pushing the fork tines in to their full depth to loosen and aerate compacted soil as much as possible.

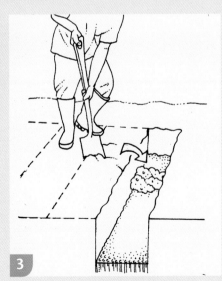

3 Now using the spade again, dig a new trench and turn this next batch of topsoil into the previous trench. Add plenty of organic matter to improve the soil quality.

4 Continue digging in this way until you reach the final trench. Having forked over the base, fill this final trench with the soil you have kept from the first.

Take care with this back-breaking work

In the 'good old days' much was made of digging: single digging, double digging, trenching, and so on. Nowadays, we tend to turn a bit of soil over and think we've worked hard. So, for those of us who are not accustomed to this kind of toil:

■ Don't be tempted to get carried away and overdo digging in your first session, especially if you are not used to such physical work. Digging exercises muscles in the shoulders, stomach and back that many of us don't know we have.

■ Keep the blade upright so that the spade achieves maximum depth with minimum effort.

■ Lift small spadefuls at a time, not mammoth ones. Remember damp soil is much heavier to lift than dry.

■ Do it little and often to protect your back from damage – no more than half an hour at a stretch.

■ Don't work when the ground is wet or frozen – you will do more harm than good. The soil is more likely to become compacted in these conditions. You can help protect the soil by standing on a scaffold plank to spread your weight.

Like nature, vegetable gardeners are always itching to fill a bare patch of soil and make the most of any available space. As a result they have developed some crafty ways of getting more out of their plot than you might have thought possible: intercropping, catch cropping, and successional sowing.

This is a combination of intensive cropping and companion planting. Both the garlic and the carrots can be harvested at around the same time, in early to midsummer, and the garlic may deter carrot fly.

Intercropping

Intercropping is the sort of thing that you might do when you find you have a tray of young lettuce plants and nowhere obvious to put them. It's a great way to work your vegetable bed really hard, so it's particularly valuable if you don't have much space. Basically, in areas where you have slow-growing veg, you can double up on the planting by squeezing in some speed merchants.

Intercropping sounds easy, and often it is, but you do need to take into account the amount of shade any of these slow- and fast-growing partnerships are going to create – nothing will thrive too close to leafy potato plants, for example – and how will you harvest your early veg without disturbing your more sedate late veg? To make intercropping work well, you need to plan quite carefully.

One popular and attractive set of plants to grow together is courgettes, sweetcorn and runner beans. In theory, the faster-growing courgettes and runner beans grow up and through the slower-growing sweetcorn. However, in reality, if you get your spacing wrong between plants, you can find yourself crawling through a jungle of leaves and stems, looking for courgettes that are so hidden away that they have managed to grow into large marrows in the meantime. The runner beans would have liked the shade, but this dense undergrowth has invited all the slugs

Making the most of any gaps that appear in the veg garden involves having something to go in when other veg come out. Here, leeks have been raised in a nursery bed to take the place of harvested new potatoes.

and snails in the neighbourhood to take up residence – and they love beans. You have been warned!

Catch cropping

There are two main periods in the year when large gaps appear in the vegetable garden: spring, before planting, and again in autumn, after harvesting but before you plant out overwintering crops. This is when you can do a bit of catch cropping. Like intercropping, it is a matter of planting fast-growers, but this time they're on their own. You harvest them just before your longer-term overwintering vegetables, such as cabbage, kale and garlic, go in.

Plants that are suitable as catch crops are usually the same characters as for fast-growing intercrops. Either sow them directly or (particularly in spring) raise them under cover to give them a quicker start. If you have a cloche or cold frame for protection, you can

plant them out quite early to get a crop even sooner.

Successional sowing

If you have never grown vegetables before (or even if you have) it is easy to end up with a huge amount of veg all ready to be harvested and eaten at about the same time. Successional sowing was invented to avoid this.

This is when you plant little and often – say, a short row of lettuce every two or three weeks – so you don't end up with twenty lettuces all at the peak of perfection on 16 June. Even when you know the theory, successional sowing isn't always easy to get right, due to uncontrollable influences – usually the weather. When it comes to veg growing, any planting plan has to be constantly adjusted and amended. But having a Plan B, or even C, is one of the joys of growing your own. You can make vegetable gardening as efficient and complex as you like.

For intercropping

SLOW GROWERS
These include parsnips, Brussels sprouts, sprouting broccoli, winter cauliflower.

FAST GROWERS
Salad leaves, radishes, spinach, baby vegetables.

To sow successionally

Suitable veg to sow successionally include radishes, salad leaves, baby veg, chicory, endive, lamb's lettuce, peas.

If you are really keen on salad and baby vegetables, it is easiest to reserve an area of your veg garden specifically for these. Sow short rows of all the crops you like, every two or three weeks – you can be more scientific about it by recording how long they usually take to get to eating point. As you finish harvesting a row, do a spot of weeding, sprinkle on some fertilizer (see page 160) and plant some more in the same place. Towards the end of the season, begin to replace the salad vegetables with overwintering crops, such as cabbage and kale, perhaps raised in your nursery seedbeds.

Storage

When you grow vegetables there are times when you have far more produce to harvest than you are able to eat. Runner beans and courgettes, lettuce and other salad leaves all go through a phase in mid- to late summer when it takes a very determined vegetable-eater to keep on top of their proliferation. So, although the best time to eat vegetables is within minutes of picking them – which is why we grow them, of course – you might need to find ways of putting them aside for enjoyment later. The A–Z of Vegetables (*see* pages 170–227) also provides some useful information on ways to store each individual type of vegetable.

Onions don't need to be plaited together in order to store well, but it is a good way to ensure they are well ventilated and out of the damp. They look attractive, too, but avoid too much warmth or they may dehydrate.

In the shed

Most root vegetables (Jerusalem artichokes, beetroots, carrots, celeriac, parsnips) can be left in the ground until they are needed or the weather turns very wet. If the weather does turn wet, these roots will keep (cleaned and dried) in a cool shed for a while, but don't leave them in there and forget about them. Check them regularly for signs of mould or rodent damage and use them as quickly as possible.

If you want to store them for a long time, put unblemished, unwashed root vegetables in a box of slightly damp sand – make sure they are not touching – and cover them over. This keeps the flesh firm.

Maincrop potatoes and onions tend to be harvested all at once in fairly large numbers. They keep perfectly well in a cool shed or garage. Garlic needs to be stored in slightly warmer conditions, though still cool, in the house. With all these, it is vital to make sure they are completely dry on the outside, with most of the soil brushed off, before storage. Potatoes are fine in paper or hessian sacks, while onions and garlic can be plaited to hang up, or stored on trays. Don't store any produce that is bruised or damaged: it will quickly rot and could spoil the rest of your harvest.

If you don't have a cool shed, use the coolest room in the house. Potatoes need to be kept in the dark to prevent them from sprouting; onions and garlic in the light.

In the kitchen

It is always better by far to pick vegetables and salads as required so that you always eat them fresh. But if you do need to store them, the best storage place is the salad drawer of the fridge. Most will keep there for a few days, and they will still be fresher than their supermarket counterparts.

Freezing

Most vegetables can be frozen. Many lose their texture and some of their flavour in the process, but this might be better than throwing them away.

Freezing is fine for broad beans and peas, as long as you do it as soon as you have picked them. Blanch them first: immerse them in boiling water for a minute or two and then plunge them into cold water and dry well before freezing.

If you have huge numbers of courgettes and tomatoes, they can be frozen, but the former are better frozen within a cooked dish, such as ratatouille, and the latter as a purée to be added to sauces, stews or pasta dishes, when defrosted.

With any veg, don't freeze any specimens that are less than perfect – they won't improve with time – and use all frozen vegetables within a few months as they still go on deteriorating in the freezer.

Juicing fresh vegetables

One of the healthiest ways of using surplus fresh produce is to invest in a juicer and convert tomatoes, carrots, beetroot and cucumbers into drinks, which can be as delicious as they are colourful. Drink these straight away, though:

vitamins are soon lost as the juice oxidizes, and it quickly changes colour or goes cloudy and then looks much less appetizing.

Green tomato chutney

This mild, sweetish chutney is lovely with mature cheddar and cold meat, and it's the perfect way to use up tomatoes that you know have no hope of turning red.

- 1.4kg (3lb) green tomatoes
- 14g (½oz) salt
- 113g (4oz) sultanas
- 170g (6oz) chopped onion
- 170g (6oz) chopped apple
- 170g (6oz) sugar
- 14g (½oz) mustard seed
- ½ teaspoon pepper
- ½ teaspoon pickling spice
- 425ml (¾ pint) white vinegar

Chop or mince the green tomatoes and put them into a basin in layers, sprinkling each with salt. Cover and leave to stand overnight. Drain and discard the liquid from the tomatoes, then put all the ingredients into a pan and cook slowly until you obtain a soft pulp. This takes about two hours. Pot the chutney into sterilized jam jars.

Storing tomatoes

If you have plenty of tomatoes at the end of the summer you could also try drying them in the oven (have it on the very lowest setting for a couple of hours with the door just ajar). However, it might be more satisfying and energy-saving to create your own tomato ketchup, chutneys and pickles, to which you could even add other surplus veg. These are easy to make and keep for a long time, although the original flavour of the vegetable will be masked to a greater or lesser extent.

Vegetables can be made into chutneys, jellies and a wide variety of preserves. This pumpkin preserve was made using lemons, sugar, salt and mixed spices.

A–Z of Vegetables

In this A–Z, each description provides the key cultivation needs of the vegetable and any special requirements it may have. For example, many plants can be started off in pots indoors, but some are better planted where they are to grow (in situ) because they dislike having their roots disturbed. Watering and weeding are mentioned many times. They are the two most important aspects of vegetable gardening and shouldn't be neglected: weed when you're feeling energetic, water when you simply want some peaceful time out in the garden. And don't forget to water every pot-raised plant before and after you plant it out into the garden, even if the soil is already damp – this is vital.

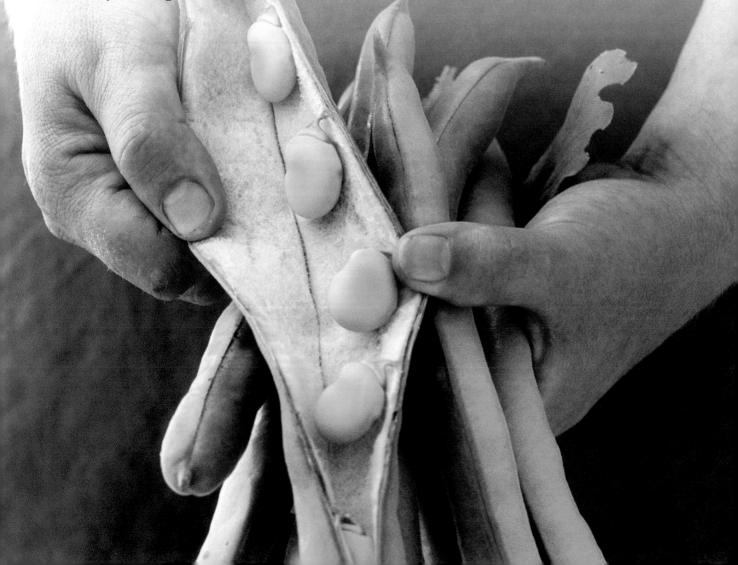

Making choices

There are some vegetables – potatoes, beans, tomatoes, lettuce – that you can be sure of finding in almost every vegetable garden up and down the country. These plants are the backbone of the veg garden: they usually grow well, they always taste good, and with a bit of effort they will produce a worthwhile crop. The A–Z describes them and how best to grow them. However, it also includes some of the more borderline creatures, such as aubergine, celery and Florence fennel, which can be a challenge and require additional cossetting and nurturing, but are worth trying if you like to eat them, as home-grown ones will always taste better than the shop-bought variety – even if they're only half the size. Some of the veg featured will do better with a little protection, and with others it is undeniable that a greenhouse or polytunnel will achieve larger yields, but on the whole you should be able to grow those featured in normal or sheltered garden conditions.

What's in a name?

Nowadays there is a huge and wonderful selection of vegetable seeds available from many different suppliers, so it can be difficult to make a choice. Within each vegetable description in the A–Z there are suggestions of particular varieties of vegetables you might like to try and grow, but if you can't find those mentioned when you are buying seed, rest assured that the majority of seeds on the market have been carefully bred to be reliable and tasty, or they have proved their worth over many years. As long as you read the catalogue or seed packet description carefully, like what you read, and it suits your growing conditions, you can't go far wrong.

Which ones to grow in pots?

Of the vegetables featured in the A–Z, only asparagus and globe artichokes are totally unsuitable for growing in containers, although no doubt somebody somewhere will be doing it successfully. This is because they are perennial plants, which means that they need lots of space to grow and time to establish before they crop well, by which time they'll have outgrown their pot. Of the rest, some are better than others for growing in containers, simply because of their particular cropping habits.

From a 'time and motion' point of view, the best plants to choose for containers are those that crop over a longish period, such as tomatoes, peppers and runner beans, or that are quick to mature, such as radishes, lettuce and other salad leaves. There are also the squash and marrow family, which do quite well in growbags, as long as there is space in the surrounding area for them to stretch out. Alternatively, you could train squashes and marrows up strong supports; there are varieties bred for just such a purpose. Potatoes are famous for their adaptability. Two or three seed potatoes (*see* pages 212–4) can be planted in a compost bag to produce a good crop with little work.

HOW IS IT DONE?
Fill the containers with a mixture of good, soilless, multipurpose compost and soil-based potting compost – half and half is a good start.

Plant larger vegetables, such as tomatoes, peppers and aubergines, individually in containers, and smaller ones, such as some chillies, two or three to a pot. Salad vegetables are best in wide shallow(ish) pots or boxes, as these will provide more leaf-growing space without taking up too much potting compost. Long root vegetables need deeper pots but can be planted quite densely. Beans, both French and runner, can be planted in groups 10cm (4in) apart in tubs or growbags. Provide them with an obelisk or wigwam of canes for support, or position them to grow up a trellis or netting against a fence or wall. Given shelter, they will do very well. Alternatively, you could choose dwarf varieties of beans, which won't need as much support, but will produce a smaller crop.

Aubergines do well planted in generous-sized pots. The plant has hairy leaves and spiky fruit stems. It is a member of the potato family with very similar-looking flowers.

Artichokes, Globe

SOW MAR, APR plant APR
harvest JUL, AUG, SEP

Globe artichokes are grown for their tasty flowerbuds, and make excellent ornamental plants, too. They have silvery leaves that are cut like a thistle's and they reach up to 1.5m (5ft) tall. One or two plants are enough for the average family. If you don't get around to eating all the buds before the flowers open, the bees will thank you.

Though not the best for flavour, 'Green Globe' is a reliable cropper producing big flower buds. It is common and widely available as seed and plants.

Cultivation

DIFFICULTY Easy; low input.

SOW under cover in late winter or in an outdoor seedbed in early spring.

PLANT out in mid-spring. Also sold as young plants.

SPACE 90cm (3ft) apart with 90cm–1.2m (3–4ft) between rows.

CARE Summer – water during dry spells when plants are carrying a crop. Mid-spring – feed each plant with slow-release fertilizer and mulch generously. Autumn – cut down old stems as plants die down. No supports needed.

YIELD Six to ten buds per plant each season.

STORAGE Artichokes will keep for a week in the salad drawer of the fridge.

Keep them happy by…

Providing a warm, sunny, sheltered spot in well-drained soil. Allow them a year to establish before you start harvesting, but don't allow flowers to develop during the first summer – snip off buds as soon as you see them. Replace plants every four to five years; in year three, pot up some of the small offsets that form round their base to start a new establishing row the following year.

Worth trying…

'Gros Camus de Bretagne' – French variety, hard to find as plants. Flavour is superb from very large heads.

'Gros Vert de Lâon' – French variety, widely available as plants. Good flavour.

'Violetto di Chioggia' – Available as seed or plants with pretty mauve buds. Fair flavour but lightish crops.

Enjoy them…

From midsummer to early autumn. Harvest half-grown (fist-sized) flower buds, using secateurs to snip through the stem about 2.5cm (1in) below the base of the bud.

Look out for…

Blackfly often attack artichoke flower buds; a light attack is no problem as the outer scales are removed before cooking, but a bad infestation is very off-putting on the plate. If you see blackfly while crops are growing, wipe them off developing buds with a damp cloth or a soft brush dipped in water. Earwigs can also be a problem. Soak the flower buds upside-down in salted water before cooking to remove them.

Artichokes, Jerusalem

plant FEB, MAR
harvest JAN, FEB, MAR AND OCT, NOV, DEC

Jerusalem artichokes are grown for their plump knobbly tubers, which are baked, fried, roasted or stewed, just like potatoes. The plants are weatherproof, even though the stems reach 3m (10ft) high, and low-maintenance, so they make a good allotment crop.

Cultivation

DIFFICULTY Very easy; low input.

PLANT egg-sized tubers 15cm (6in) deep in late winter or early spring. Save some of the best tubers from each crop to plant next year.

SPACE 40cm (15in) apart, with 90cm (3ft) between rows. Plant a double or triple row so these tall plants can support each other. This also makes a good windbreak.

CARE Use a general fertilizer when preparing the soil; no extra watering or feeding is needed. Flower buds can be removed to increase tuber yield, but in practise this is unnecessary as the yields are high, and the sunflower-like flowers are a bonus.

YIELD 2kg (4lb) per tuber planted.

STORAGE Leave them in the ground until they're wanted, as they store better there than anywhere else.

Keep them happy by...

Staking in a windy site or, if you must be neat, bang in a stake each end of a row and run long strings or plastic-coated wire either side of the plants. You'll have a bigger crop if you earth up the plants when they've reached about 45cm (18in) high.

Worth trying...

'Fuseau' – Less knobbly tubers than normal, which are easier to clean and peel for cooking.

Enjoy them...

From mid-autumn right through winter. When the plants start dying off in autumn, cut them back to 30cm (12in) high, after which you can simply dig up individual plants any time you want some tubers. Tubers still in the ground the following mid-spring will start growing again, so use them before then.

Look out for...

Save some of the best tubers to re-plant next year.

The distinctive knobbly tubers of Jerusalem artichokes. They make nourishing and flavoursome winter soups.

HOW TO earth up

Earthing up Jerusalem artichokes and potatoes encourages the shoots to root and boosts tuber production. With asparagus and celery it keeps the stems pale and tender.

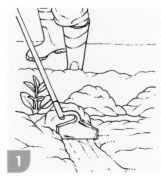

1 Plant the vegetable as normal and wait until shoots start to appear, then use a draw hoe to pull the soil up and over them and block out the light.

2 The shoots will reappear and when they are about 15cm (6in) high, cover their lower half again, then leave the plants to develop normally.

Asparagus

plant APR
harvest APR, MAY, JUN

Asparagus is pricey in the shops, to say nothing of being well travelled, so it is worth growing it yourself to enjoy it when it is really fresh. On the downside, it is a perennial and needs plenty of space. You buy it as 'crowns' from specialist growers who have raised these

for several years already. It still needs a further three years to settle in to your veg bed before you get much of a harvest, but the plants may then continue cropping for 8–20 years.

Cultivation

DIFFICULTY Easy; medium input.
PLANT each crown in a generous hole, spread the roots out well then cover with 5cm (2in) of soil. Water well. As shoots start to appear above the ground, gradually earth up the plants until they are growing along ridges up to 15cm (6in) high.
SPACE 30–45cm (12–18in) apart, with 90cm (3ft) between each row.
CARE In early to mid-spring, sprinkle general fertilizer over the asparagus beds; water if the weather is very dry during the cropping season. Hand-weed beds regularly; don't use a fork for removing weeds – asparagus plants are shallow rooted and dislike disturbance.
YIELD About 20–25 spears per mature plant.
STORAGE Don't store – eat fresh!

Keep them happy by…

Planting crowns in well-drained ground or in slightly raised beds on their own, adding plenty of organic matter during the previous winter.

Do not cut any emerging spears for the first two summers after planting, and then only take a light crop in the first few weeks of the cutting season in year three. From then on you can harvest as much as you like until early summer. In autumn, cut the yellowed or browning fern to 5cm (2in) above ground, then weed and mulch the soil generously with well-rotted organic matter.

Worth trying…

'Connover's Colossal' – An old favourite, readily available as both male and female plants – females are less prolific and shed

Thick, sturdy asparagus spears emerging from a gravel mulch, which will discourage slugs snacking on them. They are regarded as the elite among vegetables, and though it takes three years for a bed to come into regular cropping, the results will amply repay your patience.

seed via berries that ripen towards autumn; self-sown seedlings are a nuisance.

'Jersey Giant' – Long-season variety, cropping two weeks earlier than most and continuing to early summer.

'Jersey Knight' – Vigorous, heavy-cropping, all-male F1 hybrid, readily available from the mail-order firms. Thick spears and superb flavour.

'Stewart's Purple' – For those who like colour; sweet-tasting, purple spears from mid-spring.

Enjoy them…

From mid-spring to early summer. Cut spears as soon as they reach about 15cm (6in) tall. Use a strong knife to cut them off 5cm (2in) below the soil surface and then refill the hole with soil to prevent pests from getting in. After early summer, let the plants grow and complete their life cycle.

Look out for…

Self-sown asparagus seedlings grow quickly and are soon indistinguishable from those with pedigrees, except in their output, which is generally much poorer. These interlopers then overcrowd beds, reducing the yield from your chosen variety.

Thin asparagus spears usually come from weak plants that have been cropped too early, cut too heavily in previous years, or not fed sufficiently – or all three.

Slugs also like emerging spears (*see* page 280 for controls).

Asparagus beetles eat the spears and the foliage. They appear from early summer and are yellow and black and about 1cm (½in) long; their caterpillar-like larvae are grey-black. Both beetles and larvae are easily spotted and can be picked off by hand, as can the clusters of black eggs on foliage. Tidy up the browning asparagus ferns in autumn to discourage overwintering pests, and burn the cut foliage to kill any pests that still may be lurking.

Any sign of infestation is very off-putting on the plate. If you see blackfly while crops are growing, wipe them off developing buds with a damp cloth or a soft brush dipped in water.

HOW TO plant asparagus crowns

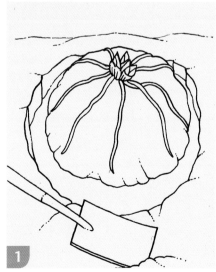

1. Prepare the soil well before planting – add organic matter the previous winter and then a fertilizer just beforehand. Dig a hole about 15cm (6in) deep and build a mound. Sit each crown on the top of the mound and arrange its roots down the slope as evenly as practical.

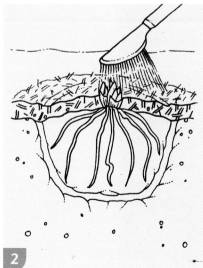

2. Ensuring that the crown will be slightly proud of the surface, and taking care not to dislodge it from its perch on top of the mound, backfill the hole with soil. Water it well, then cover the crown with about 8cm (3in) of soil and top it off with a generous mulch.

For the best flavour and texture, harvest asparagus spears before they get too long. You can use a sharp knife, but special serrated-edged asparagus knives are available.

Aubergines

SOW FEB, MAR plant MAY, JUN
harvest JUL, AUG, SEP, OCT

Aubergines are one of those vegetables that you try growing, have poor results with, and then don't bother with again. Think again – grow a couple of plants in pots in the warmest place in your garden, and given a good summer they might surprise you. If you raise plants from seed, you could try novelty varieties such as 'Calliope' (pink-striped) or 'Mohican' (white). These are decorative but the flavour is nothing special.

It is possible to get reasonable-sized fruit from aubergine plants. 'Moneymaker' is a good performer and suitable for outdoor cultivation, where it crops well in good summers.

Cultivation

DIFFICULTY Easy; low input but need the right conditions.
SOW at 21–24°C (70–75°F), in late winter/early spring. Prick out seedlings into small pots and grow on at 16–18°C (60–65°F) until late spring.
PLANT in a cold greenhouse in late spring. Alternatively, plant outside in early summer; but harden off first and wait for warm weather. Aubergine plants are often available at garden centres to save having to grow them from seed.
SPACE 60cm (2ft) apart in all directions.
CARE Water sparingly at first, increasing the supply as plants start carrying a crop, especially in hot weather. Feed weekly with liquid tomato feed once the first fruits have set. Support the main stems with canes. Plants grow to about 90cm (3ft) high and 60cm (2ft) wide outdoors, slightly bigger under glass.
YIELD Up to 1.8kg (4lb) per plant – if you are lucky.
STORAGE Keep for a couple of weeks in the fridge.

Keep them happy by…

Growing them in a warm, sheltered place. Slow growth and low yields on poor plants are usually a sign that growing conditions are unsuitable: too cold, too wet or too windy.

Worth trying…

'Black Enorma' – Fat, purple-black aubergines, but only a few per plant. Slow to reach full size, so best in a greenhouse.
'Moneymaker' – Purple, sausage-shaped aubergines; reliable, high-yielder. Fruit are produced early, so a good choice for growing outdoors as they have a good chance of maturing.

Enjoy them…

From midsummer on, as soon as the fruit are 7.5cm (3in) long or more; use secateurs to cut the prickly stem 1cm (½in) beyond the fruit. Plants will continue to crop outside until cold nights strike in early autumn – crops grown under glass will continue for another month.

Look out for…

If fruit are left on the plants too long, they will taste bitter and develop small hard seeds. Harvest while still shiny.

Greenfly can stop the plants growing, especially early on and under glass. Remove small infestations by hand or use a suitable spray (see page 279).

Whitefly and red spider mite can be a problem. Use a biological control (see page 280).

Beans, broad

SOW LATE AUTUMN OR, FEB, MAR, APR
plant MAR, APR
harvest JUN, JUL

Broad beans are a favourite in traditional vegetable gardens. They are worth growing if you have the space for a reasonable number of plants, and are prepared to provide support: home-grown and fresh from the garden, they are far superior to any that you can buy, even those that are frozen within hours of picking. The flowers have a fabulous fragrance, too.

'The Sutton' is a long-standing favourite. Its dwarf stature makes it suitable for growing in smaller gardens.

Cultivation

DIFFICULTY Easy, but need regular care and attention.
SOW under cover in pots or trays in late winter and early spring, or outdoors in situ in mid-spring. Sow in succession in early and late spring and in late autumn for a longer season.
PLANT out indoor plants in mid-spring.
SPACE 20cm (8in) apart, in double rows 20cm (8in) apart, with 45cm (18in) between the double rows. If you have plenty of space, increase the double-row spacing to 60–90cm (2–3ft), which enables the plants to cope better with dry conditions and allows for easier weeding.
CARE Water routinely if the weather is dry. No extra feeding is needed throughout the growing season.
YIELD About 5.5kg (12lb) from a 2m (6ft) double row.
STORAGE If you have any to spare, freeze them (*see* Storage, pages 168–9) as soon as you pick them.

Keep them happy by...

Erecting some good support. Insert two 1.2m (4ft) posts at the end of each double row with two horizontal strings along each side of the double row of plants, at 30 and 60cm (12 and 24in) above the ground. As the plants grow the strings will hold them up without damaging the fragile stems.

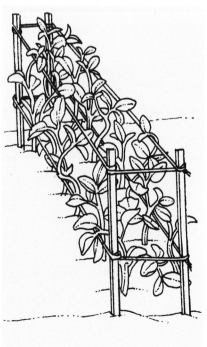

Support
Broad beans can make large leafy plants and they have weak stems, so it is important to provide strong supports. Do this when they are still small and easy to work with otherwise the job becomes much more difficult.

Worth trying...

'Aquadulce' – A tried-and-tested variety. Not a fantastic flavour, but the weatherproof plants are good from an early sowing and can also be sown in late autumn for an early spring crop.
'Imperial Green Longpod' – Bright green and tender beans in long pods on tall plants; a heavy cropper.
'Medes' – Short pods of tasty beans on mid-height plants. Only sow in spring.
'The Sutton' – Compact, 30cm (12in) tall, so needs less support. Can be sown in late autumn for an early crop in late spring; as it is short it is easy to protect early spring plants with cloches or gardener's fleece.

Enjoy them...

Once the beans inside the pods are the size of a thumbnail – over a six-week period from early summer. Pick them by pulling back the pod against its direction of growth, then twisting slightly, or snip them with scissors or secateurs. After cropping, if you don't need the space for something else, cut the plants down to about 15cm (6in) or so above the ground – if you are lucky you may get a late smattering of beans towards the very end of summer.

Look out for...

Mice and pigeons regard broad bean seed as fair game and cold, wet, early-spring weather makes them rot; if your ground is less than well-drained, sow seed later in spring or raise your plants under cover.

The black bean aphid (blackfly) is a regular pest, congregating round the plant tips and on young pods. Once pods start to appear, nip out the plant's growing tips to remove their feeding sites.

Chocolate spot causes brown markings on the leaves. Avoid this fungus by feeding plants and providing good drainage and air circulation. Rust fungus produces red-brown markings on the leaves, but it occurs too late in the season to be a problem. Pea and bean weevil chew notches in the leaves – ugly, but this seldom affects yields.

If you want lots of broad beans, it is annoying that in some years seeds planted in autumn and then overwintered can be a complete failure!

Beans, French

Dwarf
SOW APR, MAY, JUN, JUL **plant** MAY
harvest JUN, JUL, AUG, SEP

Climbing
SOW APR, MAY, JUN **plant** MAY
harvest JUN, JUL, AUG

Flageolet, haricot
SOW APR, MAY, JUN **plant** MAY
harvest SEP, OCT

Green beans are near the top of the list of veg to grow. They don't take much space or time and they are fantastic fresh – much, much better than those jet-setting imports that have seen more of the world than you. If you become really keen, there is a wide range of types: connoisseur's, heritage, purple- or gold-podded, and those that can be dried. If you have a greenhouse you can also grow green beans 'out-of-season'.

'Blue Lake' has pencil-thin cylindrical pods and white seeds.

Cultivation

DIFFICULTY Easy, but need better growing conditions than runners; average input.

SOW on a warm windowsill indoors in mid-spring; outdoors in situ in late spring to midsummer – bear in mind that they are frost tender.

PLANT greenhouse-raised plants outdoors after the danger of frost is past in late spring.

SPACING Dwarf varieties 15cm (6in) apart with 25cm (10in) between rows; climbing varieties on supports 20cm (8in) apart.

CARE Water sparingly while they are young and in dull, cool weather, more generously after they are established and carrying a crop. No extra feeding is needed if the ground was well prepared before planting.

YIELD From a 1.5m (5ft) row – dwarf 1.8kg (4lb), climbing 2.7kg (6lb).

STORAGE Fine for a week in the fridge; can be frozen (*see* storage, pages 168–9).

Keep them happy by...

Avoiding planting them if the weather is cool, dull or damp – both the seeds and the young plants can rot. For early plants or if the summer is cold, plant seeds in small individual pots indoors and keep the seed compost on the dry side. Don't rush to put plants out until conditions are warmer and drier.

Worth trying...

'Blue Lake' – Climbing variety with cylindrical green pods. Large pods can be left to dry out for haricots.

'Cobra' – Climbing, heavy and long cropper with long, slender green pods and lilac flowers; attractive in a pot, and can be grown early under glass.

'Hunter' – Climbing, heavy cropper with large, flat (like runners), very tender, tasty pods for slicing. Grow in spring and late summer/autumn under glass as well as outdoors. Seeds can be difficult to obtain; 'Helda' is similar.

'Opera' – Dwarf, reliable heavy cropper with excellent flavour. Disease resistant, so good for organic growing.

'Purple Teepee' – Dwarf, heavy cropper with dark purple pods.

'Valdor' – Dwarf, heavy cropper; tasty pale gold pods. Long season and disease resistant.

Some for drying...

'Pea bean' – Old variety with small pods of pea-sized, cream beans with maroon spots. These can be shelled and used fresh

Special notes

OUT-OF-SEASON CROPS

Sow Dwarf French beans on a warm windowsill indoors in early spring. Plant them in the greenhouse in a well-prepared soil border, growing bags or large pots from mid-spring; avoid cold spells. Harvest in late spring and early summer. Sow in midsummer for plants to grow in an unheated greenhouse for cropping in early to mid-autumn.

FOR DRYING

Leave the pods to grow to full size and they'll start to turn yellow–brown as the beans ripen. Let them dry out naturally, if possible. If damp or frost threatens, pick them and finish the drying in shallow trays in a warm, dry place indoors. Shell the pods, spread out the beans to dry further, then store in jars.

or allowed to dry in the pods on the plants. Can be difficult to find. Keep some pods for next year's seed.

'Soissons' – Climbing bean with green seeds – flageolets when dry. Fine flavour.

Enjoy them...

As soon as the pods are big enough, so you can really appreciate them at their most tender. Pick them regularly otherwise the beans get too fat and coarse and are no longer good to eat. Dry out and save these beans for next year's seed.

Look out for...

Most beans really don't like cold wet conditions, avoid these and you will avoid most problems.

Even if you don't want haricots, it is tempting to grow 'Borlotto Lingua di Fuoco' just for the attractive maroon and white speckled pods. They make especially attractive climbing plants in the flower garden, where they provide height when grown up obelisks.

Beans, runner

SOW APR, MAY plant MAY, JUN
harvest JUL, AUG, SEP, OCT

The secret with runners is to eat them while small and tender; beans that have been left to grow huge become tough and stringy. Don't feel guilty about chucking them on the compost heap, as chances are they'll be plenty more young beans as these plants always produce bumper crops. If you think you hate runners, think again. Grow them yourself, don't grow too many, eat them young and you'll love them.

These healthy runner bean plants of the variety 'Lady Di' are just beginning to produce pods.

Cultivation

DIFFICULTY Easy; low input, apart from picking.
SOW in pots on a windowsill indoors in mid-spring, or outdoors in situ in late spring.
PLANT out pot-grown specimens in early summer.
SPACE 23cm (9in) apart in rows or on wigwams.
CARE Water thoroughly in dry spells. Also spray the plants daily to increase humidity. In very dry weather, give the plants a thorough soaking then mulch them with garden compost or old newspapers. Never let the soil dry out completely. Extra feeding isn't needed for plants in well-prepared patches; for those in containers or intensive veg beds, apply liquid tomato feed weekly while plants are carrying crops.
YIELD A dozen plants will feed a family of four and allow some beans to be frozen.
STORAGE Put them in the fridge for up to a week if you must; can be frozen (*see* Storage, pages 168–9).

Keep them happy by...

Providing tall supports – canes need to be 2.5m (8ft) tall; 30cm (12in) of which needs to be pushed into the ground. Spray open flowers with water to encourage 'setting'. Never let the soil dry out completely. Yes, I know I've said that already, but it's important!

Worth trying...

'Enorma' – Very long, straight pods; tender and tasty.
'Lady Di' – Long, slender, flavoursome, stringless beans; seedless until quite well developed with a long growing season.
'Sunset' – Shortish beans with a good flavour early in the season. Pale pink flowers make this ideal for a pot or even a flower garden.
'White Swan' – A heavy cropper producing long and wide beans over a long period; white-flowered.

Enjoy them...

As soon as they are upwards of 10cm (4in) long. When they are growing quickly, many large-podded varieties are still good at 30–38cm (12–15in). Once they have developed seeds they aren't worth eating.

Look out for...

Birds may peck off the flowers and snails enjoy high-rise living on the supports and are partial to the occasional pod, as well as the leaves. Flower drop may occur in dry weather.

Beetroot

SOW MAR, APR, MAY, JUN
harvest JUL, AUG, SEP, OCT

Fresh beetroot is wonderful roasted or boiled, or even grated raw; and the leaves can be used young in salads. When home-grown and picked while still small, beetroot is sweet and full of flavour – you'll never be able to face the pickled variety again. The natural, vivid purple colour of beetroot is caused by anti-oxidants, which, it is claimed, are good for your health.

Smallish roots from an early harvest of 'Boltardy'. A tried-and-tested favourite with a good flavour, this variety is less likely to bolt than some other beetroots.

Cultivation

DIFFICULTY Intermediate; average input.
SOW early bolt-resistant varieties in early spring; other varieties from mid-spring to midsummer. For a really early crop, sow a few seeds in a greenhouse border in late winter.
SPACE Sow 'seed' 2.5cm (1in) apart in rows; thin seedlings to 7.5cm (3in) apart for babies, or 15cm (6in) apart for full-sized roots. (The 'seed' are capsules containing several seeds.)
CARE Water during dry spells to keep plants growing steadily; no extra feeding is needed. Weed to prevent young plants from being swamped.
YIELD About 2.3kg (5lb) from a 1.5m (5ft) row.
STORAGE Keep in the fridge for up to two weeks.

Keep them happy by…

Protecting plants with fleece in cold weather.

Worth trying…

'Albina Vereduna' – White globes with a sweet flavour.
'Boltardy' – Bolt-resistant, traditional roots with a good taste and texture.
'Burpee's Golden' – Globe-shaped, golden roots; superb flavour. Good for picking small.
'Cylindra' – Tall, tubular roots form above ground, up to 20cm (8in) tall; produces a huge crop from a single row; no good for baby beet.
'Detroit 6-Rubidus' – Reliable, bolt-resistant globes for early crops. Doesn't get woody, even when allowed to grow large.

Enjoy them…

As early as late spring, as baby beetroot around 2.5cm (1in) in diameter. Pull every third or fourth plant, leaving the rest with space to continue growing. Use full-sized roots as needed during summer. Roots tend to store best in the ground; lift the remainder in mid-autumn, keep under cover in a cool place to use as soon as possible.

Look out for…

Beetroot is very prone to bolting (running to seed) if sown too early or when growing conditions are difficult for them (*see* Keep them happy by…). Use varieties bred for early sowing if you suffer regular bolting. Water more regularly if your roots turn out woody.

Broccoli, sprouting

SOW APR, MAY **plant** JUN, JUL
harvest JAN, FEB, MAR

Sprouting broccoli is incredibly tasty and a very reliable winter crop, not to be confused with the summer-cropping calabrese (*see* page 186). The sprouting spears are amazingly tender for plants that grow through winter and this is one of those vegetables that is unbeatable picked and cooked within minutes. Just a few plants are enough for a real treat with hearty winter meals.

Purple sprouting broccoli in summer

'Bordeaux' and 'Summer Purple' are summer croppers, although their season is brief. Sow seeds under cover from late winter and at three-week intervals until early summer, plant out from mid-spring and have crops from midsummer. Combine these varieties with the winter ones and you could have tender shoots of sprouting broccoli all year round.

Cultivation

DIFFICULTY Easy, low input.
SOW from mid-spring/late spring in a seedbed; thin to 7.5–10cm (3–4in) apart.
PLANT out the young plants from the seedbed to the main bed in early to midsummer.
SPACE 45cm (18in) apart in each direction.
CARE Plant in very firm ground and water in dry spells. Give a general-purpose liquid feed in late summer, or use a granular feed with plenty of water to wash it in.
YIELD About 600g (1½lb) per plant.
STORAGE Keeps for up to three days in the fridge.

Keep them happy by…

Supporting plants in exposed sites. Tie main stems to stakes before the autumn winds start picking up.

Worth trying…

'Claret' – Very late – for picking in mid-spring; purple spears.
'Late Purple Sprouting' – Crops in early to mid-spring.
'Rudolph' – Very early, purple spears, ready from early to late winter; large, tasty shoots.
'White Sprouting' – Crops in early spring; green-white spears.

Enjoy them…

As soon as the colour of the developing heads is visible, cut the entire shoot 5–10cm (2–4in) long with a sharp knife. Check plants at least twice a week and don't allow any shoots to run to seed; the more you cut, the more will grow, but once they flower, they stop producing new shoots.

Look out for…

In fact, most varieties of sprouting broccoli are amazingly pest free, since the edible part forms in late winter or early spring when there are no cabbage white butterflies about. Summer varieties of purple sprouting broccoli (*see* left) may be more prone; if they strike, pick them off.

Clubroot can ruin crops and prevent you from growing brassicas for years (*see* page 184). Pigeons can be a problem: cover brassicas with fine-mesh netting or bird netting.

This plant of 'Late Purple Sprouting' broccoli should have a long cropping season and is a handsome addition to a flower border.

Brussels sprouts

SOW FEB, MAR, APR plant MAY, JUN
harvest JAN, FEB, MAR AND SEP, OCT, NOV, DEC

What a surprise that sprouts have turned out to be good for you! They contain anti-oxidants, which are thought to help fight cancer. These slightly peppery mini cabbages are not to everyone's liking, but in common with so many vegetables, the home-produced ones are far superior to anything you can buy.

Sprouts are great winter vegetables whose flavour is improved by exposure to frost. They are available for harvesting throughout the autumn and winter.

Cultivation

DIFFICULTY Easy; lowish input.

SOW at 13–16°C (55–60°F) indoors in late winter and early spring for early croppers, or in an outdoor seedbed in early spring and mid-spring for later ones.

PLANT out indoor-raised seedlings in late spring after careful hardening off. Those plants started off in seedbeds can be planted in situ in early summer.

SPACE 60cm (2ft) apart in all directions, further apart (75cm/2½ft) where there is more room.

CARE Water well in dry spells. Give a boost in the form of a general-purpose fertilizer in late summer and water in.

YIELD Around 1kg (2¼lb) per plant.

STORAGE Keep for a few days in the fridge; can be frozen (*see* Storage, pages 168–9).

Keep them happy by...

Making sure the soil is very firm; tread it down well before and after planting, using your heel around the plants. Stake in exposed sites.

Worth trying...

'Darkmar' – Heavy cropper with dark green sprouts from late autumn.

'Falstaff' – Mild, reddish purple buttons from mid-autumn to early winter.

'Trafalgar' – Sweetish sprouts produced in heavy crops from early winter to early spring; tall plants.

Enjoy them...

As soon as they are large enough to eat – from the size of a large marble. Cropping from early varieties begins in early autumn, later ones from late autumn; the latest can be picked up until early spring.

Look out for...

Pigeons, which target the young plants: use protection. Instead of forming tight buttons, sprouts sometimes 'blow' – they open out into small, flattened, green rosettes. Avoid growing them in loose soil and stake them if in doubt.

Clubroot is a threat (*see* page 184).

Cabbages

Summer- and autumn-hearting and red
sow MAR, APR **plant** MAY, JUN
harvest AUG, SEP, OCT

Winter-hearting and Savoy
sow APR, MAY **plant** JUN
harvest JAN, FEB AND NOV, DEC

Spring-hearting
sow JUL, AUG **plant** SEP, OCT
harvest APR, MAY

The name 'cabbage' encompasses a treasure trove of vegetables in a range of colours (white, green, red) and textures (smooth, crispy, deeply wrinkled). They are tasty, healthy and versatile. If you haven't yet tasted coleslaw made with your own home-grown cabbages, then make this the year that you do.

Cultivation

DIFFICULTY Intermediate; it is worth a little extra care.

SOW early varieties under cover and later types in a seedbed, thinning out the latter and transplanting them as appropriate.

PLANT out summer and autumn cabbages, including red cabbage, in late spring and early summer; winter cabbage and Savoys in midsummer; spring cabbage in mid-autumn.

SPACE Depends on the variety: allow 30cm (12in) apart for smaller ones, bigger ones need 45cm (18in). Increase spacing if you have more room.

CARE Keep watered in dry spells so that plants can grow continuously without a check. Apply a top-up general-purpose or high-nitrogen feed during the summer to encourage leafy growth; water in well.

YIELD Varies according to variety.

STORAGE Cabbages are best left attached to their stems in the ground until you want to eat them.

Clubroot

Clubroot is a problem with brassicas. It is easily brought in on young plants raised in infected ground elsewhere. The roots of plants such as cabbages, broccoli and Brussels sprouts swell and eventually rot, and the top growth is badly stunted. Once you have clubroot it stays in the ground for 20 years or more, during which time you can't grow any members of the cabbage family (it also affects flowering members of the family) – there's no 'cure'. Make sure you don't get it by raising all your own plants, by growing brassicas in well-drained soil and by liming acid soil prior to planting. The disease is less common on chalky, alkaline soils and where drainage is good (*see* pages 157–159).

It's not surprising that cabbages are popular in decorative potagers. This is the Savoy variety 'January King', which looks especially decorative when covered with frost.

Keep them happy by…

Planting them in well-prepared firm ground, weeding regularly, and taking care not to disturb their shallow roots.

Worth trying…

There are numerous cabbage varieties, so you might want to experiment. Here are some good ones:

'Cuor di Bue' (Bull's heart) – A full-flavoured winter cabbage with tight conical heads in late summer and autumn. The seeds can be hard to obtain – try the Internet.

'Golden Acre' – Summer-hearting, ball-headed cabbage; sow in late winter.

'Hispi' – Summer- and autumn-hearting; the one to choose if you grow no others. Tasty and fast growing with small hearts. Sow from late winter under cover and from early spring to midsummer outdoors. Sow under cover in mid-autumn and raise the plants in a unheated greenhouse border for cutting early in spring. 'Hispi' is also suitable as 'baby' veg: plant 23cm (9in) apart in each direction.

'January King' – Savoy cabbage tinged with red; matures in autumn and can be left in place through winter from a late-spring sowing.

'Kalibos' – Heirloom red variety with pointed heads.

'Red Jewel' – Good round-headed, red-leaved variety.

'Wheeler's Imperial' – Compact spring cabbage. Sow in summer for a spring harvest or late winter for an autumn crop.

'Winter King' – Savoy with crumpled leaves. Several sowings in late spring and early summer will stagger the crop, extending your Savoy season into late winter.

Enjoy them…

When the centre tightens up and forms a solid 'heart'. Use secateurs or a knife with a scalloped blade to cut through the stem just below the heart. Remove damaged outer leaves. Leave the rest on to protect the interior. With careful planning you should have cabbage varieties all year round.

Look out for…

Cabbage white butterflies (large and small) love brassicas, and their caterpillars eat the leaves and deposit frass (excrement), making them unfit to eat. Cover growing crops. Remove caterpillars by hand or use an organic pesticide.

Small slugs can work their way into the hearts of developing cabbages, causing damage and leaving droppings. For slug controls *see* page 280.

Pigeons like cabbages as winter forage – put bird netting in place if necessary to keep them off the crop.

Cabbage root fly lays its eggs at the base of the stem and the larvae eat the roots, causing the plant to wilt and die. Buy small collars made from roofing-felt (specifically made for protecting crops) and slip these around the base of each stem to prevent egg laying. Fine mesh properly fitted above and around the plants also helps. Clubroot can occur, *see* box.

The hearts of 'Hispi' develop in summer and autumn, making neat conical heads of fresh green leaves.

Calabrese (green broccoli)

SOW MAR, APR, MAY **plant** APR, MAY, JUN
harvest JUN, JUL, AUG, SEPT

Calabrese is a delicious and deservedly popular vegetable. It is similar to broccoli (and often known as such) but with solid cauliflower-like heads. If you cut the central head and leave the plants in the ground, you get some smaller 'spears' a few weeks later – which makes it a good-value crop into the bargain. It's also easily grown, especially in polytunnels.

Cultivation

DIFFICULTY Intermediate; needs regular care.
SOW under cover in early spring, or in an outside seedbed from mid-spring. In a polytunnel, sow in succession (about every six weeks) all year round apart from midwinter.
PLANT outdoors in late spring or early summer.
SPACE 30cm (12in) apart in each direction.
CARE It is vital to keep the plant growing steadily, so water and weed regularly and use a boost of general-purpose or high-nitrogen feed halfway through the growing season.
YIELD About 600g (1½lb) per plant.
STORAGE The heads will keep for a few days in the fridge if picked with a length of stalk.

Keep them happy by…

Protecting them from caterpillars (*see* page 279). They are very popular with cabbage whites, which will get to them anywhere (even in a polytunnel) if they are not covered with a fine-mesh netting (make sure that the netting does not touch the leaves).

Worth trying…

'Crown and Sceptre' – A large central head in summer is followed by several pickings of smaller spears in late summer and autumn.
'Chevalier' – Medium-sized heads are followed by small spears from early autumn onwards.
'Kabuki' – Compact plants that mature early for baby calabrese; grow closer together.

Enjoy them…

From early summer into autumn. Cut off the whole head and use as required.

Look out for…

They suffer the same problems as all the cabbage family, including clubroot (*see* page 184).

Although calabrese is available all year round at the greengrocers and in the supermarket, there's nothing to match the flavour of home-grown varieties, such as 'Chevalier'.

Carrots Early varieties

SOW MAR AND JUL, AUG
harvest JUN, JUL AND OCT, NOV

Carrots are fantastic eaten young, either raw or lightly steamed. When you grow your own you can experiment with all the different coloured (and shaped) varieties, which are not available in the shops. Maincrop carrots (see box) are best for real carrot enthusiasts and those who want to eat everything organic, as the organic type are expensive to buy.

Cultivation

DIFFICULTY Intermediate; pay attention and give regular care.
SOW thinly in shallow seed drills. Sow early varieties under cloches or fleece in early spring, then again in midsummer and late summer for a few quick, late pickings; cover these with fleece in the autumn to extend the growing season.
SPACE Sow as thinly as you can as thinning carrots releases an aroma that attracts carrot fly. Allow 30cm (12in) between rows.

CARE Water well during dry spells and weed regularly to keep the roots growing steadily. Take precautions against carrot fly; avoid thinning out seedlings as the scent may draw carrot flies to your crop which could ruin it.
YIELD Around 2kg (4½lb) from a 1.5m (5ft) row.
STORAGE Pull and eat early varieties. If necessary, store them in a paper sack in a cool place. Check them regularly and eat as soon as possible.

Keep them happy by...

Cultivating the soil until it is fine textured without lumps or stones before sowing seed – and don't put them in ground that has been manured in the last 12 months.

Worth trying...

'Autumn King' – Large, tapering carrots; ready in autumn but keep well in well-drained ground over winter.
'Healthmaster' – Deep red-orange carrots with increased beta-carotene; use raw for the best nutritional benefits.
'Nantes' – Sweet-tasting long roots ready in early summer from a protected late winter sowing. 'Nantes' can also be sown at the same time as other earlies. Improved forms, such as 'Nantes 2', are identical.
'Samurai' – Red-skinned carrots with pink flesh that retains its colour even when cooked. Ready in summer and autumn.
'Sugarsnax' – Long thin carrots for eating raw.
'Yellowstone' – Sweet, bright yellow carrots; best in salads.

Enjoy them...

As baby or salad carrots as soon as the first ones are big enough to use, leaving the rest to keep growing (around midsummer). Pull alternate carrots to give those left behind more room to grow (carrot flies are less trouble later in the season).

The smooth-skinned carrot variety 'Yellowstone' produces sweet roots at their best eaten raw. You'll find that home-grown carrots are markedly sweeter than those bought in the shops, especially if they are cooked within minutes of being harvested.

Maincrop varieties

If you want to grow maincrop carrot varieties, sow carrot seed in the open in mid- and late spring and early summer when the soil has had a chance to warm up. You can leave the crop in the ground, until rainy weather starts in autumn. After this they are liable to produce fine, white root hairs and resprout, so dig them up, brush them off and let them dry. Washing them encourages rot.

Look out for...

Carrot fly is almost inevitable. The best solution is to keep carrots covered with fine, insect-proof mesh throughout their lives. Grow rows of onions and spring onions around them to disguise the scent that attracts carrot flies.

There are nearly always one or two fanged roots. If your whole crop is badly affected, you have probably added too much organic matter to the veg bed too recently. Stony soil can produce the same effect though. If necessary, make a raised bed (*see* pages 150) and fill it with sieved soil mixed with old potting compost to give the carrots a good root run.

Beat the flies

There are several carrot-fly resistant varieties such as 'Flyway', 'Maestro' and 'Resistafly'. However, they often prove to be less tasty than other 'non-resistant' varieties and are not 100 per cent effective: small outbreaks of carrot fly may still occur.

Where carrot flies are a problem, try growing onions in among your carrots. Members of the onion family (alliums) are thought to discourage this pest.

Cauliflowers

Summer-heading cauliflowers
SOW JAN, FEB plant MAR, APR
harvest MAY, JUN, JUL

Autumn-heading cauliflowers
SOW MAR plant APR MAY
harvest AUG, SEP, OCT, NOV

Winter-heading cauliflowers
SOW APR, MAY plant MAY, JUN
harvest FEB, MAR, APR

Cauliflowers have undergone a change: aside from the traditional white type, which we are all familiar with, you can now get a rainbow of colours – well, green, yellow-green and purple anyway. These look pretty, although for flavour and texture you can't beat the white ones. On the downside, cauliflowers aren't a breeze to grow, but if you have space, try a few.

Cultivation

DIFFICULTY Advanced; look after well. Not time consuming.
SOW summer varieties indoors at 16°C (60°F); autumn varieties indoors or in a seedbed under cover (such as a coldframe, greenhouse border or under fleece outdoors) and winter varieties in a seedbed outdoors.
PLANT out young plants at 7.5–10cm (3–4in) tall with a good root system.
SPACE 60cm (2ft) apart for summer and autumn varieties; 75cm (2½ft) for winter varieties.
CARE Keep plants well weeded and watered through the summer. Boost the plants with a general-purpose or high-nitrogen feed around mid- to late summer.
YIELD If you are lucky, up to 1kg (2.2lb) per plant, but probably considerably less.
STORAGE Wrap in clingfilm and store in a fridge for up to a week; can be frozen as florets (*see* Storage, pages 168–9).

Keep them happy by...

Really excelling at your soil preparation; as with all brassicas, firm soil is essential.

Bend a few outer leaves over the cauliflower head as the curds bulk up (snap the leaf midrib to keep it in place). This is especially important for white varieties, which easily discolour.

Worth trying…

'All Year Round' – Traditional white cauliflowers, all seasons from successional sowings. Sow in mid-autumn and protect the plants in a polytunnel or under fleece for spring crops.

'Autumn Giant' – Reliable autumn-header, firm white curds.

'Clapton' – An autumn-header with long leaves that protect the developing heads; resistant to clubroot.

'Purple Cape' – Good variety with tasty, large, deep purple heads that keep their colour reasonably well on cooking. Takes nearly a year to grow, but the result is well worth it.

'Romanesco' – Lime-green curds form a series of pinnacles instead of a smooth flat head; good for dividing into florets for salads or steaming; keeps its colour when cooked. Ready in late summer/autumn. 'Celio' and 'Veronica' are similar.

'Trevi' – Bright green heads with a wonderful flavour; keeps its colour on cooking. Sow in late spring, eat in early autumn.

'Violet Queen' – Mauve heads ready in late summer/early autumn; turns green when cooked.

Baby cauliflowers

Mini-cauliflowers – one-per-person-size – are great fresh and for freezing. You need to buy specially bred 'baby veg' or 'patio variety' seeds. The range increases each year, but 'Igloo' and 'Avalanche' are good. Plant them closer together than normal – approx 30–45cm (12–18in) apart.

Enjoy them…

Once the developing curds form a dense, tightly packed hemisphere; cut it off just beneath the base of the head (include the collar of outer leaves as these will provide protection until you use the cauliflower). Pick as soon as the head is level all over; don't delay, as the florets soon start to shoot out individually and quickly open into flowers.

Look out for…

Cauliflowers suffer the same problems as cabbages, including clubroot (*see* page 184).

Unfavourable weather can produce small or ruined heads. If it's the weather, this is unavoidable, but inadequate soil preparation can also be a factor.

'All Year Round' is a traditional-style cauliflower with large white curds.

The cauliflower variety 'Romanesco' has vivid green heads with pointed curds.

Celeriac

sow MAR **plant** MAY, JUN
harvest JAN, FEB, MAR AND SEP, OCT, NOV, DEC

With it's lumpy misshapen roots that grow half out of the ground, no-one could call celeriac an attractive vegetable, but it certainly is tasty, and it's much easier to grow than its refined relative, celery. It is one of those veg that are pricey in the shops, so it's worth your while trying to grow a few.

Cultivation

DIFFICULTY Intermediate; pay attention to detail.
SOW in early spring on a windowsill indoors at 16–21°C (60–70°F). Prick out seedlings into small pots and continue growing in warmth (13°C/55°F minimum) on a windowsill or in a heated propagator in a greenhouse. Keep well watered and in good light, but not strong sun.
PLANT into soil containing plenty of well-rotted organic matter after hardening off and when the last frost is safely past (late spring onwards).
SPACE Minimum 30cm (12in) apart in all directions if you are restricted for space; 45cm (18in) apart if you can.
CARE Administer general-purpose liquid feed as often as every two weeks and keep plants well watered at all times. Weed regularly until plants are big enough to cover the ground and shade out weeds naturally.
YIELD A row of 1.5m (5ft) gives about 1.5kg (3½lb).
STORAGE Dig them up as you need them; keeps for a few days in the fridge.

Worth trying…

'Monarch' – A reliable variety with good-quality roots.

Keep them happy by…

Preparing the soil well: rich soil is the key to succulent roots. They hate poor, dry earth. Don't stint on food and water as the plants need to be able to grow steadily.

Enjoy them…

From early autumn, as soon as the first roots are big enough. Dig up the whole plant, rest it on a hard surface and slice off the top, including all the leaves. Remove the smaller roots. You will need a strong knife.

In mild winters you can have celeriac until early spring. Leave them in the ground until you want them.

Look out for…

Celery fly (*see* page 191) may cause problems, otherwise crop failure is usually due to cultivation deficiencies or adverse weather. However, even imperfect roots are fine for making soups.

What it lacks in beauty celeriac makes up for in flavour, but it needs really rich soil to put on weight.

Celery (self-blanching)

SOW MAR **plant** MAY, JUN
harvest AUG, SEP, OCT

Celery is delicious to eat raw and also imparts a wonderful rich flavour to a wide variety of stews, soups and other concoctions in the kitchen. However, it must be well aware of its value because it is very demanding in the vegetable garden and one of the most difficult crops to grow successfully.

Celery plants require perfect growing conditions to do well.

Cultivation

DIFFICULTY Advanced; challenging and time consuming.
SOW on a windowsill indoors at 16–21°C (60–70°F) in early spring. Prick out seedlings into small pots as soon as they are large enough to handle, and continue growing in warmth (13°C/55°F minimum) on a windowsill or in a heated propagator in a greenhouse. Keep the plants well watered and in adequate light, but not strong sun. Harden off carefully.
PLANT out when the last frost is past – from early summer.
SPACE 23cm (9in) apart in all directions. Close spacing ensures the plants shade each others' stems, which helps them to blanch. Grow them in blocks, with an edging of raised boards to prevent the stems of the plants at the edges being turned green by the light.
CARE Keep plants well watered at all times – they must never go even slightly short of moisture. Give a liquid feed regularly from planting time onwards, using a general-purpose or high-nitrogen fertilizer. Keep well weeded until plants cover the ground enough to shade out weeds for themselves.
YIELD Depends how successful you are.
STORAGE Although it will keep in a fridge for a few days, why not eat it while it's fresh?

Keep them happy by…

Providing them with rich fertile soil that contains quantities of well-rotted organic matter. Celery hates a struggle – keep the plants growing by watering and feeding assiduously.

Worth trying…

'Victoria' – A self-blanching F1 hybrid; the easiest to grow successfully.

Enjoy them…

When the sticks are an edible size – this will be late summer. Self-blanching celery isn't hardy, so use it before the first proper frost.

Look out for…

Slugs can get in between the stems and eat the plant centres, which will then fall prey to bacterial infections and rots. Take strict precautions against slugs at all times, starting several weeks before planting.

Celery fly can be a nuisance, mining the leaves and leaving blotches and ribbon-shaped tunnels. Pinch off and destroy any badly infected leaves.

Carrot fly may also attack (*see* page 188).

Chicory

SOW JUN, JUL
harvest OCT, NOV, DEC

Chicory is one of those vegetables that some people like and some hate. It is slightly bitter tasting and forms heads rather like a lettuce, which can be cooked or used in salads. Witloof varieties are usually forced, which means they are grown without light to keep the leaves tightly furled, pale and tender. Other types, of which radicchio is one (it may be sold under 'R' in seed catalogues), are grown 'normally' for salad leaves.

Cultivation

DIFFICULTY Fairly easy; forcing varieties (see box) need time and effort.
SOW In situ – thin the seedlings, but don't transplant them.
SPACE 30cm (12in) apart in all directions.
CARE Water in dry spells, and keep well weeded.
YIELD A 1.5m (5ft) row gives about 1.25kg (2¾lb).
STORAGE Remains fresh in the fridge for a week or two.

Keep them happy by...

Giving them a long growing season and ensuring conditions are as good as possible. Radicchio can be temperamental but 'Sugar Loaf' should be pretty reliable. If all else fails, it can be forced as well (*see* box).

Forcing chicory

'Witloof Zoom' is the standard forcing variety. Grow the plants as usual and in late autumn cut down the tops to 7–8cm (3in) above the ground, dig up the roots and store them in slightly damp buckets of sand or soil in a cool shed.

Forcing takes 3–4 weeks. Depending on how much chicory you eat, force 3–4 roots at a time. Plant the roots in pots of moist compost, so their tops are just below the surface, then put them in a warm, dark place. Check regularly and water lightly if necessary – don't overdo it.

When the emerging buds are 7.5–10cm (3–4in) tall, cut them off at the base to use – don't wait, as they soon start to open and spoil. The same roots should produce several more 'chicons' before they need replacing with a new batch of roots from the shed.

Pale and interesting – forced 'Witloof Zoom' chicory at the point of perfection and ready for harvesting.

Worth trying...

'Rossa di Verona' – Tightly packed leaves form mahogany-red radicchio hearts. Non-forcing.
'Sugar Loaf' – Upright, green-hearted non-forcing chicory with substantial inner leaves. Very reliable; good in polytunnels, where it can be left for some time in winter without rotting or bolting.

Enjoy them...

When they have formed hearts from mid-autumn onwards. Leave slowcoaches as they may heart up anytime until mid-spring. Forcing chicory should provide you with fare from midwinter.

Look out for...

Red varieties can stay green. Red radicchio only changes colour towards autumn, when the nights start growing cold. If it is green but has hearted up, you can still eat it.

Slugs and snails are less of a problem than they are with lettuce, they must dislike the bitter taste.

Chillies

SOW FEB, MAR **plant** MAY, JUN
harvest JUL, AUG, SEP, OCT

Chillies are very fashionable and come in a wide range of shapes, colours and 'heats': if you don't want your tongue set on fire, there are plenty of mild ones that add a pleasant zing to a meal. The plants are attractive too, and some varieties can crop quite well on a sheltered patio, though growing them under cover gives more assured results.

Cultivation

DIFFICULTY Relatively easy; low input.
SOW in pots or trays at 21–24°C (70–75°F).
PLANT in early spring by first pricking out the seedlings into 7.5cm (3in) pots. Grow them on in an unheated greenhouse from late spring; or wait a month and for some settled warm weather before putting them outside.
SPACE One or two plants of each variety should have you overflowing with chillies, but if you grow more allow 30cm (12in) between compact varieties, 45cm (18in) between normal varieties and 60cm (2ft) between rows.
CARE Water sparingly, especially in cool conditions and while the plants are small. Feed weekly with liquid tomato feed. The stems are brittle so provide support. No pruning or trimming is needed.
YIELD Some plants produce loads of tiny fruits, others only a few big ones.
STORAGE Use fresh as required or dry them and put them in clean dry jars – whole or ground up.

Keep them happy by...

Plant them in a sheltered protected spot. A cold, dull or windy site or a poor summer can spell disaster.

Worth trying...

'Apache' – Compact plants; ideal for pots and on windowsills; green/red mid-strength fruits.
'Jalapeño' – Short, mid-strength green/red chillies with a slightly cracked skin.
'Joe's Long Cayenne' – Huge cropper; very long (to 30cm/10in) slim chillies, ripening red with a rich, fairly mild flavour.
'Mustard Habanero' – Very hot chillies with an unusual shape and colour – cream to purple to orange. Best under cover.

'Jalapeño' chillies used to be the most famous, but they've been overtaken by hotter ones with more exotic names; they're still among the best for general use, though.

'Thai Dragon' – Large crops of slender, achingly hot, green then red fruits.

Enjoy them...

Green as soon as they are large enough to use (usually from midsummer), or leave them to reach full size and turn red and develop their full flavour. Snip off a whole chilli plus part of its short green stalk.

Move container-grown plants under cover in autumn to extend the season, or pull up the plant, hang it upside down in a shed or not-too-hot kitchen to continue ripening, and let the chillies dry out naturally on the plant.

Look out for...

Greenfly like the plants too. They are mostly seen early on. Wipe them off by hand or use an organic spray as soon as you see them.

Courgettes, marrows, summer squashes

sow APR **plant** MAY, JUN
harvest JUN, JUL, AUG, SEP, OCT

Once you have eaten a home-grown courgette you'll never want the thin-skinned, watery-flavoured, shop-sold ones again. Courgette plants are prolific – you'll only need one or two to have more than enough to eat. Marrows, which are more-or-less courgettes that have reached maturity, are good for stuffing and baking. Summer squashes can be grown and used just like courgettes – they only differ in shape.

Cultivation

DIFFICULTY Easy; low input.
SOW singly in small pots indoors from mid-spring.
PLANT young plants out from early summer after the last frosts. Harden them off first.
SPACE 60cm (2ft) apart in each direction for compact varieties, otherwise 90cm–1.2m (3–4ft) apart.
CARE Water young plants carefully, increasing the quantity as they grow. Ideally, apply liquid tomato feed every week while plants are carrying a crop.
YIELD More than you need from two or three plants.
STORAGE Best eaten fresh, but will keep in a fridge for a week.

Keep them happy by...

Giving them rich, fertile soil with plenty of organic matter – the more the better; you can even grow them on the compost heap. Don't plant them out too soon as they aren't hardy and you won't gain anything. They grow very rapidly once conditions are right. If fruits fail to develop it is almost always due to cool weather. Hand pollination can help. The failure of female flowers to appear is usually also due to cold weather.

Worth trying...

'Clarion' – Pale green courgettes with a very mild flavour; good for using raw.
'Defender' – An early, heavy-cropper producing dark green courgettes; resistant to the virus that can ruin courgette crops.
'Orelia' – Long yellow courgettes on a vigorous plant.
'Parthenon' – A compact parthenocarpic courgette with dark green fruits which sets without being pollinated.
'Patty Pan' – A summer squash with tasty, flying-saucer-shaped, pale green fruits.
'Sunburst' – Similar to 'Patty Pan' but with golden fruits.
'Tiger Cross' – A compact, heavy-cropping and virus-resistant bush marrow, producing large crops of tender light-and-dark green striped marrows.
See also page 219: Squashes and pumpkins.

For a good all-round, tasty traditional courgette, it is hard to beat 'Defender'.

Enjoy them...

As soon as they are big enough to use; courgettes from 10cm (4in), summer squashes from golf-ball size. Leave marrows until they are bigger (15–25cm/6–10in long). There's no need to wait until the flower has fallen off the end of the fruit. Cut through the stalk with a sharp knife. Avoid cutting into the plant or other fruit – it's easily done. Remove any rotting, misshapen or damaged courgettes at the same time, and discard. Plants will continue to crop until mid-autumn.

Look out for...

Cucumber mosaic virus can affect plants, as yellow-flecks at first, then the leaves turn increasingly yellow-patterned and crinkled and plants become stunted and unproductive. The disease is spread by aphids and by knives used for cutting crops. Choose resistant varieties where possible; many garden plants carry the disease so it is difficult to avoid. Pull out and dispose of affected plants.

Young plants that fail to thrive are often found to have virtually no roots when they are dug up. This is usually due to poor growing conditions and/or over-watering, but it may sometimes be harmful organisms in the manure or garden compost. To be on the safe side, start again with new plants in another spot.

Powdery mildew, a grey-white talcum-powder-like deposit on the foliage, often appears as nights start turning cool in the autumn, especially after a dry summer. Plants usually continue cropping lightly. Improve vigour by liquid feeding and watering generously; remove the worst affected leaves by hand.

'Patty Pan' squashes are shown here with a harvest of green marrows and yellow courgettes. Lightly steam these small squashes for a hot crunchy treat.

Extend the season

You can plant courgette seeds up to a month earlier in a greenhouse or polytunnel as long as you protect them with gardener's fleece on cold nights. However, protecting them in this way does mean that pollinating insects are less likely to reach them. To solve this problem, choose a variety that produces fruit without pollination (parthenocarpic). Also, try planting some courgettes under cover in late summer; these will provide fruit until the cold nights of autumn.

Large crops of light-and-dark green striped marrows are best cut and stored in a cool place. Do not leave them lying on the soil or their skins will deteriorate.

Cucumbers

Greenhouse
sow APR **plant** MAY
harvest JUL, AUG, SEP, OCT

Outdoor
sow APR **plant** MAY, JUN
harvest JUL, AUG, SEP

There is nothing quite like cutting your own fresh cucumbers and eating them while still standing out in the garden. They are crunchy, tasty and very moreish. It will make you wonder how those that are sold in the supermarkets got past the Trades Descriptions Act. There is little to choose between indoor and outdoor cucumbers for taste, but indoor ones are likely to have the edge on production, as they are less subject to the vagaries of the weather.

Indoors or out, 'Crystal Lemon' tends to produce more cucumbers than you dreamed you would need. It is best peeled as the skin can be tough and spiky.

Cultivation

DIFFICULTY Intermediate; won't stand neglect.
SOW seeds singly in small pots indoors – in mid-spring for greenhouse plants, late spring for outdoor plants.
PLANT on into a greenhouse in late spring, or outdoors from early summer, after hardening off the seedlings.
SPACE 45cm (18in) apart; one or two plants should suffice.
CARE Water sparingly at first and increase gradually as they come into full growth – when cropping, cucumbers need large amounts of water during hot weather. Feed regularly with general-purpose liquid feed. Cucumbers need support. To support: tie the main stem of indoor plants to a vertical bamboo cane, adding ties as the plant grows; outdoor plants need a wigwam, netting or other firm support. For good-sized fruit you should also prune them. To prune: remove all sideshoots from the bottom 60cm (2ft) of the plant; allow higher sideshoots to develop. By the time each of these has grown about 15–20cm (6–8in) long, they should be carrying a tiny cucumber with a flower at the tip. Nip out the end of the shoot, one or two leaves beyond the developing fruit. Check plants twice a week – nip out the tips of sideshoots and tie up the main stems to keep them under control. They grow very fast. If you don't mind having lots of smallish cucumbers, then nipping out sideshoots and thinning fruit is less important.

Keep them happy by...
Giving them a warm, sunny, sheltered spot, especially outdoors. The plants are not hardy and hate cold, wet, windy conditions. Be very careful not to over-water young plants, but do make sure you provide plenty of water when they are cropping. It's essential to keep plants growing steadily otherwise developing cucumbers may abort.

Worth trying...
'Burpless' – An unromantic name, but a good description; tender, crunchy, medium-sized fruit. This F1 hybrid is the best of all the outdoor varieties.
'Carmen' – Heavy-cropping, F1 hybrid for the greenhouse; resistant to powdery mildew and several other diseases.
'Crystal Lemon' – Heavy-cropping outdoor variety with small, round, yellow fruits. One plant is enough.
'Flamingo' – An all-female F1 hybrid for the greenhouse; slender, long fruits.

'Long White' – Mild-flavoured outdoor variety with short, cream-skinned fruits.

'Passandra' – All-female F1 mini cucumber – the fruits reach 15cm (6in) long; disease-resistant; grow under cover.

Enjoy them…

The cucumbers are ready as soon as their shape fills out all the way along and they look big enough. You can eat them while quite tiny and they're delicious, but it takes practise to know exactly when the flesh turns from being slightly tangy to being juicy – it's when they're about the circumference of a 10p piece. Use secateurs to snip through the narrow stem connecting the cucumber to the plant – don't pull or twist them off or you'll drag the plant down or break off long lengths of stem that should carry the next lot of cucumbers.

Look out for…

The plants are susceptible to powdery mildew which may appear at the end of the season (*see* courgettes, pages 194–5). Choose disease-resistant varieties.

Cucumber mosaic virus can sometimes infect plants (*see* courgettes, pages 194–5), so choose virus-resistant varieties where possible.

Red spider mites invade crops under glass. They spin minute webs and suck the sap from the leaves, which begin to yellow. Discourage them by keeping the atmosphere damp; if necessary, use a biological control (*see* page 280).

Sex discrimination

It is easier to grow all-female hybrid varieties of cucumber. With other varieties the risk of pollination is great and this makes the fruit bitter and full of seeds. If you must try them, put insect-proof screens over all greenhouse openings to keep out pollinating insects. Remove male flowers every few days – they're the ones without a baby cucumber growing behind them.

'Burpless' is a long-standing, well-proven outdoor variety. If you want classic straight green fruit, it will do you proud. This particular plant is being grown up a decorative wicker obelisk – an alternative to runner beans for bringing height to a potager.

Endive

SOW MAY, JUN, JUL
harvest JAN, FEB, MAR AND SEP, OCT, NOV, DEC

Endive is like chicory in flavour and use but it is very different in appearance, with frizzy leaves in loose heads. If you like the bitter taste, it is a useful salad crop as it grows through the winter, making you less likely to have to trot down to the supermarket for a bag of sterilized green leaves.

Cultivation

DIFFICULTY Intermediate; get the details right and it's fine.
SOW In situ in rows 30cm (12in) apart from mid-spring; make successive sowings to have endive from early autumn to spring.
SPACE 30cm (12in) apart by gradual thinning.
CARE Water sparingly, increasing the supply slightly as plants mature. Plants remaining in the ground as winter approaches won't need watering, as rainfall should be adequate.
YIELD A 1.5m (5ft) row will produce 5–6 heads.
STORAGE Leave in the ground until they are needed.

Keep them happy by…

Protecting plants that you intend to harvest through the winter. They will usually do quite well until late winter, but you can help by covering them with cloches or fleece for protection until you are ready to blanch them (*see* box, below).

Worth trying…

'Moss Curled' – Called 'frisée' in France; large heads of filigree foliage; tender and tasty when blanched. 'Kentucky' is similar.

Enjoy them…

By cutting the whole plant at the stem just above the ground. Trim off the tough outer leaves. Use the soft, tender, yellowish leaves at the centre of the rosette.

Look out for…

Slugs and snails like to hide inside blanching pots, where they snack on the tender heads of endive; check the blanching pots regularly and remove slugs by hand, but also take anti-slug and snail precautions throughout the growing season (*see* page 279).

Blanching

When they are three months old, choose a few of the biggest plants to blanch. Blanching helps to reduce bitterness in the flavour of the leaves. Stand a heavy bucket or large clay flowerpot (with drainage hole blocked up) upside down over the top. Leave the pot in place for three weeks.

Alternatively, bunch up the outer leaves round the heart and use raffia or soft string to tie them in place – the result will be slightly less pale, but you will have fewer problems with worms or slugs. When one batch is ready, start to blanch a few more.

A few crunchy endive leaves drizzled with salad dressing and popped between two slices of granary bread make a good snack lunch.

Home-grown endives may not reach the prodigious size of those you can buy in a French market, but 'Moss Curled' will provide enough leaves to keep you happy.

Florence fennel

Under cover
sow APR plant JUN, JULY
harvest AUG, SEP

Outdoors
sow MAY plant JUN, JUL
harvest AUG, SEP

The swollen white bases of Florence fennel plants taste like aniseed and provide a touch of class when used raw in salads; they are even better cooked, particularly roasted with other vegetables in olive oil. It is not always reliable, especially in dodgy summers, and is easiest to raise under cover.

Cultivation

DIFFICULTY Advanced; not time consuming but demanding.
SOW Start plants off indoors in spring; sow three seeds each in small pots. Remove two and keep the strongest seedling.
PLANT Harden off seedlings carefully before planting in a greenhouse border or polytunnel in late spring, or outside in a sunny, sheltered spot from midsummer – wait for a prolonged warm spell.
SPACE 23–30cm (9–12in) apart in each direction.
CARE Water carefully – they need little water at first but must not dry out. As they grow and the weather warms up, increase watering and ensure the soil stays moist at all times. Feed with a general-purpose feed. Cover outdoor-grown plants with fleece at night if it's chilly, even in summer.

Keep them happy by...

It's essential to grow plants fast and without a check or the 'bulbs' will be too tough and the plants will bolt prematurely.

Worth trying...

'Goal' – F1 hybrid, produces large bulbs with a good aromatic fennel flavour.
'Victorio' – Fast-growing F1 hybrid variety with short, squat bases.

Enjoy them...

When they are the size of a tennis ball. Don't delay, or by the time you've used one or two the rest will have bolted. Pull the whole plant up, trim off the root and lower leaves and cut the foliage back to a few centimetres above the top of the 'bulb'.

Look out for...

Bolting is their main pastime, making them useless for eating. Any little discomfort sets them off – dry soil, poor growing conditions, lack of organic matter, sudden swings in temperature...all have an effect.

Slugs and some underground pests also enjoy them (*see* page 279 for controls).

If you can grow Florence fennel well, you will have every reason to be proud of yourself. They are a challenge, but worth it if you like the flavour.

Garlic

plant FEB, MAR AND NOV
harvest JUN, JUL, AUG

This little health-giving, breath-affecting bulb needs no introduction. It is an excellent addition to the vegetable garden and good value for time. If you grow onions, you can grow garlic. Don't plant garlic bought from the greengrocer's: choose properly prepared bulbs from a garden centre or seed catalogue.

Cultivation

DIFFICULTY Easy; low input.

PLANT whole cloves, ideally in late autumn. Autumn-planted garlic is ready earlier and usually makes larger bulbs, since it has a longer growing season. Choose the biggest cloves for planting and discard tiny ones. Push the cloves into the soil so the tip is a couple of centimetres (1in) below the surface.

SPACE 15cm (6in) apart in each direction.

CARE Check occasionally and carefully replant any cloves the birds pull up. Water both autumn- and spring-planted garlic in dry spells in summer.

YIELD A 1.5m (5ft) row produces about 10 bulbs.

STORAGE Some varieties store well, others need using quite quickly. (*See* Worth trying, right.) 'Wet' garlic is like a fresh vegetable and needs using promptly.

Garlic has been grown commercially on the Isle of Wight for many years, which accounts for the names, although the varieties probably originated elsewhere. 'Solent Wight' is a pale-cloved bulb ready to use from midsummer.

Keep them happy by...

Drying them well after harvesting and storing them in the house rather than a shed, where the cooler atmosphere may start them into growth.

Worth trying...

'Lautrec Wight' – Pink cloves with a white skin; stores until early spring.

'Purple Wight' – Early variety with purple-tinged cloves, ready for use 'wet' from early summer. Stores until early winter.

'Solent Wight' – Bred for the British climate; ready from midsummer.

'Purple Modovan' – Vintage, very pungent variety with mauve-tinged skin; use within four months.

Enjoy them...

From early summer as 'wet' garlic – the plants are still leafy but there are reasonable-sized heads underground. Pull only what you need. Harvest the rest when the foliage starts to dry off naturally – midsummer (autumn-planted) or late summer (spring-planted). When it has turned brown, dig up the plants and let them finish drying off on the ground in the sun. Try slicing up the stalks and using them as you would the cloves.

Look out for...

Rust disease (red spots on the foliage) can kill the leaves prematurely, resulting in smaller heads of garlic. It's often worse on ground that is poorly drained or rich in nitrogen fertilizer, but particularly where members of the onion family have been grown before, or debris from infected plants has been left behind or is in the compost. Destroy affected foliage, don't grow the onion family in that site for 4–5 years, and practise strict crop rotation (*see* page 153).

Bolting sometimes just happens. Don't worry about it: some varieties bolt easily but it doesn't affect their ability to produce a good bulb.

Elephant garlic

Elephant garlic is not a true garlic, being more closely related to leeks. It has a thick stem and a huge underground 'head', up to 10cm (4in) across, of a few enormous cloves. It is brilliant for roasting and has a sweet mild flavour. Use within four months.

Kale

SOW APR, MAY, JUN **plant** MAY, JUN, JUL
harvest JAN, FEB, MAR, APR AND DEC

Kale is a member of the cabbage (brassica) family, but
has its own characteristic flavour and softer leaves that
wilt to be delicate and tender when steamed. If you are
looking to eat vegetables in season, then it is a must as it
is harvested through the winter months, when few other
fresh veg are available.

Cultivation

DIFFICULTY Easy; low input.
SOW in pots or seed trays.
PLANT Transplant into beds as and when the seedlings are
large enough to handle.
SPACE 45cm (18in) apart in each direction.
CARE Keep watered in dry spells through the summer.
YIELD Up to 1kg (2¼lb) per plant.
STORAGE Keep leaves on the plant until needed.

Keep them happy by…

Planting in firm soil – after all, kale is a brassica and this is what
brassicas like.

Worth trying…

'Black Tuscany' ('Nero di Toscana') – Upright plants (can be
spaced 30cm/12in apart); rich flavour from long and narrow,
bobbly deep-green leaves. It can be picked from late summer
to early spring of the following year.
'Pentland Brig' – Tender, tasty, dual-purpose curly kale: pick
leaves in winter and the succulent shoots in spring; use the
latter like broccoli spears.
'Redbor' – Bronze-purple curly kale with crinkly leaves that can
be used young in salads.

Enjoy them…

By picking a few leaves as soon as they are big enough, but
don't take too many at once. Take your main harvest from early
winter (from a mid-spring sowing) onwards. Leave the plants in
situ over winter, as they enjoy a new spurt of growth in spring
and produce a quick crop of succulent young leaves before
running to seed.

Look out for…

Caterpillars can be a nuisance, but they are less of a problem
with kale than on many other brassica crops. Remove them by
hand or use an organic pesticide; keep the plants covered with
insect-proof mesh if it's a real problem.

Clubroot is an ever-present threat (*see* page 184).

Though lacking the exotic appearance of some of its relatives,
'Pentland Brig' is a reliable kale with plenty of flavour.

Kohl rabi

SOW APR, MAY, JUN
harvest JUL, AUG, SEP

This odd-ball vegetable tastes like a mild turnip when cooked, slightly sweeter raw. If you like it, you should give it a go as you'll rarely find it in the shops; if you don't know it, grow it for something unusual to show your friends – you'll probably end up liking it too.

Cultivation

DIFFICULTY Intermediate; medium input.
SOW in situ from mid-spring.
SPACE Gradually thin out plants to 15cm (6in) apart in each direction.
CARE Keep well watered throughout the life of the crop – it's vital the plants never have a check to their growth, otherwise you'll end up with tough hard balls of fibrous matter.
YIELD A 1.5m (5ft) row produces about 10 'balls'.
STORAGE Keeps for up to two weeks in the fridge.

Keep them happy by...

Providing well-prepared, fertile soil with plenty of rich organic matter.

Worth trying...

'Blue Delicacy' – late purple variety of kohl rabi with a mild, turnip-like flavour.
'Kolibri' – Purple globes with white flesh; a juicy F1 hybrid.
'Logo' – Fast growing with white globes; slow to bolt.
'Supershmelze' – Green globes with white flesh; can grow huge, but is not widely available.

Enjoy them...

When the first globes reach golf-ball size (use these raw); work through the crop, eating them all before they reach tennis-ball size. Pull up whole plants, top-and-tail the globes and peel as thinly as you can.

You can grow purple, white or green kohl rabi – they all taste similar, it's just the colour that alters. The different colours do best at different temperatures; white kohl rabi for early crops and purple for later in the season.

Look out for...

It can develop a woody texture, splitting or bolting due to poor growing conditions or a shortage of water.

Clubroot (*see* page 184) could attack, but as the plant grows quickly it is rare. Luckily, caterpillars are not that partial to the leaves either.

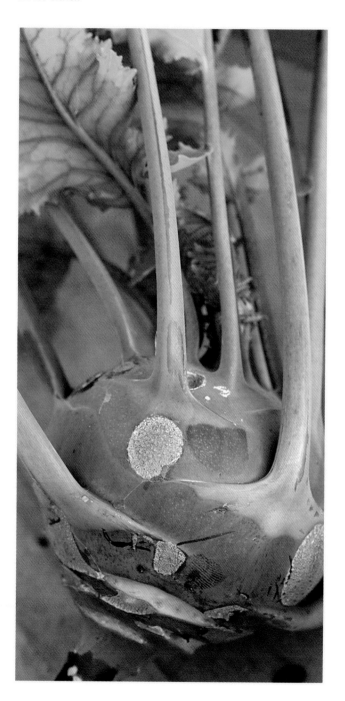

Leeks

SOW MAR, APR plant JUN
harvest JAN, FEB, MAR AND SEP, OCT, NOV, DEC

Leeks are one of those vegetables that are perennially in vogue, and it's easy to see why. Tasty with a good texture, they are extremely versatile in cooking, have a long cropping season and are easy to grow. Grow two or three different varieties to have continuous supplies right through autumn, winter and early spring, and grow summer baby leeks too.

Cultivation

DIFFICULTY Easy; little input.

SOW in seed beds in spring.

PLANT Transplant seedlings when they reach 15–20cm (6–8in) tall.

SPACE 15cm (6in) apart, in rows 30cm (12in) apart.

CARE Plant into fairly firm soil: make a hole 7.5–10cm (3–4in) deep for each seedling using a big dibber or a thick piece of cane. Drop each seedling in place without firming the soil around the roots. 'Puddle' them in with a watering can so the planting holes fill with water.

YIELD A 1.5m (5ft) row produces about 2kg (4½lb).

STORAGE Leave in the ground until needed; they keep in the fridge for up to a week.

Keep them happy by…

Providing good growing conditions and plenty of water. Bolting can occur if plants aren't completely happy.

Worth trying…

'Apollo' – An F1 hybrid with good rust resistance; bred for winter use.

'King Richard' – An early cropper (early autumn to early winter); long, slender stems.

'Musselburgh' – A reliable old variety that withstands hard winters; early winter to early spring.

'Porbella' – Good cropper over a long season from mid-autumn to late winter.

Enjoy them…

A few at a time as soon as they reach a usable size. If you are growing several varieties, it makes sense to use the earlier maturing ones first as they won't last so well through winter.

Look out for…

Just like onions and garlic, leeks are prone to bolting. Some years are worse than others. Use bolters instantly, even if they are still small, otherwise they'll be inedible. Leeks sown very early indoors (in midwinter), tend to produce more bolters than those sown outside in late spring.

They suffer rust, as do all members of the onion family (*see* garlic, page 200); salvage what you can by harvesting leeks to use early. Look out for rust-resistant varieties.

Baby leeks

'King Richard' gives a naturally early crop of long, slender leeks and is ideal for raising babies. Prepare the ground well – as for a seed bed. Sow thinly, making several sowings at three-weekly intervals from early spring to early summer. Thin the seedlings to 2.5cm (1in) apart, but don't transplant. Water carefully and give a regular feed with a general-purpose liquid feed. Start pulling baby leeks when they resemble spring onions. They'll crop from early summer until early autumn. If you have a polytunnel, a sowing in early spring will give you a late spring crop.

Right the way through the winter, leeks can be harvested. Only when the ground is frozen will they be unavailable.

Lettuce and various salad leaves

Aside from the lettuces, there is a wide variety of other leafy plants that can be grown for use in salads (some are also suitable for stir fries and braising). You can grow the plants individually or as a mixed sowing for 'cut-and-come-again'; pre-mixed seed packets are available. Most are easy to grow and can have a long cropping period from successional sowings, (*see* page 167) it's a matter of you choosing the varieties you like best and having a go.

Cultivation

DIFFICULTY Most are easy to grow well, some need a little attention.

SOW Make early sowings in pots or seed trays in a propagator, on a windowsill, or in a cold greenhouse. Prick seedlings out into pots and transplant as the weather improves.

SPACE According to the variety, but usually in rows 30cm (12in) apart.

CARE Lettuces and lettuce-based mixtures need plenty of water and good soil, the rest mostly like water but are less fussy about soil conditions.

Lettuces and salad leaves make an attractive display in the garden – but they're also irresistible to slugs and snails, so you do need to be vigilant.

Look out for...

Slugs and snails are a big threat to most salad leaves. Take precautions continuously, using a biological control from several weeks before sowing (*see* page 279).

Flea beetles make pinprick holes in many salad leaves, especially if the spring and early summer are dry. Attacks rarely kill plants, but the damaged foliage looks uninviting in a salad bowl. Help plants to get established by good soil preparation and generous watering; cover with insect-proof mesh. Greenfly may take a shine to lettuce and lamb's lettuce in particular; brush them off to prevent a build up.

With pre-mixed salad leaf seeds, one variety is often stronger or faster growing than anything else. When you spot the culprit, hoick some of it out while it is young to maintain a better balance of leaf types.

Bolting can occur in hot or dry conditions, particularly in poor soil; remove bolted plants to the compost heap as the salad leaves will taste bitter.

Chinese mustard greens

SOW MAY, JUN, JUL, AUG
harvest JUN, JUL, AUG, SEP, OCT

These are members of the cabbage family and like firm soil and similar growing conditions to other brassicas. They can be grown under cover or protected by gardener's fleece for a longer season. They are suitable for cooking or eating raw in salads.

SPACE 15–20cm (6–8in) apart.

HARVEST As you thin out young leaves, take alternate plants to eat as babies, leaving the rest to grow larger.

The hot, spicy leaves of fresh Chinese mustard greens.

Lamb's lettuce Corn salad, mâche

SOW JAN, FEB, MAR AND SEP, OCT, NOV, DEC
harvest JAN, FEB, MAR, APR AND OCT, NOV, DEC

Providing salad leaves through the winter, lamb's lettuce is best grown under cover or protected with fleece.

SPACE 2.5cm (1in) apart, in rows 15cm (6in) apart.
HARVEST when plants are 2.5cm (1in) across.

Tasty lamb's lettuce.

Mizuna

SOW MAY, JUN, JUL, AUG
harvest JUN, JUL, AUG, SEP, OCT

This is a member of the cabbage family and likes similar growing conditions to other brassicas.

SPACE 30cm (12in) apart.
HARVEST Use the plants as cut-and-come-again and they will provide leaves through the winter.

Young mizuna leaves.

Lettuce

SOW MAR, APR, MAY **plant** APR, MAY
harvest JUN, JUL, AUG, SEP, OCT

The best-known salad vegetable comes in a wide choice of forms, colours, and leaf shapes. Prefers rich, fertile, loose soil. Keep weeds down and water well.

SPACE According to variety.
HARVEST Hearting types are best enjoyed when they have formed a heart; others can be eaten as soon as they're big enough.

Neat conical heads of 'Cos' lettuce.

Pak choi

SOW APR, MAY, JUN, JUL, AUG
harvest JUN, JUL, AUG, SEP, OCT

A member of the cabbage family and requiring similar conditions to other brassicas, pak choi is a great salad vegetable but also wonderful braised or steamed.

SPACE 15–20cm (6–8in) apart.
HARVEST Start pulling whole plants as soon as the bases swell to 2.5cm (1in) in diameter, otherwise the last leaves will have become coarse by the time you get to eat them.

Crunchy pak choi.

Purslane

SOW MAR, APR, MAY, JUN, JUL
harvest APR, MAY, JUN, JUL, AUG, SEP, OCT, NOV

Unlike other salad leaves, purslane has succulent foliage and can cope with hot, dry summers. The seeds may be more difficult than other salads to obtain.

SPACE 7.5cm (3in) apart, in rows 23cm (9in) apart.
HARVEST A few leaves at a time; the plants will continue growing and providing leaves throughout summer.

Succulent purslane leaves.

Rocket

SOW MAR, APR, MAY, JUN, JUL, AUG, SEP
harvest APR, MAY, JUN, JUL, AUG, SEP, OCT, NOV

Another member of the cabbage family, but this one grows under almost any conditions, even on a bright windowsill through winter.

SPACE 10–15cm (4–6in) apart.
HARVEST Pick a few leaves from each plant and leave them to grow; watch out for bolting.

Well-grown rocket.

Onions

Spring onions
SOW MAR, APR, MAY, JUN, JUL
harvest JUN, JUL, AUG, SEP

Winter-hardy spring onions
SOW AUG, SEP, OCT
harvest FEB, MAR, APR, MAY, JUN

Bulb onions – summer, from sets
plant MAR, APR
harvest AUG, SEP

Bulb onions – overwintering, from sets
plant SEP, OCT
harvest MAY, JUN, JUL

Onions are a nice easy crop to grow and you can have something oniony to harvest pretty much all year if you're clever. They might be reasonably cheap in the shops but it's not like eating your own. And it is great to have spring onions and red onions on the doorstep; both make an ordinary salad into something special, as well as being great for cooking.

Cultivation

DIFFICULTY Easy; little input.
SOW a short row of spring onions every 3–4 weeks from early spring to midsummer, then sow an overwintering variety from late summer to mid-autumn. Sow thinly and thin out if the seedlings are overcrowded.
PLANT maincrop (summer) onion sets in early spring, and overwintering onion sets in autumn.
SPACE Thin spring onions to 2.5cm (1in) apart, and allow 15cm (6in) between rows. Plant onion sets 10cm (4in) apart, in rows 20cm (8in) apart.
CARE Keep plants watered in dry spells so they don't suffer a check to their growth, which may encourage bolting.
YIELD Depends on the variety; about 1.3–1.8kg (3–4lb) from a 1.5m (5ft) row.
STORAGE Most maincrops will remain in good condition from early autumn until late winter. Keep them in the light to avoid sprouting. Use overwintering onions within a month or so after they have been harvested.

It's worth growing 'Red Baron' for its appearance alone, but it is also a good cropper and keeps well.

Keep them happy by…

Weeding regularly; when you plant, make sure your onion hoe will fit between your rows, to make weeding less of a chore. Keep the soil evenly moist when they are growing.

Worth trying…

'Garnet' – Maincrop, new version of 'Red Baron'; slightly earlier to mature.

'North Holland Blood Red' ('Redmate') – Reliable, purplish red spring onion for spring sowing; grows on to produce red onions that keep until the following spring.

'Overwintering White Lisbon' – Very hardy spring onion, reliable for autumn sowing in the open (protect with fleece ideally) but best under (cool) cover.

'Radar' – Gold-skinned overwintering onion; good for cold areas or bad weather.

'Red Baron' – Maincrop (summer) red onion with a fantastic flavour, mild enough for salads; keeps well through winter.

'Rosanna' – An improved version of an old favourite maincrop; pink flesh and red-brown skin.

'Senshyu' – Japanese overwintering onion with semi-flattened bulbs.

'Sturon' – Reliable, tasty maincrop (summer) onion; bolt resistant; keeps well through winter.

'White Lisbon' – Classic, white-skinned spring onion for spring/summer sowing; grows on to produce white, silver-skin-type golf-ball-sized onions.

Enjoy them…

As soon as they are big enough. Use the thinnings of spring onions as you would chives, then pull alternate plants as baby spring onions; any left to grow can be used like mild onions. With maincrops, bend the tops over once the leaves start naturally turning yellow or brown to assist ripening; lift the bulbs when completely ripe and leave them in the sun to finish drying before storing in shallow trays in an airy shed. Use overwintering onions fresh from the ground from the time the first few reach usable size (around late spring); keep pulling them as needed.

Look out for…

As with all members of the family, bolting is a problem in some seasons. Choose a bolt-resistant variety and, where possible, buy heat-treated sets, which reduces the risk of bolting.

Mildew, a white or grey fungal growth, is disfiguring and debilitating. Cut off affected foliage and do not store bulbs.

White rot, an unpleasant disease, is quite common in onions, including spring onions; it spreads rapidly and has no cure. The foliage of affected plants turns yellow, then white cotton-wool-like stuff with black blobs in it develops near the base of the plant. The fungus that causes white rot remains in the soil so you won't be able to grow members of the onion family there for years (some say 8, others about 20). Destroy affected plants and foliage and grow onions elsewhere. Practise crop rotation (*see* page 153) to minimize the risk of the disease occurring.

Seed or sets?

As onion seed is short-lived and must be sown fresh, it seems sensible to let someone else take on the task of sowing it. Commercial growers raise young onions until they have made small bulbs called sets. At this point, like any other bulb, they can be harvested and sold. Sets are simply small onions which, when planted, become quickly established and grow into proper-sized onions without the hassle of growing onions from seed.

Parsnips

SOW MAR
harvest OCT, NOV, DEC

Baby-size parsnips
SOW MAR
harvest JUL, AUG, SEP

When you grow traditional parsnips, you have to be patient as they take about nine months to reach hearty roasting size, and they need space. But you can enjoy parsnips much sooner as babies, which take up much less space and save you a packet on what you would pay in the shops. You will need proper baby-parsnip seed as normal parsnip seedlings stay very thin until quite late in their life, so cannot be eaten early.

'Avonresister' is one of the best varieties to grow if you're worried about canker and prefer small portions.

Cultivation

DIFFICULTY Intermediate; low input.
SOW Thinly, about 2.5cm (1in) apart, in situ in deep, rich, fertile soil where manure was not used the previous winter; wait for mild weather if the soil is cold and wet.
SPACE Thin 'normal' parsnips to 15cm (6in) in several stages, babies to 5cm (2in). Space the rows 30cm (12in) apart, less to produce baby veg.
CARE Water in dry spells and weed regularly.
YIELD A 1.5m (5ft) row produces about 1.8kg (4lb); less for babies.
STORAGE Leave them in the ground until needed unless it's very wet, in which case lift them and store in a frost-free shed.

Keep them happy by...

Giving them a well-prepared site that has been deeply dug, is not too stony and has not recently (within the last year) been manured. On stony soil, build a raised bed (*see* page 150). Fanged roots (they are still edible) will be more common if you can't provide these growing conditions.

Worth trying...

'Arrow' and 'Dagger' – Good baby varieties; but try other new baby varieties too.
'Avonresister' – One of the stalwarts of the veg garden; resistant to canker, less likely than most to bolt in adverse conditions and produces good crops even on poor ground. Smallish roots, so space 7.5–10cm (3–4in) apart.
'Tender and True' – The one for flavour; long roots with small cores.

Enjoy them...

From summer (babies) onwards. Dig up roots as required (after the foliage starts turning yellow).

Look out for...

Parsnips can be affected by canker. The roots develop brown scabs, especially round the top, which eat into the flesh. Less-damaged roots can be used once the canker is removed, but some are ruined. It is thought that canker may be caused by too much organic matter or by too much or too little rain. There is no cure; grow canker-resistant varieties, such as 'Avonresister'.

Plants may bolt, making the root fibrous and inedible. It's down to poor growing conditions, sometimes the gardener's fault, sometimes not.

Peas

Early varieties
SOW MAR, APR AND JUN, JUL
harvest JUN, JUL AND SEP, OCT

Maincrop varieties
SOW APR, MAY, JUN, JUL
harvest JUL, AUG, SEP

Mangetout and sugarsnaps
SOW APR, MAY, JUN
harvest JUN, JUL, AUG, SEP

If you want to grow peas, from a time, effort, and result point of view it is best to stick to mangetout and sugar snap types, which are much better than the shop offerings – to say nothing of being less travelled. Shelling podded peas is fun, but it is difficult to do maincrop peas as well as the 'two hours from picked to frozen' brigade, who have the help of all sorts of high-tech equipment. Mangetout and sugar snaps are unaffected by maggots, which can ruin whole crops of 'normal' peas.

Cultivation

DIFFICULTY Intermediate; reasonable input.
SOW Make two or three staggered rows in a flat-bottomed drill about 20cm (8in) wide, so the seeds are about 7.5cm (3in) apart in each direction.
PLANT If you have raised early crops under cover, plant them out in staggered rows, with plants 10–15cm (4–6in) apart in each direction.
SPACE 45cm (18in) between sets of rows for short varieties; 90cm (3ft) for tall varieties, to allow access.
CARE Keep plants watered in dry weather and weed regularly.
YIELD A 1.5m (5ft) row produces about 2.3kg (5lb).
STORAGE Eat fresh. If you want to keep them, freeze them as soon as you pick them (*see* Storage, pages 168–9).

Keep them happy by...

Providing plant support. After sowing, push pea sticks in along the rows of short-growing varieties. Tall varieties are best with 2m (6ft) posts and horizontal wires holding up pea netting.

Worth trying...

'Alderman' – Traditional, 2m (6ft) tall, shelling variety, late to start cropping, but productive over a much longer cropping season than dwarf pea plants. Sow early spring to midsummer.
'Feltham First' – Round-seeded shelling pea suitable for the very earliest sowings in late winter. These dwarf plants, 45cm (18in) tall, need little support.
'Golden Sweet' – Tall mangetout (2m/6ft) with mauve flowers, pale green leaves, red leaf nodes and yellow pods; very decorative, so great for a potager (*see* page 147).
'Hurst Green Shaft' – A delicious second-early or maincrop variety, 75cm (2½ft) tall. Long and heavy cropping.
'Kelvedon Wonder' – Wrinkle-seeded shelling variety on dwarf plants 45cm (18in) tall with good flavour. Sow early spring to midsummer; ideal if you only want to buy one packet of pea seed.
'Oregon Sugar Pod' – Tall mangetout reaching 1m (40in) tall, with a fairly long cropping season; grow outdoors from early spring to midsummer, or early/late under cover.
'Sugar Ann' – Tall sugar snap variety, 1.5m (5ft) high; needs support but crops for a reasonable length of time.

Who could resist a pea like this? 'Hurst Green Shaft' living up to its descriptive name with its young peas just beginning to swell.

'Sugar Snap' – Early sugar snap variety; dwarf 75cm (2½ft) tall so needs little support; can be sown early under cover.

Enjoy them…

When they reach a usable size. Mangetout pods are best at 5cm (2in) long; they never get fat but they can get stringy, so pick and discard any that have 'gone beyond it'. Sugar snaps are best at about 4cm (1½in) long but can be shelled if they've grown too large. Check the progress of shelling peas by popping open one or two of the biggest pods – use them while young, tender, and sweet; don't let them grow big, they get tough and starchy.

Look out for…

Seeds may be eaten by mice or other rodents, and can succumb to cold, wet soil at sowing time.

Powdery mildew (grey-white talc-like powder) on young leaves and tips of shoots can spread to cover whole plants. Old plants and any under cover are prone, and it is worst on dry soil. Keep plants well watered and ensure good air circulation.

Pea weevil makes irregular notches in the margins of leaves; all but the most badly infested young seedlings nearly always

Continuous cropping – for pea fans

■ Plant early and late-shelling pea varieties and make successional sowings for a long season, or choose a tall heritage variety, such as 'Alderman', which has a longer season.

■ Plant tall mangetout varieties; these should crop for six weeks or more.

grow out of it without problems. The weevils, if you spot them, are 6mm (¼in) long and buff-brown with six legs and a short pair of forward-facing antennae.

Maggot larvae of the pea moth tunnel into the pods of shelling peas to eat the seeds and deposit their mess. They can ruin a whole crop of plants at the same time. Either sow early or late, as these crops seem to be less susceptible, or use insect mesh. Mangetout and sugar snap peas don't seem to be affected.

Foot-and-root rot kills the roots – they turn black and the young plants turn yellow. It may be due to overwatering poorly established small plants in cold, dull weather, or an organism in the soil. Put new seeds or plants in a different patch of ground and practise crop rotation (*see* page 153).

For peas out of season

Sow all varieties in trays of multipurpose compost in a cold greenhouse or cool windowsill indoors in late winter.

Shelling peas Harden off seedlings before planting out in a mild spell about a month later. Protect young plants with gardener's fleece. Round-seeded varieties (it'll say on the packet) are best for very early sowings (gamblers might even like to sow them in autumn to overwinter outdoors and produce an early spring crop – results are not guaranteed).

Sugar snaps and mangetout Plant in a greenhouse or polytunnel border once the weather turns milder, usually from late winter. In early spring, sow a few rows of pea seed in situ under cover.

It's also worth sowing a wide row of 'Oregon Sugar Pod' mangetout into a polytunnel border in autumn; plants should overwinter, even if they look rather ropey, to produce a very early crop the following spring.

The secret of growing mangetout and sugar snap peas is to harvest them young and crisp before the pods become tough or stringy.

Peppers

SOW FEB, MAR **plant** MAY, JUN
harvest JUN, JUL, AUG, SEPT

Home-grown peppers are like a more concentrated version of the ones you can buy in the supermarket; they are perhaps less thick-fleshed and juicy, but far more flavoursome. It is easy to get the green fruit, but ripening to red is more likely on indoor plants than those peppers grown outdoors.

Cultivation

DIFFICULTY Easy; little input.
SOW in a heated propagator or on a windowsill indoors at 21–27°C (70–80°F). Prick out the seedlings into individual small pots when large enough to handle, and grow on at 16–19°C (60–65°F).
PLANT Transfer the young plants to an unheated greenhouse in late spring or put them outdoors in early to midsummer. Harden off before planting out – they are frost-tender.
SPACE 45cm (18in) apart; they can grow individually in pots or two to a growbag.
CARE Water in after planting, then water sparingly until plants are growing strongly and starting to flower or bear fruit.

Keep them happy by…

Feeding weekly with liquid tomato feed after the first flower opens to encourage plenty of fruit. Support plants by tying the main stem to a cane.

Worth trying…

'Bell Boy' – Heavy cropping and reliable, often sold as plants in garden centres. The fruits start green, ripening to red. There are other 'Bells' in various colours.
'Big Banana' – Long, tapering peppers to 25cm (10in). Green, ripening through yellow to red.
'Matador' – Bull-horn-shaped sweet peppers; red when ripe.
'Redskin' – Compact, bushy plants, good for containers, with large numbers of oblong green peppers, ripening to red.

Enjoy them…

Green as soon as they are big enough to use – they probably won't grow as big as the ones you buy in the shops. If you want red peppers, leave green peppers to ripen, but be aware the plant won't produce any more fruit during this time. For a larger crop, it is best to use them green and then red. To pick, don't tug or twist since the branches are easily damaged.

Look out for…

Greenfly affect peppers, especially youngsters under cover. Check plants regularly and wipe off greenfly with damp tissue, or use an organic insect spray.

Outdoor plants can fail to produce fruit if growing conditions are poor (lack of sun, cold, dull or windy weather); overwatering can also cause crop failure. In a poor summer, try to move them into a conservatory or enclosed porch for shelter, or drape them with fleece at night and on cold or windy days, for extra protection.

A green pepper ready for harvesting. Cut the short stem with secateurs to avoid damaging the plant.

Potatoes

First earlies
chit FEB, MAR **plant** MAR, APR
harvest MAY, JUN, JUL

Second earlies
chit FEB, MAR **plant** APR
harvest JUN, JUL, AUG SEP

Maincrop
plant APR
harvest SEP, OCT, NOV

Today, a huge range of potato varieties is available to gardeners: bakers, chippers, mashers, salad spuds, novelty and coloured ones, and heirloom varieties – as well as a selection of disease-resistant ones, ideal for organic growing.

Spuds are not grown from seed, nor from any sprouted leftovers you have in your vegetable rack. Instead, you must buy 'seed' potatoes, which are available from garden centres and via mail order in late winter or early spring. These are tubers grown especially for the job and certified disease-free. The ideal seed potato is the size of a hen's egg, but you will find bigger and smaller ones.

Potatoes are known as first earlies (new potatoes), second earlies and maincrop, depending on how early or late in the season they are ready for harvesting. It is traditional to 'chit' first and second early varieties (*see* box) to get them started into growth before planting them out when the weather warms up a little. This gives them a head start as their growing season is shortish. You don't need to chit maincrop spuds, since they have a much longer growing season.

Cultivation

DIFFICULTY Easy; little input apart from regular earthing up (*see* how to earth up, page 173).
PLANT First earlies in early spring; second-earlies a week later and maincrop potatoes a week after that. Plant all tubers 13cm (5in) deep.
SPACE Earlies 30cm (12in) apart in rows 60cm (24in) apart; second-earlies and maincrops 40cm (15in) apart in rows 75cm (2½ft) apart.
CARE Hoe between rows to keep down weeds until the potato shoots are 15cm (6in) high, then earth up the plants (*see* how to earth up, page 173). If frost threatens, earth up as soon as

Chitting

Chitting involves sitting the tubers in a box, such as an old egg box or seed tray, with the growing end facing upwards – recognizable by the cluster of tiny buds ('eyes') on it. Keep them in good light but out of direct sunlight. When the shoots are 1–2.5cm (½–1in) long, the potatoes are ready for planting.

the shoots appear above ground. Except in a long dry summer, you shouldn't need to water potatoes.
YIELD Much depends on variety.
STORAGE Harvest first and second earlies as you need them; they are fine in a cool place for a week or so. Store maincrops, dry and with the soil brushed off, in brown paper or hessian sacks in a cool dark place.

Keep them happy by...

Checking for signs of slug damage. Potatoes are popular with keeled slugs. These live underground and burrow into the tubers, making them prone to rotting. Slugs love organic matter, particularly if it isn't very well rotted, so only plant potatoes on ground that had compost or manure dug in at the start of the previous season. Use the biological control for slugs (*see* page 279); using slug pellets on the soil surface has little or no effect on keeled slugs. Where slug damage is a regular problem, look for potato varieties with in-bred slug resistance.

Worth trying...

FIRST EARLIES

'Duke of York' – Pale yellow tubers for new potatoes or to grow on as later maincrop potatoes; a good choice if you only have room for one variety.

'Foremost' – Firm, waxy, white, salad new potato. Eat hot or cold.

'Mimi' – Small, pink-flushed tubers; compact foliage makes this ideal for container growing.

'Pentland Javelin' – Delicious white waxy potato, ideal salad potato; disease resistant.

'Rocket' – Fast-growing early; large crops of round white tubers; disease resistant. Try it very early under cover.

SECOND EARLIES

'Charlotte' – An attractive and highly popular, superb salad potato with golden skin and firm, waxy, cream-coloured flesh.

'Edzell Blue' – Purplish skin gives this tasty Victorian variety its name. The very floury white flesh makes it a fabulous masher; it tends to crumble when boiled.

'Estima' – Large oval, yellow-fleshed tubers, excellent as summer bakers; plants do well even in dry summers.

'International Kidney' – Of 'Jersey Royal' fame (only when grown there), this has kidney-shaped tubers with a waxy texture.

'Kestrel' – True potato-shaped, off-white tubers with purple rims around eyes. A good all-purpose variety; fair disease resistance.

MAINCROP

'Golden Wonder' – A late maincrop – harvest it after other maincrops. It has red-brown skin and a superb flavour that improves with age. Best for baking, roasting and frying.

'King Edward' – Old favourite with red-variegated tubers, known for its superb flavour, with cream-coloured flesh. Good for roasting and baking, but needs good growing conditions to do well.

'Mayan Gold' – Long, slender golden tubers with firm, golden, nutty-flavoured flesh. Great deep-fried whole or roasted; breaks up when boiled.

Exercise restraint

Unless you have a vast vegetable garden, or an allotment, and the storage capacity to match, it is far wiser to concentrate on growing some tasty earlies (new potatoes) and second earlies, than maincrop potatoes which are inexpensive to buy in the shops. New potatoes have an unbeatable flavour and texture when cooked soon after digging up. If you want to grow maincrop potatoes, pick one or two varieties that you won't get in the shops, such as 'Pink Fir Apple'. If you need more inspiration there are fascinating websites dedicated to potatoes of all kinds, including 'heritage' types.

Easily the most popular salad and new potato, 'International Kidney' (the name derived from its distinctive shape) is better known as 'Jersey Royal' when imported from that Channel Island.

'Picasso' – White-skinned potato decorated with splashes of pink. Cream-coloured tasty flesh. Good for all uses.

'Pink Fir Apple' – An old variety that makes the most fabulous potato salad and is also great baked, if you like a crispy skin. A very late maincrop with long, slim, knobbly tubers, best left in the ground until late autumn. Stores well right through winter.

Extra-early new potatoes under cover

For really early potatoes, buy seed potatoes as early as possible (midwinter, ideally) and chit them immediately (*see* box, page 212). When the shoots are 6mm (¼in) high, wait for a spell of mild weather (around early spring) and plant three tubers 13cm (5in) deep in a 40cm (15in) pot filled with a half-and-half mixture of John Innes No. 3 potting compost and multi-purpose compost, or plant six in a growbag and keep it in a frost-free greenhouse or conservatory with plenty of light. Once all risk of frost is past, the container can be moved outside, but for the very earliest crops,

continue growing them under cover. You could be picking your first new spuds by late spring.

'Mimi' is compact and good for growing like this; other potatoes grown in containers need stem support – the sort sold for supporting bushy herbaceous plants are ideal.

Enjoy them…

From early summer (first earlies), midsummer (second earlies) and autumn (maincrops). Use a fork carefully to dig up each plant individually, pushing the tines in 30cm (12in) or so away from the base and loosen the soil. Take a handful of stems at the base and gently pull – a lot of the potatoes will come up with the roots. Sift through the soil for the rest. Dig up second earlies in the same way.

Earlies often produce enough fair-sized tubers for a meal, even before the plants start to flower (flowering is a good indication that the crop is ready). Use your fingers to pull a few out without disturbing the plants, which will continue to grow.

Maincrops keep quite well in the soil even after the haulm (foliage) has died down, but need lifting before the weather turns wet to prevent attack by black keeled slugs. They may also start to grow again, which affects their keeping qualities.

Look out for…

Tubers affected by scab (irregular corky patches on the skin) look unattractive but are still edible – peeled. The disease is more prevalent on light soil that dries out badly in summer, especially on chalky ground, so adding plenty of organic matter a season before planting does help.

Potato blight is the most serious potato disease. Outbreaks are most likely during a wet summer; affected plants develop brown patches on the leaves (in damp conditions you'll also see white fungal rings around the brown spots on the backs of the leaves) in late summer and the foliage very quickly yellows and dies off. Early potatoes are rarely affected, since the tubers have usually been lifted before blight strikes, but if midsummer is rainy, start spraying plants with Bordeaux mixture to prevent the disease. Once it gets hold there's no cure. Dig up affected crops straight away and use tubers that are sound. Destroy the remains of affected plants; do not compost them.

Several different viruses affect potatoes: the edges of the leaves roll inwards, or leaves may develop yellow mosaic patterns. Viruses are often spread by aphids feeding on the leaves, but often occur when people save their own tubers to replant instead of buying seed potatoes. Affected plants are stunted with low yields.

It is best not to try to peel a 'Pink Fir Apple', but they taste just as good with the skin on.

There is nothing like harvesting potatoes to bring out the big kid in you. It's like striking oil.

Radishes

Summer radish
SOW MAR, APR, MAY, JUN, JUL, AUG
harvest MAY, JUN, JUL, AUG, SEP

Winter radish (including Chinese, Japanese, Mooli)
SOW JUL
harvest AUG, SEP, OCT, NOV

Radishes are the traditional accompaniment to a typical English salad, but can do so much more besides in stir fries and as crudités. They are a very quick crop – the quickest in fact, but this doesn't make them all that easy to grow. There are also oriental and winter radishes with large roots ready to pull in autumn and winter – they are worth trying for a change.

Cultivation
DIFFICULTY Easy; average input to provide what they need.
SOW In situ in succession throughout the growing season.
SPACE Thin summer radish seedlings to 2.5cm (1in) apart; allow 15cm (6in) between rows. Thin winter radishes to 5–7.5cm (2–3in) apart with 30cm (12in) between rows.
CARE Keep plants watered and well weeded. Thin out seedlings early.
YIELD As many as you like to sow.
STORAGE Summer ones are best eaten the day they are pulled, but will keep for a few days in the fridge. Winter ones can be stored for a short while in a cool dry place.

Keep them happy by...
Planting them in good, rich, well-drained fertile soil; but not anywhere that's recently had organic matter dug in or roots may split or fork.

Worth trying...
'French Breakfast' – Traditional cylindrical summer radish; red with a small white area at the base; very reliable.
'Mantanghong' or 'Beauty Heart' – Chinese winter radish; huge, tennis-ball-sized with green rind over red flesh. Crisp and sweet; make good 'vegetable crisps' or crudités.
'Mirabeau' – Long thin radishes with the traditional pink and white colouring; suitable for early sowing under cover as well as outdoors.
Mooli – Various types of Japanese winter radish with often

These 'French Breakfast' radish can be sown straight into the ground from early spring until mid-summer and will be ready for harvest in three to four weeks.

huge, hot-tasting, long, tapering to cylindrical white roots; used in oriental cookery.
'Scarlet Globe' – Popular, traditional, round, cherry-red summer radish; can be sown early/late under cover for out-of-season crops.

Enjoy them...
As soon as the first summer radish reaches useable size. Don't delay – they grow fast and then turn tough and woody, or bolt. From late summer if they are winter radishes. You'll have to dig, not pull, them up. Any left in the ground by late autumn should be dug up and stored in a dry, frost-free shed. Mooli varieties keep quite well until midwinter.

Look out for...
Poor soil, hot or dry conditions can all cause bolting.
Overcrowding or leaving it too late before thinning out seedlings will prevent roots developing freely.
Flea beetle can attack (*see* lettuce, page 204); a severe attack can kill small seedlings but is unlikely to harm bigger plants.

Shallots

plant FEB, MAR
harvest JUL, AUG

No longer grown simply for sloshing about in vinegar, shallots are now considered superior versions of onions. They have a more delicate appearance and lovely mild flavour and are as easy as onions to grow, with fewer problems. No reason not to pickle them still, though, if you prefer. Like onions, you buy them as sets; each set produces a cluster of offsets.

Cultivation

DIFFICULTY Easy; little input.
PLANT with a trowel, just covering them with soil.
SPACE 20cm (8in) apart in rows 30cm (12in) apart.
CARE Weed frequently and water in prolonged dry spells.
YIELD Up to 1.8kg (4lb) from a 1.5m (5ft) row.
STORAGE Spread them in shallow trays in a frost-proof shed or garage, or hang them up in a net in the shed roof; they'll last through winter.

Keep them happy by...

Planting the sets out of sight, under the soil. If they get pulled up shortly after planting, birds are the culprits. Replant them so that the tops are just covered this time. The problem stops when the shallots start taking root.

Worth trying...

'Golden Gourmet' – Large, golden-brown bulbs. Good flavour and a good keeper.
'Hative de Niort' – Very neat, small, globular, identical shallots popular for showing; not a very heavy cropper and can be difficult to find as sets.
'Jermor' – Tall, lean, upright shallots. Coppery skins and pink-tinged flesh; superb flavour.
'Prisma' – New variety; disease resistant with red skin and white flesh.
'Red Sun' – Rounded bulbs with rich, red-brown skin; good flavour and a long keeper.

Whereas with onions the single set, or bulb, grows bigger, with shallots it splits to produce a number of offsets.

Enjoy them...

After the leaves have turned yellow naturally in late summer. Lift clumps carefully with a fork, shake off the soil and put them on the ground to dry off in the sun before storing.

Look out for...

Poor growing conditions can cause crop failure or small offsets. This could be due to poor infertile soil, cold wet weather or lack of water. Have you been a good weeder? Shallots, like all onions, hate competition from weeds.

Onions growing with shallots in a well-tended vegetable bed.

Spinach

Summer spinach
SOW MAR, APR, MAY
harvest MAY, JUN, JUL, AUG, SEP

Autumn spinach
SOW AUG, SEP, OCT
harvest SEP, OCT, NOV

Spinach is so convenient to buy in neat bags, ready washed, but it is also pretty easy to grow and you can have it much cheaper and fresher that way, still bursting with health-giving nutrients. Most of the modern varieties are dual-purpose: you can eat them raw in salads when the leaves are tiny and then cooked when they're bigger.

Cultivation

DIFFICULTY Easy; low input.
SOW Thinly in rows in situ, or scatter in large tubs or in an intensive salad bed. If you want baby salad leaves, sow every 4–6 weeks during the sowing season. (Note: not all seeds are suitable for sowing in autumn; check the packet.)
SPACE By thinning to 2.5cm (1in) apart for baby leaves, or 7.5cm (3in) for cooking-size leaves – use thinnings in salads.
CARE Water and weed assiduously. It's essential for the plants to grow steadily without a check. Seeds sown in early summer are less likely to succeed as the summer months are too hot and the soil too dry for most spinach varieties; if they do grow they are likely to bolt. Grow other salad leaves (*see* pages 204–6) during the height of summer.
YIELD Up to 2.3kg (5lb) from a 1.5m (5ft) row.
STORAGE Best eaten just-picked, but will keep for a couple of days in the fridge and can be frozen (*see* Storage, pages 168–9).

Keep them happy by…
Providing rich, fertile soil containing enough nitrogen.

Worth trying…
'Bordeaux' – Bright red leaf stalks and leaf veins make this ideal for baby salad leaves. Can also be sown in late winter and from late summer to autumn.
'Galaxy' – Mildew-resistant variety for baby leaves. Can be grown through the winter under cover, even on a bright windowsill.
'Medania' – All-round variety for sowing in spring or summer to produce 'baby' spinach leaves, also in autumn to grow under cover for cutting the following spring.

Enjoy them…
As baby leaves as soon as they are big enough to use, usually within a month of sowing. Cut the crop little and often. For cooking, start cutting leaves when the plants reach a suitable size (6–8 weeks after sowing) – don't wait too long or they will bolt and the leaves won't be so tasty.

Look out for…
Downy mildew can affect crops, especially those under cover, particularly in cold, dull, humid weather; modern disease-resistant varieties fend off all but the worst attacks.

Bolting is triggered by high temperatures, shortage of water or poor soil with insufficient organic matter, but spinach plants are not long-lived anyway and all run to seed eventually. Sow frequently for a continuous supply.

The leaves of spinach 'Bordeaux' are coloured by rich red stalks and veins, which makes them pretty in the garden as well as tasty on the plate.

Perpetual spinach

SOW APR, MAY, JUN, JUL
harvest JUL, AUG, SEP, OCT

Perpetual spinach is excellent for providing you with a spinachy vegetable nearly all year round. It is less fragile than 'real' spinach, the same plants are easily capable of surviving the hotter summer months and on through winter in milder areas. In flavour and texture, it's very much like Swiss chard, but without the thick midribs. Only one variety is usually available.

Winter crops

Remember to sow a row or two of perpetual spinach in midsummer under cover. The resulting plants will stay in perfect condition through the winter and start growing again in spring, producing enormous crops of large, tender, unblemished leaves until they run to seed in late spring.

Alternatively, sow perpetual spinach seed outdoors in midsummer and protect the plants with fleece over winter. They can survive the cold without protection, but the leaves will be battered and unfit to use.

Cultivation

DIFFICULTY Easy; little input.
SOW thinly in rows where you want the plants to crop.
SPACE seedlings by thinning to 15cm (6in) apart with 30cm (12in) between rows.
CARE Keep plants watered in dry spells and weed regularly.
YIELD Up to 2.3kg (5lb) from a 1.5m (5ft) row.
STORAGE Best eaten just-picked, but will keep for a couple of days in the fridge.

Enjoy them...

As soon as the leaves are big enough to use; don't over-pick plants – cut little and often from all over the row and allow plants to recover between times.

Look out for...

Slugs can be a nuisance, but this is really a trouble-free crop.

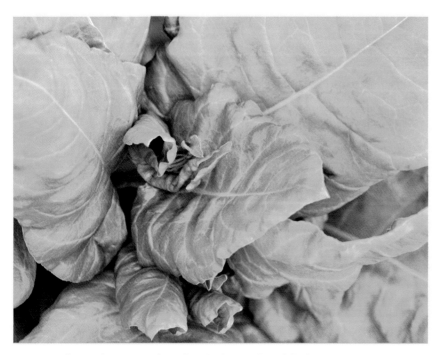

Perpetual spinach is more robust than 'real' spinach and the leaves are more shiny and a bit tougher – they don't cook down to such a pulp. The taste is also slightly different, but just as good.

New Zealand spinach

SOW APR, MAY, JUN
harvest JUN, JUL, AUG, SEP, OCT

The shoots of New Zealand spinach are excellent steamed, but not for use raw in salads. It thrives in the hot conditions that 'normal' spinach hates. The same plants crop all summer right up to the first proper frost. Under cool cover the cropping season is slightly longer and the plants may self-seed, or you can collect the seed.

Sow the seed in a hot, sunny, sheltered spot with well-drained soil. Thin the seedlings to 15–20cm (6–8in) apart, with 45cm (18in) between rows. Water sparingly, if at all; keep well weeded until plants cover the ground, when no weeds will be able to grow.

Start picking as soon as plants are a just a few inches high; cut or snap off tips of shoots about 2.5–5cm (1–2in) long. Pick little and often, at least two or three times a week to keep plants productive – that is, bushy and leafy.

Squashes and pumpkins

SOW APR **plant** MAY, JUN
harvest OCT

Squashes and pumpkins make huge plants and need plenty of room – and they don't repay the space with quantity, it must be admitted – but they are easy to grow and kids love them. While they can be good for soup, pumpkins are usually more popular for making Halloween lanterns, while squashes tend to be more versatile and are great roasted or added to seasonal autumn stews and pies. (For summer squashes, *see* under courgettes, page 194).

Squashes are renowned for their odd shapes, and few are odder than the aptly named 'Turk's Turban' – bright orange, streaked with cream and green; best roasted for its roast-chestnut flavour.

Cultivation

DIFFICULTY Easy; low input after good soil preparation.
SOW singly in pots on a windowsill indoors or in a heated propagator in the greenhouse at 18–24°C (65–75°F). Grow on at 13–18°C (55–65°F) – a cool room or shaded, sheltered cold frame is ideal.
PLANT Harden off and plant when the last frosts are safely past, from late spring. After planting, surround each plant with a ring of soil, about 30cm (12in) from the stem; fill this with water each time you water.
SPACE 90cm (3ft) apart.
CARE Water sparingly at first. As the plants get going, water regularly to keep the soil moist and feed with liquid fertilizer. Weed until the plants cover the ground and smother the competition. Slowly reduce the feeding and watering towards the end of summer to encourage the fruit to start ripening, and as early autumn arrives, carefully remove foliage overshadowing the fruits to allow the sun to reach them and develop their full colour.
YIELD Three fruits per plant.
STORAGE Allow the fruits to dry in the sun, turning them over so the underneath can dry too. Store them in a dry, frost-free shed or garage where they should keep for several months; alternatively, bring them indoors to a dry, coolish room.

Keep them happy by...

Planting them in very rich, very well-manured soil or dig a large hole in autumn and spend winter filling it with materials you'd usually put on the compost heap. In spring, cover it with a mound of soil and plant there. You can even grow them on the compost heap – put a few inches of soil on top first.

Worth trying...

'Avalon' and 'Harrier' – versions of the butternut squash (the light-bulb-shaped, beige squash that greengrocers sell). The true butternut is unlikely to ripen even in a good summer, but these have been bred for our weather conditions.
'Becky' – The ideal Halloween pumpkin.
'Crown Prince' – Medium-sized, squat, steely blue-grey pumpkins with orange flesh; good for roasting and pumpkin soup.
'Hasta La Pasta' – Long, bright orange, marrow-like squashes; it yields 'vegetable spaghetti', obtained by baking whole then removing the shredded flesh in the centre using a fork.
'Sweet Dumpling' – Small, green-striped, cream squashes produced at the rate of 4–6 per plant. Delicious baked and stuffed whole or sliced and roasted.

Enjoy them…

Once they are ripe; allow them to grow to full size on the plant then cut them carefully, leaving a short length of stem. Pick them all up off the ground by mid-autumn, before sitting on cold, damp ground causes rotting on the undersides of the skins.

Look out for…

Mosaic virus (*see* courgettes, page 194) can affect pumpkins and squashes – look out for yellow mottling on the leaves and poor growth. Pull out and destroy affected plants.

Mice and larger rodents may nibble the skins of pumpkins, especially before they ripen and harden; make sure your compost heaps are not home to such wildlife before planting in them.

Slugs may damage young fruits while the skins are very soft, and damaged areas deform as the fruits grow larger. It's not usually a problem unless you want a perfect specimen for showing; deep wounds may allow in fungal organisms, which cause rot in a damp season.

In a good year you can have many more pumpkins and squashes than you can eat, but they store well and are very decorative.

Growing a monster

Choose the right variety, such as 'Atlantic Giant', 'Big Max', 'Dill's Giant Atlantic', 'Hundredweight', 'Sumo Giant'.

Start plants and harden off as normal. Plant using the pit-full-of compost method. After planting, cover the plant with a cloche or fleece for protection (uncover it on fine days), until it grows too big or the weather really warms up.

Allow three fruits to set and start to swell, then select the largest and remove all the rest. This means the plant directs all its energies into just the one fruit. Weed, water and feed as normal. If you are really keen, bury the trailing stems in very good soil, only just covering them. They will grow roots to help feed your monster pumpkin.

To improve your chances and choice, grow several plants, spaced 2–3m (6–10ft) apart.

'Atlantic Giant' is capable of growing to enormous proportions.

Swedes

SOW MAY, JUN
harvest JAN, FEB AND SEP, OCT, NOV, DEC

Perhaps because it is cheap and not very pretty, the poor old swede has a reputation for being staid and boring, but mashed with carrots or potato and with some butter and pepper added, it is a great comfort food. Perhaps it would be more popular if we called it by its more exotic American name of rutabaga?

Cultivation

DIFFICULTY Easy; little input.
SOW seeds thinly in situ in early summer – timing is critical.
SPACE seedlings by thinning in several stages until they are 23cm (9in) apart, allow 40cm (15in) between rows.
CARE Hoe regularly and water well in dry weather – keep the soil evenly moist, as wide fluctuations between wet and dry conditions can cause the roots to split and spoil.
YIELD Up to 6.8kg (15lb) from a 1.5m (5ft) row.
STORAGE They keep best in the ground until needed, but dig them up if your garden is on heavy clay or if prolonged freezing temperatures are forecast.

Keep them happy by…

Giving them an open, airy situation in full sun; don't grow them crowded together or overshadowed by surrounding crops.

Worth trying…

'Brora' – A new variety with excellent flavour, purple skin and yellow flesh.
'Invitation' – Modern variety with purple-flushed skin, bred for resistance to clubroot and mildew.
'Marian' – The traditional flavoursome variety with purple tops and yellow-cream bases; very resistant to mildew and clubroot.

Enjoy them…

Towards autumn when the roots become big enough to use; you don't have to wait until they are the size of the ones in the shops. Pull individuals as you want them and leave the rest to continue growing.

Look out for…

They can suffer clubroot like all brassicas (*see* page 184). Choose a resistant variety.

Powdery mildew can also be a problem; again the answer is in your choice of variety.

The swede is long overdue for a comeback – it's a tasty, hearty root vegetable that's also pretty easy to grow and a great addition to winter soups and stews.

Sweetcorn

sow APR **plant** MAY, JUN
harvest JUL, AUG, SEP

For true fans, the only way to eat sweetcorn is picked fresh from your own crop and cooked minutes later. The sugars start to turn to starch as soon as the cob is removed from its parent, so every minute counts. If you find frozen or tinned sweetcorn too sweet it could be that you are eating the supersweet varieties; try growing a 'normal' variety – you may find it more to your taste.

Cultivation

DIFFICULTY Easy to intermediate; lowish input.
SOW one seed per small pot on a windowsill or in a heated propagator at 16–21°C (60–70°F) in spring. Grow on in slightly cooler temperatures. Harden off for planting out when the frosts are over, in early summer.
PLANT sweetcorn in blocks not rows, as the plants are wind-pollinated and this is the best way of ensuring good pollination.
SPACE 45cm (18in) apart in each direction.
CARE Cover young plants with fleece on cold nights to help them establish quickly. Water in dry spells. No support is needed, even though the plants grow quite tall.
YIELD Two cobs per plant.
STORAGE Eat as soon as picked, or freeze as soon as picked.

Keep them happy by...

Planting them slightly deeper than the soil level in the pot. This encourages tillering – putting out small side shoots and more roots – and makes the plants more stable.

Worth trying...

'Applause' – Supersweet F1 new(ish)comer.
'Incredible' – Sugar-enhanced, reliable variety; ripens mid-season.
'Minipop' – For baby corn cobs 10–15cm (4–6in) long; plant all baby varieties only 20cm (8in) apart and pick before pollination (the tassels are still silky and pale).

Modern varieties of sweetcorn, such as 'Golden Bantam' are bred for reliability in our unreliable climate. They are late-ripening, so good for extending the cropping season when grown with an earlier one, such as 'Sundance'.

'Sundance' – 'Normal' F1 variety with 18cm (7in) cobs; matures early and crops reliably, even in poor summers.

Enjoy them...

As soon as the cobs ripen in late summer. You can tell they are ripe as the silky tassels turn brown and dry up, but you should double-check by testing the cobs too: peel back a little of the leaf-like green sheath to expose a few kernels and press a thumbnail into one or two – if clear liquid spurts out the cob is not quite ripe; when it's ready to pick the juice is milky.

Look out for...

Poor pollination can mean that you have gappy cobs – areas without kernels. They are still edible.

Fruit fly larvae distort the developing tips of young plants so that they grow stunted and twisted and produce unusable, underdeveloped cobs. Protect young plants with insect-proof mesh and pull out and destroy affected plants.

Swiss chard

SOW APR, MAY, JUN, JUL
harvest JUL, AUG, SEP, OCT

Swiss chard is a great green vegetable, like a mild spinach but with more substance – it doesn't cook down to mush. As well as being quite tasty, it looks attractive in the garden with its big shiny leaves and white leaf stalks. There are also varieties with orange or pink leaf stalks and leaf veins and these look wonderful with the morning or evening sun shining through them.

Cultivation

DIFFICULTY Easy; little input.
SOW in mid-spring to midsummer in rows outside.
SPACE 15cm (6in) apart with 30cm (12in) between rows.
CARE Keep plants watered in dry spells and weed regularly.
YIELD 1.4kg (3lb) from a 1.5m (5ft) row.
STORAGE Pick and use fresh rather than store.

Worth trying ...

'Bright Lights' – A mixture of red-, white- and yellow-stemmed varieties; its decorative qualities are its main asset. The thinnings can be used to brighten salads.

Ruby chard – Slender bright red stems and purple-tinged dark green leaves; it is not quite such a strong grower as Swiss chard, so grow it if you want decoration as well as food.

Keep them happy by...

Doing next to nothing; they are very easy to please.

Enjoy them...

As soon as individual chard leaves are big enough to use, around midsummer from early sowings. Use a sharp knife to cut through the stem at the base of the plant, taking care not to slice into neighbouring stems. Early-sown chard plants are usually finished by the autumn, but midsummer-sown crops often withstand a mild winter. If there's a really cold spell they may die down, but regrow in spring to produce a short-lived crop of tender leaves before running to seed in late spring. The leaves can be steamed or cooked like spinach; the leaf stalks boiled like celery, but most folk stick to cooking just the leaves since the flavour of the stalk is nothing to write home about!

'Fordhook Giant' has long, thick, white, flattened and ribbed stems with glossy, crinkled, dark green leaves; connoisseurs are sure that the flavour is better than that of the coloured varieties. It reaches the large size of 55–68cm (22–27in) tall and 30cm (12in) across.

Look out for...

Snails can make a meal of them, but they often prefer to hide in the bigger leaves, which you won't want to eat anyway. Check them carefully when you wash them before cooking. Otherwise this is a trouble-free crop.

Tomatoes

Indoor
SOW FEB, MAR **plant** APR, MAY
harvest JUL, AUG, SEP, OCT

Outdoor
SOW MAR **plant** MAY, JUN
harvest JUL, AUG, SEP, OCT

Cherry, plum and giant beefsteak, yellow, brown, white and striped – you could eat a different tomato on almost every day of the year, so great and wide is the choice. They are not the most accommodating of plants, though, being quite demanding and prone to almost as many problems as there are varieties, but even if you experience difficulties one year, you're sure to succeed the next. In the end, home-grown tomatoes are worth it.

Cultivation

DIFFICULTY Intermediate; they crave attention – don't turn your back on them.

SOW seeds on a windowsill indoors or in a heated propagator at 18–21°C (65–70°F) from late winter to early spring for plants for growing in an unheated greenhouse, or mid-spring for growing outside. You can sow a little bit later if you live in a cold area; it makes no sense to have plants that are 60cm (24in) tall at planting time – 30cm (12in) is better.

PLANT in the greenhouse (in soil borders or pots) from mid- to late spring, avoiding cold spells. Plant outdoors after the last frost is safely past, usually late spring to early summer.

SPACE 60cm (24in) apart in borders under cover; outside plant them 75cm (2½ft) apart with 90cm (3ft) between rows.

CARE You'll need to support the plants and feed, water, tie up and trim them regularly. Anticipate spending a bit of time on caring for your tomato plants every week on top of routine watering (*see* box on page 226 for specifics).

YIELD Varies with the type.

STORAGE Eat fresh, or make into sauces to freeze (*see* Storage, pages 168–9).

Worth trying…

'Ailsa Craig' – Traditional and popular cordon for outside or under cover; medium-sized round, red fruits. Often available as young plants at garden centres at planting time.

'Brandywine' – US beefsteak cordon variety for under cover; large pink fruits with outstanding flavour and potato-like leaves.

'Gardener's Delight' – Hugely and deservedly popular cordon for outdoors or under cover; huge trusses of sweet, cherry-sized tomatoes are among the first to start ripening.

'Green Grape' – Cordon best grown under cover or on a very warm and sheltered patio; bite-sized green fruits ripen from jade green to yellowy, lime green; exceptionally sweet and mild, almost like a real grape.

'Ildi' – Cordon for under cover or outside; bunches literally dripping with small, sweet, teardrop-shaped, yellow fruit that ripen in succession – almost too many to eat.

'Marmande' – A French beefsteak cordon with lobed, red fruits for growing outside; 'stop' the plants (remove the tops of the

If you have a penchant for really big 'meaty' tomatoes, you can't go far wrong with 'Brandywine', but you do need to grow it in a greenhouse or polytunnel.

main stems) after two or three flower trusses have set fruit, as they can't support a huge crop.

'Roma' – Bushy variety reaching waist-high for indoors or outside; flavoursome and nicely shaped, red plum tomatoes, lots of juice and few seeds.

'Sungold' – Cordon for outdoors or under cover; lots of small orange-yellow cherry tomatoes of superb flavour.

'Tigerella' – Cordon best under cover; striking large, striped fruit with a tangy taste; the fruit are light and dark green at first, ripening to orange-yellow then to red with orange stripes.

'Tornado' – Outdoor bush variety that does well even in a poor summer, with very well-flavoured, medium, round, red fruits.

'Tumbler' – Compact, trailing, easy-to-grow bush tomato, ideal for hanging baskets, window boxes or tall containers; it produces a modest crop of small, round, red tomatoes.

Enjoy them…

Straight from the plants when they have ripened fully. Indoors this can be from midsummer, outdoors from late summer. If you aren't going to eat them straight away, snip them off just above the green calyx to help them keep better. In a good season, plants will continue to ripen fruit until late autumn under cover, early autumn outdoors.

In late summer, start removing new flowers (they'll never fruit) and remove the growing tip (or tips, in bush varieties). Reduce the amount of watering drastically. Remove a few of the lower leaves, especially those that are already yellowing, to allow more light and air to circulate.

When you want to clear the plants, remove any full-sized green tomatoes and put them in a dark place indoors. Don't put them on a sunny windowsill – this makes them shrivel up without ripening. You could put them in a box with a ripe apple or banana, since the fruit gives off ethylene gas, which hastens maturity – though not flavour, but it's better than nothing.

Look out for…

Tomatoes suffer from many ailments.

Soil-borne diseases build up when they are regularly grown in the same soil. Eventually your crop will hardly be worth having. Problems are more common in soil borders under cover and can be rectified by digging out and replacing the soil as far as possible or using growing bags or pots instead.

Split fruit occurs as result of stress, caused when plants are alternately wet and dry at the roots. Avoid it by watering little

It's always so tempting to try different tomato varieties – there are so many of them – but in the end, among the cherries, 'Gardener's Delight' always comes out near the top.

and often. It's common on outdoor plants during a dry summer when there's suddenly lots of rain. Pick affected fruits – they're usually the riper ones anyway – and purée them so they don't go to waste.

Blossom end rot is a sunken, black leathery patch on the base (or blossom end) of the tomato. It is most common in container plants – especially those in growing bags – and is due to the plants occasionally being allowed to dry out. To prevent it, water regularly. Plants grown in the ground are rarely affected. Outdoor tomatoes are susceptible to potato blight (see page 214). Keep a close watch for early symptoms (brown patches on the leaves), particularly if there is rain in early and midsummer, and, as with potatoes, spray outdoor tomatoes with Bordeaux mixture as a precaution. Repeat every fortnight and you may save the crop. Once leaves start looking dead and both ripe and unripe fruit develop brown, rotten-looking patches, it's too late. Tomatoes grown under cover are less likely to be affected but they aren't totally immune, since the spores can enter through ventilators and doors. A few blight-resistant varieties are starting to become available.

Botrytis affects different parts of tomato plants in different ways: fluffy, grey sunken patches on stems, grey mouldy flowers that drop off without setting fruit, small, round, translucent 'ghost spots' on the skin of green tomatoes. It's more of a problem under cover; avoid it by ventilating more and limiting watering to the base of the plants to avoid excess humidity in the air. In a particularly bad case, use a suitable fungicide.

Whitefly are little white flies that live on the undersides of the leaves and fly out when you tap the plant. They suck sap and secrete sticky honeydew, which may then grow sooty mould. They are difficult to control as the young are tough and scale-like. Use a biological control (*see* page 280) under glass. They're less of a problem outdoors, but if you have had an attack last year grow companion plants; fuzzy-leaved marigolds, *Tagetes minuta*, grown alongside the tomato plants will help deter them. Sticky traps can be effective, but they can also catch beneficial insects.

'Tigerella' has a slightly tangy flavour and its colour really makes a difference in salads.

Keeping them happy

PLANTING

You are almost always going to get a better crop from plants grown under cover, but it is worth having a few plants outdoors in a sunny sheltered spot.

In a greenhouse, plant into a soil border that's been well prepared or use pots 40cm (15in) in diameter and filled with a mixture of John Innes No. 2 potting compost and multipurpose compost (half and half). In the ground outside, plant tomatoes in a warm sheltered spot and give them slightly more room (*see* Cultivation notes). Growing bags are another choice, either under cover or outdoors, but limit yourself to two plants in each one and do take extra care with the watering – it can be difficult to get right.

WATERING

Immediately after planting, give each plant ½ litre (1 pint) of water, then let it go slightly short of water until the first flowers open. Gradually increase watering when the green fruits start to swell. Container-grown plants carrying a crop of ripening fruits need watering once or twice daily; those in the ground can make do with every few days. Into the soil beside each plant, sink a 10cm (4in) plastic flowerpot or an upside-down plastic bottle with the bottom cut off, pour the water into this so that the water goes straight to the roots.

FEEDING

Start feeding with liquid tomato feed while the young plants are still in their pots, prior to planting out. After planting, feed once a week, make this twice a week once they start carrying a crop.

SUPPORTING AND TRAINING

Cordon (single-stemmed varieties) need a single cane. Bush varieties do better with three shorter canes to support their bushier shape. Tie the main stems to the canes to stop them being weighed down by the developing crop and breaking. Tie in new growth every week. With cordon tomatoes, remove all the sideshoots that grow in the angle where each leaf joins the main stem. This needs doing every week. Bush tomatoes don't need their sideshoots removed; if they grow too big and bushy, however, you could thin out the growth a bit.

Turnips

Under cover
SOW MAR AND AUG, SEP
harvest MAY, JUN AND OCT, NOV

Outdoors
SOW APR, MAY, JUN, JUL
harvest JUN, JUL, AUG, SEP

As far as baby vegetables go, it is hard to beat turnips. At this size they are still tender and have a wonderful flavour, not to mention a range of interesting colours that look great on the plate. You can eat them raw when they are young, too, and if you do let them grow a bit big, you can always stew or bake them with other veg for what nowadays is an unusual treat.

Like swedes, turnips have a reputation for being staid in the taste department, but that's only because the ones we remember eating were probably months old before they reached our plate. Fresh home-grown turnip is something altogether different.

Cultivation

DIFFICULTY Easy; low input.
SOW Early under cover, later outdoors, thinly in situ.
SPACE 2.5cm (1in) apart for baby veg; 5cm (2in) apart for normal crops. Allow 15–20cm (6–8in) between rows.
CARE Water regularly and keep well weeded to avoid competition and to ensure the plants grow steadily without a check, otherwise they tend to become fibrous and tough.
YIELD 1.4–1.8kg (3–4lb) from a 1.5m (5ft) row.
STORAGE They keep for a few days in the fridge.

Keep them happy by…

Remembering that they are a member of the brassica family and need to be given similar growing conditions: especially well-prepared firm ground.

Worth trying…

'Atlantic' – Traditional-looking, reliable turnip, like a flattened ball with a purple top; good for sowing early and late under cover, as well as outdoors. Known to the French as 'navets'.
'Golden Ball' – A round turnip with flavoursome golden flesh; grow outdoors.
'Snowball' – Long-established turnip with sweet white flesh.
'Tokyo Cross' – If you can find it, it is great for sowing under cover. Produces its pure white little balls of flavour in six weeks.

Enjoy them…

When they are almost 2.5cm (1in) across. Pull them up gently. Turnips more than 5cm (2in) across are too fibrous and lacking in flavour, by this stage they are only fit for the chickens.

Look out for…

It is a brassica and prey to clubroot (*see* page 184). There are currently no resistant varieties.

Turnip gall weevil is caused by a larva living inside the root, which it hollows out, causing distortion that looks similar to clubroot. Cut a root open: if it's gall weevil you'll find the tunnel; if it's clubroot the flesh will stink. Gall weevil isn't a problem – just throw away affected roots.

Flea beetle likes turnips and will sprinkle leaves with tiny round holes. Use insect-proof mesh, tucked in well around the plants, to protect turnip crops as a severe infestation will check their growth underground, which you don't want at all.

A–Z of Herbs

It may seem like a bit of a cliché, but no vegetable garden is complete without a selection of culinary herbs, and once you start cooking with your own home-grown vegetables it is a natural step to grow your own herbs to accompany them.

Herbs to grow

Herb plants are available from garden centres and supermarkets but it is also well worth a visit to a herb farm, where the proprietors will be able to provide you with lots of advice about growing, storing and using these plants. Start out with a few tried-and-tested favourites and then expand your herb collection as you expand your repertoire of recipes. Remember, too, that many herbs don't like the rich, moisture-retentive growing conditions that you have created in your vegetable patch, so provide them with what they need.

Basil

SOW MAY, JUN
plant JUN, JUL, AUG
harvest JUN, JUL, AUG, SEP, OCT

Basil is among the most popular culinary herbs. Its soft, bright green leaves and wonderful clove scent make it a great addition to the vegetable garden or kitchen windowsill. It is slow growing from seed, but the intense flavour of home-raised basil leaves is worth the wait.

Cultivation
DIFFICULTY Intermediate; it needs above average input.
SOW and plant in pots on windowsills indoors at room temperature all year round, or in a greenhouse or conservatory in summer. Thin out very overcrowded seedlings, but allow several young plants to grow in the same pot to make a bushy 'plant'.
PLANT these potfuls outside in a container filled with multipurpose compost, or plant them in the ground in a warm, sheltered sunny spot in well-drained humus-rich soil.
SPACE Individual potfuls about 15cm (6in) apart.
CARE Water sparingly, little and often; use a general-purpose liquid feed regularly on container plants to encourage them to remain leafy. As soon as flower buds appear at the tips of the shoots, nip them off to encourage further leafy growth.
STORAGE Basil can be dried, but its flavour is never as good.

Keep it happy by...
Giving the seedlings warmth; seeds started indoors are more likely to succeed. The plants also like plenty of sun and fertile soil. Sow new plants every month or so, to maintain supplies.

Worth trying...
'Genovese' – A cultivar renowned for its fragrance and the traditional basil for pesto, but a good all-rounder as well.
Bush basil – A compact, dome-shaped bush with small leaves.

The most commonly grown basil is 'Genovese' – it's the one sold in supermarkets. It has shiny, soft leaves that are bursting with a clean clove and mint taste.

'Ararat' – This variety has green leaves flecked with purple.
'Kemangie' – This is also called lemon basil and combines basil and lemon flavouring.
'Neapolitana' – This variety has very large crinkled leaves with a good strong flavour.
'Purple Ruffles' – The chief attraction of this basil is its extravagantly ruffled, rich purple leaves.

Enjoy it...
Start picking little and often as soon as the leaves are big enough to use. Don't remove whole shoots as this will set the plants back.

Look out for...
The seedlings are prone to damping off and young plants may develop black stem bases due to cold or damp conditions.

Greenfly is common, especially on indoor plants. Move plants grown in pots outside in summer to improve ventilation and to enable natural predators to do their bit. Avoid using pesticides as you are going to eat the leaves!

Bay

plant MAY, JUN, JUL
harvest YEAR ROUND

Bay is a versatile herb that is used in any number of dishes, from stews and soups to marinades and sauces, and is a key ingredient in bouquet garni, along with parsley, thyme and other herbs. The leaves are tough so are usually removed before the food is served. The plant itself is an evergreen that is capable of growing into a large bushy tree in southern counties, but is usually seen trained as a smallish, globe- or cone-shaped shrub, often in a large container.

Cultivation

DIFFICULTY Easy; low input.

PLANT small specimens outside after the last frosts; they need good growing weather to become established before winter.

SPACE You are unlikely to need more than one bay plant. Give it plenty of space.

CARE Water and liquid-feed pot-grown plants throughout summer. In winter, bring trained pot plants into a greenhouse or sheltered corner of the garden; water sparingly if the compost dries out. Plants growing in open ground only need pruning and are otherwise self-sufficient. Use secateurs to prune the shape back into trained plants in mid-spring; remove whole leaves, don't cut into them.

STORAGE You won't need to store any as you can pick leaves fresh all year round.

Training a standard

You will need a single-stemmed plant. Push a cane into the pot or soil beside the stem and tie it in to keep the growth straight. Remove sideshoots until the plant reaches the top of the cane, then nip out the very tip of the plant to encourage sideshoots to develop all round the top. When they are 7.5–10cm (3–4in) long, remove tips to encourage them to branch. Continue doing this until you have a dense head of foliage. Prune in spring to maintain its shape; and again in late summer.

Sometimes called bay laurel, bay makes an attractive addition to the herb garden and keeps it leaves all year round.

Keep it happy by…

Growing it in a bright sunny spot and providing pot-grown plants with plenty of water and food in the growing season.

Worth trying…

Bay (*Laurus nobilis*) – Only this species is available. It has oval, dark, evergreen shiny leaves.

Enjoy it…

At any time of year. Choose undamaged, full-sized but young leaves for cooking.

Look out for…

Pot-grown specimens are particularly prone to scale insect attack. These browny yellow creatures attach themselves to the undersides of leaves, usually along the main veins. Their sticky secretions encourage sooty mould, which is unattractive and spreads quickly. Wash the leaves with a soft cloth or cotton wool ball wetted with soft soap or washing-up liquid (diluted as you would for washing up) to remove the pests and the mould.

Chives

plant APR, MAY, JUN, JUL
harvest MAY, JUN, JUL, AUG, SEP

Chives are among the best known of herbs. The mildly onion-flavoured leaves are hollow and tubular and wonderful chopped up in salads, particularly potato salad. They are one of the ingredients for *fines herbes*: the others are traditionally chervil, parsley and tarragon. The rounded heads of lavender-purple flowers appear in early summer, decorating the vegetable garden and attracting bees. Chive plants are perennial and can be lifted and divided at almost any time to increase your stocks. They may even gently self-seed.

Cultivation

DIFFICULTY Easy; virtually no input.
PLANT pot-grown clumps in late spring or summer.
SPACE Clumps about 15cm (6in) apart.
CARE Water in new plants and weed when necessary.
STORAGE They don't store unless dried, so pot up a clump and bring it indoors for use over winter.

Keep them happy by…

Watering during dry periods. You can remove the spent flowerheads by simply pulling gently on the flowering stem, which will come out neatly from the base of the plant. Do this as necessary through the summer.

Worth trying…

Chives (*Allium schoenoprasum*) – This is the only widely available form. Its rounded heads of flowers are 2.5cm (1in) across on 15cm (8in) stalks and held just above the tops of the plants. White chives (*Allium schoenoprasum* 'White Form') – White-flowered chives are rare but sometimes sold by herb nurseries. Garlic chives, Chinese chives (*Allium tuberosum*) – The flat, narrow leaves of this perennial species have a mild garlic flavour. The plants are taller than common chives, at 30cm (12in) high, and have clusters of white flowers at the top of the stems in summer.

Enjoy them…

As soon as the leaves are long enough to cut. Cut the leaves at their base, about 2.5cm (1in) above the ground, and take a few from each clump so that the appearance of the plant isn't spoiled.

Dig up and divide a clump of chives at the end of summer. Plant a couple of small clumps into small pots and replant the rest in the garden. Cut down the top growth in the potted clumps to 2.5cm (1in) and bring them indoors. They will respond by re-shooting, providing you with fresh leaves over winter.

Look out for…

Chives can grow spindly if overcrowded by other plants or if in too much shade. Move them into the light. Lanky plants with yellowing or broken and bent leaves can be cut down to 2.5–5cm (1–2in) above the ground and will soon make fresh new growth.

Chives produce generous quantities of small lavender-purple flowerheads, which are long lasting and beloved by bees.

Coriander

SOW MAY, JUN, JUL
harvest JUN, JUL, AUG, SEP

Coriander is well known for its deeply cut, aromatic leaves, which are added to soups, salads and all manner of other dishes, but its seeds are also invaluable and have a delicate but exotic spicy flavour. They are used in the subtle Indian spice mixture garam masala. There are coriander varieties bred specially for leaf production; they are well worth going for as they have a long season, otherwise you tend to get flowers and seeds far too quickly.

Cultivation

DIFFICULTY Intermediate; needs some special care.
SOW in rows or patio containers every six weeks or so from late spring until midsummer. You can also sow coriander on the kitchen windowsill to have fresh leaves all year round. To harvest coriander seed, you need to sow by May.
SPACE The seedlings of seed-bearing varieties 7.5–10cm (3–4in) apart, with 30cm (12in) between rows. With leaf coriander thin only if the plants are very overcrowded and use the thinnings in the kitchen.
CARE Water sparingly as seedlings may damp off if allowed to get too wet.
STORAGE Dry the seeds on a shallow tray then store them in screw-top glass jars in a cool, dark place. Grind them just before use for maximum flavour.

When well grown, coriander is a lush plant with delicate divided foliage.

Keep them happy by...

Making sure you weed around the plants. Coriander doesn't like being crowded and you are less likely to get a good crop of seeds if it is. And put them somewhere warm, sheltered and sunny – they won't thrive in cool conditions.

Worth trying...

FOR SEEDS 'Moroccan' and the species (*Coriandrum sativum*) – These will produce heads of tiny white flowers on stalks about 60cm (2ft) high, followed by seeds. 'Moroccan' is particularly fast to flower and set seed.
FOR LEAVES 'Cilantro' and 'Leisure' – These are leaf varieties of coriander and particularly good for later sowings. You can grow them as a cut-and-come-again crop, keeping them around 10cm (4in) tall.

Enjoy them...

As leaves as soon as they are big enough to use: the same plants should re-shoot several times if you are careful to leave at least 2.5–5cm (1–2in) of growth above the base of the plant.

For seeds it is best not to cut the leaves at all. The flowerheads start to produce green seeds towards the end of the summer. When these turn buff-brown, cut the stems and hang them upside down in a warm, airy place out of direct sun. Tie paper bags over the heads to catch any seeds that drop.

Look out for...

A cold wet summer can mean the plants struggle. In this case place pots of leaf coriander on an indoor windowsill. Seed coriander can be grown in the soil border of a greenhouse or polytunnel, but watch out for high humidity, which can cause fungal disease.

Dill

SOW APR, MAY, JUN
harvest MAY, JUN, JUL, AUG

This statuesque herb has pale green feathery leaves on tall stems and flat flowerheads like yellow cow-parsley. It is a decorative plant for a flower border as well as the corner of your veg garden. Dill has an aniseed taste and it is popularly used for baking and poaching fish, particularly salmon, but the feathery leaves can also be used as a garnish, like parsley, and their unique flavour is pleasant in green salads. They are also used in mustard sauces.

The leaves of dill are so feathery as to be hardly leaves at all. A full-grown plant makes a magnificent specimen.

Cultivation

DIFFICULTY Easy; virtually no input.

SOW in pots indoors or on a patio from mid-spring. For leaves you can make successional sowings (through the winter if indoors), but for seeds you need to start early and plant the seedlings out for a long season of growt h.

SPACE Seedlings to 10–15cm (4–6in) apart by removing a few from the pots; don't disturb the roots.

CARE Water sparingly in dry spells, but be careful as the plants dislike wet conditions.

STORAGE Cut the flowerheads when the seeds have formed and dry them upside down in a dry airy place. Put paper bags loosely over the heads to prevent any seed falling where you don't want it. Store the dried seeds in a screw-top glass jar until they're needed.

Keep it happy by…

Providing an open, sunny, well-drained growing site for your seed-producing specimens and grow leaf-producers in containers for best results.

Worth trying…

Dill (*Anethum graveolens*) – This is the species and the usual variety that is grown. It reaches 90cm (3ft) tall if it is allowed to flower and set seed.

'Mammoth' – This variety is grown specifically for seed production. It is less leafy and runs to seed early.

Enjoy it…

As soon as there is enough leaf to harvest. The plants can be used as a cut-and-come-again crop. Regrowth will occur, but sow a new batch of seeds once you are about halfway through the first for continuous supplies. Avoid using the leaves of seed plants if you want to avoid spoiling your garden display; the seeds form towards the end of the summer and can be collected straight off the plants.

Look out for…

The plants are susceptible to poor conditions – a wet, cold summer, or heavy, wet soil can spell disaster. Keep some indoors so that at least you get something, no matter what the weather is like.

Fennel

SOW APR, MAY, JUN, JUL
harvest MAY, JUN, JUL, AUG, SEP

This herb is quite like dill but a little more robust, producing taller (1.5–1.8m/5–6ft) cane-like stems of feathery leaves; it is an attractive addition to any garden, vegetable or decorative. The seeds and leaves are delicately aniseed flavoured. The leaves are traditionally used in fish cooking, and are also good with eggs and in salads, while fennel seeds are a necessity for many Indian and Middle Eastern dishes. A handful of fennel seeds are also good to chew as a breath freshener.

Like dill, fennel has feathery leaves, though they are somewhat darker and finer. The flat yellow flowerheads last throughout the summer months.

Cultivation

DIFFICULTY Easy; virtually no input.
SOW a few seeds in a pot in spring, thin them carefully and plant the whole clump without breaking up the rootball.
SPACE One plant will be plenty, give it at least 60cm (2ft) in each direction.
CARE Fennel needs little care apart from watering until it is established. At the end of autumn, cut down the stems to 2.5–5cm (1–2in) above the ground and the plants will re-grow next spring.
STORAGE Cut the flowerheads when the seeds have formed and dry them upside down in a dry airy place. Put paper bags loosely over the heads to prevent any seed falling where you don't want it. Store the dried seeds in a screw-top glass jar until they're needed.

Keep them happy by…

Raising them in a pot to begin with; although your own plants will self-seed like mad, bought seeds sown in the open don't do so well.

Worth trying…

Fennel (*Foeniculum vulgare*) – This is the usual green-leaved form with strong, feathery leaves and yellow cow-parsley-like flowers throughout summer and early autumn.
Bronze fennel (*Foeniculum vulgare purpureum*) – This has dark bronze-purple foliage and is excellent in decorative borders with tall plants such as common foxgloves and delphiniums, as well as pale pink roses. It self-seeds producing a mixture of purple-leaved and green-leaved seedlings.

Enjoy them…

As soon as the leaves are large enough. Use young leaves as these are most tender and have a better flavour.

Look out for…

Self-seeding is the only problem, so remove fading flowerheads if you don't want seeds to form.

Self-sown seedlings

If you don't deadhead your fennel, you will get abundant self-sown seedlings. If you want them, fine, if not, pull out unwanted ones while they are still tiny, otherwise their tap roots will break off when you pull and the plants will regrow.

Lemon grass

SOW FEB, MAR, APR, MAY
harvest YEAR-ROUND

A principal ingredient in Thai cooking, as well as other exotic cuisine, lemon grass is a somewhat coarse plant, capable of reaching 1.2m (4ft) high, with rough grassy leaves. A native of India, it is tender, so in the British winter it needs to be cosseted in the warm as a houseplant, although it will survive in a sheltered place outside over the summer. Keep it away from areas where young children play as the leaves are very sharp-edged – one of its other common names is barbed-wire grass.

The sleek but sharp-edged foliage of lemon grass.

Cultivation

DIFFICULTY Easy; low input.
SOW Indoors at room temperature in spring or early summer.
PLANT As an alternative to growing from seed, you can root a piece of bought lemon grass in a jam jar of water. Pot it up when the roots are 1cm (1½in) long, which won't take very long, except in winter.
SPACE Grow on in pots; two or three lemon grass plants will give you all you need.
CARE Keep the plants in a sunny situation; in winter they need a temperature of at least 13°C (55°F) or even warmer – room temperature. In summer, move them to a conservatory, where they are quite heat-tolerant if they are kept well watered, or put them out on a warm, sunny patio. Water generously, particularly in summer.
STORAGE The harvested stems stay fresh for some time in the fridge, or in a jar with their bases in about 2.5cm (1in) of water.

Keep them happy by...

Watering generously during hot dry weather. Repotting or dividing as the plants grow bigger.

Worth trying...

Lemon grass (*Cymbopogon citratus*) – This is the only form. It makes a dense clump of grassy leaves reaching 30cm (12in) across and 75cm (2½ft) high in a couple of years. It can be kept in check in a smaller pot, but will need plenty of regular feeding and watering to flourish.

Enjoy them...

As soon as the plants have developed slightly swollen, whitish stem bases – after about a year. The best way to harvest stems from an established plant is to divide the clump and replant one or two stems, keeping back what you need for the kitchen.

Look out for...

No problems, except for those sharp leaves.

Marjoram and oregano

SOW APR
plant MAY, JUN
harvest MAY, JUN, JUL, AUG, SEP

Marjoram and oregano both belong to the same genus – *Origanum* – and are similar in flavour, though oregano is usually more pungent. They are excellent combined with tomatoes, such as in pizza topping, and as a complementary flavouring for meat, particularly lamb; oregano is the main herb used in Greek salad. The bushy plants are easy to look after and are attractive with strongly aromatic leaves and tiny pink or white flowers which are loved by bees and butterflies.

Cultivation

DIFFICULTY Easy; very low input.
SOW thinly in pots on a windowsill indoors; plant out as potfuls rather than pricking out seedlings.
PLANT them out from mid-spring after the last frosts. As two or three plants will provide you with plenty of leaves, it is often simpler to buy them (cheaply) from garden centres and nurseries. This will also make it easier to grow several different varieties. Over the growing season, the sprawling stems often grow roots, and these roots can be removed to make new plants in midsummer.
SPACE Plant 23cm (9in) apart, or use them as decorative plants around the garden or in pots.
CARE Water in well, and water in very dry spells. Remove the dead flowerheads. Sweet marjoram does not survive the winter, so pull out old plants in late autumn. Leave perennials over winter, giving them a haircut in mid-spring.
STORAGE In a good growing season the leaves will contain plenty of aromatic oils and the best can be dried for storage in a screw-top glass jar.

Keep them happy by…

Providing them with a warm, sheltered growing position with plenty of sun and they will produce very aromatic leaves.

Worth trying…

Greek oregano (possibly as subspecies of *O. vulgare*) – This variety has bristly aromatic leaves and is the one for Mediterranean cookery and barbecues. It could do with winter protection as it is not reliably hardy.
Pot marjoram (*Origanum onites*) – This is the best for general use. It is an evergreen perennial, 30cm (12in) wide and high, with deep mauve flowers in midsummer, usually grown from cuttings.
Sweet or knotted marjoram (*Origanum majorana*) – This strongly aromatic, slightly floppy plant reaches about 30cm (12in) high and has clusters of tiny white flowers. It is grown as an annual.
Wild marjoram (*Origanum vulgare*) – Reaching 45cm (18in) high and wide, this small, evergreen, spreading plant has slightly hairy leaves and very small mauve flowers. It grows wild and is highly aromatic but does not develop a particularly strong flavour. The cultivar 'Aureum' has attractive golden leaves.

Enjoy them…

As soon as the plants have enough growth.

Look out for…

Poor growing conditions – cool weather and lots of rain – affect the strength of the flavour. Put some in well-drained pots on a sunny patio to recreate their baking homeland.

Wild marjoram (above left) and its golden-leaved variety 'Aureum' (above right) make pretty garden plants and are very popular with insects, particularly bees, but they aren't the best for cooking flavour.

Mint

plant APR, MAY, JUN
harvest MAY, JUN, JUL, AUG, SEP

Mint sauce with lamb and chopped mint on new potatoes, peas or broad beans are classic British uses of this herb, but it can do so much more besides: mint is excellent as a tea infusion, in flower arrangements (where it also acts as a fly repellent), and it also adds character to some Middle Eastern dishes. When well grown they are attractive plants with deliciously aromatic leaves.

Cultivation

DIFFICULTY Easy; will grow with no input, but better results come from harder work.
PLANT Buy young plants of named varieties from herb farms, nurseries or garden centres and plant them in humus-rich, fertile, moisture-retentive soil.
SPACE One plant of each of your favourite varieties is enough; allow 45cm (18in) between them. Mint can spread rapidly; to avoid this plant it in a largish bottomless container, such as an

Pineapple mint (*Mentha suaveolens* 'Variegata') looks unusual with its milky white variegation and has a good compact habit, but it lacks culinary virtues.

old bucket, sunk into the ground but with about 5cm (2in) of the rim showing.
CARE Water in new plants and water regularly in dry spells. Mulch and feed with a general-purpose fertilizer each spring when new growth first appears.
STORAGE The leaves can be dried for winter use but this is a herb best used fresh.

Keep it happy by…

Not cutting it back in midsummer. This has been traditional to encourage more leafy shoots, but, in fact, the flowers don't harm the plant in any way and they attract bees and butterflies, which is never a bad thing. When the flowers have faded, cut the flowered stems down to 5–7.5cm (2–3in) above ground and new shoots will soon appear.

Mint quickly exhausts the soil, so dig it up in spring every other year just as growth re-starts and replant one strong young section in a new site with freshly prepared ground.

Worth trying…

Apple mint (*Mentha suaveolens*) – This has large, slightly hairy, crinkly leaves and branching spikes of lilac flowers. The delicate flavour is good for mild mint sauce or jelly.
Eau de cologne mint (*Mentha* x *piperita* f. *citrata*) – Not surprisingly, the dark green, smooth leaves of this mint smell of eau de cologne. It's good with potatoes and peas, and is the very best variety for cutting for decoration.
Spearmint, or garden mint (*Mentha spicata*) – This is the commonest kind, with almost shiny, deep green leaves that have serrated edges, and mauve flowers. It's the best mint for mint sauce or to cook with new potatoes or peas.

Enjoy it…

As short sprigs as soon as the plants are growing well. You can continue harvesting throughout summer. Pot up some rooted stems or take 10cm (4in) cuttings in late summer for continued supplies of leaves over winter.

Look out for…

Mint falls prey to powdery mildew in mid- to late summer, just after it has flowered. Cut the plant to 5–7.5cm (2–3in) above the ground, feed and water it well and apply a 2.5cm (1in) mulch; strong new shoots should soon appear.

Mint rust produces small orange-red spots on the foliage. Pick off and destroy affected leaves.

Parsley

SOW MAR, APR, MAY
harvest MAY, JUN, JUL, AUG, SEP, OCT

No kitchen garden is complete without parsley: plant it and find ways to use it, such as in stocks, sauces, as a traditional garnish, in potato salads, green salads and as a partial or total replacement for the basil in pesto sauce. The flat-leaved type is considered superior to the curly-leaved type in cooking, but this, as we all know, is excellent as a garnish. Parsley is best grown afresh each year as it runs to seed very quickly in its second season.

Cultivation

DIFFICULTY Easy; low input once it has germinated.
SOW Thinly where you want it to grow, or in small pots; plant these out without disturbing the rootball as parsley doesn't transplant well. Thin in situ seedlings as necessary. Sow seeds in pots on the windowsill for a year-round indoor supply, every three months should be sufficient.
SPACE Thin plants to 15cm (6in) apart with 15cm (6in) between rows.
CARE Water regularly. Remove yellowing leaves. Replace plants when they seem 'tired' or if they start running to seed.
STORAGE It is really best eaten fresh, so keep those indoor pots going over winter. Alternatively, freeze it in bunches in plastic bags or chopped up and made into ice-cubes.

Keep it happy by...

Sowing in quite rich, moisture-retentive soil – parsley is greedy. Feed the plants every few weeks using a general-purpose liquid or soluble feed. This ensures that they grow strongly with that rich green colouring and flavour.

Worth trying...

Flat-leaved parsley – This is the non-frilly, flat-leaved type, which is sometimes called French or Italian parsley. It makes bushy plants of about 30cm (12in) high, with deeply serrated and shiny leaflets.
'Lisette' – An improved curly-leaved variety with clouds of leaves on plants reaching 60cm (24in).
'Moss Curled' – The favourite curly-leaved variety, with rich green very frilly leaves on short plants.

Enjoy it...

As individual leaves, removed complete with stalks, as soon as they are large enough. Choose good specimens, leaving behind the youngest and oldest.

Look out for...

Seed germination can be very slow. Low temperature is almost always the problem. Try a pot indoors in temperatures above 16°C (60°F). Thin them slightly if necessary and pot on the whole clump.

Bolting will occur when you least want it to happen. Sow regularly to always have a fresh supply.

'Moss Curled' parsley is the one we Brits tend to favour, and for good reason: it has a lovely rich colour and very good flavour.

Rosemary

SOW APR, MAY, JUN, JUL
harvest APR, MAY, JUN, JUL, AUG, SEP, OCT

Rosemary leaves are wonderful for flavouring roast potatoes, vegetables and meat, particularly lamb; they are widely used in Mediterranean cooking and salad dressings, and a few sprigs chucked on barbeque coals will fill the air with fragrance. Beside all this, the shrubby plants with their blue flowers make a decorative contribution to any garden and some varieties can survive and produce their highly aromatic leaves in the least promising conditions, even in a shady, north-facing spot in milder areas, though they do prefer something warmer.

Cultivation

DIFFICULTY Easy; very low input.

PLANT As a young potted specimen, readily bought from herb farms, nurseries or garden centres, in a warm sheltered spot with well-drained soil. One or two will be enough, unless you want to make a low hedge.

SPACE Allow 60–90cm (2–3ft) between rosemary and its neighbours; if you are planning a low hedge of rosemary, 30cm (12in) is adequate.

CARE Water new plants in and keep them watered in dry spells until they are well established.

STORAGE If you aren't too greedy, you should be able to pick leaves throughout the year. However, rosemary does store well: when you prune or clip the plants, save the tips (about 15cm/6in long) to dry. Wash them then dip them for a second or two in boiling water followed by cold water. Hang them in small bunches away from sunlight.

Keep it happy by…

Trimming plants in midsummer after the first flush of flowers. Remove long straggly branches to prevent splitting at the base.

Worth trying…

Common rosemary (*Rosmarinus officinalis*) – This is the widely available species and it reaches 90cm (3ft) or more high and wide; it's attractive in the garden and good for culinary use. Prostratus Group (also known as *R. lavandulaceus*) – This compact, low-spreading rosemary is slightly less hardy than other kinds. It has light blue flowers and highly aromatic leaves that aren't the best for cooking. It can be clipped formally and is

'Miss Jessopp's Upright' – As the name suggests, this version is tall and vertical, perhaps reaching 1.5m (5ft) high; it has pale violet flowers speckled with deeper blue. It is good for training as a mid-height hedge.

good in a pot by the kitchen door or even in a hanging basket. 'Severn Sea' – This is a smaller, mound-shaped plant, more or less 75cm (2½ft) high and wide. 'Tuscan Blue' – An upright type with dark blue flowers.

Enjoy it…

As sprigs when the plants are large enough. The shrubs are evergreen, so you can cut for cooking at any time of year, though the flavour is most intense during the growing season.

Look out for…

Rosemary has few problems but a recent invader from the continent, rosemary beetle, is proving to be a pest, mainly in south-east England but also in other parts of Britain. The beetles are small, oval, metallic-green with purple stripes and they eat the foliage of rosemary and other Mediterranean herbs, especially lavender, thyme and sage. At present, there's no chemical deterrent to protect plants against rosemary beetle, so pick them off by hand.

Sage

plant APR, MAY, JUN, JUL
harvest APR, MAY, JUN, JUL, AUG, SEP, OCT

With its soft leaves in green, purple or variegated with white, sage is an attractive garden plant as well as being the traditional ingredient in stuffing. Don't limit yourself to using it with onions, its talents are much more varied: butters, sauces, breads, in place of a bay leaf in almost any dish and with vegetables as well as meat.

Cultivation

DIFFICULTY Easy; low input.
PLANT Young specimens – easily purchased from garden centres and herb farms – in a sunny and sheltered spot with well-drained soil.
SPACE You'll only need one culinary variety but allow 60cm (2ft) between it and it's neighbours. Ornamental sages need less space – 45cm (18in) will do.
CARE Water in new plants; once established, sage is fairly drought tolerant. Prune plants in spring to tidy their shape.
STORAGE Pick perfect leaves in summer, dip them briefly into boiling water then cold, and lay them out thinly on baking sheets to dry in the airing cupboard or another dark, warm, dry place. Store them in screw-top glass jars.

Common sage is capable of making huge mounds of soft sage-green foliage. It makes a wonderful garden plant as well as a good culinary herb.

Replacement cuttings

Take cuttings, 10cm (4in) long, from the tips of strong, healthy stems in early summer. Remove the lower leaves. Fill a 10cm (4in) pot with a mix of half and half potting grit and multipurpose compost and insert up to five cuttings. Stand the pots indoors out of direct sun. Pot them in late summer and keep under cover for the first winter.

Keep it happy by...

Giving it plenty of time to get established before winter sets in. It is hardy, but will do better this way. Take cuttings of older plants (5 or 6 years old) in late spring or early summer to ensure you always have some sage (*see* box).

Worth trying...

Common sage (*Salvia officinalis*) – This is a wide and low, bushy plant 60cm (2ft) high and 90cm (3ft) wide. Its heavily aromatic leaves are soft, textured and grey-green; the purple-blue flowers attract bees.
Golden sage (*Salvia officinalis* 'Icterina') – This attractive sage grows to 45cm (18in) high and has gold and light green leaf variegation. It is quite a strong grower and is good for cooking and in flower arrangements.
Purple sage (*Salvia officinalis* 'Purpurascens') – Smaller than the species at 45cm (18in) high and a little wider, this has wonderful purple-grey leaves that are just as good for cooking, and purplish flowers.
Tricolor sage (*Salvia officinalis* 'Tricolor') – Although pretty with its mauve, cream and green variegated leaves and blue-toned flowers, this sage is slow and its growth is fairly weak. It is better as an ornamental and in flower arrangements than for cooking and is likely to succumb to winter wet if you don't have it in ideal growing conditions; take cuttings just in case.

Enjoy it...

As soon as the plants are large enough not to miss a few leaves. It is best from early spring to autumn, after which the leaves wither and are not pleasant to use. Dry some for winter.

Look out for...

Sage suffers from attack by rosemary beetle (*see* page 239).
   Wet weather can kill off some stems. Old sage bushes tend to flop open and the central thick woody stems don't produce new leaves. As a last resort, cut them back hard in spring, or just prune regularly in spring so as to avoid needing to do this.

Thyme

plant APR, MAY, JUN, JUL
harvest YEAR ROUND

There is an enormous range of thyme cultivars and many are ornamental as well as culinary. It's fun to make a collection, but bear in mind that some aren't really very useful for cooking. As an added bonus bees love the flowers, which appear from early to midsummer. In the kitchen thyme is one of the traditional ingredients of bouquet garni and its strongly aromatic flavour adds zing to breads, stuffings, stews, risottos and a variety of fish and meat dishes.

Cultivation

DIFFICULTY Easy, when grown in the right conditions; low input.

PLANT Pots of thyme plants are easily and cheaply bought at garden centres and herb farms. Plant them in a sunny spot with poor, very well-drained soil.

SPACE Bushy, upright types 23cm (9in) apart, but allow 30cm (12in) for spreading varieties.

CARE Water in and provide water during very dry weather while they are establishing themselves; after this, watering is rarely necessary. Give plants a trim to improve their shape and remove any dead stems in spring. Take cuttings to replace plants every third year (*see* rosemary, page 239), but make the cuttings smaller) from midsummer to early autumn.

STORAGE Dry surplus thyme in summer, but not when it's flowering. Dip whole stems briefly in boiling water then cold water, then hang them upside down to dry in an airy place out of direct sunlight. When perfectly dry, rub the leaves off the stems with your fingers and store them in screw-top jars in a cool, dark place.

Keep them happy by...

Providing really poor, really well-drained soil. Use lots of grit to make it that way, or grow them in raised beds or containers in a half and half mixture of John Innes No.1 and potting grit. Don't feed them; they like it tough. Plant them early in the growing season, as even though thyme is a hardy perennial, the plants will find it easier to survive if they are well established by winter.

Worth trying...

Caraway thyme (*Thymus herba-barona*) – A very low, creeping species only 5cm (2in) or so high, spreading up to 30cm (12in),

Common or garden thyme (*Thymus vulgaris*) is a mound-forming thyme, reaching about 30cm (12in) high and two-thirds as wide. This popular culinary thyme has dark green narrow leaves with a strong flavour and aroma, and dark mauve-pink flowers.

with caraway-scented shiny green leaves and delicate rose-purple flowers.

Lemon thyme (*Thymus* x *citriodorus*) – This is a diminutive bushy plant, 15cm (6in) high with a mild lemony flavour. 'Aureus' has yellow leaves.

Orange thyme (*Thymus* x *citriodorus* 'Fragrantissimus') – This thyme's small grey leaves are strongly orange scented; its flowers are pale pink or white and appear in June/July; good for putting under duck while it's roasting.

Thymus x *citriodorus* 'Bertram Anderson' – This is a spreading, dual-purpose variety – good for cooking and ornament. It is 10cm (4in) high but up to 60cm (2ft) wide, with mildly lemon-flavoured, gold-variegated leaves and mauve-pink flowers.

Enjoy them...

As short shoot tips when the plants are well established. Regular harvesting ensures you get plenty of new shoots to cut. Thymes can be picked all year round, though the warm sun of summer produces the best flavours.

Look out for...

They are sensitive to unsuitable growing conditions. Too much wet will cause their demise, particularly through the winter, and avoid humus-rich soil at all costs.

Plant care and propagation

Gardening can be enormously creative, but, as anyone who's ever pulled on a welly knows, there's a deal of day-to-day upkeep to consider too. Now, I know that sounds dull, but once you know what you're doing and why, it needn't be dull at all. It can be enormously rewarding. Routine jobs, like weeding and watering, keep you close to the plants, the soil, and all the other living things, helping you to get to know them better. And there's little more satisfying than raising new plants from old, to add that personal touch to your garden.

Pruning

Pruning has been described as the removal of parts of a plant for a particular purpose, but it's not usually that simple. Often there will be several objectives rather than just one. Before you prune anything, you must have an idea of what you hope to achieve and how the plant should respond. Knowing how it will look once the pruning is complete (and through the coming seasons) should influence what you do.

Some plants can be left largely to their own devices and will still grow reasonably well. After all, many trees and shrubs grow happily in the wild and are never pruned, although you might want to cut them back a little to suit the size and shape of your garden. At the other end of the spectrum, some plants are constantly clipped – often two or three times each season, in the case of topiary – resulting in amazing garden 'sculptures'. Generally, though, a bit of routine pruning is beneficial for plants; to improve their health, vigour, performance and shape or to restrict its size (*see* pages 244–5).

Remember that pruning will not solve all of the growth, performance and habit problems a plant may experience, and no amount of pruning will ever correct or control a plant when it's growing in the wrong place. For instance, a large tree may have to be cut back severely on an annual basis, to the

point where it bears no resemblance to its true natural form and habit, simply because it has been planted too close to a house or building. Similarly, a hedge of the highly vigorous × *Cupressocyparis leylandii* (Leyland cypress) will never look right in a small suburban garden, no matter how often it's cut back, and it will dwarf and shade neighbouring plants in no time.

Always use the right tools. Secateurs are fine for smaller stems, but never strain them. Use loppers and pruning saws for larger stems or branches.

These are both examples of the wrong plant in the wrong place and, sadly, the only realistic solution is to remove them and replace them with other plants that are more suited to the surroundings.

Why prune?

There are a number of reasons for pruning: to encourage strong, healthy growth, to increase flower or fruit production, and to create a more pleasing, balanced shape and restrict growth. Pruning can also perform a more specialized function – you can use pruning techniques to train young trees and shrubs, or to create special effects such as coloured stems or large leaves in certain species. Some plants need regular attention to give of their best, while others may require only an annual trim or some formative pruning in their early years.

Health and vigour

Pruning trees and shrubs for health and vigour involves removing shoots, branches, stems or leaves that will have a detrimental effect on the plant if they are left alone. Parts of a plant that are infected with fungal disease or that have died back should be taken out as soon as possible in order to prevent problems increasing and affecting healthy tissue.

Overcrowded plants are prone to attack by fungal diseases because the air flow through the branches is reduced, and where shoots rub together in the wind it creates an open wound through which spores can enter and attack. Pruning trees and shrubs to remove any stems or branches whose woody tissue has been invaded by fungal or bacterial diseases can (if done in time) prevent the spread of many diseases and often prolong the life of the plant. Removing thin, weak, spindly shoots, which are most vulnerable to attack, and thinning out the growth in the centre of a plant to allow a good flow of air around the branches, both help to make life more difficult for diseases such as mildews and pests such as aphids, thus reducing the need for spraying.

With some plants, if a branch or stem has been twisted, broken or split as a result of wind or other damage (for instance, soft shoots being killed by frost or wind chill), the wound almost always gets infected or becomes a sheltering site for pests that may attack other parts of the plant. Here, pruning is used to remove the damaged growth before

Even established trees benefit from pruning; removing weak, spindly or crossing branches will improve health and appearance. Raising or thinning crowns also increases the light level for plants growing below.

the attack can progress. The plant may take several years to recover and regain its natural shape afterwards, but a sacrifice made in the short term can extend the life span of the remaining parts of the plant.

Shaping

It is necessary to prune some woody plants constantly throughout their lives to maintain their habit. This can range from the occasional cutting back of a few stems to retain an attractive form, to regular and essential trimming of more complex shapes. The most obvious example of the latter is in topiary, when clipping

What happens if you don't prune?

Some trees and shrubs will grow quite happily without regular pruning, although in the average garden some pruning will probably be necessary to keep the plant under control. Few gardens have sufficient space for a tree to be allowed to grow entirely unchecked.

However, often when plants are left to grow naturally without any pruning, they develop faults that can lead to the production of misshapen shoots and stems. These may result in further damage later in the plant's life. This problem is quite common with trees and shrubs where branches develop too closely together – branches rub together, causing injury, or narrow forks form, which are prone to splits and breaks when the stems become larger. Even a plant such as magnolia, which often needs very little pruning once established, will benefit from pruning and training as a young plant to prevent any of these common faults developing.

Maintenance pruning can also reduce the risk of damage to a plant from pests and diseases, by creating the type of conditions that make the plant less prone to attack.

plants into a particular shape, for instance a cone, a sphere or a spiral, or more elaborate creations such as bird or animal forms. Such plants become living statues (*see* below). Hedges may also need to be clipped or trimmed regularly (up to three times a year) to maintain their shape.

Balance

Young plants, especially woody ones, tend to produce lots of strong vigorous growth. This is followed by a period of fairly balanced growth, with equal energy going into both flower and fruit production and leaf and shoot development. Later, as the plant ages, there is a greater emphasis on flowers and fruit, with much less new leaf and shoot growth.

One of the main purposes of pruning is to keep a balance between the two types of growth. Some pruning each year may be necessary to encourage more flowers and fruit

Some plants, such as shrubby willows (*Salix*) or dogwoods (here, *Cornus alba* 'Sibirica') are best pruned hard every year in early spring. They respond by producing a crop of bright young stems that make a vivid display in winter.

in the early stages of the plant's life. As the plant matures, the emphasis will shift towards encouraging new shoots to form to replace older ones, to sustain the plant. It is easy to forget that flowering and fruiting can often put a huge strain on a plant, and so it needs sufficient green leaves to manufacture food to support it during this period.

Special effects

You can use pruning techniques to create a variety of special ornamental effects. For instance, some plants respond to annual hard pruning by producing stunning new shoots or leaves. If hard pruned,

Cotinus coggygria 'Royal Purple' (purple-leaved smoke bush) and *Sambucus nigra* f. *laciniata* (cut-leaved elderberry) will produce a few stems with very large, brightly coloured leaves – these are popular with flower arrangers, who use their impressive foliage as background 'greenery' in their displays. *Corylus avellana* 'Contorta' (contorted or corkscrew hazel) and some dogwoods (*Salix* or *Cornus* species) respond to hard pruning by producing striking twisted stems or brightly coloured young shoots respectively (*see* above).

Pruning for effect can also involve altering the growth habit of a plant to suit a particular situation.

Topiary is the triumph of the gardener (armed with pruning shears) over nature. These gigantic and fantastical coffee pots are the result of decades of regular trimming.

For instance, a flowering quince (*Chaenomeles*) or a pyracantha can be grown as a freestanding shrub in a border, or – if pruned differently – the same plant may be grown successfully as a wall shrub or a hedge.

Fruit and flower production

With many wall shrubs, climbing plants and fruit trees, pruning and tying growths into set positions will maximize the quantity of flowers or healthy, undamaged fruit, as well as limit the amount of growth a plant produces each year.

A fruiting plant left to its own devices will usually produce large amounts of small fruits. By pruning to reduce the number of stems, you can direct the plant's energy into making fewer, larger fruits. This, coupled with the practice of 'fruit thinning', to remove a

Many wall shrubs need pruning to encourage the stems to grow up and along the wall, rather than outwards. This peach (*Prunus persica* Peregrine') has been trained into a fan shape.

proportion of the fruits where overcrowding has occurred, can be used to improve fruit size and quality.

To produce a good crop of fruit from trees growing in a confined space, fruit growers prune and train the trees into specific shapes, such as cordons, espaliers and fans (*see* pages 268–269 and above).

Size restriction

The size of a plant can be controlled by regularly pruning out shoots. However, this is an ongoing process that must be repeated frequently, and one that does not in itself

Many plants, including wisteria (here, *W. floribunda* 'Alba') flower better when they are trained horizontally. Make sure the wall can take the weight – the flowering branches can be very heavy.

slow or restrict the plant's growth. For this, you need to root-prune. Cutting through the roots of a plant checks the flow of water and nutrients to the stems, thereby limiting the growth potential of the plant and consequently its height and spread. (Bonsai could be considered the ultimate example of effective root pruning combined with regular trimming.)

To produce the desired effect, root pruning can be carried out in one operation or in stages. Either way, it will slow the plant's growth for several years, after which it may need to be repeated.

Many plants display a characteristic known as apical dominance, where the growing tip (apex) of a shoot dominates the growth of that stem. No side (or 'lateral') shoots develop in the area immediately below the growing point and the result is a very slender, vertical plant. This isn't always desirable, for several reasons: bushier, fuller growth may be required, and in some cases horizontal branches produce better flowers or fruit. The problem of apical dominance can be overcome by pruning.

To create bushy, multi-branched plants you need to break apical dominance, either by bending a stem into a horizontal position (*see* below) or by removing the shoot tip (*see* right). The former reduces the flow of sap to the terminal bud and the latter stops sap flow completely. Both methods will lead to the growth of sideshoots, along with a new growing point (usually from the highest bud). With young plants, removing the tip is often referred to as 'pinching' or 'pinching out' – you can either snap off the tender shoot tip between your finger and thumb, or cut

it off with a sharp knife. With woody plants, you should cut off the growing point (and often part of the stem, too) using a pair of sharp secateurs.

Horizontal shoots

Many climbing plants can be coaxed into better flower development and producing more shoots by bending the long, trailing growths down into a horizontal position and tying them in place. This will have the effect of encouraging flower buds to form along the entire length of the shoot, rather than just on the growing point. It is no

coincidence that when you see wisteria growing on house walls it is invariably the horizontal branches that are covered in flowers (*see* opposite).

Fruit growers increase the yield of their apple trees using this technique; tying new young shoots into a horizontal position encourages fruit buds to form along the entire length of the shoots, while also allowing more sunlight to reach the fruit, since the branches are evenly spaced. The end product is fruit that is better coloured and easier to see and pick. These horizontal shoots need to be tied into this position for only one or two years until they become woody and fixed in position. They then remain horizontal, but any new shoots that form as extensions of these will try to grow vertically again, so you will need to train these horizontally or prune them out.

Apical dominance can be broken in two ways, with slightly different effects:
① Removing the tender growing tip from young plants or shoots to encourage the plant to branch outwards.
② Bending a stem until it is horizontal to encourage the growth of more sideshoots.

Types of pruning

There are four main types of pruning: formative, maintenance (or routine), renewal, and renovation (or rejuvenation). The type of pruning you decide to do will depend on what you want to achieve, the type of plant you are pruning, and the plant's stage of development. As a general rule, younger plants need more pruning in order to create a good framework of branches and stems.

Work put in when a plant is young yields long-lasting results. A standard bay (*Laurus nobilis*) is not difficult to produce, but it does take patience.

Formative pruning

This is used mainly for young or developing plants. The aim is to create even growth and overall development, but it can also be used to shape plants into a particular structural framework. Even plants that you intend to grow 'naturally' (so that they follow their normal growth habit) need some pruning in the early stages to prevent problems later on. For instance, if you don't prune a tree when it is young, it may form narrow-angled branches, which are very vulnerable to splitting as the plant gets older. Also, some trees and shrubs that have their buds in opposite pairs have a strong tendency to develop into 'forked' stems – where two buds at the top of a shoot grow at an equal rate. They eventually create a narrow fork that can easily split, and this can lead to half of the crown or top of the plant being lost if one shoot breaks. Again, formative pruning will reduce the chances of forked stems occurring.

The amount of formative pruning you undertake depends to a large extent on the type of plant and the way in which it has been grown in its early years. For example, if you've propagated a plant yourself you'll need to train it from scratch. However, if you buy a container-grown fruit tree or shrub that has been partially trained from a garden centre or nursery, there will be very little formative pruning to do because the work has been started for you.

Standard plants

Possibly the most common form of formative pruning is the creation of 'standards', where a plant (usually

Many trees, including this crab apple (*Malus*), will have a more attractive shape if they are pruned when young. Remove the lowest branches to give a clear trunk, cut out any badly placed shoots, and shorten leggy growth.

a tree) is trained on a single stem (or 'leg') with a cluster of branches (or 'head') at the top. Sometimes the stem and head are of the same plant, or they may be different varieties. In the case of a 'weeping' standard, the top is often a trailing ground-cover plant that has been grafted onto a straight stem to create the effect. With these types of plant a separate pruning regime is required for each stage of the plant's development; one type of formative pruning is used to create the stem and another to form the head.

Maintenance pruning

As the name suggests, this is the type of pruning carried out to keep plants healthy and growing and performing in the way you want them to. This type of pruning (also known as routine pruning) is aimed at retaining a balance between growth and flowering or fruiting.

Some plants, such as *Brachyglottis* (syn. *Senecio*), *Callistemon* (bottle brush), *Hebe* and lavender (*see* below), have a natural tendency to become bare and 'leggy' at the base so they are routinely pruned after flowering to shorten the top growth. This allows plenty of light into the base of the plant and encourages shoots to form lower down the stems. Many of these shrubs thrive in plenty of light, and one of the main reasons for them developing a sparse growth habit with bare wood at the base is because of top growth shading the lower levels of the plant and causing the foliage to die.

Other forms of maintenance pruning include dead-heading (removing old flowers, *see* page 264) and removing unwanted suckers (*see* page 267).

Renewal pruning

This technique is often used for pruning established fruit trees, but it can also be used on established shrubs where minimal pruning is required. It involves very little cutting but it will help keep established plants growing well. Renewal pruning involves the removal of older growth to make room for new shoots to grow as replacements; fruit growers often refer to it as 'replacement' pruning.

Ornamental cherries and apples

Many ornamental cherries can also be pruned in this way, particularly those that produce flowers only on the shoot tips. If you prune these plants overall to stop them spreading too far, you will be removing flower-bearing wood each time. By removing complete branches and making way for other branches to grow naturally, and creating room for replacement shoots, only a small amount of flower is lost. This strikes a balance between losing some flowering wood and allowing other shoots to form that will bear future generations of flowers.

Apple trees with a tip-bearing (or partially tip-bearing) habit, such as the cooking apple *Malus domestica* 'Bramley's Seedling' (*see* page 250), often crop better when pruned by this method.

Some plants become scruffy and short-lived when left to grow naturally. Lavender should be shorn back to low buds in spring to keep it compact and looking neat.

shoots of similar size and thickness. In this case, renewal pruning consists of cutting out a number of shoots each year (usually the oldest and most unproductive) with a saw or loppers, as close to ground level as possible, to create space for new, vigorous replacement shoots. No other pruning is normally required, other than trimming any shoots that are damaged when the large stems are removed. If this regime is followed regularly, after four to five years all the older shoots will have been replaced by new ones.

Renovation (rejuvenation)

Whichever word you use, this type of pruning amounts to the same thing: implementing a severe pruning regime to give a misshapen, overgrown, tired and neglected plant a new lease of life. In short, it is the rescue operation that you attempt when the only other option is to remove the plant and start again. However, as with most things in the life of a gardener, success is not guaranteed and, with some plants, failure is inevitable. Conifers seldom regrow if you prune into old, brown growth; the exceptions are *Taxus baccata* (English yew) and *Thuja plicata* (western red cedar), which will both recover. As a general rule, conifers are usually replaced rather than hard pruned. Several other plants are also unable to come back from this type of pruning –

Weeping trees

Renewal pruning is very useful as a method for pruning plants with a weeping habit, where the newer shoots tend to emerge and arch over previous generations of branches. The problem with this type of growth habit is that the older branches become shaded by the newer, stronger shoots and suffer from a lack of light. The growth becomes weak or dies off and large quantities of dead or dying wood

can accumulate, which may harbour pests and diseases. Where this is the case, simply remove the lower, older shoots and branches; this will either allow in sufficient sunlight to encourage new shoots to emerge, or create enough room for the younger shoots to spread and grow naturally.

Ornamental shrubs

A number of ornamental shrubs can be renewal pruned, because these tend to form a dense clump of mainly broad-leaved evergreens such as *Ceanothus*, *Coronilla*, *Cytisus*, *Genista*, *Lavandula* and *Santolina*.

If a plant is a suitable candidate for renovation (*see* below), it is worth having a go, especially if the plant is valuable or otherwise difficult to replace. If it is healthy and vigorous, albeit neglected, it should respond. If it does not, dig it out and replace it.

Renovating gradually

Renovation must be carried out in stages: it is not an overnight mission, so it does require patience. It will usually involve cutting back (hard) half of the plant one year and the other half the following year, so it may be two or three years before you see the plant really start to look happy again. Flowering may take a year longer. With a hedge, the need to renovate in stages is a great advantage because it means you can keep a certain amount of privacy and shelter while the plants recover.

If the plant responds well to the first year's pruning it will produce a quantity of strong, vigorous shoots. In some cases there may be far too many new shoots for your intended purpose. They may also (inevitably!) grow in completely the wrong place, and usually all together. So part of the second stage of renovation is to select for retention those new shoots that will produce a strong, well-balanced plant and to 'thin out' or remove the others (always remove the spindliest, weakest shoots first).

If at the end of it all you find that your rescue mission has been a success, the effort will have been worthwhile. For a gardener, it is enormously satisfying to see a much-loved but neglected plant restored to its former glory.

Rejuvenate large plants like this *Magnolia* × *loebneri* 'Leonard Messel' and *Camellia japonica* 'Mercury' by cutting back over two or three years.

Plants suitable for renovation pruning

Abeliophyllum

Aucuba

Callistemon

Calycanthus

Camellia

Carpenteria

Chaenomeles

Chimonanthus

Cornus

Cotoneaster

Daphne

Eucryphia

Garrya

Hydrangea anomala subsp. *petiolaris*

Ilex

Kalmia

Magnolia × *soulangeana*

Mahonia × *media*

Malus

Osmanthus

Pyrus

Rhododendron

Schizophragma

Wisteria

Before you whip out your pruning loppers, decide what it is you're trying to achieve. Ask yourself why you are pruning the plant and what you expect from it after it has been pruned. Next, you need to make sure that you have the equipment to do the job and that it is in excellent condition. Hacking away at stems with rusty or blunt tools will cause more damage than just about anything else.

Planning your pruning

It is easy to forget that pruning provokes growth, and the way you prune will determine how the plant responds. With any type of pruning, you can divide it up into the cuts you *need* to make (necessary cuts, or the 'four Ds') and the cuts you *would like* to make (desirable cuts).

The cuts you *need* to make are those that protect the health and well-being of the plant you're pruning. The cuts you *would like* to make are those that will shape or form the plant – these are the cuts that will influence the growth and general performance of the plant.

Choosing the right tool

First, decide which tool is most appropriate for the task. The tool you use will depend on the thickness of the stem or branch that you're intending to cut, and it's quite possible you'll need at least two cutting implements to cope with the difference in stem size and thickness. For woody shoots up to 1cm (½in) thick, use secateurs. For thick, woody shoots 1–2.5cm (½–1in) thick, and for inaccessible stems, long-handled pruners, or loppers, are ideal. For very thick branches you'll need to use a pruning saw. A garden knife is also useful for light pruning tasks. (For information on tools, *see* pages 256–9.)

Necessary cuts

There are some basic rules to follow when you start pruning any plant, and these should make the task of pruning easier. First, inspect your plant and make decisions about what to remove and what to leave. The essential parts to cut out are known as the 'four Ds', which makes them easier to remember:

- Dead
- Damaged
- Diseased
- Dying

The four Ds are all necessary cuts and should always be carried out before any other pruning. There is nothing more annoying than doing quite a bit of work on a stem or branch only to find that it is diseased at the base and should have been cut out at ground level or where it meets the main trunk.

Dead wood

First, remove any dead branches from the plant you're pruning. Dead wood makes no contribution at all to the plant and will form a perfect site for the eggs of insect pests and spores of fungal diseases to survive the winter successfully and emerge to attack the plant in the following spring.

The dead wood may be hard and dry so, wherever possible, remove it with a saw – cutting through it with secateurs or loppers can be very hard work and will quickly blunt your tools (this is because they are designed to cut through live, green, sappy wood). With some plants it's very difficult to tell which stems are dead and which are alive, especially if you are pruning in the winter when the plants are dormant. If in doubt, do the scrape test (*see* Don't forget, below).

Using the right tool for the job is vital. If you tackle thick stems like the ones of this dogwood (*Cornus*) with secateurs, you'll mash up the stems (and probably damage the blades into the bargain).

Don't forget

Whenever you are not sure if a shoot is alive, there is a simple but effective test you can do. Scrape away a small amount of bark with your fingernail or a clean knife. If the wood below the bark is a greenish white, there is a very good chance that the growth in this area is still alive. If you find dry, brown or grey wood under the bark, the area you have exposed is almost certainly dead. You can repeat this process along a stem or branch to find out the extent of the dead areas. (Not all plants have greenish-white live tissue under the bark: berberis, magnolias and mahonias all have live tissue that is orange or yellow.)

Alternatively, you could wait until growth starts, when it will be much easier to distinguish between live shoots and dead ones.

Damaged branches and stems

Plants with damaged branches and stems are difficult to make a decision about, mainly because you need to determine what degree of damage you are prepared to accept and what is severe enough to need to be removed for the health of the plant.

Where branches and stems are broken, make a pruning cut into healthy wood below the damaged area. A split stem exposes the inner tissue, and this type of wound very rarely heals because it is continually opening and closing every time the branch or stem moves. It is vulnerable to the entry of fungal spores, which can eventually cause the entire plant to die.

The difficulty comes where the damage has been caused to stems and branches by rubbing or scraping – either two branches rubbing together, or where stems and branches are rubbing against some type of foreign body, such as a tree touching its supporting stake and ties or, most often, climbers and wall shrubs chafing against a wall, fence, or other support structure when the wind is blowing. Any form of damage will tend to create an open wound that, particularly with rubbing, never gets the chance to heal because it is constantly being reopened. A large amount of the plant's energy will be diverted into producing callus (healing tissue) in an attempt to close the wound.

With wounds on climbing plants and trees where the injury is caused by contact with the supports or ties, the very least you need to do is re-tie stems and branches so that they are no longer loose. If the damage is severe, some pruning will be needed to remove the damaged parts.

Diseased growth

You will need to remove any branch, shoot or root that shows signs of disease (or severe pest infestation) in an attempt to safeguard the remaining parts of the plant. This may involve paring away some bark with a sharp knife to remove the early signs of a disease attack or, in a lot of cases, taking away complete branches to halt the progressive spread of a fungus or bacterium. The main problem is knowing how much to remove. It is best to remove as little growth as possible, but it is also important to be sure you have eradicated the problem completely.

In many cases, branches and stems that are being attacked by fungal or bacterial diseases will give clues to their rate of progress if you know

where to look. For instance, you may see a coloured staining in the wood, which may be present just under the bark or running through the centre of the stem. The best way to be sure you have removed all traces of infection is to cut back beyond these areas of staining in the hope that you have removed all the diseased parts.

Dying parts

Wilting shoots and leaves or peeling bark are often signs that a plant, or a section of a plant, is dying. It is well worth pruning these sections out as a precaution, but don't just leave it there – always investigate further to see if you can identify the cause. The main justification for removing any shoots you think are dying is to try to prevent any infection spreading through the plant. Diseases such as coral spot fungus will establish on dead shoots and twigs and then start to invade the living parts of a plant.

Leaves and stems that are affected by diseases should be removed as soon as they are spotted.

To encourage the annual production of colourful stems in shrubs such as this *Cornus alba* (dogwood), you need to hard prune in spring.

Desirable cuts

When all the necessary cuts have been made, you can begin to prune your plants for appearance. Always start with a plan and have some idea of what the plant should look like

This single-tier espalier apple on a dwarfing rootstock creates a low step-over hedge. Having apples growing close to the ground can be convenient, but can also attract ground-living pests.

when you have finished. You should also know what you want the plant to do – for instance, if you want more flowers, prune accordingly.

Where the plants' overall appearance is more important than flowering, particularly where they are being grown as hedges or for topiary, try to imagine each plant after it has responded to being pruned. Hard pruning encourages strong, vigorous growth, but this is frequently at the expense of flowers – at least during the first season after pruning, and sometimes even longer.

When you prune or train a plant, the main objective is to improve the performance of that plant. This can be for better foliage colour, brightly coloured stems, more or larger flowers, or more or better fruit. When you do this, though, you always need to consider the plant as a whole, rather than focus solely on one aspect. A plant cannot thrive and give you large, delicious fruits every year if you keep cutting the leaves off, or if you prune off all of the shoots that are producing flower-bearing growths for the following year.

Don't forget

Pruning often has to strike a balance between how you would like your plant to grow now and its appearance in future seasons. It is much easier to work with a plant's natural growth habit rather than trying to force it to develop in a totally unnatural way.

Tools for the job

Knives, secateurs, loppers, saws and extending-reach pruners all have their uses when pruning, with shears and clippers being used for trimming hedges and topiary. Having the correct tool for the task makes working much easier and produces considerably better results.

Hand tools

You will need a decent set of hand tools for carrying out the wide range of pruning tasks in the garden. It is well worth investing in good-quality equipment at the outset.

Pruning knife

A pruning knife is a heavy knife with a curved blade that enables you to get a 'slicing' action when cutting. The handle is also curved, or has a bulbous base, to give a better grip. It is used mainly for light trimming or finishing off cuts made with a saw, such as trimming ragged bark.

Secateurs

For most types of lighter pruning, including cutting woody shoots up to approximately 1cm (½in) thick,

the best tool is a pair of sharp, well-maintained secateurs. There are two basic types, which vary in their cutting action. 'Bypass' secateurs have two curved metal blades that pass one another very closely and cut rather like a pair of scissors. 'Anvil' types have a single, straight-edged cutting blade that closes down onto an anvil (a bar of softer metal or plastic), giving a guillotine-like cutting action.

Some anvil-type secateurs have been designed to incorporate a ratchet. The blades can be locked into position around the branch, and then the ratchet is released to cut through the branch in stages. These are good for gardeners with a small hand span, but they have a relatively slow cutting action.

A pruning knife is perfect for cutting soft stems or for tidying up saw cuts.

Shears

These are long-bladed pruners, also known as 'clippers'. All have a bypass cutting action and are intended mainly for cutting hedges or lawns, with the longer cutting blades covering an larger area quickly. Often the handles are of similar length to the blades and they are joined together at a central pivotal point. They should be well balanced, strong,

Anvil and bypass secateurs

All secateur types can produce good, healthy cuts if they are used correctly. However, anvil-type secateurs (see below left) are not suitable for plants with hollow or brittle stems because their guillotine-like cutting action can crush the stems and cause damage.

In the case of hollow- or brittle-stemmed plants, use bypass secateurs (see below right), which cause less crushing and bruising. This will also reduce the risk of shoots dying back. Don't stint when buying secateurs; a sturdy pair, well maintained, can last a lifetime.

Anvil secateurs

Bypass secateurs

Loppers make the best job of thick, woody stems. The blades are larger than those of secateurs and the long handles make the job less strenuous.

light and comfortable to use. Most have straight blades with a deep notch at the base of the blade for cutting thicker stems.

Some shears have a blade with a wavy edge, which acts to trap the shoots being cut through and thereby give a cleaner cut. It is also possible to get 'one-handed' or 'single-handed' models, in which the blades are operated by squeezing a lever against the handle to open and close the blades, but these tend to have small blades and are suitable only for light trimming.

Tool maintenance

All tools need to be frequently maintained to keep them operating efficiently and comfortably. Oil all moving parts regularly and when blades become clogged with dry sap, rub them clean with emery paper. When the blades become blunt they may be sharpened, either on an oilstone or, in the case of powered tools, sent in for servicing.

Long-handled pruners (loppers)

These are basically strong secateurs with long handles that give extra leverage when cutting stems or branches that are too thick to be tackled with secateurs – for branches about 1–2.5cm (½–1in) thick. The cutting mechanism can be either bypass or anvil type, and there are a few variations on the basic design: some have a ratchet, to make it possible to cut in stages, and others have a gear mechanism on the blade and handle to provide extra leverage and make cutting easier. Versions with extending handles, to increase leverage, are also available (*see* page 258).

Pruning saw

These saws are intended for use on stems and branches that are too large for loppers to cut through – that is, branches that are more than about 2.5cm (1in) thick. There are three main types: single-edged, double-edged and bow saws.

Some single-edged saws have a fixed, straight blade. Many of these are designed to fold, or retract, so that the blade closes back into the handle (like a penknife), and the saw fits neatly into a pocket when not in use. Others have a slightly curved blade – these are based on the 'Grecian saw', which has a curved blade and sloping teeth. Both are designed to cut on the pull stroke. Most taper to a sharp point,

which makes them very useful for getting access to small spaces in the narrow angles between branches.

The traditional double-edged pruning saw has a tapering blade with a broad, blunt end and teeth on both sides. One side has small teeth for cutting through dry, dead wood, while the other has much coarser teeth designed to cut cleanly through living, wet, sappy wood.

Bow saws have a sprung metal frame, curved in the shape of a bow, holding a wide blade with coarse teeth. The blade is held under tension by the frame to make cutting easier. This type of saw gives a rough cut and is intended for cutting through larger branches and trunks (it was originally designed for sawing logs). There is also a smaller version called a half-bow saw, with the metal frame tapering to a sharp point at one end; this is used for cutting through smaller branches and working in situations where space is restricted. Bow saws cut on the push stroke.

The pruning saw – essential for making clean cuts in stems that are too thick for loppers to cope with.

Long-arm pruners

These are 'loppers on a pole' and consist of a pole 2–3m (6–10ft) in length, with a hooked end and curved blade at the tip; the blade is operated by a lever or pull toggle at the opposite end. These tools are more specialized and are used for pruning tree branches that would normally be out of reach (unless a ladder or stepladder is used), and some are capable of cutting through branches up to 4cm (1½in) thick. Some models have extending poles, and there is at least one version with a set of shear blades attached – these are designed for clipping tall hedges from a ground-level position.

Long-arm pruners are a simple but effective way of reaching high branches.

Pole saw

A pole saw consists of a fixed or extending pole 2–3m (6–10ft) in length, with a saw attachment fitted to the tip. The saw is usually a curved Grecian type that cuts on the 'pull' stroke, which is much easier for pruning over head height. These are used for pruning tree branches that would normally be too high to reach without a ladder or stepladder.

Powered tools

Where you plan to undertake large amounts of very similar types of pruning – perhaps clipping a large hedge – powered tools can save a lot of work (*see also* pages 260–1).

Cutter-bar hedge trimmer

This involves a scissor-like action of either one moving (reciprocating) blade and one fixed blade trapping and severing the stems, or two moving blades cutting through the shoots. These trimmers have a cutter bar onto which the moving blades are fixed, and usually cut on both sides of the cutter bar; there are models that will cut on only one side, and these are usually the ones that are capable of cutting through thicker material.

These trimmers can be powered by various means. Petrol is used in heavier machines, which are ideal for cutting through thicker shoots. These are often favoured by professional gardeners. Mains electricity is at present the most

Battery-operated hedge trimmers are useful for topiary. They are cordless, light, and easy to manoeuvre.

common power source. Most machines are lightweight and give a good-quality finish, but the cable can be a restriction in terms of both mobility and safety (*see* page 261).

Rechargeable batteries are increasing in popularity – this is mainly because of advances in battery technology, lighter batteries with a longer working life and rapid recharging, and freedom of movement. There is also an increasing range of lightweight trimmers that can be safely held and operated in one hand. These are designed for light work, such as trimming the soft new growths on plants trained as topiary.

Rotary hedge trimmer

This tool is relatively new and quite different from the traditional mechanical hedge trimmers used by home gardeners. Rotating blades are enclosed within a mesh grid that allows the plant stems to protrude through; they are then severed and shredded by the blades rotating at high speed. Rotary trimmers also have a 'cassette' fitted behind the blades to collect the prunings, which are chopped down to a tenth of their original volume. At present, all available models are powered by mains electricity.

Telescopic hedge trimmer

These trimmers (*see* below) usually consist of cutter-bar trimmers on the end of an extendable (occasionally fixed) pole, often providing an extra reach of up to 3m (10ft). The cutting head or bar can be adjusted through a range of angles. This variety of movement enables the user to cut both the sides and top of the hedge from a standing position. These machines usually have their power source on the opposite end of the pole from the handle, to balance the overall weight of the engine and cutter.

Again, these can be powered by various means. Petrol-powered trimmers are ideal for really heavy-duty work and where large areas of hedge may need trimming, or where electricity supply may be a problem. These tend to be much heavier machines and are often very noisy. Mains electricity is the most popular power source, with cables plugging into the base of the telescopic arm. Most are lightweight, but the trailing cable can be a hazard.

With rechargeable batteries, the cutting unit and extending pole are quite light. However, the battery unit can be heavy, so with many of these trimmers the battery is fixed to a belt and fitted around the user's waist to distribute the weight more evenly and reduce fatigue.

Pole pruner

The cutting action of a pole pruner is usually chainsaw-like, with linked, sharpened saw teeth driven around a fixed guide bar; some types of pole pruner have a circular cutting blade with a high-speed toothed disc. These can be used for trimming branches on trees or thicker stems on neglected hedges or tall shrubs. These devices can have fixed or telescopic poles, usually with a drive unit at the base to counterbalance the guide bar and a chain or disc on the other end.

Some of the chainsaw types can be detached from the pole and used as small chainsaws for work at ground level.

For heavy work, petrol-driven engines provide the power; both mains electric and rechargeable batteries can also be used, although the battery-powered units tend to be smaller and have a limited work time from each charge. Some of the petrol-powered units can be used to prune plants at ground level, particularly where shrubs and dense thickets of woody growth need cutting down.

Nylon-line trimmer (strimmer)

This machine can be used to prune ground-cover plants that are cut down to soil level on a regular basis. A central spool or 'head' rotates at high speed, and the cutting is done either by a spinning disc with 'teeth' around the edge, or by a length of nylon cord.

Chainsaw

A chainsaw is useful for sawing large branches and for major felling jobs. There are electric and petrol-driven models. They can be dangerous, so they should always be operated by someone who has been trained to use them (*see* page 261).

For large areas of hedge, particularly high hedges, an extendable, telescopic hedge trimmer is ideal.

Protective clothing and safety

Pruning can be a dangerous undertaking: it involves using sharp tools – often powered – and if you're not careful you may find yourself balancing on a wobbly stepladder placed on uneven ground. If you plan to use a stepladder, make sure there is someone with you to hold it stable. Take good care when bending and stretching, and wear protective clothing to prevent injuries from prickly plants and sharp branches.

Sap from *Euphorbia* plants is an irritant. Protect hands with gloves.

Gloves

Have you ever tried pruning a rose without wearing gloves? At the very least, it is wise to wear a pair of sturdy gardening gloves to protect your hands (and forearms if the rose is a large shrub), as this is far better than dealing with the thorns and scratches. Strong leather gauntlets are a good start, but choose a pair with supple leather so that you can feel what you are doing when you are handling the plants.

The real danger comes when you start to use power tools for pruning and trimming, especially where the tools concerned are operating at high speed to cut through plant stems and branches. Always wear good-quality gloves when operating such machines.

Some plants, such as *Euphorbia* species (*see* above), exude sap that is very irritating to the skin. For trimming plants like this, a pair of rubber gloves will suffice.

Eye protection

All too often gardeners suffer from eye injuries. Most of these are caused by bending too close to the stubs of cut plants or canes (which have a very small 'profile' when viewed end on). Another risky time is when you are gathering up prunings, which often brings them close to your eyes. In these circumstances, eye protection in the form of goggles or safety glasses is worth considering.

With powered equipment, splinters or shards of stems and shoots can fly about in all directions, so you should always wear eye protection, regardless of whether your trimmer is powered by petrol or electricity. Also, when shredding prunings, the shredder may 'spit' small pieces of woody stem (especially from dry prunings) back out of the hopper.

Ear protection

Some sort of ear protection is essential when using powered pruning tools, so always wear earplugs or ear-defenders whenever possible. This is even more important if the machines are running for long periods. The best type of ear protection is something that muffles the noise rather than blocking it out completely. If you can't hear anything at all, if someone spots a hazard you have not seen you may not be able to hear their shouted warning. Petrol-driven tools and trimmers are particularly noisy.

Cable safety

With pruners and trimmers powered by mains electricity, the biggest drawback is the trailing cable. You spend most of your time wondering where it is and making sure you don't trip over it, cut through it or get it caught in some obstruction. Always try to have the cable positioned behind you, and well away from what you are cutting. You can buy gadgets that clip to your belt or clothing and hold an electric cable, while still allowing it to run freely but not impede movement while working.

Much of the health and safety emphasis is placed on avoiding cutting through a 'live' cable, and rightly so, but making sure that any cables are not going to wrap around feet or legs is every bit as important. Falling over while holding a power-driven trimmer or pruner (while it is running) is extremely dangerous.

Safety precautions

■ Tree-felling and the removal of large branches should be carried out by a profession tree surgeon. Never attempt to remove any tree over 5m (15ft) high.

■ When using a chainsaw, do so from the ground; for branches above waist height, always hire a tree surgeon.

■ Regular tetanus injections are advisable to eliminate the risk of infection from the tetanus bacterium, which is carried in soil and can enter through breaks in the skin. Adult boosters last for up to ten years, after which time they will have to be renewed.

■ Never trim plants in wet weather and wait until the plants themselves are dry.

■ Work from the ground wherever possible. Do not stretch out to reach growth while up a ladder.

■ Don't compost or shred diseased plant material, since it can infect other plants. Instead, burn it or dispose of it as waste.

Chainsaw safety

Chainsaws have the potential to be extremely dangerous, especially when the person using them has had no training. Ideally, it's best to employ a professional tree surgeon to do the work for you. However, if you do decide to hire a chainsaw, always insist on a demonstration and thorough instructions on how the machine works. If you are using one for the first time, make sure there is someone close by while you work, just in case things go wrong.

Don't forget

For any gardening equipment powered by mains electricity, always use an RCD (residual current device), also often referred to as a circuit breaker or trip switch. This device will make sure that the electricity supply to the cable stops instantaneously should you accidentally sever the power cable. If you have to use an extension cable, choose one with a brightly coloured outer casing that is easy to see – this greatly reduces the risk of cutting through it accidentally.

The chainsaw is probably the most dangerous of all pruning tools. Consider hiring a professional tree surgeon for major jobs.

Essential techniques

There is a wide selection of pruning tools to choose from (including your fingers!). The tool you select for a particular job will be determined by the reason for removal and the type of growth you are dealing with. Clean, precise cuts will heal better than rough and ragged ones, so all cutting blades should be kept clean and sharp.

Pruning with tools

Correct use of pruning tools is vital for your safety and the health of the plant. Using tools incorrectly can damage the plant and lead to infection and disease.

Using cutting tools

When using double-bladed cutting tools, such as secateurs, loppers and pole pruners, never twist or lever the blades to try to speed up the cutting process. This will only strain the pivotal nut that holds the blades in place; once this has been damaged, the blades will be misaligned and unable to make clean cuts. If you find you are having to twist or lever, it means you are using the wrong tool for the job.

When you position the blades for cutting, make sure the stem is centrally placed between the tips and the pivotal point of the blades, erring on the side of the pivotal point. This will give you the firmest possible grip on the stem. Making cuts with the tips of the blades is likely to strain or force them apart.

When using a pruning saw, always cut a branch off close to a trunk or main stem. Don't leave a stump that will die back and don't cut flush to the stem. If you leave a 'collar' at the base of the branch (*see* box, opposite) it will encourage

bark to grow over the wound and will heal better.

Use a gardening knife to smooth the rough edges of pruning cuts to prevent infection.

Where to cut

The position of a pruning cut on the stem or branch of a plant is very important as it can have a direct bearing on how well (and how quickly) a cut may heal – and in some cases whether a cut can heal at all. It also affects how quickly the plant responds to the cut – that is,

When using double-bladed tools, such as loppers (above) or secateurs, cut near the pivotal point of the blades rather than the tips.

Where and how to make a cut

For plants that have buds arranged alternately on the stem (below left), make a diagonal cut just above a bud. The cut should slope down behind the bud. Ideally, the cut will be at an angle of about 25 degrees. Where a plant has opposite buds (below right), and an angled cut is difficult, make a horizontal cut straight across the stem, just above a pair of buds. In both cases, cut about 6mm (¼in) above the bud.

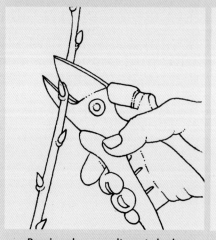

Pruning above an alternate bud

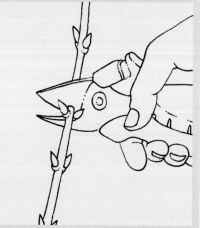

Pruning above a pair of opposite buds

how quickly new growth will spring from the pruned section.

A plant's growth hormones are concentrated in the area of the buds. As well as encouraging growth, these hormones promote healing. So it makes sense to make your cuts close to a live bud (though not so close that you risk damaging it). As a general rule, the ideal place to cut is 6mm (¼in) above the bud. (The only time you might not want to cut close to a bud is when you are trying to discourage growth, such as when you completely cut out unwanted stems.) Remember that the direction in which the bud points is an indication of the direction that the new growth will take once the stem is pruned. So if you want new growth to spring to the right, don't cut above a bud that is pointing to the left.

How to cut

Wherever possible, stems should be cut at a slight angle to encourage sap or rainwater to drain off rather than accumulate on the cut surface (where it will inhibit the healing process). Note that the angle should be slight (say, 25 degrees); if it is greater than this, you negate much of the benefit of making the angled cut because you increase the surface area of the cut – the greater the surface area the greater the area of entry for harmful bacteria or viruses.

The buds on most plants are arranged either alternately or in opposite pairs on the stem. For plants with alternate buds, it is easy to make the angled cut (the cut should slope down from the bud). For plants with opposite buds, there is no alternative but to cut straight across, just above the pair of buds, as shown opposite.

Removing large branches

It is often difficult to estimate the size and weight of a branch, and they always seem to be larger and heavier than you think – especially if they are removed or reduced in the summer, when they are full of sap. For very large branches, it is safer to hire a professional tree surgeon to carry out the work. If you are removing a large branch yourself, It is always best to remove it in stages, rather than try to cut it off all in one go, to avoid the branch ripping away and damaging the tree trunk.

Make the first cut *underneath* the branch being removed (*see* below left), about 30–45cm (12–18in) away from the trunk. The cut should slice about a quarter of the way through the branch. Make a deeper cut in the top of the branch, a few centimetres away from the first. The bulk of the branch should then fall gently away, leaving a stump.

To remove the stub (*see* below right), make a third cut close to the trunk. Take care to leave the collar (ridge of bark where the branch joins the trunk), as this will help the wound to heal and reduce the chances of infection. Wound-sealant paint is available, but this may do more harm than good (*see* box, page 265).

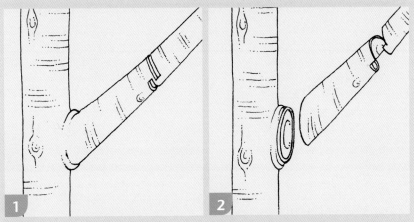

1 Make two cuts in the branch: one beneath, the other in the top.

2 Make a third cut to remove the stub, leaving a 'collar' on the tree.

The large branch on the right-hand side of this *Robinia pseudoacacia* 'Frisia' is likely to break off if its weight is not reduced by pruning. It is best to remove large branches in stages (*see* box, left).

Hand-pruning techniques

Soft shoots, dead flowers and suckers (*see* page 267) are often more easily removed by hand than with pruning tools.

Dead-heading

Dead-heading (the removal of dead flowers) is one of the simplest forms of pruning. It involves removing any old, spent flowers in order to prevent seeds forming. It is a way of 'fooling' the plant into thinking it hasn't yet reproduced, and as a result it will often prolong flowering. To dead-head a plant, pluck off any dead blooms when they start to fade and turn brown. The way in which you do this depends on the type of flower you are dealing with, and whether it has long or short stems. In the case of thicker, woodier stems, for example those of roses, you will need to use secateurs.

If you are dead-heading long-stemmed plants, such as pelargoniums, remove the stalk as well as the dead flower. Break it off cleanly at the point where it grows out from the main stem of the plant.

Finger pruning

This technique (sometimes known as 'pinch pruning') involves using your fingers rather than tools to prune. It is used to remove soft young growth of some plants, such as fuchsias and penstemons. You can use either the fingernails of your thumb and fore-finger to pull out the sideshoots, or if they're small, rub them out with the side of your finger.

Stopping One of the aims of finger pruning is to make young plants branch and form an attractive bushy shape. Many plants have a natural tendency to grow upwards, becoming tall and lanky rather than filling out nicely. This is known as 'apical dominance' (*see* page 247). Plants whose stems display apical dominance have natural hormones that encourage the bud at the stem tip to keep growing so that the stem gets longer and longer. However, if the gardener nips out the tip at the end of the stem, the hormones are deflected to the next buds down, which are then triggered into growth to produce sideshoots. This pruning technique is often

known as 'stopping', as a plant's natural growth habit is checked. It is best carried out when potting up rooted cuttings.

Pinching out The same technique is also used on mature plants with soft growth, to maintain a neat habit. For instance, the plant may be growing in a lopsided way and you'll want to create a more balanced shape by removing over-long shoots. You should also remove shoots that have been damaged by frost or pests and diseases. Removing the damaged shoot gets rid of the unsightly plant part as well as any unwanted pests present, and it acts as a trigger to the plant to produce a new shoot. This technique of removing growing shoots on mature plants is sometimes known as 'pinching out'.

With short-stemmed flowers, such as camellias, nip the dead heads off with your fingers just behind the flower.

Keeping pruned plants healthy

Pruning is generally beneficial for plants, but in some cases it can take its toll. The removal of leafy shoots can deprive the plant of its source of energy, and stimulating more vigorous flowering or fruiting will put further demands on the plant. In addition, pruning can leave a plant vulnerable to infection or other damage, such as excessive 'bleeding'. But don't be put off by all this – if you follow a few simple rules you should be able to avoid problems before they arise.

An annual mulch of organic matter, such as garden compost (above) or horse manure, will keep plants healthy and, combined with fertilizer, will help to reduce the chance of infections taking hold after pruning.

Feeding and mulching

Pruning can check a plant's growth potential, especially if pruned while it is actively growing. For this reason, to get the best results, feed plants soon after they have been pruned. Most plants pruned between spring and midsummer need a general fertilizer that contains a balanced combination of nutrients, including nitrogen, phosphates and potassium, together with essential trace elements. However, in some cases you may need to use a different type of fertilizer. For example, if you were pruning a hedge in spring you would feed it with a fertilizer that contains high levels of nitrogen to promote new growth; pruning the same hedge in late summer and feeding it with a fertilizer that is higher in phosphates and potash will encourage the production of slower, harder growth that can withstand the winter cold much better.

If you're undertaking a major renovation programme of a neglected plant (*see* pages 250–1), feeding is particularly important, as you will be putting more strain on the plant. Remember, it is better to apply several small feeds rather than one large one, as this will help to provide steady new growth rather

than very soft, sappy shoots that are susceptible to pests and diseases.

After you've applied fertilizer, it's a good idea to apply a mulch, such as well-rotted farmyard manure or garden compost. Mulching provides low levels of valuable plant nutrients, it helps to keep the plant's roots at an even temperature and retains moisture in the soil. If the mulch is deep enough (ideally 8–10cm/3–4in deep) it will also suppress weeds that would compete with the plants for water, nutrients and (if they grow tall enough) light.

Preventing infection

Every time you saw off a branch, or cut a root or shoot with a knife or secateurs, there is always a chance that the wound you have made can become infected. Until the cut surface has hardened and dried, the wound is open to fungal and bacterial rots entering the plant. If undetected or left untreated, the infection may lead to the eventual death of the plant.

It is worth remembering that healthy, vigorous, well-fed plants are much more able to fight off infection naturally than poor, weak, sickly plants ever could. The speed at which a pruning wound heals is always a good indication of how

healthy a plant is; rapid healing of a cut is a sure sign that a plant is healthy and growing well.

Timing

One way to reduce the chance of infection is to prune during the summer, when wound healing takes place more rapidly and there are far

Natural healing process

Traditionally, gardeners used wound paint to cover a pruning wound. These used to contain fungicides or tar extract, but these toxic substances have been phased out in favour of treatments containing natural plant resins. However, extensive research has now shown that there is really no benefit to be gained from using any type of wound paint. Indeed, these treatments may actually seal fungal spores into the cut and aid infection rather than healing. This has led to a trend away from using wound treatments and towards encouraging the plant's natural immune system to heal the wounds.

fewer fungal spores drifting in the air to land on cut surfaces and open wounds. Many *Prunus* species (members of the cherry family) are pruned at this time to reduce the risk of infection by silver leaf fungus, which is a common cause of death in these plants. *Acer* species (Japanese maples) are often pruned while they are actively growing to counter possible infection from coral spot fungus, which frequently invades live growth after establishing itself on dead twigs.

The timing of pruning in relation to the growth cycle of the plant is also important. For example, broad-leaved evergreens and conifers tend to have two surges of growth each year, one in spring and one in late summer or early autumn; so, for the most rapid healing of pruning cuts, you should prune just before these growth surges.

Techniques and tools

The rapid healing of pruning cuts is closely linked to making good, clean pruning cuts using the correct technique (*see* pages 262–3). Generally, you should make as many cuts as possible close to a branch join or fork, often referred to as the 'branch bark ridge', which is the slight swelling at the point where a branch joins another branch or the main trunk of the plant. This is the most important area, as it is where an open wound will heal most rapidly and where the naturally occurring chemical and physical barriers within the wood that offer resistance to the invasion of rot-causing fungi are found. So, by pruning at this point, the plant's own natural 'immune system' has the best possible chance of protecting it against the invasion of fungal decay.

Like the other species of maple, *Acer shirasawanum* 'Aureum' is one of the plants that are especially prone to coral spot disease and 'bleeding'. It is therefore best pruned in the summer.

To help pruning cuts heal quickly, it is essential that all cutting implements, such as saws, knives, loppers and secateurs, are clean and sharp. Clean, precise, carefully positioned cuts will always heal more quickly than rough-edged cuts with bruised woody tissue and torn or jagged bark.

Dieback

Sometimes a shoot or branch starts to turn brown and die off from the tip downwards. This is called 'dieback' and is caused by disease. Any affected shoots should be cut out as soon as you see them. Prune well below the dead area so that the disease cannot infect the rest of the plant.

Preventing 'bleeding'

Another type of pruning damage can occur in those plants that are prone to excessive sap loss – known as 'bleeding' – through the cut surfaces. Some plants can lose a lot of their strength and vigour if they are allowed to bleed sap for long periods, and this will slow down the sealing and healing process on the newly cut surface, so the wound remains vulnerable to infection. To make matters worse, where bleeding occurs the section of stem immediately beneath the pruning cut may start to die back away from the wounded area, leaving bare dead stumps or sections of branch that will need to be pruned out later.

One way to overcome these problems is to prune plants that are at risk – namely, *Acer* (maple), *Aesculus* (horse chestnut), *Betula* (birch), *Vitis* species (vines) and *Juglans* (walnut) – in mid- to late summer, when they are in full leaf, rather than in winter or spring.

The leaves will draw up water, which then evaporates from the leaf surface (a process called 'transpiration'). Because the pull of the leaves is so strong, much of the sap is drawn past the open wounds, allowing them to start healing more quickly.

Removing suckers

Many trees and shrubs have a suckering habit, which means that they produce new shoots, or 'suckers', from their roots; some other plants may produce suckers after they have been pruned hard or if they have been damaged.

Suckers may spread out from the roots around the plant you have pruned, or they may grow from the stem or trunk of the plant, either at or just above ground level. Most suckers do not actually damage the plant, but they may sap its energy. However, if the plant concerned has been propagated onto a rootstock – for instance in the case of a rose – the

Plants prone to suckering
Ailanthus
Aralia elata and cultivars
Celastrus
Clerodendrum
Corylus avellana 'Contorta'
Embothrium
Fallopia aubertii, *F. baldschuanica*
Gleditsia
Hippophae
Kerria japonica
Malus (fruiting and ornamental)
Populus
Prunus (fruiting and ornamental)
Pyrus (fruiting and ornamental)
Rhus typhina
Robinia
Rosa (species and shrubs)
Syringa cultivars
Tilia
Wisteria

problem is more severe, because the unwanted, more vigorous shoots of the stock plant will eventually take over and replace the grafted cultivar.

All suckers should be removed as soon as you see them. Where plants produce sucker growths from a rootstock, try to rip or pull them from the plant at the point of origin, rather than cutting them off. If you cut them off, some dormant buds are more likely to remain at the base of the shoot to produce new suckers. If the suckers have formed a clump some distance from the plant, pull or dig them out with a spade.

Rhus typhina is a wonderful small tree with elegant, fern-like foliage. However, it suckers profusely and the shoots can appear some distance from the plant. Be careful where you plant it and remove suckers as they appear.

The aim of training is to create a very productive tree growing in a confined space in its own 'microclimate'. The tree is usually grown against a support structure and is regularly pruned and tied in to achieve a particular shape. The microclimate protects more frost-tender plants, or encourages hardier ones to flower and fruit slightly earlier than normal.

Fan

This shape is often used for plants grown against a wall or fence, particularly ones that need shelter or warmth. Although the pruning and training method is quite intensive, when done well these plants can be attractive in winter – even when they are just a framework of bare shoots.

When the tree is young, the main stem is pruned to encourage a

These are all space-saving ways of growing trees. They are highly ornamental and, in many cases, improve flowering or fruiting.
① A fan-trained morello cherry.
② A line of cordon-grown apples.
③ A pear trained as an espalier.
④ An olive tree grown as a standard.

branching habit. The resulting sideshoots ('laterals') are pruned, trained and tied in to create an evenly spaced framework of branches that go on to produce flower- or fruit-bearing shoots. The shoots may be tied to canes as they grow and are gradually moved into position over several months to make sure the support surface is evenly covered with tiered shoots, all with a similar amount of growing space.

For most plants, pruning in both spring and summer will be necessary to maintain the shape of the fan. This will also help to maximize the growth potential of the tree.

Cordon

A cordon consists of one or more main stems, which form the main framework of the tree or shrub, and side branches trained to form fruit-bearing spurs. Many single-stemmed cordon apple trees are grown as 'oblique' cordons, planted and trained at an angle of 45 degrees, to restrict the natural vigour of the plants and to encourage more fruit production.

Redcurrants and gooseberry plants can also be trained as cordons, but these are usually grown as upright stems, often with two or more stems (apples can also be cultivated as multi-stemmed upright cordons). The problem with this method is trying to balance the growth evenly between the number of stems involved.

Like fans, cordons will need pruning at least twice a year – once while they are growing and once while dormant. They will also need regular tying in and

training to direct the growth into the desired shape and direction. The main advantage of training plants like this is that heavy crops of fruit can be produced in a relatively small area.

Espalier

This is possibly the most difficult type of training. The aim is to create several tiers of perfectly symmetrical branches, evenly spaced along a single, vertical main stem. A very strong support system of horizontal wires running along a wall or fence, or between stout posts, is essential. Although this shape is most commonly associated with apples and pears, pyracanthas grown as wall shrubs also work well as espaliers.

The tiers of branches are formed by cutting the growing tip out of the main stem to create a minimum of three new shoots: one to grow upwards to act as a replacement for the main stem, and at least two others to be trained out in opposite directions horizontally. This process is repeated each year until the desired number of tiers is formed. As with other methods of training, the shoots are pruned and tied to canes before they can be bent down into a horizontal position. This is the tricky bit, because the tree is being forced to grow against its natural habit.

Both summer and winter pruning are needed, with the lateral shoots being trimmed to form fruiting spurs along the entire length of the horizontal branches.

Standard

Standard trees have a clear stem (with no branches) and a crown or 'head' of branches on the top. There are two types: 'natural' and 'grafted' standards.

Natural standard The framework of branches that forms the head of a tree will develop naturally on the extension of the main stem, known as the 'central leader', which continues to grow upwards as the tree ages. With weeping standards, the head is made of lax, weeping branches formed above the clear stem or 'leg', often with the branches trailing down almost to the ground.

Grafted standard A plant with a vigorous rootstock is grown to form a single upright stem or 'leg', with the side branches being cleared from the stem in stages over two, three or four years, depending on the plant. Once this stem has reached a height of 1.5–2m (5–6ft), the top is cut off and another plant (usually a cultivar chosen for its decorative qualities) is grafted onto the top. If the graft is successful, a new head forms, which may be upright or weeping in habit. Weeping forms of ash, birch, beech, pussy willow and cherry (as well as upright types of cherry) are often sold as grafted standards.

Training climbers and wall shrubs

True climbers are at least partially self-supporting, so they often need little more than a bit of encouragement to scramble over another plant or structure – they will do the rest. However, in the early stages, you should give them a good start with some formative training. Wall shrubs need all the help they can get because they are shrubs, not climbers; support and constant tying in will be necessary to make sure they stay in place.

Climbers

You might think that a climber is a climber, but where plants are concerned it is seldom that simple, and it is easy to choose a plant with the wrong method of support for a particular site. For instance, climbers that use sucker pads to cling as they grow do not grip well onto wooden surfaces unless the wood is painted, so they need much more training until they do finally take hold. (Climbers with aerial roots, on the other hand, seldom have any trouble, which is why ivy can get just about anywhere.)

Plants with tendrils will not coil around supports that are too thick or of a large diameter, and most wooden trellis is too thick for plants such as clematis. This means that the first shoots have to be tied in regularly, but the second flush will cling to these older shoots for support, rather than the trellis itself. This may well be all right at the time, but when the plants are pruned and the older stems are removed the support for the younger stems goes too.

The tendrils of clematis have evolved from modified leaves. Ideally, their support should be no thicker than a pencil, so the plants can grip on easily. You often see clematis being trained around the downpipe from a roof gutter, with yards of string being used to try to make the plant climb. In that situation, the easiest option is to plant the climber as close to the downpipe as possible, then wrap sections of chicken wire around the pipe, leaving a 15cm (6in) cavity between the pipe and the wire and guiding the plant to grow in this cavity. The shoots will naturally grow out into the light, so they will cling to the wire (and soon disguise it). More sections of wire can be added as the plant gets taller.

There are various types of support for climbers and wall shrubs.
① A tree is a good support for many climbing plants, such as this hydrangea.
② Climbers and wall shrubs can be tied into trellis fixed against the wall.
③ A wigwam in a container is ideal for a climber if there is not room for a trellis.
④ A strong fence can support a trained wall shrub, such as this ceanothus.

With wisteria the most important part of training is to keep the stems separated where possible; otherwise they tend to twine around themselves and each other rather than around the support. Pruning is a twice-yearly task, while training is an ongoing process of tying and guiding shoots into the areas where you want them to grow.

Wall shrubs

Only a regime of regular pruning and training makes these plants grow against a wall or fence in a way that sometimes contradicts their natural growth habit. One of the easiest ways to train a wall shrub, keep it neat and tidy and have a good display of flowers, is to use some form of trellis or similar structure, with a large gauge of mesh; it must be strong enough to take the often considerable weight of the plant it is supporting.

Fasten the frame to the wall or fence, using spacers between the support and the structure it is attached to; a gap of 5–8cm (2–3in) between the two fixtures will leave enough space for the plant to grow into. Tie the plant to the trellis. As the wall shrub grows, it will naturally want to grow outwards, towards the light and away from the trellis; where this is the case, you just need to gently push the main stems back under the trellis frame to keep it against the fence or wall. As these main stems produce sideshoots, these will also grow out towards the light, and they can be trimmed back to four or five leaves (or buds if it is winter). These growths will often form flowering spurs. As the plant grows, the leaves will obscure most, if not all, of the trellis once the plant is established.

Regularly tie the plant back against the support structure to make it grow in the direction you would prefer. To get a better flowering performance out of most wall shrubs and climbers, try to train as many growths as possible into a horizontal position. This will cause a redistribution within the plant of natural hormones, which influence flower production in certain parts of the plant. Rather than getting long, erect shoots with a few clusters of large flowers at the top, bending stems down into a horizontal position and tying them into place will encourage the formation of flowers along the entire length of the shoot, giving far more flowers and a much better display (*see also* page 247).

Propagation

There are several very good reasons to have a go at propagating your own plants, not least that you can increase your range of container plants at very little expense. Top of the list of reasons though must be the great satisfaction that is to be had from watching a plant grow that you've sown or rooted yourself.

Methods

There are lots of ways to propagate container plants, using all parts of the plant. Sowing seed is probably the most common way to propagate but other methods include taking cuttings (from the roots, stems, shoots or leaves), dividing plants, and propagating by layering, air layering, grafting or budding. Not all of these are applicable to every plant, and some techniques are much easier than others. Grafting and budding are normally practised only by very experienced growers.

Sowing seed

Seed is easy to sow, usually fairly inexpensive (free if you collect your own and you get lots of plants from it. However, the results aren't always predictable, because of genetic variation, so you may get some plants that are better than the parents and some that are less good.

For the best chances of germination, sow fresh seed if possible. However, some seed can last for a surprisingly long time: poppy seed has been found to be viable after 70 years. If you do store seed, it's best to put it in an airtight glass jar in a dark, cool but frost-free place. The most important factors for seed germination are temperature and moisture. Seed is unlikely to germinate if it's too hot or too cold, or the compost too dry. A germination temperature of 18–21°C (65–70°F) suits most plants.

Seed sizes vary considerably, from the dust-like seeds of some begonias to the coconut. Each will have its own requirements when it comes to germination. Some seeds (particularly trees, shrubs and some alpines) need chilling before they can germinate, so you'll need to put them outdoors over winter or in a refrigerator for six weeks before sowing. Many types of seed need covering with a layer of compost after sowing, while others require exposure to light. You can maintain high humidity around the seeds by putting a sheet of glass or plastic over the seed tray until the seeds have started into growth. Stand seed in good light but not direct sunlight, as the sun may scorch the young shoots. If it's a very bright spot, such as a windowsill, you may have to shade the plants with fine netting.

Each seed has a supply of food inside that is sufficient to keep the seedling alive as it grows up to the light. Planting the seed too deeply means the food will run out before it gets to the surface. Generally, the smaller the seed, the lower the reserves and the nearer the surface it should be sown.

Sowing the seed too thickly or leaving the seedlings in too dark a place will result in them becoming long and straggly.

Some seeds are very fussy about the ambient temperature, requiring it to be within a particular range and constant before they'll deign to show themselves. If you want to grow seed like this, you'll need to invest in a heated propagator. Many seeds, however, are far less particular and will reward you handsomely for what really amounts to very little effort.

Some seeds should be sown beneath the surface of the compost, such as beans (left); others should be scattered over the surface and left uncovered, such as poppy seed (right). If you buy seed, the packet instructions will tell you what to do. If you collect your own seed and have no idea how to sow it, work on the principle that the larger the seed, the deeper it should be sown.

HOW TO sow small seed

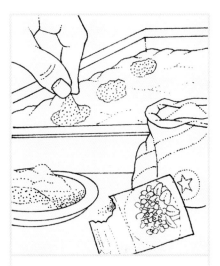

Fill a pot with seed compost and firm it down gently. Scatter the seed onto the compost, ensuring you get a thin, even distribution over the surface. If the seed should be covered, sprinkle over sieved compost until it disappears from view. Then stand the pot in tepid water until moisture has soaked up to the surface.

Place the pot inside a loose plastic bag or a propagator and put it in a light spot but not in direct sunlight. Check daily. If the compost dries out, water again in the same way. When the first seedlings germinate, discard diseased or damaged seedlings. Once the seedlings have opened out the first true leaf, they need transplanting, or 'pricking out'.

Mix very fine seed, such as begonia, with fine sand, then sow it in 'pinches' or scatter it evenly over the surface of the compost. The seed should be evenly distributed through the sand for easy handling. The sand helps you see where you have sown the seed.

HOW TO transplant or 'prick out' seedlings

Fill a clean seed tray with fresh compost and firm it gently. Then take a dibber and use it to gently loosen clumps of seedlings and separate the roots from the compost. Don't handle the stems. Carefully lift each seedling and lower it into a finger-sized hole in the new compost, spacing the seedlings about 3.5cm (1½in) apart.

Ensure the seed leaves rest just above the surface of the compost. Gently firm compost around the seedling to cover the roots and fill the hole. Water them in, either by standing the tray in water or by using a fine rose on a small watering can. Place the seedlings in a bright spot, but out of direct sunlight. Keep the compost moist.

Keep a close eye on their progress and, after six weeks, begin feeding the plants once a week with a general-purpose liquid fertilizer. When the tray is full of roots, the young plants will be ready for potting up into larger pots filled with fresh, sterilized compost, such as John Innes No. 1. Handle the young plants very carefully.

Taking cuttings

Unlike growing plants from seed, propagating from cuttings gives you a predictable result, because the cuttings grow to resemble the parent plant almost exactly. Some may be demanding to root and require a propagator, but many can be rooted in pots. You may have to try several times to establish which type of cuttings works for which plants and the best time of year to take them.

Softwood cuttings

Also called tip or shoot-tip cuttings, these are cuttings of soft, fast-growing new shoots, taken in spring and summer before the growth begins to harden and turn brown and woody. If you haven't grown plants from cuttings before, start with easy ones, such as pelargoniums, osteospermums or fuchsias, as they root easily. Softwood cuttings of most plants will root between spring and early autumn. Fill a 10cm (4in) pot with cutting or seed compost to just below the rim, then prepare your cuttings as shown here.

Pelargoniums are among the easiest plants to propagate from softwood cuttings, ideally taken in summer.

HOW TO propagate softwood cuttings

1 Using a sharp knife, remove lengths of strong, healthy shoot from the plant. (Always take more cuttings than you need in case some don't root.) The best plants for this method are pelargoniums, fuchsias, argyranthemums, penstemons, tender perennials and osteospermums.

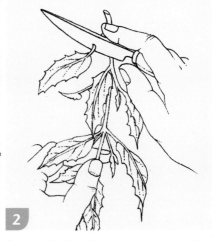

2 Remove the basal leaves from each cutting and trim it just below a leaf joint. For most plants, you should have a cutting of about 8cm (3in) long, with two to three leaves at its tip. (Note that fuchsias should be 2.5–5cm/1–2in.) If necessary, dip the cut stem bases in hormone rooting powder.

3 Using a pencil or thin stick, dib the cutting into damp seed and cutting compost. Don't push the cutting in too far: its remaining leaves should be clear of the compost. By placing cuttings around the edge of a pot, you should be able to fit several cuttings into one pot.

4 Thin-leaved cuttings need humidity. Place a clear plastic bag over the pot and hold it in place with an elastic band (this acts as a mini-greenhouse and keeps the humidity high until the roots form). Once new growth starts (in about four to six weeks), the cutting is ready for potting.

Semi-ripe cuttings Semi-ripe cuttings are best taken in mid- to late summer as the growth begins to harden on the current season's shoots. They're less likely to wilt than softwood cuttings, because they're slightly tougher, but they will take longer to root. Many shrubs, such as camellias and lavender (*Lavandula*), as well as evergreen herbs, conifers, box (*Buxus*) and heathers (*Calluna*), root well when taken this way. Look for young shoots that are just starting to turn brown and woody.

Hardwood cuttings These are taken from growth that is one year old, in autumn or early winter. You can take several cuttings from one long shoot, cutting just above a leaf at the top and just below at the base. They will take the whole winter to root, but be patient: the worst thing you can do is keep pulling them up for a look (you will break any new roots as they form).

Lavender is easily propagated by taking semi-ripe cuttings in summer.

HOW TO propagate semi-ripe cuttings

1 Select a shoot from a healthy plant, ideally about 8cm (3in) long, with about 1cm (½in) of brown, woody stem at the base. If it is a sideshoot, pull it away from the plant (with a short 'heel' of main stem) and if it is a shoot-tip cutting, cut it away about 8cm (3in) below the shoot.

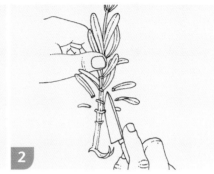

2 Using a sharp garden knife, remove the lower leaves from the lower two-thirds of the stem, as well as any thorns from prickly plants. Pinch out any sappy shoot tips. Trim the heel to remove any long whiskers. The prepared cuttings should be about 10cm (4in) long.

3 For plants that need help in order to root, such as clematis, dip the cut end into a saucer filled with hormone rooting powder and tap off the surplus. Push the cuttings around the edge of a pot filled with damp seed and cutting compost or multipurpose compost.

4 Cover the pot with a clear plastic bag, held in place with an elastic band. While the plants are rooting, stand the pot in a well-lit spot, but out of direct sunlight. Check the cuttings after two or three weeks and once they have rooted, pot them up separately.

Hormone rooting preparations

With some plant cuttings, such as those of clematis, it can be extremely difficult to get them to root without a little extra help from a hormone rooting powder or gel. Others, such as pelargoniums, do not need it – in fact, it will make the stem rot. If you can't find out whether to use it for a particular plant, you can always hedge your bets by planting up two pots of cuttings – one treated with rooting preparation, one untreated. Bear in mind that hormone rooting powders and gels have a limited life, which will be shortened further if they become contaminated. Tip out only a small amount into a saucer for immediate use and close the container again. When you have finished, throw away any powder remaining in the saucer, rather than tipping it back into the container.

Taking hardwood cuttings is an ideal propagation method for deciduous shrubs with long, straight stems such as roses, dogwoods (*Cornus*), willows (*Salix*), hazel (*Corylus*) and vines (*Vitis*). Some plants, for instance dogwoods, willows, forsythias and philadelphus, root more easily than others and can be inserted direct into the garden soil or into a pot of compost to root. Others need a hormone rooting preparation as well as compost.

Division

This is one of the simplest ways to propagate plants. Digging up and dividing old perennials is a good means of splitting large clumps of plants where the centre of the plant often dies off. This method is suited to plants that have spreading root systems or produce new growth from the base, such as hostas, daylilies (*Hemerocallis*) and some primulas. It allows you to keep the healthier outer parts, discard the old pieces and multiply your stock. As you replant, you can give the new pieces of plant more space and fresh compost to keep them growing and healthy. Most perennials should be divided between late autumn and early spring, but not during extreme weather conditions.

You can also use division to multiply your bulbs, such as irises, lilies (*Lilium*), tulips (*Tulipa*), daffodils (*Narcissus*), snowdrops (*Galanthus*) and hyacinths (*Hyacinthus*), and improve flowering. Simply lift and divide the bulbs if they're overcrowded, splitting 'daughter' bulbs away from the parent, and replanting in another container.

HOW TO propagate hardwood cuttings

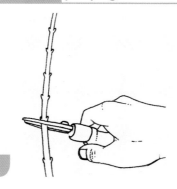

1 Using secateurs, remove a length of healthy stem from the current year's growth. Make a straight cut. If there are sideshoots present, trim them off.

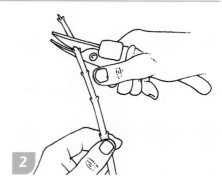

2 Trim the top of the shoot, making a sloping cut just above a bud. The cutting should be about 20cm (8in) long. You may need to dip the base in hormone rooting powder.

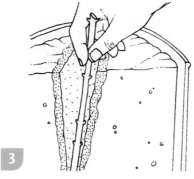

3 Fill a pot with free-draining cutting compost and moisten the compost well. Make a small slit trench in the compost. Insert the cutting into the trench, base first, leaving only the top third of the cutting showing above the surface.

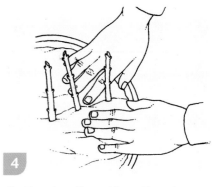

4 Continue inserting cuttings, then close the trench by firming compost around it. Water well and stand the pot in a well-lit, frost-free, sheltered spot outside over winter. Once the cuttings have rooted, pot them up separately.

Root and leaf cuttings

Root cuttings are an unusual means of propagation that works for plants that do not respond well to division, for example the alpine types of phlox, campsis, wisteria and *Anemone × hybrida*. It can be done while plants are dormant, between winter and early spring. Dig up an established plant and wash the roots in a bucket of water. Select a young, fleshy root and cut it into sections with a clean, sharp knife, making a straight cut at the top and a slanted cut at the base. Pull off any fibrous side roots. Roots of around a pencil's thickness can be pushed vertically into pots of John Innes No. 1 or multipurpose compost so that the tip is just buried. Thinner roots can be laid horizontally in trays of compost. Once you see new shoots emerging, pot up the plants individually.

Leaf cuttings are a way of propagating plants that don't have any stems, such as African violets (*Saintpaulia*), *Begonia rex* and many succulents. Root African violet leaves complete with their leaf-stalks individually. Cut a healthy leaf from *Begonia rex*, slice it up into sections, about 3cm (1½in) square, remembering which is the top and bottom of the leaf. Insert the cuttings into seed compost, burying the bottom 1cm (½in) of the leaf section and leaving the rest sticking out. Keep the cuttings in a warm propagator. When a young plant has been produced at the bottom of each of them, pot them up individually.

HOW TO divide clump-forming perennials

1 Using a trowel, work your way around the sides of the pot containing the perennials to be divided (here, hostas). Tip the pot upside down to release the rootball.

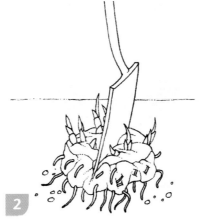

2 Where the roots divide naturally, dig through the clump with a sharp spade to divide it in two. Repeat if required to produce more, smaller clumps.

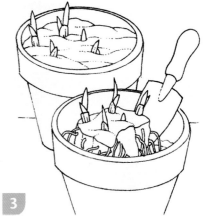

3 Plant the smaller clumps immediately into new containers filled with compost. Don't delay or the plants may dry out. Water thoroughly after planting.

Which propagation method?

	BEST PROPAGATION METHOD	SEASON
BULBS, CORMS AND RHIZOMES	Division	Late autumn to early spring
ANNUALS AND BIENNIALS	Seed	Depends on flowering times and temperatures needed for germination
PERENNIALS		
Perennials with spreading root systems and producing lots of shoots from the base *Achillea, Aster, Astrantia, Helianthus, Hemerocallis, Heuchera, Hosta, Lychnis, Ophiopogon, Phormium, Primula, Sedum, Veronica*	Division	Late autumn to early spring
Bushy herbaceous perennials that root quickly and have long stems *Argyranthemum, Diascia, Gazania, Impatiens, Osteospermum, Pelargonium, Penstemon, Solenostemon*	Softwood cuttings	Spring or summer
TREES, SHRUBS AND ROSES		
Shrubs that root easily *Fuchsia, Helichrysum petiolare, Hydrangea, Viburnum*	Softwood cuttings	Spring or summer
Conifers, many evergreen shrubs and some deciduous shrubs *Aucuba, Berberis, Buxus, Callistemon, Calluna, Camellia, Ceanothus, Choisya, Cistus, Cotoneaster, Cytisus, Elaeagnus, Erica, Garrya, Griselinia, Hebe, Ilex, Lavandula, Magnolia grandiflora, Mahonia, Olearia, Pieris, Prunus (evergreen), Rhododendron, Rosmarinus, Skimmia, Weigela*	Semi-ripe cuttings	Mid- to late summer
Deciduous shrubs with long, straight stems *Cornus, Corylus, Forsythia, Philadelphus, Rosa, Salix, Vitis*	Hardwood cuttings	Mid-autumn to early spring

Plant problems and remedies

All sorts of things can go wrong when you're growing plants; the reasons can be lack of care, inclement weather conditions or pests and diseases. The best way to avoid problems is to prevent them from happening in the first place – by keeping plants healthy – but if problems do occur it's much easier to deal with them if you catch them early.

Many of the problems associated with plants can be controlled by taking simple steps to maintain good hygiene. Fungal spores can remain dormant for long periods of time until the conditions they need for growth are right. Microscopic as they are, they may be on the wall, floor or woodwork and on any of the pots, trays or tools that you're using. Similarly, the eggs of insects may remain hidden, waiting for suitable conditions for the larvae to hatch. There are several simple precautions you can take to reduce or even eradicate this threat. First, wash all your pots and trays in a disinfectant solution before you re-use them and clear away old pots and compost before they can attract fungal spores. Cut away any growth that looks damaged before it can infect the rest of the plant or pass to others and remove dead leaves from in and around the containers – this is important all year, but especially in autumn. Wash down the walls around your plants with disinfectant solution in late autumn. If you have a greenhouse, use a citrus-based cleaning solution to clean the walls and floor, paying particular attention to the crevices around the glazing.

Examine plants frequently to see whether watering, feeding, repotting or weeding are necessary, and remember to dead-head and prune as needed. Also, check for pests and diseases and treat the condition promptly if needed. Lift out dead plants straight away and, before replacing them, try to determine the cause of death – if they've been attacked by a soil pest you shouldn't use the same compost for replacement plants.

Common pests

As with plants in the open garden, plants in containers are susceptible to pests. Even plants on a balcony or terrace can fall prey to attack – slugs and snails can travel great distances vertically, as long as the wall is moist, and have been reported as high as a fourth-floor balcony.

Some problems can be lived with, as long as the aesthetic effects of the attack don't bother you. Try to avoid chemical sprays: they're damaging to the environment and, along with the foes that you want to be rid of, they often eradicate friends – the beneficial insects that you want to encourage (see page 280). The development of resistance in some insects also means that chemical controls are not always as effective as you think.

There are now biological controls for many pests (see box, right): these target only the bad guys, so do not adversely affect the beneficial bugs. The great thing about containers is that they provide a limited environment, which is ideal if you want to introduce predators – for

Biological controls

Almost every garden pest has a predator, so once you know the enemy you can release it and hope that it annihilates garden pests on your behalf. Great advances have been made recently in the use of nematodes (microscopic eelworms), predatory insects and selective bacteria that will keep the population of pests under control. These methods of control cause no environmental damage, use no toxic chemicals, are safe around children and pets, are easy to apply and pose no problem with resistance. The only limiting factor is that they need a mild temperature to live and become active, so the treatments don't work outside in winter. Insect predators, such as hoverflies and lacewings (whose larvae feed on aphids), are ideal for use in a greenhouse or enclosed area.

Predators eat the pest (or its eggs or larvae); pathogens infect the pest with a fatal disease; parasites live on (or in) the pest, ultimately killing it; nematodes are parasitic worms.

PEST	BIOLOGICAL CONTROL OR PREDATOR
Aphid	*Aphidius* species (parasitic wasp larva)
Caterpillar	*Bacillus thuringiensis* (pathogenic bacterium)
Mealy bug	*Cryptolaemus montrouzieri* (pathogenic nematode)
Red spider mite	*Phytosieulus persimilis* (predatory mite)
Scale insect	*Metaphycus helvolus* (parasitic wasp)
Slug	*Phasmarhabditis hermaphrodita* (pathogenic nematode)
Vine weevil larva	*Steinernema kraussei* (pathogenic nematode)
Whitefly	*Encarsia formosa* (parasitic wasp)

example eelworms to deal with soil-level pests such as slugs and snails. You simply water on a preparation containing the eelworms (nematodes) and they will do the work for you. Also, many pests can simply be removed by hand – the simplest and often the most effective remedy.

Below are some of the most common garden pests, the problems they cause and recommended treatments to get rid of them.

Ants
Ants can kill plants, not by eating them but by tunnelling along their roots and causing them to dry out. They also like to 'farm' aphids for their honeydew – in effect they are running a protection racket! **Prevention and control** The trick is to keep things damp so that they go elsewhere. They also dislike the smell of mint, so planting a low-growing form of it such as pennyroyal (*Mentha pulegium*) can help deter them.

Aphids
The distortion of shoot tips and new leaves is a symptom of aphids. There is also a sticky coating on leaves (honeydew), sometimes with black sooty mould. **Prevention and control** Remove and destroy badly infected plants. Catch them early before the populations build up. Spray the foliage with a sharp jet of water, and wipe off any small infestations with your fingers. Organic controls include insecticidal soap (based on fatty acids), derris (derived from tropical plants) and pyrethrum (derived from a type of chrysanthemum). As with many other pest problems, encouraging the pest's predators in the garden is helpful (*see* page 280). Aphid predators include ladybirds, lacewings, wasps, spiders and hoverflies.

Caterpillars
The most obvious signs of caterpillars are holes eaten in leaves, flowers and seedpods. The plant may be completely defoliated. **Prevention and control** Remove caterpillars by hand. For large infestations, use a biological control (*see* opposite). You can use this in conjunction with a pheromone trap to let you know when the moths are laying eggs and make the treatment more accurate, as the bacteria have to come into contact with the caterpillars quickly or they will die.

Earwigs
Small, circular notches or holes in leaves and flowers often indicate that earwigs are present on a plant. **Prevention and control** You may consider a small amount of damage from earwigs as acceptable, because they do eat aphids, one of the greatest garden pests. However, they can wreak havoc with some types of flower (such as dahlias), in which case you will want to reduce their numbers. A pot filled with shredded paper or straw will serve as a trap as well as an earwig hotel – depending on whether you're trying to catch them or encourage them. Place the stuffed pot upside down on top of a cane and leave it overnight. Adult earwigs will use it as a hide-away. In the morning, you simply empty the trap, or you treat it as a mobile hotel and transfer it to a place where the earwigs can do some good – to an aphid-infested container plant, for example.

Froghoppers
These insects produce clusters of frothy bubbles on stems and leaves, looking like spittle or discarded washing-up water (the bubbles are sometimes known as 'cuckoo spit'). Each cluster conceals the nymph of the froghopper, which as an adult looks like a cross between an aphid and a grasshopper. They do no harm at all, but you may consider the 'spit' aesthetically displeasing. **Prevention and control** If you want to get rid of them, you can spray with a jet of water or pick off by hand as soon as they are spotted.

Leaf miners
These cause pale green or white wiggly lines on leaves. They are an aesthetic nuisance rather than harmful. **Prevention and control** Pull off affected leaves as soon as they are spotted. Use a biological control if necessary.

Lily beetles

These eat holes in leaves, flowers and seedpods of members of the lily family, from mid-spring to late summer. The plant can be completely defoliated. The black mucky deposits on stems and leaves are the beetle larvae concealed in their own excrement. **Prevention and control** Small numbers of plants can be protected by picking the adults and grubs off by hand. You must be vigilant, however: despite their bright red colour, lily beetles are remarkably adept at

avoiding detection. Inspect the plants regularly, picking off the beetles and wiping off the black residue containing the grubs. They overwinter in the soil, so plants that have suffered heavy attack should be repotted into a clean pot with fresh compost.

Red spider mite
Signs of red spider mite are stunted growth, and curled and mottled leaves covered with a fine webbing that protects the breeding colonies. Do not confuse these mites with the small, fast-moving red spiders (which are totally harmless to plants).

Prevention and control Spray the undersides of leaves frequently with water, and maintain high humidity (as they prefer dry conditions). Use a biological control (*see* page 278) or spray with insecticide as soon as the damage is spotted.

Scale insects
Scale insects cause stunted growth and yellowing of leaves. There is a sticky coating on the lower leaves, sometimes with black sooty mould present.
Prevention and control Barrier glue around the stem stops the larval stage moving to new parts of the plant. Apply a biological control in summer (*see* page 278) or an insecticide in late spring or early summer.

Slugs and snails
Overnight, you find that holes have been eaten in plant tissue. Damaged seedlings are usually killed.

Prevention and control Apply a mulch of sharp gravel around the plants as a barrier. Copper bands around pots deliver a small electric shock to these pests, discouraging them from reaching the plant. Beer traps can be effective, but remember to empty them every day. There are also biological controls (*see* page 278).

Vine weevils
The larvae of the vine weevil eat the roots of plants, causing the whole plant to wilt or collapse. Small, semi-circular notches bitten out of the leaf edges are caused by the adults.
Prevention and control Keep the compost surface clear of debris (which can hide adult female insects). Use a thick mulch to stop the female laying eggs in the compost. Apply parasitic nematodes or add insecticide granules to the compost (*see* page 278).

Whitefly
These cause the leaves to develop a yellow, freckled appearance; there is a sticky 'honeydew' (whitefly excrement) on the upper surface of lower leaves and a form of sooty mould.
Prevention and control Use yellow-coloured sticky traps to attract and catch flying adults. Introduce a biological control in summer (*see* page 278) or apply an appropriate insecticide in late spring and early summer.

Beneficial creatures
There are many garden creatures that can help you in the campaign to kill off pests, without you doing a thing other than providing a safe, undisturbed, preferably chemical-free haven in which they can live a quiet life, away from predators. Birds are the great friend of the gardener – you could attract them to your garden by feeding them in winter and providing clean water and shelter in the form of trees and shrubs. Hedgehogs are also helpful – again, provide them with somewhere to shelter: a couple of rotting logs among shrubs is perfect. If you have a pond, you'll encourage frogs and toads, both of which eat pests that live near or on the ground. There are also numerous beneficial insects – ground beetles feed on soil pests, velvet mites eat small insects such as red spider mite, centipedes feast on mites, slugs and other insects, and lacewings, wasps, hoverflies, spiders and ladybirds all devour aphids. Encourage insects to stay in your garden over winter by postponing your autumn tidy up until spring, leaving them with plenty of hiding places.

Unwanted visitors
Neither animals nor insects recognize boundaries and if something attracts them, they will investigate it, whether we want them to or not. For some uninvited guests, there are chemical controls that can be used, but there are certain steps we can take to make the garden uninviting without having to resort to this. If you know there are cats in the vicinity, for instance, then don't plant catmint (*Nepeta* × *faasenii*) that will attract them.

Common diseases

Diseases are caused by bacteria, fungi and viruses. Fungi and bacteria are encouraged by poor weather conditions, while viruses are often transmitted by insect pests. All problems are exacerbated by poor husbandry.

Botrytis Also known as grey mould, this results in yellowing and browning of leaves. The stems may rot at ground level. The plant becomes covered with a grey, felt-like mould.
Prevention and control Prune out affected stems and burn. Maintain good air circulation and hygiene. Isolate the affected plant. Pick off faded leaves and flowers regularly.

Canker Small sunken areas of bark enlarge and restrict growth, leading to stem die-back.
Prevention and control Prune out affected branches or cut out affected area and paint the wounds with copper-based fungicide as soon as symptoms are spotted. Remove and burn badly affected plants.

Coral spot Individual branches of trees and shrubs wilt in summer and grey-brown staining may be found under the bark. In autumn the dead bark is covered in small, salmon-pink blisters.
Prevention and control Prune to remove affected wood and burn infected material immediately. Prune in summer when there are few fungal spores in the air. Dispose of prunings.

Downy mildew Discoloured, yellowing leaves have white patches beneath. Plants often die slowly in autumn.
Prevention and control Use disease-resistant cultivars. Avoid overcrowding and maintain good air circulation around containers. Remove and burn badly infected plants.

Fireblight Flowers and young shoots of trees and shrubs in the Rosaceae family blacken and shrivel. Leaves wilt and turn brown; shoots die back.
Prevention and control Grow as few susceptible plants as possible. Remove and burn any plants with these symptoms.

Powdery mildew White, floury patches appear on young leaves. Shoots are distorted and there is premature leaf fall.
Prevention and control Keep plants well watered as mildew thrives in dry conditions. Prune out infected stems in autumn to prevent spores overwintering. Spray fungicide on the young leaves (the fungus cannot penetrate old leaves) at the first signs of infection.

Root rot Foliage turns yellow, branches die back from the tips, and affected roots usually turn black.
Prevention and control Avoid heavy watering and improve drainage. Never use unsterilized compost. Dig up and burn affected plants. Choose varieties known to be tolerant or disease resistant.

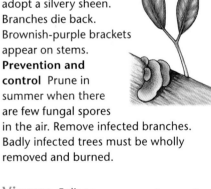

Rust Leaf surface has yellow blotches, the underside has bright orange or brown patches of spores; leaves eventually drop off.
Prevention and control Increase plant spacing to enhance air circulation. Remove all affected parts.

Silver leaf Leaves of trees (especially *Prunus*) adopt a silvery sheen. Branches die back. Brownish-purple brackets appear on stems.
Prevention and control Prune in summer when there are few fungal spores in the air. Remove infected branches. Badly infected trees must be wholly removed and burned.

Viruses Foliage is small, distorted, or grouped in rosettes. Leaves develop yellow coloration.
Prevention and control Buy healthy, virus-free plants. Control potential carriers (insect pests) and clear away weeds, which may harbour viruses. Remove and burn affected plants, and do not propagate from them.

Index

A

Abies koreana 60
Acanthus 40
   A. spinosus 55
Acer 117, 266
   A. campestre 63, 65
   A. palmatum 'Bloodgood' 51
   A. platanoides 'Drummondii' 44
   A. shirasawanum 'Aureum' 266
Achillea 40
   A. filipendulina 'Gold Plate' 45, 55
Aconitum 33
Aeonium 'Zwartkop' 27, 117
aeration 72, 103–4
Ajuga reptans 29, 33, 43
Alcea rosea 'Nigra' 27
Alchemilla mollis 29, 33, 40, 42
Allium 29, 42
   A. hollandicum 26, 65
Alnus
   A. glutinosa 'Imperialis' 72
   A. incana 'Aurea' 72
Alternanthera dentata 117
Amelanchier lamarckii 72
Anchusa azurea 45
Anemone
   A. blanda 59
   A. x hybrida 29, 55, 276
annuals 56–7, 115
Anthemis tinctoria 45, 65
Anthriscus sylvestris 27, 117
antirrhinums 56–7
ants 279
aphids 278, 279
Aquilegia 28, 29
   A. alpina 18
arbours 46, 66
Arbutus unedo 60
arches 10, 24, 46
architectural plants 20, 26, 50, 119
Armeria maritima 29
Artemisia 'Powis Castle' 51
artichokes, globe 172
artichokes, Jerusalem 173
Arum 33
   A. italicum subsp. *italicum* 'Marmoratum' 44, 121
arum lilies 120
asparagus 171, 174–5

Aster x *frikartii* 29, 55
Astilbe 40
Astrantia 29
   A. major 'Sunningdale Variegated' 44
Atriplex halimus 51
aubergines 171, 176
Award of Garden Merit (AGM) 55

B

balconies 113, 278
bare-root plants 126
bark chippings 124
basil 111, 229
bay 121, 230, 248
beans, broad 177–8
beans, French 171, 178–9
beans, runner 115, 166, 171, 180
beech 36, 49, 62
beetroot 115, 181
Begonia
   B. rex 276
   B. x tuberhybrida 117
Berberis thunbergii 47, 51
Bergenia 40, 66, 72
Betula
   B. nigra 72
   B. pendula 65, 117
   B. utilis var. *jacquemontii* 49
biennials 56, 57
birch *see Betula*
birdboxes 31
black plants 27, 117
blackthorn 31, 63
'bleeding' (sap loss) 267
borders
   bulbs 58–9
   container plants in 113–14
   layered planting 36, 39
   planting plans 18–19
'borrowed' features and views 21, 24, 25
botrytis 281
boundaries 20, 21, 24
box *see Buxus sempervirens*
Brachyglottis 51, 249
broccoli, sprouting 182
Brugmansia 33, 113
Brunnera macrophylla 29, 44
Brussels sprouts 183

buckthorn 63
Buddleja 30, 31
   B. davidii 'Black Knight' 47
bulbs 58–9
   in borders 58–9
   compost 123
   in containers 59, 110, 118, 131
   division 276, 277
   in grass 59
   natural survivors 65
butcher's broom 67
Buxus sempervirens 18, 22, 33, 34, 37, 39, 62, 65, 117, 145

C

cabbages 184–5
calabrese 186
Calamagrostis x *acutiflora* 'Overdam' 44, 121
California poppy 29, 57, 68
Callistemon 249, 251
Camellia 14, 50, 68, 132, 138, 139, 251, 264
Campanula 40, 42
   C. poscharskyana 29, 65
canker 281
Capsicum anuum 'Black Pearl' 117
Carex
   C. buchananii 26, 37, 65
   C. comans 139
   C. morrowii 'Fisher's Form' 44
   C. oshimensis 'Evergold' 33, 65
Carpinus betulus 47, 62, 65
carrots 144, 187–8
Caryopteris x *clandonensis* 45
catch cropping 167
caterpillars 278, 279
catmint 30, 280
cauliflowers 188–9
Ceanothus 45, 50, 60, 251, 271
celeriac 190
celery 191
Centaurea montana 65
Centranthus ruber 29, 30, 65
Ceratostigma willmottianum 45
Cercis siliquastrum 49
Chaenomeles 246, 251
   C. x superba 'Crimson and Gold' 33
chainsaws 259, 261

Chamaecyparis lawsoniana 63
chicory 192
Chilean glory flower 57
chillies 193
Chinese mustard greens 204
Chionodoxa 58, 59
   C. luciliae 65
chives 147, 231
Choisya ternata 'Sundance' 51
Chusan palm 117
clay cap 14
Clematis 14, 113, 270
   C. 'Comtesse de Bouchaud' 65
   C. 'Étoile Violette' 53, 65
   C. 'Huldine' 53
   C. 'Jackmanii' 53
   C. 'Marie Boisselot' 120
   C. 'Perle d'Azur' 61
   C. tangutica 65, 69
   C. 'Warszawska Nike' 52
climate 14
climbing plants 52–3
   annuals 57
   containers 126–7
   natural survivors 65
   partners 52
   roses 53
   for screening 61
   self-clinging 52–3
   small gardens 121
   training 270–1
cloches 146, 167
clubroot 158, 184
Cobaea scandens 53, 57
cocoa shells 124
Colchicum 33
   C. speciosum 'Album' 59
   C. 'Waterlily' 59
cold frames 146, 167
coleus 117
colour, effective use of 20–1, 35, 41–5, 119
compost bins 146, 147, 160, 161
composts 160–1, 164
   loam-based 122
   loamless 122–3, 135, 136
   making 160
conifers 63, 132, 138, 250, 266
container-grown plants 126
containerized plants 126
containers 106–39

bulbs 59, 118, 131
choosing 107–9
colour schemes 119
composts and additives 122–3
cottage-garden 115
drainage 125, 139
feeding 136–7
grouping 118
overwintering 138–9
planning and designing 116–21
planting 126–31
repotting 127, 132–3
seasonal 118, 127
siting 116
top-dressing 133
toppings 124
vegetables 115, 142, 149, 171
water features 114, 117
watering 116, 134–5, 138–9
year-round displays 118
contemporary gardens 26–7, 117, 119
Convolvulus
    C. cneorum 51
    C. sabatius 119
copper beech 62
coral spot 281
cordons 268
Cordyline australis 26, 37, 40
coriander 232
Cornus 251, 253, 276
    C. alba 33, 44, 50, 51, 65, 73, 245, 255
    C. controversa 'Variegata' 44
    C. kousa 117
    C. mas 61
    C. sanguinea 63
Corylus 276
    C. avellana 'Contorta' 117, 245, 267
    C. maxima 'Purpurea' 51
cosmos 56–7
Cotinus coggygria 51, 61, 245
Cotoneaster 31, 251
    C. horizontalis 33, 40, 69
    C. simonsii 65
cottage gardens 28–9, 115
courgettes 166, 194–5
courtyard gardens 22, 26, 113
crab apple 30, 248

Crambe cordifolia 40
Crataegus 30, 63
    C. laevigata 72
    C. x lavalleei 'Carrierei' 60, 65
    C. monogyna 63
    C. persimilis 'Prunifolia' 60
Crocosmia 40, 45
Crocus
    C. speciosus 59
    C. tommasinianus 65
Cryptomeria japonica 40
cucumbers 196–7
    x *Cupressocyparis leylandii* 36, 63, 243
cuttings 274–6
Cyclamen 29, 40, 58
    C. coum 59
    C. hederifolium 44, 59, 65, 66
Cynara cardunculus 40

D

Dahlia
    D. 'Bishop of Llandaff' 42, 45
    D. 'Chimborazo' 43
damp gardens 72–3
Daphne 33, 251
dead-heading 57, 249, 264
decking 27, 82–3
deep beds 148–9
Delphinium 40, 45
design 8–73
    computer-aided design 18
design challenges 20–5
design plan 16–19
    planting plans 18–19
    principles 10–11
    site analysis 12–15
    wish list 17
    see also garden styles; planting schemes; site
Dianthus 29, 111
Dicentra spectabilis 120
dieback 266
digging 86–8, 148–9, 155, 164–5
double digging 165
forks and spades 155
no-dig systems 148
single digging 87, 164
Digitalis 29, 30, 33, 40, 44, 56, 57

D. purpurea 65, 120
dill 233
distance and depth, 20, 21, 25, 41, 116
dividing plants 276–7
dogwood *see Cornus*
domed plants 40
Doronicum orientale 65
downy mildew 281
driveways 79
drought-tolerant planting 14, 26, 27, 70–1
Dryopteris wallichiana 73

E

earthing up 173
earwigs 279
Eccremocarpus scaber 57
Echinops ritro 29
Elaeagnus 'Quicksilver' 51
elder *see Sambucus*
electrical safety 261
elephant garlic 200
endive 198
Epimedium 66
Eremurus 40
Erigeron karvinskianus 29, 65
Eryngium 29, 30, 44
    E. alpinum 45
    E. giganteum 26, 29, 65
Erysimum latifolium 58
Escallonia 68
    E. laevis 'Gold Brian' 51
Eschscholzia californica 29, 57, 68
espaliers 269
eucalyptus 68
Euonymous
    E. europaeus 31, 61, 63
    E. fortunei 33, 44, 51, 52, 65, 66
    E. japonicus 'Microphyllus' 22, 62
    E. planipes 61
Eupatorium 72
    E. maculatum Atropurpureum Group 40, 73
Euphorbia 33, 42, 260
    E. amygdaloides var. *robbiae* 65, 67
    E. 'Blackbird' 27
    E. characias 18, 26, 29, 44, 55

E. cyparissias 'Fens Ruby' 40
E. myrsinites 71
E. polychroma 40, 69
evening primrose 30

F

Fagus sylvatica 47, 62
family gardens 32–3, 91
fan training 246, 268
Fargesia nitida 26
    x *Fatshedera lizei* 40, 65, 67
Fatsia japonica 26, 37, 40, 50, 67, 121
feeding
containers 136–7
lawns 96–8
after pruning 265
vegetables 159–60
fences 24, 68
fennel 234
ferns 40, 43, 44, 120
fertilizers 97–8, 123, 136–7, 137, 159–60, 265
Festuca glauca 37
Ficus carica 40
filler plants 39, 40
fireblight 281
Florence fennel 199
flower shows 27
focal points 11, 21, 116
Foeniculum vulgare 40
forget-me-nots 28, 29, 57
formal gardens 34–5
forsythia 42, 52, 276
foxgloves *see Digitalis*
Fritillaria meleagris 59
froghoppers 279
frost and snow 138, 139
frost pockets 14, 144
fuchsias 68, 138

G

Galium odoratum 66
Galtonia candicans 59
garden styles
    contemporary 26–7
    cottage 28–9, 115
    family 32–3, 91
    formal 34–5
    wildlife 30–1

garlic 168, 200
Gaultheria procumbens 37
Geranium
    G. 'Ann Folkard' 69
    G. *macrorrhizum* 'Album' 65, 66
    G. x *magnificum* 33, 65
    G. *pratense* 'Black Beauty' 27, 59
    G. *psilostemon* 29, 55
    G. 'Rozanne' 18, 45, 55
Geum rivale 29
Ginkgo 49
Gleditsia 49, 267
    G. *triacanthos* 'Sunburst' 72
globe artichokes 171
grasses
    natural survivors 65
    variegated 44
gravel gardens 14, 15, 36, 70
greenhouses 147, 278
ground-cover plants 44, 70
guelder rose *see Viburnum opulus*
Gypsophila paniculata 40

H

Hakonechloa macra 26
hanging baskets 110–11, 121, 128–30
hawthorn *see Crataegus*
hazel *see Corylus*
Hebe 50, 68, 138, 249
    H. *pinguifolia* 'Pagei' 51, 65
Hedera 31
    H. *canariensis* 'Gloire de Marengo' 44
    H. *colchica* 'Sulphur Heart' 44
    H. *helix* 44, 65
hedge trimmers 258–9
hedges 36, 62–3
    clipping 63
    formal 35
    native hedging 63
    planting 63
    plants 62–3
    renovation 63
    step-over hedges 255
    windbreaks 68
height, creating 46–7
Helenium 40

Helianthemum 'Wisley White' 18, 51
Helichrysum italicum 'Korma' 51
Helictotrichon sempervirens 26
Helleborus 27, 29, 55
    H. *foetidus* 66
Hemerocallis 276
    H. 'Corky' 45, 55
herbs 111, 121, 147, 228–41
Hermodactylus tuberosus 27
Hesperis matronalis 29
Heuchera
    H. 'Obsidian' 117
    H. *villosa* 'Palace Purple' 117
Hibiscus syriacus 45
Hippophae rhamnoides 31, 51, 69
holly *see Ilex*
hollyhock 29
honeysuckle *see Lonicera*
horizontal plants 40
hormone rooting powder 275
hornbeam 62
horticultural fleece 139
Hosta 40, 66, 117, 276
    H. 'Halcyon' 41
    H. *sieboldiana* 26, 40
    H. 'Wide Brim' 44
Humulus lupulus 'Aureus' 40, 65
humus 70, 72, 158
Hyacinthoides hispanica 66
Hydrangea 68
    H. *anomala* subsp. *petiolaris* 53, 251

I

Iceland poppy 57
Ilex 29, 31, 36, 60, 249, 251
    I. x *altaclerensis* 'Golden King' 33
    I. *aquifolium* 44, 47, 65, 121
    I. *crenata* 'Convexa' 62
Imperata cylindrica 117
intercropping 166–7
Inula hookeri 29
Ipomoea 33
    I. *lobata* 57, 115
Iresine herbstii 'Purple Lady' 117
Iris 29, 40, 44, 276
    I. *foetidissima* 66
    I. 'Harmony' 59
    I. *pallida* 'Variegata' 26, 44

    I. *pseudacorus* 'Variegata' 41, 44
    I. *sibirica* 45, 55, 65
ivy *see Hedera*

J, K

Jasminum
    J. *nudiflorum* 33, 65
    J. *officinale* 33
Judas treee 49
Juniperus communis 37, 47, 69
kale 201
Kniphofia 40, 45
kohl rabi 202

L

Laburnum 33
lamb's lettuce 205
Lamium maculatum 'White Nancy' 44
Lathyrus
    L. *latifolius* 65
    L. *odoratus* 115
Laurus nobilis 121, 230, 248
Lavandula 29, 30, 51, 249, 251
lavatera 68
lawns 20, 32, 75, 76–7, 84–105
    aerating 103–4
    bulbs in 59
    edgings 95
    feeding 96–8
    maintenance 36, 76, 89
    mowing 92, 96, 101–2
    pros and cons 77
    scarifying 103
    seeding 89, 90–2
    site preparation 86–8
    siting 84–5
    striped lawns 102
    top-dressing 105
    turfing 89, 93–4
    watering 92, 94, 99–100
leaf miners 279
leeks 167, 203
lemon grass 235
lettuce 205
Leucojum aestivum 65
Libertia 40
light and shade 10, 20, 21, 45

lighting 117
Ligustrum vulgare 63
lilac 68
Lilium regale 44, 59
lily beetles 279–80
liming 158
Limnanthes douglasii 29, 30
Liriodendron tulipifera 13
long, narrow gardens 22–4
Lonicera
    L. *nitida* 33, 36, 51, 62
    L. *periclymenum* 'Graham Thomas' 65
    L. *pileata* 65
    L. x *purpusii* 'Winter Beauty' 65
love-in-a-mist 29, 56
low maintenance gardening 36–7
Luma apiculata 'Glanleam Gold' 44
Lunaria annua 29, 121
Lupinus 40, 44
Luzula sylvatica 'Marginata' 65, 66
Lychnis x *haageana* 117

M

Magnolia 14, 68, 117
    M. x *loebneri* 'Leonard Messel' 251
    M. x *soulangeana* 251
Mahonia 50
    M. x *media* 18, 45, 47, 251
Malus 30, 248, 251, 267
    M. *domestica* 249, 250
manholes, covering 114
manure 70, 159, 160, 265
maple *see Acer*
marjoram 236
marrows 194–5
Matteuccia struthiopteris 40, 43, 120
Meconopsis cambrica 45
Mentha suaveolens 'Variegata' 44, 237
Mespilus germanica 72
Michaelmas daisies 31
microclimates 12, 14
mint 30, 146, 237
mirrors 21, 24, 25, 114
Miscanthus sinensis 44, 65, 121
mizuna 205

moisture-loving plants 72, 73
mood, creation of 45
morning glory 57
Morus nigra 48
mulching 70
    after pruning 265
    container plants 124
Myosotis 28, 29, 57

N

Narcissus 276
    N. 'Jack Snipe' 18, 59, 65
    N. 'Tête-à-Tête' 45, 59
nasturtiums 57
Nectaroscordum siculum 65
Nepeta 29, 30, 280
Nerine bowdenii 59
New Zealand spinach 218
Nigella damascena 29, 40, 45, 56
nutrients 96–7, 136, 159

O

obelisks 46
onions 168, 206–7
Ophiopogon planiscapus
    'Nigrescens' 27, 117
opium poppy 29
oregano 236
organic gardening 32, 97, 160
organic matter 65, 72, 158,
    162–3, 164
oriental poppy *see Papaver*
    orientale
Origanum vulgare 'Aureum' 33
Osmanthus 251
    O. x *burkwoodii* 65, 121
    O. heterophyllus 18, 37, 44, 50,
    65

P

pak choi 205
palms 113, 117
Papaver 29, 30, 43
    P. nudicaule 57
    P. orientale 28, 45, 65
    P. somniferum 29
parsley 147, 238
parsnips 208

passageways 114, 121
paths 10, 11, 15, 20, 23, 25, 75,
    78–9, 79
patios 75, 80–1, 110, 112
paving 11, 15, 21, 66
peas 115, 209–10
peat 157
Pelargonium 111, 116, 117, 138,
    264, 274
Pennisetum glaucum 117
Penstemon 'Andenken an
    Friedrich Hahn' 55
peppers 137, 171, 211
perennials
    cottage garden 29
    division 277
    herbaceous 54–5, 65
perforated/seep hoses 100
pergolas 10, 11, 24, 46, 53, 61,
    66, 80
periwinkle *see Vinca*
perlite 123
perpetual spinach 218
Persicaria 72
    P. amplexicaulis 'Firetail' 45, 73
pests and diseases 72, 278–81
biological controls 30, 278–9, 280
Philadelphus 52, 276
    P. coronarius 'Aureus' 51, 59
    P. 'Silberregen' 18
Phillyrea angustifolia 62
Phlomis fruticosa 33, 51, 65
Phormium 37, 40, 50, 109
    P. cookianum subsp. *hookeri*
    'Cream Delight' 44
    P. 'Maori Queen' 26
    P. 'Platt's Black' 27
    P. tenax 'Dazzler' 117
Phyllostachys nigra 27, 47, 60
Physocarpus opulifolius 51
pinching out 247, 264
pinks 14, 29
pipework and cabling 15
Pittosporum tenuifolium 27, 51,
    121
planting schemes
    colour 41–4
    grouping plants 39, 54
    mood 45
plant shapes and textures 39–1
play equipment 32–3

plug plants 126
poached-egg plant 29, 30
poisonous plants 33
poles 47
Polygonatum x *hybridum* 41
Polystichum setiferum 120
ponds and pools 24, 30–1
Portuguese laurel 60
potagers 115, 147
potatoes 168, 212–14
Potentilla fruticosa 65
powdery mildew 281
Primula veris 29
privet 36, 63
problem gardens 64–73
propagation 272–7
    cuttings 274–5
    division 276–7
    from seed 272–3
protective clothing 260
pruning 242–71
    aftercare 265–7
    apical dominance problem
    247, 264
    formative pruning 248–9
    fruit and flower production
    246, 249
    maintenance 249
    purpose of 243–5
    renewal pruning 249–50
    renovation 250–1
    reversion problem 249
    root pruning 246
    safety 260–1
    techniques 253–5, 262–4, 266
    tools 243, 253, 256–9
    training trees and shrubs
    268–71
Prunus 266, 267
    P. cerasifera 'Nigra' 60
    P. lusitanica 60, 65
    P. persica 'Peregrine' 246
    P. spinosa 31, 63
    P. 'Spire' 47
Pulmonaria 29
    P. 'Lewis Palmer' 55, 67
    P. saccharata 44
pumpkins 219–20
purslane 206
Pyracantha 31, 45, 246
Pyrus 251, 267

P. calleryana 'Chanticleer' 47
P. salicifolia 'Pendula' 49

R

radishes 215
rain shadows 85
raised beds 32, 37, 121, 143, 149
    150
recycling 15, 28–9, 109
red spider mite 280
Rhamnus
    R. alaternus
    'Argenteovariegata' 44
    R. cathartica 63
Rheum 40
    R. palmatum
    'Atrosanguineum' 40
rhododendron 14, 50, 251
Rhus typhina 267
Ricinus communis 33, 40
Robinia 49, 263, 267
    R. pseudoacacia 'Lace Lady' 48
rocket 206
Rodgersia
    R. aesculifolia 73
    R. podophylla 40, 41, 43
roof gardens 27, 82
root rot 281
root-balled plants 126
Rosa 267
    R. 'Adélaïde d'Orléans' 53
    R. 'Compassion' 53, 65
    R. 'Fru Dagmar Hastrup' 65
    R. 'Geranium' 45, 47
    R. glauca 65
    R. 'Golden Showers' 53
    R. 'Graham Thomas' 45
    R. 'Madame Alfred Carrière' 53
    R. 'Roseraie de l'Haÿ' 71
    R. rugosa 31, 69
    R. spinosissima 69
    R. 'Winchester Cathedral' 18
rosemary *see Rosmarinus officinalis*
Rosmarinus officinalis 33, 65, 71,
    239
rotavators 156, 162
rowan *see Sorbus*
Rubus
    R. cockburnianus
    'Goldenvale' 51

R. thibetanus 51, 67
Rudbeckia 40, 72
Ruscus aculeatus 67
rust 281
Ruta 33

S

safety
    containers 116
    poisonous plants 33
    pruning 260–1
    water features 33
sage 240
salad leaves 152, 204–6
Salix 245, 276
Salvia
    S. involucrata 'Bethellii' 43
    S. lyrata 'Purple Knockout' 117
    S. officinalis 'Purpurascens' 51
Sambucus 61
    S. nigra 27, 44, 51, 59, 65,
    117, 245
    S. racemosa
    'Sutherland Gold' 51
Santolina 29, 251
    S. chamaecyparissus 'Lemon
    Queen' 26, 51
Sarcococca 50
    S. confusa 33, 65, 66
Scabiosa atropurpurea
    'Chile Black' 27
scale insects 280
scarifying 103
Scilla 59
    S. siberica 65
screening 15, 22, 60–1, 112–13
sea buckthorn 31, 69
seaside gardens 68
Sedum 27, 30, 37, 40
    S. erythrostictum 'Frosty Morn'
    44
    S. 'Herbstfreude' 55, 71
    S. spectabile 26, 30
seed beds 156
seeds
    seed and cutting compost 123
    seedlings, pricking out 273
    sowing 272–3
    successional sowing 167
    watering 70

self-seeding 29, 56
Sempervivum tectorum
    'Atrorubens' 26
sempervivums 27, 37
shade and shady gardens 12, 13,
    20, 44, 49, 66, 66–7, 67, 114
shallots 216
shelter 12, 14, 68, 138
shrubs 50–1
    colourful 51
    container-grown 133
    deciduous 50–1
    evergreen 50
    natural survivors 65
    propagation 277
    pruning 51, 250
    screening with 60
    as trees 61
    wall shrubs 271
shuttlecock fern 43
silver leaf 281
Sisyrinchium 40
    S. striatum 26, 44, 65, 71
site 12–15
    analysis 12–15
    aspect and orientation 13
    existing plants and features
    14–16
    shape and proportions 10,
    12–13, 20–5
    site plan 17
    survey 16–17
    topography 13, 14
Skimmia japonica 'Rubella' 37
sloping sites 13, 34, 81, 84
slugs and snails 72, 280
small gardens 120–1
soil 14, 157–8
    chalk 14, 157
    clay 14, 72, 157
    drainage 14, 72
    improvement 65, 70, 72,
    158–9, 164
    loam 157
    peat 157
    pH (acidity/alkalinity) 14,
    157–8
    sandy 14, 157
    testing 14, 158
soil pan 145
Solanum crispum 'Glasnevin' 65

Solenostemon scutelarioides
    'Chocolate Mint' 117
Solomon's seal 41
Sorbus 30, 49
    S. aria 'Lutescens' 65
    S. aucuparia 47, 49, 72
    S. commixta 49
    S. hupehensis 49, 65
    S. 'Joseph Rock' 49
Spanish bluebells 66
sphagnum moss 129
spinach 217–18
spindle *see Euonymous*
Spiraea
    S. 'Arguta' 40
    S. japonica 'Goldflame' 51
sprinklers 100
square garden plots 22
squashes 194–5, 219–20
Stachys byzantina 65
standards 230, 248–9, 269
stepping stones 79
Sternbergia lutea 59
Stipa
    S. gigantea 26
    S. tenuissima 18, 29, 35, 37,
    40, 45, 65
strawberry tree 60
structural plants 39
successional sowing 167
succulents 27, 37, 135
suckers 267
swedes 221
sweet peas 29, 57, 115
sweet rocket 29, 57
sweet williams 56, 57
sweet woodruff 66
sweetcorn 166, 222
swimming pools 32
Swiss chard 115, 151, 223

T

table displays 111
tamarisk 68
Taxus baccata 29, 33, 34, 36, 39,
    47, 60, 62–3, 121, 250
Tellima grandiflora 33, 72
terraces/terracing 14, 20, 34, 81
terracotta pots 108, 110, 115
tetanus 261

Teucrium fruticans 51
Thalictrum
    T. aquilegiifolium 40
    T. delavayi 29
Thuja plicata 63, 250
Thymus 30, 111, 241
    T. citriodorus 33
Tolmiea menziesii 'Taff's Gold' 66
tomatoes 137, 169, 171, 224–6
tools 36, 125, 155–6
    maintenance 257
    pruning tools 243, 253, 256–9
topiary 21, 35, 77, 245
Trachycarpus fortunei 117
trees 47, 48–9
    canopy 49, 85
    choosing 48–9
    container-grown 133
    for damp gardens 72
    for wildlife gardens 30
    natural survivors 65
    overhanging lawns 85
    planting under 66
    propagation 277
    screening with 60–1
    training 268–9
    tree-felling 261
    weeping trees 250
trellis 22, 27, 61
triangular gardens 24
troughs, tubs and barrels 108,
    111, 114
tulip tree 13
Tulipa 108, 131, 276
    T. 'Ballerina' 65, 71
    T. 'Couleur Cardinal' 45
    T. 'Dillenburg' 58
    T. 'Queen of Night' 27
turf stacks 86
turnips 227

V

valerian 68
variegated plants 44, 249
vegetable gardening 140–225
    baby vegetables 152
    benefits of 141–2
    container growing 115, 142,
    149, 171
    crop rotation 153

intensive cropping 166–7
potagers 115, 147
tools and equipment 155–6
vegetable storage 168–9
watering 144, 147
what to grow 151–2
vegetable plot 143–5
aspect 144
drainage 145
layout 146–7
preparation 162–5
shelter 145
soil 144, 157–60
Veratrum nigrum 27
Verbascum 40
Verbena bonariensis 22, 29, 30, 33
vermiculite 123
Veronica umbrosa 'Georgia Blue' 65
Veronicastrum 40
vertical planting 40, 47, 121

Viburnum
V. davidii 40, 50
V. lantana 63
V. opulus 31, 45, 51, 63, 65, 73
V. plicatum f. *tomentosum* 'Mariesii' 40
V. rhytidophyllum 61
V. sargentii 'Onondaga' 51
V. tinus 'Variegatum' 44
Vinca
V. difformis 67
V. major 67
V. minor 33, 120
vine weevils 125, 280
Viola 29
V. cornuta 40
V. riviniana Purpurea Group 27, 29, 62, 65
viruses 281
Vitis coignetiae 65

W
wall planters 111
wallflowers 29, 56, 57, 58
water features 21, 45
containerized 114, 117
ponds and pools 24, 30–1, 32
safety issues 33
water-retaining crystals 123
watering
containers 116, 134–5, 138–9
lawns 92, 94, 99–100
vegetables 144, 147
waterlogged soil 145
wayfaring tree 63
weeds and weeding 162, 163
tools 155
weed-proof fabric 124
weedkillers 156, 163
Weigela 44, 51
western red cedar 63, 250
wheelbarrows 156

whitefly 280
wide, shallow gardens 25
wildlife gardens 30–1
willow and hazel structures 29, 32, 77
wind chill 138
windbreaks 68, 112
window boxes 111, 121, 126
windy gardens 14, 68–9, 138
Wisteria 251, 267, 271
W. floribunda 'Alba' 246
W. sinensis 53

Y, Z
yew *see Taxus baccata*
Yucca 40, 50
Y. filamentosa 'Bright Edge' 18, 26, 44
Zantedeschia aethiopica 120
zinnias 56–7

Picture credits

Key t = top; b = bottom; l = left; r = right; c = centre

All photographs by Jonathan Buckley except the following:
Alamy/Lifestyle David J Green 259. **Julia Brittain** 16l, 28t, 112bc, 66br. **DK Images** 163. **FhF Greenmedia** 261. **GAP Photos** Elke Borkowski 80tl; Zara Napier 92, Elke Borkowski *169*. FhF Greenmedia *185*. Marcus Harpur *166*. Michael Howes *182*. Lynn Keddie 195t. Rice/Buckland *168*. **The Garden Collection** Andrew Lawson 34, 66bc, Liz Eddison *111*, *119tr*, *119br*, *129l*, *130*; Andrew Lawson *119tl*; Jane Sebire *115(2)*; Nicola Stocken Tomkins *124(2, 3)*, *129rl*, Derek St Romaine *186*. Nicola Stocken Tomkins *241*. **Garden World Images** S. Keeble 95(3), Trevor Sims *224*. **Sue Gordon** *175r*, 214r. **Harpur Garden Library** 256bl. **Marianne Majerus** 258t. S&O Matthews 250. **Andrew McIndoe** 84, 85b, *87tr*, *91br*, *98*, *124(1)*, *131(1, 3)*, *144t*, *147cr*, *167*, 183, 194, 206b, 212, 215. **Clive Nichols** 75b, *78t*, *79t*, 83t. **Photolibrary** Mark Winward *91bl*, David Askham 227. **Photolibrary/Fresh Food Images** Janet Bligh 105b. **Howard Rice** 258bl, 268r. **Science Photo Library** Malcolm Thomas 254. **Maddie Thornhill** 256t. **Robin Whitecross** 190, 192, 203, 211, 216, 221

Thanks also to the following designers and owners:
Rosemary Alexander, Stoneacre, Kent 144br. Darina Allen, Ballymaloe Cookery School, Co. Cork, Ireland 9. Maureen Allen, St John's Road, Walsall 8, 25, 113. Audley End, Essex 155. Janet Bonney 152t. Christopher Bradley-Hole 95(1). Gill Brown 46t, 109bl, 112, 115t. Fiona Bruce 75t. Declan Buckley 24. Tommaso del Buono & Paul Gazerwitz, RHS Chelsea Flower Show 2008 149b, 232. Alan Capper 117(3). Beth Chatto, Beth Chatto Gardens, Essex 15, 43b, 48t, 72, 245t. Veronica Cross 58l. Helen Dillon, Stephen Firth & Chichester College students, RHS Chelsea Flower Show 2005 26t. Fergus Garrett 114. Diarmuid Gavin 27, 82, 83. Anthony Goff 2–3, 85t, 275. Rose Gray, The River Cafe, London 228. Maurice Green 11. Robin Green & Ralph Cade 116, 121l, 142. Bunny Guinness 143t. Diana Guy,

Welcome Thatch, Dorset 121r. Trudi Harrison 91. Jeffery Hewitt 111. Jim Honey & James Dyson 117(1). Wendy & Leslie Howell 68. Kevin Hughes 64, 78br. Paul Kelly 9. Virginia Kennedy, Rosendale Road, London 60tr. Dominique Lafourcade 79t. Rani Lall 21, 60br, 77t, 242; Little Court 75b. Pam Lewis, Sticky Wicket, Dorset 31bl, 44b. Christopher Lloyd, Great Dixter, East Sussex 35br, 42, 58r, 59, 60bl, 78bl, 106, 118, 136, 156r, 245b, 246t, 251, 269l. The Lodge, Slindon, Hampshire 220t. John Massey, Ashwood Nurseries, Staffordshire 19, 48, 46tr, 66, 139tr, 263, 267. Mr and Mrs Mogford 255b, 268r. Christina Oates 81t. Dan Pearson 49c. Pots and Pithoi 119tl. Sarah Raven, Perch Hill, East Sussex 29, 56l, 57b, 77, 87, 88, 94t, 98, 100r, 108, 110, 136, 149t, 168t, 170, 260, 268l. Pam Schwerdt & Sibylle Kreutzberger 38. David & Mavis Seeney 50b, 62t. Haruko Seki & Makoto Saito, RHS Chelsea Flower Show 2008 35bl. Gill Siddell 89, 99, 146b. Carol & Malcolm Skinner, Eastgrove Cottage Garden Nursery, Worcestershire 28b, 41, 62b. Penny Smith 12. Sue & Wol Staines, Glen Chantry, Essex 5r, 26, 50t, 147t, 255t. Georgina Steeds 119tr. June Streets 32, 77b. Tom Stuart-Smith: 46tl. Joe Swift & Sam Joyce for The Plant Room 52, 46b, 81b, 269r. Kathy Taylor 83t. Xa Tollemache, RHS Chelsea 1997 34. Carole Vincent 107, 119(2). Sue Ward, Ladywood, Hampshire 20, 120, 44t, 160t. Wayford Manor, Somerset 10, 49br, 53c. Cleve West 33t. West Dean Gardens, West Sussex 45t. Kim Wilde & Richard Lucas, RHS Chelsea Flower Show 2005 160b. Wilkins Pleck 78t. Gay Wilson 8, 61t, 76t, 80r. Adam Woolcott & Jonathan Swift, Chelsea Flower Show 2007 166. Helen Yemm: Eldenhurst, East Sussex 13, 22, 30; Ketley's, East Sussex 14, 39, 45b 46b, 70, 143b; London 23.

While every effort has been made to trace and acknowledge all copyright holders, the publisher would like to apologize should there be any errors or omissions.

Alan Titchmarsh
how to garden

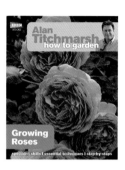

Growing Roses

specialist skills | essential techniques | step-by-steps

Pests and Problems

specialist skills | essential techniques | step-by-steps

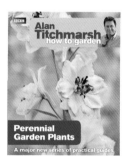

Perennial Garden Plants

A major new series of practical guides

Container Gardening

A major new series of practical guides

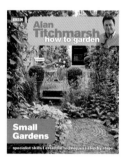

Small Gardens

specialist skills | essential techniques | step-by-steps

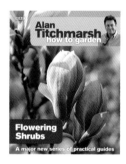

Flowering Shrubs

A major new series of practical guides

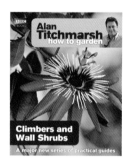

Climbers and Wall Shrubs

A major new series of practical guides

Growing Fruit

A major new series of practical guides

Pruning and Training

A major new series of practical guides

Vegetables and Herbs

A major new series of practical guides

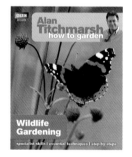

Wildlife Gardening

specialist skills | essential techniques | step-by-steps

Gardening in the Shade

A major new series of practical guides

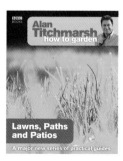

Lawns, Paths and Patios

A major new series of practical guides

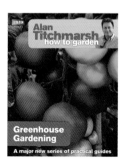

Greenhouse Gardening

A major new series of practical guides

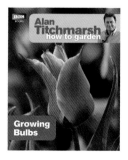

Growing Bulbs

A major new series of practical guides

Garden Design

A major new series of practical guides